CU00923302

Confabulation
Views from neuroscience,
psychiatry, psychology,
and philosophy

Confabulation
Views from neuroscience, psychiatry, psychology, and philosophy

Edited by

William Hirstein

Professor and Chair of Philosophy,
Elmhurst College, Elmhurst,
Illinois, USA

OXFORD
UNIVERSITY PRESS

OXFORD
UNIVERSITY PRESS

Great Clarendon Street, Oxford OX2 6DP

Oxford University Press is a department of the University of Oxford.
It furthers the University's objective of excellence in research, scholarship,
and education by publishing worldwide in

Oxford New York

Auckland Cape Town Dar es Salaam Hong Kong Karachi
Kuala Lumpur Madrid Melbourne Mexico City Nairobi
New Delhi Shanghai Taipei Toronto

With offices in

Argentina Austria Brazil Chile Czech Republic France Greece
Guatemala Hungary Italy Japan Poland Portugal Singapore
South Korea Switzerland Thailand Turkey Ukraine Vietnam

Oxford is a registered trade mark of Oxford University Press
in the UK and in certain other countries

Published in the United States
by Oxford University Press Inc., New York

British Library Cataloguing in Publication Data

Data available

Library of Congress Cataloging in Publication Data

Data available

Typeset in Minion
by Cepha Imaging Private Ltd., Bangalore, India
Printed in Great Britain
on acid-free paper by the
MPG Books Groups, Bodmin and King's Lynn

ISBN 978-0-19-920891-3 (Pbk)

10 9 8 7 6 5 4 3 2 1

Contents

Contributors

German E Berrios
Department of Psychiatry,
University of Cambridge, The
Academy of Medical Sciences,
United Kingdom

Quin Chrobak
Department of Psychology,
Kent State University, Kent,
Ohio, United States

Max Coltheart
Macquarie Centre for Cognitive
Science (MACCS), Macquarie
University, Sydney, Australia

Gianfranco Dalla Barba
Institut National de la Santé-et-de-la
Recherche Médicale, Paris, France;
Dipartimento di Psicologia,
Università degli studi di Trieste,
Trieste, Italy

John DeLuca
Kessler Medical Rehabilitation
Research and Education Corporation,
New Jersey, United States

Todd Feinberg
Beth Israel Medical Center,
M. Bernstein Institute,
New York, United States

Lauren French
School of Psychology, Victoria
University of Wellington,
Wellington, New Zealand

Aikaterini Fotopoulou
Institute of Psychiatry,
King's College London,
London, United Kingdom

Maryanne Garry
School of Psychology, Victoria
University of Wellington,
Wellington, New Zealand

Kenneth Heilman
Department of Neurology,
McKnight Brain Institute,
University of Florida,
Gainesville, Florida,
United States

William Hirstein
Department of Philosophy,
Elmhurst College, Elmhurst, Illinois,
United States

Elizabeth Loftus
University of California, Irvine,
Department of Cognitive Sciences,
Irvine California, United States

E. Lorente-Rovira
Hospital Clínico, Valencia (AVS)
and CIBERSAM, Spain

Peter J. McKenna
Benito Menni Complex Assistencial
en Salut Mental, Germanes
Hospitalàries del Sagrat Cor de Jesús,
Sant Boi de Llobregat, and
CIBERSAM Spain

Alfred Mele
Department of Philosophy,
Florida State University,
Tallahassee, Florida,
United States

V. S. Ramachandran
Center for Brain and
Cognition, University of
California, San Diego, California,
United States

Martha Turner
Institute of Cognitive
Neuroscience and Department of
Psychology, University College
London, London, United Kingdom

Thalia Wheatley
Dartmouth College, Hanover,
New Hampshire, United States

Maria Zaragoza
Department of Psychology,
Kent State University, Kent,
Ohio, United States

Introduction: What is confabulation?

William Hirstein

Introduction

What is confabulation? It may be preferable to start with an example since the natural starting point – a definition of the term 'confabulation' – is still a difficult and controversial topic. 'I was at the office, doing the year-end inventory', a former office worker might reply, when asked about what he did yesterday, even though he has been retired for 20 years. There are two types of memory patients: those who know they've lost memory capacities and those who don't. Memory confabulators will not acknowledge that their memories are impaired and instead will produce confabulations when asked questions about their pasts. Confabulators seem to believe their claims, and the consensus among those who study them is that they are not deliberately lying, even though they have an obvious motive to do so in most occasions, to appear normal and healthy.

Confabulation in the clinic can be severely debilitating, and this provides another good motive to try to understand it. One's credibility is a core feature of one's identity. The brain damage that causes confabulation can turn rock-solid providers of information into people little more reliable than pathological liars. This is a large enough change to make people who knew the patient before come to see him or her as a different person. How can confabulators be of basically sound mind, yet not see their glaring errors? One approach to take in response is to argue that confabulation shows how modularized our cognition is: when we lose our somatosensory representations of the left arm – to use another type of confabulation as an example – we also lose any ability to make intelligent judgments about what the left arm is doing.

This collection is focused on delineating the basic parameters of confabulation. How exactly is the term to be defined? What are the clinical symptoms of each type of confabulation? Which brain functions are damaged in clinical confabulators? What are the neuropsychological characteristics of each type?

The phenomena of confabulation – the serene confidence, the isolated islands of deficit, and the creativity of the responses – lie at the confluence of streams of thought pursued by several different disciplines. Psychologists study confabulating patients in order to learn more about human memory. They also study the patients' willingness (or rather their stunning lack of willingness) to admit ignorance rather than to give a false answer. Both traditional neurologists and neuroscientists study the lesions of patients, using several different brain imaging techniques and sometimes by studying the brain of patients after their deaths. Cognitive neuropsychologists study how the specific lesions have specific effects on brain function and, ultimately, on outward behavior. Philosophers are interested in several questions that bear on confabulation. How is our knowledge system structured? Is it, for instance, a single homogeneous net or web of beliefs, or do we have different kinds of knowledge, perhaps represented in the brain in different ways? How do we understand the minds of others? What is the relation between knowledge and merely believing that one knows? What is the relation between knowing that p and feeling certain that p?

We should pause to consider how lucky we are since it is not clear how often in the future all these disciplines, psychology, neuroscience, psychiatry, and philosophy will be able to interact in such a vital way. Only the most jaundiced old lab heeler would deny that the sciences of the mind and brain have entered a renaissance, thanks mainly to the rapid progress of neuroscience. Lines of inquiry can move easily across disciplines for those who are willing to follow them. One type of line of inquiry moves downward in the theoretical apparatus that we have set up to understand the world. In a sort of epistemic digestion, philosophers first size up the meal, and then scientists emulsify those products into simples consumable by any decent junior high-school student. A second line of inquiry moves in the opposite direction; the inquirer takes a finding in neuroscience and ponders what meaning it might have for our everyday mental lives, or even our fundamental nature. Confabulation is a rich phenomenon that supports both of these lines of inquiry and many others moving across the disciplines in all directions.

The problem of defining 'confabulation'

Anyone broaching the topic of confabulation is faced immediately with a huge problem: there is no orthodox, problem-free definition of 'confabulation'. The one simple definition available seems to have major problems. The concept of confabulation was initially restricted to false claims presented as memories, and then grew to include other types of cases. 'Konfabulationen' was first applied as a technical term by the German neurologists Bonhoeffer, Pick, and Wernicke in the early 1900s to false memory reports made by their patients, who suffered from an amnesic syndrome that later came to be known as Korsakoff's amnesia. When asked about what they did yesterday, these patients do not remember, but will report events that either did not happen, or happened long ago. During the remainder of the 20th century, however, the use of 'confabulation' was gradually expanded to cover claims made by other types of patients, many of whom had no obvious memory disorder. This list grew to include patients who deny that they are injured, paralyzed, or blind; split-brain patients; patients with misidentification disorders (i.e. they make false claims about the identities of people they know); and patients with schizophrenia, as well as normal people and children reporting memories.

This traditional definition of 'confabulation' contains three criteria: confabulations are (1) false (2) reports (3) about memories. There are significant problems with each of the three, however. First, relying on falsity alone to characterize the problem with the patient's claim can produce arbitrary results. If a Korsakoff's patient is asked what day of the week it is and happens to state correctly that it is Tuesday, we may still want to consider this a confabulation since he has, e.g. been wrong the previous four times he answered this question, and we have good reason to believe he is confabulatory in general. Second, the idea that confabulations are reports, or stories, implies that confabulations must be in a linguistic form, yet several researchers have categorized non-linguistic responses as confabulations. One group had patients (undergoing Wada testing in which one hemisphere is temporarily disabled) pointing to fabric samples with one hand to indicate which texture of fabric they had been stimulated with on the other hand. Another research group had patients reproduce from memory certain drawings that they had seen, and referred to cases in which the patients added extra features to the drawings which were not actually present as confabulations. Other researchers applied the term 'confabulation' to the behavior of patients who produced meaningless drawings as if they were correctly reproducing designs seen earlier. Finally, the problem with calling confabulations *memory* reports at all is that even in Korsakoff's syndrome, many confabulations are simply made up on the spot and not traceable to any actual memories. Making confabulation by definition only a disorder of memory also rules out by fiat the other putative cases of confabulation by, e.g. split-brain patients, misidentification patients, and patients who deny illness. One could take Moscovitch's pithy description of confabulation as 'honest lying' as a starting point for a broader definition. To confabulate is to make a false claim without an intent to deceive. But one then feels obliged to begin listing the exceptions, joking, kidding, being ironic or sarcastic, or even telling a story, none of which count as confabulating. This definition would also include all cases in which people mistakenly say false things as confabulations, and it has the same problem noted above of categorizing as non-confabulations those cases in which an obviously confabulatory person happens to answer a question correctly.

Those using 'confabulation' in the broader sense are choosing to ignore any memory criterion, and hence must be assuming something else to be the core feature of confabulation. Neurologist Norman Geschwind's classic pair of articles entitled, 'Disconnexion syndromes in animals and man', published in the journal *Brain* in 1965, must have played a role in popularizing the broader sense of 'confabulation'. Geschwind used the word in a natural-sounding way that had nothing to do with memory, speaking for instance of a patient who 'gave confabulatory responses to visual field testing when there was no stimulus in the field....' (Geschwind, 1965, p. 597). 'I have seen a confused patient', he said, 'who gave confabulatory responses when asked to name objects held in his hand' (p. 597). Similarly, patients who deny that they are paralyzed have been claimed to confabulate when they provide reasons for why they cannot move ('My arthritis is bothering me', 'I'm tired of following your commands'). Another type of patient will deny blindness and attempt to answer questions about what he sees, producing what have been called confabulations. Misidentification patients have been said to confabulate when asked what the motives of the 'impostor' are, or why someone would go through the trouble to impersonate someone else ('Perhaps my father paid him to take care of me'). Similarly, when the left hemispheres of split-brain patients attempt unsuccessfully to answer questions without the necessary information (which is contained in their right hemispheres), this has also been called a confabulation.

There may be something broader than memory that encompasses all of these syndromes. Memory is a part of what constitutes our knowledge. Another part of our knowledge is contained in our current perceptions, of what we are seeing, of our own bodies, and of the people and things around us. The following broader definition is based on the idea that confabulation syndromes involve malfunctions in different knowledge domains, coupled with executive system damage (Hirstein, 2005). According to this two-phase approach, confabulation is caused by damage to two different brain systems. First, a perceptual or mnemonic system is damaged, the patient goes blind, loses his memory, or loses his ability to represent his body. But then a second line of defense has to fail since damage of only the first sort would produce someone who admitted the problem and sought help. If such a person did make up a memory, or a perception, as we all are prone to do, he would eventually realize that he was doing this. The brain's system of executive processes, tasked with checking, testing, and improving both mnemonic and perceptual states (Miller and Cohen, 2001; Fuster, 2002), must also fail before a person becomes confabulatory.

(One-stage theories have been proposed for specific confabulation syndromes, but I am not aware of any that has been proposed to cover the entire set.) According to this epistemic definition of 'confabulation':

Jan confabulates that p if and only if:

(1) Jan claims that p.

(2) Jan believes that p.

(3) Jan's thought that p is ill-grounded.

(4) Jan does not know that her thought is ill-grounded.

(5) Jan should know that her thought is ill-grounded.

(6) Jan is confident that p.

'Claiming' is broad enough to cover a wide variety of responses by subjects, including drawing, and pointing, as well as reports of all types. The second criterion captures the sincerity of confabulators. The third criterion refers to the problem that caused the flawed response to be generated, the first-phase problem. The fourth criterion refers to the failure of the second phase, the failure to reject the flawed response. The fifth criterion captures the normative element of our concept of confabulation: If the confabulator's brain (or specifically, her executive processes) were functioning properly, she would not make that claim. The last criterion refers to another important aspect of confabulators, the serene and complete certainty they have in their communications.

People will normally acknowledge their deficits. In order for confabulation to occur, there must be additional damage, one step up in the cognitive hierarchy, to processes that monitor the memory or perceptual representations, according to a two-phase approach. And here is where the modularization is surprising since it happens at the cognitive level, which is supposed to be much less modular or encapsulated than the lower perceptual levels. Confabulation may indicate that to a large degree, we have no global ability to monitor representations of all sorts, but rather we possess a set of monitoring abilities or executive processes, each of which is able to monitor a subset of our representations. An alternative scheme to this is that the executive processes at least attempt to do their work on every representation in consciousness, but that they are only successful on a subset of those.

Thus, there are currently two schools of thought on the proper scope of the concept of confabulation: those who remain true to the original sense and so believe that the term should only be applied to false memory reports and a growing number of those who believe that the term can be usefully applied to a broader range of disorders. An examination of the etymology of the term 'confabulation' itself turns out not to be terribly helpful. The Latin root '*con*' means with, while '*fabulari*' means to talk or converse, so that its original meaning was simply to talk with. When the German neurologists at the turn of the 20th century began using '*konfabulation*', they probably meant that their memory patients were creating fables when asked about their pasts. The patients were fabulists – fable tellers.

Types of confabulations

If the confabulation syndromes do form a natural family, this should start to become apparent if we lay out the data in a perspicuous manner. Researchers have recorded confabulation in the following cases:

Memory confabulations

Confabulations about memories are a defining characteristic of Korsakoff's syndrome and a similar syndrome caused by aneurysm of the anterior communicating artery. Alzheimer's patients will often produce memory confabulations, and children up to a certain age are also prone to reporting false memories, apparently because their brain's prefrontal areas have not yet fully developed, while the Alzheimer's patients' prefrontal lobes have been compromized by amyloid plaque lesions. All of these confabulators have an initial memory retrieval problem, coupled with a failure to monitor and correct their false 'memories'. In contrast, there exist many memory patients with damage only to more posterior parts of the memory system (e.g. to the hippocampus or other parts of the temporal lobes) who freely admit that they cannot remember and are not at all prone to producing confabulations. They have the first type of damage required to produce confabulation, but not the second since their frontal lobes are intact.

The patients with aneurysms of the anterior communicating artery – a tiny artery near the anterior commissure that completes the anterior portion of the Circle of Willis – provide our best clue about the locus of the frontal problems in memory confabulation. The location of the anterior communicating artery (ACoA) makes the posterior orbitomedial cortex an area of suspicion in confabulation. **John DeLuca** has written extensively on both the clinical and theoretical aspects of the confabulations produced by patients with damage to the ACoA. Here, he provides for us a concise overview of ACoA syndrome, especially with regard to confabulation, including several examples of actual confabulations from patient interviews.

But of course we are all capable of producing false memory reports on occasion. Researchers have lately developed several ways to provoke false memory reports in normal people, something that allows us to further probe the memory system itself, and its vulnerabilities, especially as it might pertain to witness testimony. **Lauren French**, **Marryanne Garry,** and **Elizabeth Loftus** are part of a flourishing research paradigm in psychology that is beginning to delineate the important variables that affect whether or not one is able to produce false memories in normal people. They argue that false memories in normal people are often produced by the very processes that normally function to help us reconstruct memories as we recall them. An important larger point this makes is that normal people do confabulate, and this should militate against restricting the use of the term 'confabulation' to clinical patients. One powerful technique for doing this is simply to prod the person into saying something after she has admitted not having a memory. **Quin Chrobak** and **Maria Zaragoza** review the specific variables at work behind this phenomenon and present some interesting new findings of their own.

Confabulations about intentions and actions

Patients who have undergone a split-brain operation will tend to confabulate about actions performed by the right hemisphere. In a typical experiment, commands are sent to the right hemisphere only (by presenting them briefly in the left visual field), but the left hemisphere, unaware of this, confabulates a reason for why the left hand obeyed the command. There are many cases of confabulations about actions and intentions that do not involve the right hemisphere or any obvious lateral element, however. Similar sorts of confabulations can be elicited by brain stimulation. For example, the patient's cortex is stimulated, causing her arm to move. When asked why the arm moved, the patient claims that she felt like stretching her arm. Hypnotized people may also confabulate, e.g. the subject is given a hypnotic suggestion to perform a certain action, but then confabulates a different reason for it when asked.

Patients with hemiplegia of the left arm may also claim that they moved when asked to by their attending physicians. Or, they may produce a confabulation about why they did not move when asked. **Kenneth Heilman** has been systematically testing several different hypotheses about why a certain group of patients with brain damage which causes paralysis or great weakness of their left arms are unaware, or deny, that there is anything wrong with them. His contribution here chronicles the steady progression of testing and refinement of his hypothesis, according to which denial of disability is due to malfunction in a complex, multiply parallel system for representing our bodies. Just as in the case of memory, where paradigms have been developed to elicit confabulations from normal people, in the study of action and intention, experimental paradigms have recently been developed to produce confabulations about actions from normal people. In her contribution, **Thalia Wheatley** summarizes these findings and offers a novel solution to the question of what differentiates normal mistakes from pathological confabulation.

Perceptual confabulations

Patients with Anton's syndrome are at least partially blind; but they insist that they can see. Their posterior damage typically involves bilateral lesions to the occipital cortex, causing the blindness, coupled with prefrontal damage, causing the inability to become aware of the blindness (according to a two-phase approach). Split-brain patients will also confabulate when asked about what they perceived, given certain situations. The easiest way to demonstrate this is to have the patient close his eyes while you place an ordinary object such as a key in his left hand. Then, ask him to identify the object in his hand. The right hemisphere 'knows' that it is a key, but it cannot produce speech. But the patient, or at least his left hemisphere, won't admit ignorance, and instead will confidently produce plausible but false answers: a pen, a lighter.

The patients who deny paralysis have a condition referred to as *anosognosia*, meaning unawareness of illness. They typically have a loss of one or more somatosensory systems for representing features of the affected limb. Apparently, certain types of damage (e.g. to the right inferior parietal lobe) can cause both the somatosensory problem, and at least temporarily affect prefrontal functioning enough to cause the confabulated denials of illness (Berti et al., 2005). Some patients will deny that the affected limb is even their own. In his extensive clinical experience with different types of confabulating patients, **Todd Feinberg** has become increasingly suspicious that certain patterns in their confabulations might indicate some sort of unified and psychologically interesting process at work behind them.

Perceptual confabulations are also issued by patients suffering from the misidentification syndromes (especially Capgras' syndrome). A popular approach here is to argue that these patients have a malfunction at the perceptual level to a process that produces a feeling of familiarity and/or emotional warmth at the sight of a loved one. This produces a sense of foreignness when the patient looks at his e.g. father that he explains by producing a confabulation about an impostor. The patient is unable to realize the implausibility of his claim due to additional frontal damage, adherents to this approach typically claim. There is an intriguing similarity between asomatognosia and Capgras' syndrome. The asomatognosic claims that this is not his arm, the Capgras' patient claims that this is not his father. In both cases, the very familiar is claimed to be not associated with the self. **V. S. Ramachandran** and I propose a theory designed to allow us to begin to systematize our thinking about these syndromes.

What about the delusions of those with schizophrenia? In their contribution, **Peter McKenna, Elvira Lorente-Rivera,** and **German Berrios** examine first the early history of confabulation as a symptom among a certain subtype of schizophrenics, and then describe the dynamics of this type of confabulation. **Max Coltheart** and **Martha Turner** use information about confabulations from delusional patients in order to explore a broader sense of 'confabulation', intended to apply to both memory patients and delusional confabulators. In this broader sense, confabulation is 'providing an answer to an unanswerable question'. Confabulators, whether they are also deluded or not, seem to have false beliefs. They certainly make false claims, while giving no appearance of lying or conscious deception. Are the deluded patients self-deceived in claiming that their arms are fine? Using his theory of self-deception – those curious occasions when we believe something even though we possess good evidence that it is false – **Alfred Mele** examines this question. One prototypical example of this is the doctor who believes that he is fine, even though he is aware that he has several symptoms that he would diagnose as indicating a serious cancer if he saw those symptoms in someone else. What about the patient who denies that his arm is paralyzed and says he's merely tired? Is this perhaps a case in which the patient is both self-deceived and confabulating?

There is an important commonality among several of the perceptual confabulation syndromes: they involve either right hemisphere damage or disconnection. When the right hemisphere is the primary source for a type of knowledge, for instance knowledge of the body, knowledge of the actions of the left hand, knowledge of the contents of the left visual field, and in many people, knowledge of how to recognize other people, damage or disconnection seems to set the stage for confabulation. A second type of damage is required if the two-phase theory is correct. There may be cases here in which the same event that damaged or disconnected a right hemisphere knowledge source also damaged or disconnected an executive process tasked with monitoring knowledge from that source. This would be more likely to happen if the executive processes tasked with monitoring representations produced by the right hemisphere tended themselves to be located primarily in the right hemisphere.

Confabulations about emotions

False attributions of emotions can count as confabulations. For example, in one experiment, people were given an injection of adrenaline without their knowledge, but attributed their inability to sleep to, e.g. nervousness about what they had to do the next day. We may all be guilty of confabulating about our emotions on occasion, perhaps due to the combination of our feeling responsible for giving coherent accounts of our emotions and the opacity of our emotions to cognition. The emotion itself is ill-grounded because it was produced in a non-normal way – the shot of adrenaline. Perhaps the people who confabulated were people who have trouble describing their emotions (i.e. they were alexithymic), or perhaps the example does show that we are not good at monitoring our emotions. We cannot apply the sorts of cognitive manipulations here that we can when we, e.g., check for contradictions. Given the right hemisphere's greater role in producing and perceiving emotions, there may also be a lateral element to the neural locus of confabulations about emotions.

Confabulation in general

It appears that there are confabulations about every type of intentional state, that is, every type of mental state with representational content. Even the emotions that we confabulate about at least present themselves as having a specific representational content, e.g. I am anxious *about my upcoming exam*. In theory, given the brain's large number of knowledge sources, there are many more confabulation syndromes than those listed here, but they should all follow the same pattern, damage to a posterior knowledge system (either perceptual or mnemonic), coupled with damage to prefrontal executive processes responsible for monitoring and correcting the representations delivered by that epistemic system. There are important functional links between the posterior orbitomedial cortex and the corpus callosum. Given the existence of dense interconnections between the left and right orbitomedial cortices, cutting their commissures may have the same effect of lesioning them directly.

One feature that may link all or most of the confabulation syndromes is reduced autonomic activity. There is a common finding in confabulators of a hypo-responsive, or unresponsive autonomic system. Korsakoff's patients show damage to noradrenergic structures. People with orbitofrontal damage and sociopaths (who may be confabulatory) show reduced autonomic activity to certain types of stimuli. Capgras, patients show reduced responses to the sight of familiar people. Patients with neglect and flattened affect show either no, or greatly reduced, skin conductance activity (Heilman et al., 1978). This may explain the tendency of confabulators to be unconcerned about their problems when confronted with them. It may indicate that our doubts need to be bolstered by autonomically generated feelings of uncertainty before we actually attend to them and begin to revise our beliefs. There may be several different prefrontal areas, each tasked with checking a certain type of representation, but all of these areas might stop actions based on ill-grounded representations by initiating inhibitory autonomic activity.

Most writers today agree that there is an intimate connection between intentional states and consciousness itself, although just what 'intimate' means is still under dispute. One version, from Searle (1990), is that intentional states must be either actually or potentially conscious. Each type of confabulation involves a type of conscious state, a perceptual state, a memory, an intention, and so on. According to one way of understanding executive processes, each of them takes the current conscious state as its input and performs an operation on it. The primary goal, shared by all the executive processes, is to improve the effectiveness of that person's actions. Subsidiary to this, many of the executive processes of interest in confabulation have the goal of improving the quality of the representations (e.g. beliefs, perceptual representations) of that particular person's cognitive system. As the play of consciousness proceeds, each executive process attempts to perform its specific operation on the current thought. We use executive processes to check memories, but we also use them to check thoughts of all sorts against our memories. As each watcher of the play of consciousness falls asleep, the potential for a type of confabulation opens up. **Gianfranco Dalla Barba's** contribution to this volume also explores the relation between consciousness and memory confabulations. Beginning with several examples from the clinic, Dalla Barba moves to an analysis of the phenomenology of remembering, and then to more philosophical issues about our consciousness of time.

Several of the contributors touch on the question of motivational factors at work behind confabulations. **Aikaterini Fotopoulou** looked at memory confabulations and spontaneous confabulations and found a positive bias in both, beyond our normal human tendency to be positive. Feinberg argues that what he calls personal confabulation (in which the patients 'represent themselves, their personal experiences, and their problems and preoccupations in a story') to be motivated. Mele, on the other hand, argues that motivation is not playing a role in the confabulations of Capgras' syndrome patients or anosognosics.

Conclusion

Making a sincere claim to someone, especially in response to a specific request, is similar in many ways to giving a present. We tell people things because we care about them. The present may be small or large. It may be expected or a complete surprise, and it may be of great value, or absolutely worthless. False or ill-grounded claims make bad presents; their normal value is nothing or worse than nothing since we may still waste time and energy because we believed the claim. Our minds track the value of these presents with great accuracy, especially when we are considering offering one. We do not give away valuable information to just anyone. We also do not give worthless things to people for no reason. We do not deliberately make false claims to our friends, and lying to random strangers is fairly close to being pathological. To care about someone is care about what you say to him or her. Confabulators fail exactly here, they dispense worthless claims sincerely, while seeming not to care that they are disbelieved. Their claims seem valuable to them, but they are actually worthless because they were generated by malfunctioning brain processes.

Why don't they know that they don't know? Why doesn't the Anton's patient know that he doesn't know how many fingers the doctor is holding up? Why doesn't the anosognosic know that his arm is paralyzed? Why doesn't the split-brain patient know that he doesn't know what stimulus his right hemisphere was exposed to? Why doesn't the Korsakoff's patient know that he doesn't remember what he did yesterday? Why doesn't the Capgras' patient know that he is misperceiving his father? There are many deeper questions, about what confabulation means for our conception of our nature. How does confabulation relate to artistic creativity, for instance? The recent appearance of cases in which people who had no previous interest in art or music became obsessed with them after stroke or other brain damage raises the question as to whether this sudden creative outburst might be a release or disinhibition of something that was already there, perhaps in the same way that some types of confabulation seem to be due to disinhibition. Within the realm of social psychology, does confabulation belong to that set of phenomena in which we humans in general tend to rate our intelligence, our abilities, our confidence as higher than they really are, or should be? The hope is that this volume marks the beginning of an interdisciplinary research paradigm on confabulation. Perhaps it will show that confabulation is much more than just an odd foible we humans are prone to, but is instead deeply revealing of our mental lives and what lies behind them.

References

Berti, A., Bottini, G., Gandola, M., et al. (2005). Shared cortical anatomy for motor awareness and motor control. *Science, 309* (5733), 488–491.

Fuster J. (2002). Physiology of executive functions: The perception-action cycle. In *Principles of Frontal Lobe Function* (eds. D.T. Stuss and R.T. Knight). Oxford, Oxford University Press.

Geschwind, N. (1965). Disconnexion syndromes in animals and man. *Brain, 88*, 237–644.

Heilman, K. M., Schwartz, H. D., Watson, R. (1978). Hypoarousal in patients with the neglect syndrome and emotional indifference. *Neurology, 28*, 229–232.

Hirstein, W. (2005). *Brain Fiction: Self-Deception and the Riddle of Confabulation.* Cambridge, MA, MIT Press.

Miller E.K. and Cohen J.D. (2001). An integrative theory of prefrontal cortex function. *Annual Reviews of Neuroscience, 24*, 167–202.

Searle John, R. (1990). Consciousness, explanatory inversion and cognitive science. *Behavioral and Brain Sciences, 13* (4), 585–595.

Chapter 1

Confabulation in anterior communicating artery syndrome

John DeLuca

Advancements in technology and medicine have increased the survival rate from surgery for cerebral aneurysms over the past four decades. Increased survival has directed attention away from issues of mortality toward those regarding quality of life. As such, questions regarding quality of life have been at the forefront of research with patients surviving aneurysms of the anterior communicating artery (ACoA). It is now well known that aneurysms at the ACoA frequently lead to significant neurobehavioral impairments (DeLuca and Diamond, 1995; Schnider, 2008). The most profound neurobehavioral deficits observed following ACoA aneurysm include a severe memory deficit, confabulation, and personality change. These three features have been widely referred to as the 'ACoA syndrome' (see DeLuca and Diamond, 1995) for a review) and have been the focus of much neurobehavioral research.

Ruptured ACoA aneurysm is the most consistently reported etiology which can result in severe, long lasting and spectacular confabulation (Schnider, 2008). The present chapter will focus on the behavioral and neural mechanisms of confabulation following ACoA aneurysm.

ACoA: Background information

An intracranial aneurysm is an abnormal enlargement of a blood vessel resulting from a flaw in the blood vessel wall. Cerebral aneurysms are the fourth leading cause of cerebrovascular accident (behind artherothrombosis, embolism, and intracerebral hemorrhage), accounting for 5–10% of all strokes (Dombovy, Drew-Cates and Serdans, 1998). Saccular or 'berry' aneurysms are the most common type and occur primarily at bifurcations or branch points of the vasculature. Cerebral aneurysm is fairly common, with a prevalence of 2.3–5% in adults (McCormick, 1984; Rinkel et al., 1998). The prevalence of aneurysms is also higher in females, in individuals with a family history of subarachnoid hemorrhage, atherosclerosis, suspected pituitary adenomas, and autosomal dominant polycystic kidney disease (Rinkel et al., 1998).

The ACoA lies at the anterior portion of the Circle of Willis, interconnecting the two anterior cerebral arteries just rostral to the optic chiasm. About 90–95% of saccular aneurysms lie at the anterior portion of the Circle of Willis, most commonly the ACoA, the origin of the posterior communicating artery, the first major bifurcation of the middle cerebral artery, and the bifurcation of the internal carotid into the middle and anterior cerebral arteries (Victor and Ropper, 2001). The ACoA is one of the most common sites of cerebral aneurysm in humans and is the most frequent site of cerebral infarct following aneurysm rupture (McCormick, 1984). Infarcts are often observed along the distribution of the anterior cerebral arteries, and the small perforating arterial branches directly off of the ACoA itself (Alexander and Freedman, 1984; Bornstein et al., 1987). The vascular territory of these ACoA branches involves the paraterminal gyrus (including the septal nuclei), anterior cingulum, the genu of the corpus callosum, columns of the fornix, optic chiasm, substantia inominata, the mesial anterior commissure, and the nucleus basalis of Meynert, and the anterior hypothalamus (Tatu et al., 1998).

What is confabulation?

The lack of a generally accepted definition of confabulation is a problem that should not be underestimated. Some have argued that confabulation encompasses a broad range of fabricated, distorted, or misinterpreted verbalizations including cortical blindness (Anton's syndrome), denying problems with paralyzed limbs, duplication syndromes, or neologisms from Wernicke's aphasia. While these are all manifestation of unawareness, it is unclear that they are all confabulation (see DeLuca, 2000; Hirstein, 2005). Confabulation following ACoA aneurysm involves distortions of memory. As such, confabulation is defined here as 'statements or actions that involve unintentional but obvious distortions of memory' (Moscovitch and Melo, 1997).

At a minimum, confabulation involves both distortions of the content and of the temporal context. That is, confabulatory recollections frequently include additions, distortions, or elaborations of events which either actually or plausibly occurred. This is illustrated by the following example of an ACoA patient (previously published in DeLuca, 2000):

> Doctor: What did you do today?
>
> Patient VR: Today I got up this morning and visited the rehabilitation institute ... then I went home and I was expecting some material and we received it. Then I came to the rehabilitation institute, no I actually went to the Jimsburg store and we had a small meeting there. Then I came to the hospital and we had lunch and, then met with you....

Doctor: What did you do this past weekend?

Patient VR: There was a friend that used to work at the Jimsburg store, that moved away, that was a friend of mine for 10 years or so, who came by my house for a visit with his family. We went to New York City, and as a matter of fact, we stopped by the Jimsburg store to say hello to one manager that he also has become friendly with, but this store is not operating anymore….

Several key aspects of confabulation are illustrated here. First, content distortion is illustrated by the fact that, despite having been in the hospital for several weeks, patient VR states that he has been home and had a meeting at work, yet he also correctly incorporates his knowledge about the rehabilitation hospital and the Doctor's role in it. Second, the impaired temporal context is evident when patient VR mentions the 'Jimsburg store', which he previously owned but he had actually sold years earlier. The story about the friend's visiting, going to New York City, and then seeing a mutual friend from the store actually occurred, but years earlier (verified by his spouse). The third point illustrated by this excerpt is impaired self-monitoring. While first indicating that he had visited the Jimsburg store with his friend, in the same sentence he acknowledged that the store is no longer operational. Patient VR could not realize the temporal, or the logical implausibility of being at the store and the hospital.

Thus, ACoA confabulators often exhibit a combination of temporal displacement of actual events from the past into the present, as well as the distortion of events which may be salient in the immediate environment. For researchers and clinicians, the fascination lies in the patient's lack of self-monitoring regarding the implausibility of the temporal and content displacement, therefore resulting in theories to understand what drives such behavior.

Severe confabulation following ACoA aneurysm appears acutely, occurring in 3–15% of patients (DeLuca and Diamond 1995; Schnider, 2008), and typically lasts for a period of weeks to months, sometimes years, although rarely (Talland, 1965; Weinstein, 1996; Schnider, 2008). Spontaneous confabulation following ACoA aneurysm is always coupled with a dense amnesia which persists with the resolution of the confabulation (e.g. Benson et al., 1996; DeLuca and Locker, 1996; Kapur and Coughlan, 1980). Immediately following surgery for ACoA aneurysm repair, confabulation is typically marked by confusion and disorientation, with either lethargy or agitation in some patients and anosognosia. This stage usually clears within days to a few weeks and is then dominated by the obvious confabulation, amnesia, and anosognosia (organic impairment of awareness of one's own disabilities). The confabulation can then persist even after the patient becomes oriented, usually for a few weeks to months. However, some writers confuse the confabulation for 'disorientation,' but often these can be differentiated. DeLuca and Cicerone (1991) showed that confabulation persisted in ACoA patients even with the return of orientation to person, place, month, and year, compared to a heterogeneous group of patients with a hemorrhage elsewhere in the brain, whose 'confabulation' resolved completely with the return of orientation. ACoA patients frequently hold firm convictions regarding the veracity of their confabulation and defend them readily, even when faced with the illogical nature of their statements.

A distinction between confabulation and delusion is also important. While some confabulations may be difficult to distinguish from a delusion, confabulations typically involve specific episodes or events, while most delusions concern false beliefs (Weinstein, 1996). The American Psychiatric Association defines delusion as 'A false belief based on incorrect inference about external reality that is firmly sustained…. The belief is not one ordinarily accepted by other members of the person's culture….' (American Psychiatric Association, 1994, p. 765). While 'fantastic' confabulations (see below) appear delusional, they typically resolve with improved orientation and transition into more credible 'momentary' confabulations.

Subtypes of confabulation

Korsakoff (1889, 1955) conceptualized confabulation along a continuum based on severity. However, most subsequent authors formed dichotomous distinctions of confabulation, primarily based on severity. For instance, Kraepelin (1904, 1907, 1919) proposed two subtypes: (1) *Simple* confabulation, which represented minor distortions or recall of fact, time, or detail, and (2) *Fantastic* confabulation, which consisted of bizarre, exaggerated, florid, or impossible verbalizations. More recently, Berlyne (1972) referred to 'momentary' (i.e. provoked by questions probing the subject's memory, consisting of temporal displacement of actual memories) and 'fantastic' (i.e. spontaneous, grandiose) confabulation, respectively these terms were originally proposed by Bonhoeffer in 1904 (see Schnider 2008). Kopelman (1987) distinguished between 'spontaneous' and 'provoked' confabulation, which mirrors the fantastic and momentary distinction. Despite the rise of numerous dichotomous theories, the question as to whether confabulation reflects a continuum of severity versus distinct subtypes remains a controversial issue even today.

Based largely on the difficulties in making sense of all the various permutations of behaviors associated with confabulation (e.g. intrusions, provoked, fantastic, bizarre, acting out, etc.), Schnider (2008) broke from the dichotomous tradition and proposed four forms of confabulation: (1) *intrusions or 'simple provoked confabulations'*, which are intrusions or distortions of single elements; (2) *momentary confabulations*, which are false statements upon incitement, are conceivable or plausible, can be provoked or spontaneous, and can range from simple statements to elaborate stories; (3) *fantastic confabulations* are those which have 'no basis in reality', are illogical, and are not associated with behaviorally acting upon their false beliefs; and (4) *behaviorally spontaneous confabulations*, which presumably occur concurrently with severe amnesia and disorientation and are marked primarily by patients acting-out their false beliefs. While these four forms of confabulation are informative, there is no general consensus that confabulations fit neatly into these four categories.

Other than the bizarre fabrications which are grandiose, clearly false, and have no basis in reality (i.e. fantastic confabulation), behaviorally spontaneous confabulation provides some of the most spectacular and compelling behavioral episodes. Episodes in which patients are found acting on their confabulations are not uncommon following ACoA aneurysm. For example, ACoA patient RR would frequently use the phone in his hospital room asking for his secretary and would become disturbed when the operator was unclear regarding the nature of his inquiry. On several occasions, RR would approach the nurse's station asking when and where his next meeting was to take place, demanding to speak to his secretary behind the desk. One day, ACoA patient BJ managed to leave the locked brain injury ward and was nowhere to be found. The nurses and his physician hurried to my office looking for suggestions for what to do. I suggested paging him overhead since BJ already thought that he was at work. Within minutes, BJ answered the page (as he would have done at work) and was found easily.

What is interesting about Schnider's new classification is that it provides an improved demarcation and between confabulatory behaviors. For example, in Kopelman's dichotomy, spontaneous confabulation could be either plausible or illogical. Schnider's classification allows for further differentiation of spontaneous confabulation into 'momentary,' 'fantastic,' and 'behaviorally spontaneous,' respectively. Consider the following confabulation from an ACoA patient:

Doctor: What month is it?

Patient OJ: Its December 199x and we're gathered together here under the aegis of ----- college thinking about the year past and the year to come and inevitably thinking about the holiday too and the way it marks that change from one year to another. And the ways in which our perhaps eighteen or twenty people in our group and several other groups totaling perhaps 60 to 65 people, who are around the hotel going to the same kind of workshops and jam sessions as we are. There's an alternative or second purpose to this which is to advance a second and ongoing project related to the development of teaching techniques at ----- college, specifically related to the involvement of off-campus people in teaching.... The old campus people ... are part of a program which allows them to go on a summer tour with their families in their automobiles and has them stop at this hotel-motel for a period of time.

Several years later, after patient OJ recovered from his confabulation but remained amnesic (although improved), I showed him a tape of this response and he explained that this confabulation was based on an actual summer trip to England that was taken and funded by his prior college employer and, indeed, included various families involved in learning about teaching activities. As such, this confabulation would be considered 'momentary' by Schnider. Note also that confabulation started out by simply asking the month, to which OJ responded correctly, but then 'spontaneously' elaborated that answer into an unrelated confabulation, which he now switched to the summer, as well as an entirely different topic. Incidentally, the impaired temporal context and content confusion were clear in that OJ had been in the hospital for several weeks. It should be noted that upon questioning, he was consistently oriented to person, place, month, and year. But clearly, the confabulation could not be reconciled with his orientation (i.e. poor self-monitoring).

A few minutes later during the same interview, patient OJ was asked:

Doctor: What did you do last night?

Patient OJ: Last night we were involved in this experience, trying to find out as much as possible what would happen when these people; first of all, these people to some extent who had been deprived of their stimulation due to exposure to these drugs, would react when stimulated by exposure to, [and] at least appeared like people from outer space or machines from outer space or institutions from outer space.... Maybe because these institutions from outer space were designed by us because and therefore not as different as they might be if designed by people from other times.

Clearly, OJ was exhibiting fantastic confabulation here, which was illogical and not based on reality. Nonetheless, it is clear that multiple forms of confabulation can be experienced within the same person and at the same time following ACoA aneurysm, even while oriented.

Despite Schnider's new four-factor model, a major issue in the literature has been whether provoked and spontaneous confabulations represent two distinct forms with different neuropathological mechanisms or if each is an extreme on a continuum from a single underlying mechanism. Support for the continuum hypothesis was presented by DeLuca and Cicerone (1991). These authors examined confabulation both when ACoA patients were initially disoriented and continued weekly until they regained orientation to person, place, and time. Results showed that as patients progressed from the disoriented to oriented state, confabulation changed from spontaneous to provoked in nature.

Since these were the same subjects under the two orientation conditions, differences between types of confabulation were unlikely to be due to differences in lesion location. Furthermore, both spontaneous and provoked forms of confabulation were often observed in the same patient under either orientation condition, suggesting that the two forms of confabulation did not require different lesion locations. DeLuca and Cicerone (1991) concluded that confabulation following ACoA aneurysm may represent differences in degree and not in kind.

The hypothesis that forms of confabulation represent different degrees of a common disorder has been supported by other studies (e.g. Shapiro et al., 1981; Dalla Barba, 1993). Several authors have noted that a more substantial degree of frontal lobe pathology is required to manifest spontaneous versus provoked confabulation. For instance, Kapur and Coughlin (1980) reported an ACoA patient whose confabulation changed from fantastic (i.e. spontaneous) to momentary (i.e. provoked) over several months, with this change paralleled by improvements on tests of 'frontal lobe functioning.' Fischer et al. (1995) reported that ACoA patients with spontaneous (or more severe) confabulations had more extensive lesions involving the ventral frontal lobes, basal forebrain, and striatum, compared to ACoA patients with 'momentary or provoked' (or less severe) confabulations whose lesions were restricted to the basal forebrain.

In contrast, several authors have suggested that spontaneous and provoked confabulations reflect different underlying pathologies. Berlyne concluded that 'fantastic confabulation seems to be a distinct entity having nothing in common with momentary confabulation...' (1972, p. 33). Schnider et al. (1996) reported a double dissociation between spontaneous and provoked confabulations. These authors classified patients as either spontaneous (but included only behaviorally spontaneous confabulators) or provoked (i.e. emitting intrusions on a verbal list learning task) confabulators. In this study, provoked but not spontaneous confabulations were correlated with performance on measures of verbal learning and verbal fluency. In contrast, only spontaneous confabulations were associated with difficulties on temporal order processing on a continuous recognition task. Based on this double dissociation, the authors concluded that the two forms represent different disorders rather than different degrees of the same disorder. The authors state that provoked confabulation was not associated with a specific lesion and that spontaneous confabulation was 'only found in patients with lesions of the posterior orbitofrontal cortex or structures directly connected with it.' In 2008, Schnider reconceptualizes the spontaneous confabulation reported in Schnider et al. (1996) as 'behavioral spontaneous confabulation.' He argues that acting out one's confabulation represents a more severe case subtype, mediated by different neural mechanisms, and a unique syndrome, dissociated from other forms of even spontaneous confabulations (Schnider, 2003; Schnider, 2008).

In summary, the dichotomy between differences in confabulation which reflect differences in severity versus distinct forms, first established at the turn of the 19th century by Korsakoff and Kraepelin, respectively, remains with us. There is no definitive support for either hypothesis at the turn of the 20th century. This work remains burdened by the lack of a clear definition and conceptualization of what confabulation truly is.

Confabulation: An 'unaware' or 'aware' phenomenon?

Clinicians and researchers have formulated a variety of different perspectives on confabulation over the past 100 years. Frequently, these are dichotomous in nature. One such broad dichotomy is between the aware and unaware forms of confabulation. The first conceptualizes confabulation as an 'unaware' process, a perspective that stems primarily from the neurological literature. The second recognizes a conscious awareness aspect to confabulation, which tends to reflect work from the psychiatric literature.

Korsakoff in the late 1800s first discussed the notion that patients were conceptualized as unaware of their confabulations. Korsakoff (1889, 1955) described patients who verbally present seemingly erroneous recollections that they defended with conviction as accurate or correct. He was able to trace many of these recollections and found that they were usually true but had been displaced in time. Many researchers since then have recognized that confabulation is frequently a temporal displacement of an actual event in the patient's life, although this event can be embellished with intrusions and distortions (Talland, 1965; Ptak and Schnider, 1999). Importantly, confabulators are unaware that they are confabulating, nor are they aware of the temporal displacement of their confabulations. Regarding one confabulator, Talland (1965) writes, 'The patient himself is almost certainly not aware of the gaps in his knowledge when he confabulates; he transposes information from an earlier period in his life, condenses or distorts material without consciousness of his deficit or of the confabulatory process, and hence without intent' (Talland, 1965, p. 57).

Consider the following discourse with ACoA patient OJ (previously published in DeLuca (2000)).

> Doctor: You indicated that last night you were working on a number of projects at home …, what would you say if I told you were actually here in the hospital last night?
>
> Patient OJ: I'd be surprised, because my experience, what I learn from my eyes and ears tells me differently…. I'd want some evidence. I'd want some indication that you knew about my private world before I gave any cognizance.

Doctor: Would you believe me?

Patient OJ: Not out of the blue, especially since we haven't even met (an illustration of the patient's amnesia).

Doctor: What if your wife was here and she agreed with me, what would you think at that point?

Patient OJ: I'd continue to resist, but it would become more difficult.

Patient OJ was firm about the veracity of his recollections, resisting attempts to convince him otherwise. It was clear from his statements as well as his behavior and affect that there was no explicit intention to actively 'fill gaps in memory.' Ptak and Schnider (1999) reported a case of an amnestic ACoA patient whose confabulations could always be traced back to actual experiences. The patient was unaware of his amnesia and defended the veracity of his behaviorally spontaneous confabulations, often arguing with hospital staff.

A handful of studies were designed to experimentally examine the temporal context hypothesis (Moscovitch and Melo, 1997; Schnider et al., 1996; Gilboa et al., 2006). Schnider et al. (1996) found that on a continuous recognition task, all spontaneous confabulators, but no nonconfabulating amnesics, confused present with previously acquired information. More recently, Gilboa et al. (2006) and Moscovitch and Melo (1997) have argued that defective temporal order is not the cause of confabulation, but is a symptom of a more fundamental deficit in strategic retrieval (see below).

In summary, the temporal displacement notion that confabulators are unaware of their confabulations and that these confabulations are often temporal displacements of actual events has been recognized for over 100 years and is widely accepted today by many researchers and clinicians.

By the turn of the 19th century, a second line of thinking regarding the nature of confabulation emerged, conceptualizing confabulation as active fabrication. Early researchers such as Bonhoeffer (1901) and later Van der Horst (1932), from Schnider (2008) proposed that confabulation reflects a desire to fill gaps in memory, termed 'confabulation out of embarrassment.' According to this model, confabulators contrive a story and fill-in gaps in memory in order to hide themselves from embarrassment. Obviously, such gap filling requires some awareness of a memory disorder on the part of the patient. This model gained prominence during the 20th century despite the fact that there was very little scientific empirical support for it. In fact, the few studies which empirically examined gap filling behavior did not support this hypothesis (Moscovitch and Melo, 1997; Schnider et al., 1996). Nonetheless, the gap-filling model is maintained even today. For instance, the DSM-IV defines confabulation as '… the recitation of imaginary events to fill in gaps in memory'

(American Psychiatric Association, 1994, p. 157). Psychiatry textbooks also define confabulations as conscious gap filling, with a conscious wish to deceive (Whitlock, 1981). Benson et al. (1996) describe confabulation as 'compensation for loss of memory by the fabrication of details' (Benson et al., 1996, p. 1239).

Other early conceptualizations of confabulation included '…a disturbance in symbolism, comparable to that which occurs in dreaming, … wish-fulfilling fantasies,… the means whereby sexually traumatic material could be expressed and gratified' (Weinstein and Lyerly, 1968, p. 348). Some believe that premorbid personality traits are important determinants in who will eventually confabulate (Talland, 1965; Weinstein and Kahn, 1955). However, there is very little evidence to support these early conceptualizations of confabulation, which typically rely on subjective observations of behavior and on case reports or a case series. No systematic experimentally controlled studies have been conducted.

Such 'motivational' accounts of the content of confabulation have been examined more recently in cases studies of ACoA patients (Fotopoulou et al., 2007; Turnbull et al., 2004). These studies suggested that the content of confabulation was based on a 'positive emotional bias', whereby self-representations rely predominantly on positive characteristics (see Hirstein, 2005). For instance, compared to five healthy controls, the confabulation in an ACoA patient included significantly more positive self-representations and an overall positive valence. However, others have suggested that the positive emotional bias may simply be a consequence of lesion location (involving anterior limbic structures) rather than an element of 'wish fulfillment' (Schnider, 2008). Despite these new and interesting studies, the data in support of positive bias are still based on only a handful of ACoA patients and still have methodological issues which need to be addressed.

In sum, confabulation following ACoA aneurysm involves both the temporal displacement of actual events and distortions of the content. ACoA confabulators believe and defend their confabulations and are not engaged in an intentional effort to fill-in gaps to avoid embarrassment or hide a memory disorder. Motivational theories of the confabulation content are still in need of further study.

Neurobehavioral models of confabulation

Much has been learned regarding the neuroanatomical underpinnings of confabulation following ACoA aneurysm. In the 1950s, confabulation was attributed to diffuse cerebral toxicity without structural localization. Talland (1965) suggested that the neuroanatomical structures responsible for ACoA confabulation are the same as that observed following Korsakoff's syndrome (lesions of the mammillary bodies and the dorsal-medial nucleus of the thalamus). In 1982, Gade showed that the amnesia associated with the ACoA syndrome was associated with basal forebrain lesions due directly to the interruption of blood flow from perforating arteries from the ACoA itself. Although Gade (1982) made no claims regarding confabulation, Alexander and Freedman (1984) showed that confabulators had infarcts in the ACoA territory on CT scan. They speculated that the ACoA syndrome was due to the damage to the septal area, altering the cholinergic communication with the hippocampus. A similar proposal for the amnesia was presented by Damasio et al. (1985) and later expanded by Meyers et al. (2002). Since the 1960s, three overall neurobehavioral models of confabulation have been proposed: (1) the *memory impairment model*, which focuses on importance of impaired memory in confabulation; (2) the *executive dysfunction model*, which states that frontal/executive dysfunction is the key element responsible for confabulation; and (3) the *dual-lesion model*, which states that confabulation is observed only in the presence of both a significant memory disorder and frontal/executive dysfunction.

The association of confabulation with impaired memory or amnesia has long been recognized. The memory impairment model states that amnesia is a prerequisite for confabulation to be present (Talland, 1965). Yet, both Korsakoff and Kraepelin recognized that defective memory alone could not account for confabulation. There are several lines of evidence showing that the memory impairment hypothesis is inadequate in explaining confabulation. First, not all amnesic patients confabulate (Moscovitch and Melo, 1997; Parkin, 1984; Schnider, 2008). Second, confabulation resolves in most ACoA patients over a period of weeks or months, yet little or no change is observed in the severity of memory loss (e.g. Benson et al., 1996; DeLuca and Locker, 1996; Kapur and Coughlan, 1980). Third, lesions restricted to the basal forebrain, resulting in impaired memory, do not produce spontaneous confabulation (Abe et al., 1998; Berti et al., 1990; Morris et al., 1993; von Cramon et al., 1993) but provoked intrusions are not uncommon (Fischer et al., 1995; Phillips et al., 1987).

The *executive dysfunction model* hypothesizes that confabulation is a consequence solely of executive impairment due to frontal system dysfunction, resulting from disinhibition, lack of self-monitoring, and decreased awareness (Benson et al., 1996; Johnson et al., 1993; Kapur and Coughlin, 1980). The notion that damage to the frontal lobes is necessary for spontaneous confabulation is now well established (Schnider, 2008). Several studies have shown convincingly that damage to the ventromedial and orbitofrontal regions of the frontal lobes are crucial for spontaneous confabulation following ACoA aneurysm (Luria, 1973, 1980; Stuss et al., 1978; DeLuca and Cicerone, 1991; Moscovitch and Melo, 1997; Vilkki, 1985; Fischer et al., 1995; Ptak and Schnider, 1999; Schnider et al., 1996; Gilboa et al., 2006). In addition, several studies show that confabulation diminishes as performance on tests of executive functioning improves (e.g. Kapur and Coughlan, 1980; Popagno and Baddeley, 1997, Nys et al., 2004). Confabulation has been shown to be associated with decreased perfusion of the bilateral orbitofrontal cortex, with improvements in confabulation related to increased frontal lobe perfusion (Benson et al., 1996; Mentis et al., 1995). It should be noted that while improvements in frontal/executive measures are associated with diminished confabulation, the severity of impaired memory remains unchanged in these studies.

The executive model of confabulation also hypothesizes that a memory disorder is not required for confabulation to be observed and that executive dysfunction alone is sufficient to result in confabulation (Johnson, 1991). Unfortunately, there are only a few studies which support this claim, and the few that do (e.g. Kapur and Coughlan, 1980; Papagno and Baddeley, 1997) have been problematic (see DeLuca, 2000 for more details). The fact that not all patients with frontal/executive dysfunction confabulate is a major problem for the executive dysfunction model. For example, some studies have shown that executive failures did not differentiate between spontaneous confabulators and non-confabulating amnesics (Schnider et al., 1996; Schnider and Ptak, 1999).

The *dual-lesion hypothesis* is the third neurobehavioral model which states that confabulation (spontaneous confabulation) requires both amnesia and executive dysfunction in order to be expressed (Cunningham et al., 1997; DeLuca, 1993; DeLuca and Diamond, 1995; Moscovich and Melo, 1997; Schnider et al., 1996; Ptak and Schnider 1999; Fischer et al., 1995; Stuss et al., 1978; Wheatly and McGrath, 1997). There is considerable support for this model.

DeLuca (1993) found that only ACoA patients with both frontal/executive dysfunction and amnesia confabulated. Moscovitch and Melo (1997) showed that the degree of memory impairment did not differ between confabulating and non-confabulating amnesics, indicating that amnesia is not sufficient, but may be necessary for confabulation to be observed. They did find that intensity of confabulation was associated with more impairment on frontal/executive tasks. Fischer et al. (1995) divided nine acute ACoA patients into 'spontaneous' confabulators and 'provoked' confabulators. They found that 'spontaneous' confabulation required disruption of both the basal forebrain and frontal systems. Lesions restricted to either the basal forebrain or orbital frontal structures resulted in 'provoked' or transient confabulatory responses.

Gilboa et al. (2006) compared four confabulating amnesic patients (three were ACoA) with eight non-confabulating ACoA subjects whose memory and executive function skills ranged from impaired to average or above average performance. They found that while ventromedial prefrontal cortex damage was associated with confabulation, spontaneous confabulation required additional damage to the orbitofrontal cortex. While some ACoA patients in the non-confabulating group may have had some degree of memory and/or executive dysfunction, clearly all four confabulators had severe memory and executive dysfunction.

The major problem with the dual-lesion model is that not all persons with a combination of memory and executive dysfunction confabulate. These, however, are studies primarily from etiologies other than ACoA. It may be that the specific frontal lobe lesions required for confabulation are those particularly vulnerable to ACoA aneurysm, and hence can be used to further refine the critical frontal structures needed for spontaneous confabulation.

In summary, the dual-lesion hypothesis, which states that memory confabulation requires both a lesion resulting in significant amnesia (i.e. basal forebrain) and damage to the frontal/executive system, provides the most convincing explanation for confabulation following ACoA aneurysm. The ventromedial prefrontal cortex as well as the orbitofrontal region (i.e. in the distribution of the anterior cerebral artery) are the crucial damage sites within the frontal lobes for spontaneous confabulation to be displayed.

Cognitive explanations of confabulation

There are two primary theories that discuss the neurocognitive mechanisms responsible for spontaneous confabulation: the temporality hypothesis, which states that confabulations are true memories displaced in time, and the strategic retrieval hypothesis, which suggests that confabulation results from retrieval failure for which 'monitoring' plays a critical role (Gilboa and Moscovitch, 2006).

Support for the temporality hypothesis comes from a series of studies by Schnider's group who examined two runs of a continuous recognition paradigm, one hour apart. Behaviorally spontaneous confabulators showed disproportionate deficits on the second run whereby they erroneously chose stimuli that were relevant on the first run but not the second run (Schnider et al., 1996; Schnider and Ptak, 1999; Schnider et al., 2000). They termed this finding 'temporal context confusion' (TCC). TCC appears to be due to an inability to suppress previously activated memory traces of events dating back hours, weeks, or years. TCC not only reliably separates confabulators from non-confabulators, but it also precisely parallels the recovery from behaviorally spontaneous confabulation (Schnider et al., 2000, 2008).

The strategic retrieval hypothesis is supported by Moscovitch and Melo (1997). Their first premise is that confabulation is more of a problem in retrieval than encoding, consolidation, or storage. They postulate that it is impaired *strategic retrieval*, which requires an active, self-initiated, goal-directed, and an effortful systematic memory search, and not a deficit in passive search processes (i.e. *associative retrieval*), which is responsible for confabulation (Moscovitch, 1989). Moscovitch and Melo further state that defective temporal order processing is not the cause of confabulation. Rather, impaired temporal processing is the result of a more fundamental problem in the strategic retrieval of the memory trace and defective self-monitoring of this trace. They hypothesize that the primary deficit resulting in confabulation is not simply the severity of the impaired strategic search at input (i.e. searching for the memory trace), but an impairment in the monitoring at output (i.e. monitoring what was retrieved). Therefore, confabulation is the consequence of a faulty outcome from a disturbed strategic search and results from improper monitoring, evaluation, and verification of the recovered memory trace (Rapcsak et al., 1998).

Gilboa and Moscovitch (2006) followed up on their previous work and conducted a series of three studies to directly contrast the temporality and strategic retrieval hypotheses. They studied four confabulating patients (three ACoA) and eight non-confabulating ACoA patients, the results of which supported the strategic retrieval theory of confabulation, emphasizing the post-retrieval monitoring of the memory trace as a critical component. Gilboa and Moscovitch (2006) concluded that 'TCC plays a major role in spontaneous confabulation (behavioral or verbal), and may be necessary for it to occur, but it is not sufficient as a single causative mechanism' (Gilboa and Moscovitch, 2006, p. 1413).

Schnider (2008) believes that what is required in addition to TCC is impaired episodic memory as measured by delayed recall. This is because increased TCC in the presence of normal explicit memory does not predict behaviorally spontaneous confabulation (Schnider, 2008). Interestingly, this supports the dual-lesion hypothesis described above. Importantly, both Schnider and Gilboa and Moscovitch agree that spontaneous confabulation require both ventromedial and orbitofrontal lesions.

Taken together, cognitive theories on the mechanism of confabulation stress impaired self-monitoring and strategic retrieval mechanisms as critical elements responsible for spontaneous confabulation. It appears that TCC may be necessary for spontaneous confabulation, but may be a submechanism resulting directly from impaired strategic retrieval of the memory trace.

Treatment for confabulation

Studies have reported a wide range of recovery following ACoA aneurysm, both in the time-frame of recovery (Okawa et al., 1980; Schnider, 2008) and in the pattern and degree of recovery (Stenhouse et al., 1991). Up to 84% of ACoA survivors are able to return to work (Teissier du Cros and Lhermitte, 1984; Hori and Suzuki, 1979). However, it is also well documented that many patients still manifest significant neuropsychological, psychological, and psychosocial consequences, even in the absence of obvious neurological deficits (e.g. Bornstein et al., 1987; Ljunggren et al., 1985; Sonesson et al., 1987). Neurobehavioral factors that have been shown to affect recovery include post-operative cognitive abilities (Bottger et al., 1998), post-operative personality changes (Alexander and Freedman, 1984; Okawa et al., 1980), and post-operative emotional issues (Vilkki et al., 1990). A variety of surgical and post-surgical factors have also been related to recovery (see Table 1.1).

The time frame for neurobehavioral recovery typically ranges from 1–2 months post-aneurysm to 6 months post-aneurysm. For example, Okawa and colleagues (1980) noted that in most of their cases, post-operative confabulation began to disappear 1–3 months following surgery, disappearing completely within 6 months. Alexander and Freedman (1984) reported that most patients continued to improve for months following ACoA aneurysm, during

Table 1.1 Factors affecting outcome following ACoA aneurysm

Information
Duration of surgery
Duration of temporary clipping
Edema
Hydrocephalous
Increased intracranial pressure
Induced focal perfusion
Infarction
Ischemia
Subarachnoid hemorrhage (SAH)
Following aneurysm rupture
Surgical technique
Timing of neurosurgery
Vasospasm

which time confabulation, 'denial,' and confusion cleared. However, confabulation can persist well beyond this time-frame, up to 1 year and beyond in some ACoA patients (Kapur and Coughlan, 1980; Schnider, 2008). While very mild confabulation can last for only days, such behavior should not be confused with the acute confusional state often observed post-operatively (DeLuca and Cicerone, 1991).

Very few studies have been performed evaluating cognitive rehabilitation efforts with ACoA patients, especially those with severe impairments. Treatment for confabulation is generally conducted within the framework of a comprehensive rehabilitation plan. Intervention for confabulation has focused largely on improving awareness. It has been suggested that awareness training can significantly reduce confabulation (DeLuca, 1992) and improve awareness of impaired memory (Schacter, 1987). Briefly, unawareness of deficit is not a unitary construct. For instance, confabulators could become aware that they indeed confabulate but not be aware of when they are actually engaged in such behavior. DeLuca (1992) outlined a program which treats confabulation at each of the three stages of unawarness: intellectual awareness, the ability of the patient to understand that they confabulate; emergent awareness, the ability of the patient to be aware that they are confabulating when actually engaged in such behavior; and anticipatory awareness, becoming able to identify in advance circumstance which may result in confabulation (see DeLuca, 1992 for details of the program). Unfortunately, no systematic studies evaluating the effectiveness of such a program have been published.

Because of the fantastic and bizarre presentation of severe (behaviorally spontaneous) confabulation, physicians often attempt medications as an approach for treatment. Unfortunately, there are no controlled studies on the efficacy of such treatment in ACoA patients on confabulation. Dopamine agonists have been the medication of choice, but with mixed findings at best (Pihan et al., 2004; Schnider, 2008). The effect of dopamine agonists can be observed within a few days, even with low doses, making such medications ripe for therapeutic trials.

Given the paucity of studies examining the effectiveness of rehabilitation interventions for confabulation in ACoA patients, this area is clearly ripe for further investigation.

Conclusions

Confabulation following ACoA aneurysm is not uncommon, often resulting in some of the most spectacular episodes of confabulatory behavior observed following damage to the brain. Work with ACoA patients has resulted in some significant advances regarding the nature of confabulation. Few believe currently that ACoA confabulators consciously fill-in gaps to hide a memory disorder. The traditional notion of dichotomous forms of confabulation has given way to conceptulizations of up to four forms of confabulatory behavior. In addition to amnesia, it is now clear that damage to both the ventromedial and the orbitofrontal regions is necessary for spontaneous confabulation. While temporal confusion remains a hallmark of spontaneous confabulation in ACoA patients, recent studies suggest that this may be a result of impaired strategic retrieval along with compromised self-monitoring. One area which has received little attention is rehabilitation and treatment. Such work promises to be a fruitful area of future inquiry.

References

Abe, K., Inokawa, M., Kashiwagi, A., and Yanagihara, T. (1998). Amnesia after a discrete basal forebrain lesion. *Journal of Neurology Neurosurgery Psychiatry,* **65**, 126–130.

Alexander, M.P., and Freedman, M., (1984). Amnesia after anterior communicating artery aneurysm rupture. *Neurology, 34,* 752–757.

American Psychiatric Association (1994). DSM-IV: *Diagnostic and Statistical Manual of Mental Disorders.* Washington, DC, American Psychiatric Association.

Benson, D.F., Djenderedjian, A., Miller, B.L., et al. (1996). Neural basis of confabulation. *Neurology,* **46**, 1239–1243.

Berlyne, N. (1972). Confabulation. *British Journal of Psychiatry,* **120**, 31–39.

Berti, A., Arienta, C., and Papagno, C. (1990). A case of amnesia after excision of the septum pellucidum. *Journal of Neurology, Neurosurgery and Psychiatry,* **53**, 922–924.

Bonhoeffer, K. (1901). Der Korsakowsche Symptomenkomplex in seinen Beziehungen zu den verschiedenen Krankheitsformen. *Allgemeine Zeitschrift fur Psychiatrie,* **61**, 744–752.

Bornstein, R.A, Weir, B.K, Petruk, K.C, and Disney, L.B. (1987). Neuropsychological function in patients after subarachnoid hemorrhage. *Neurosurgery,* **21**(5), 651–654.

Bottger, S., Prosiegel, M., Steiger, H.J., and Yassouridis, A. (1998). Neurobehavioural disturbances, rehabilitation outcome, and lesion site in patients after rupture and repair of anterior communicating artery aneurysm. *Journal of Neurology, Neurosurgery and Psychiatry,* **65**(1), 93–102.

Cunningham, J.M., Pliskin, N.H., Cassisi, J.E., Tsang, B., and Rao, S.M. (1997). Relationship between confabulation and measures of memory and executive function. *Journal of Clinical and Experimental Neuropsychology,* **19**, 867–877.

Damasio, A.R., Graff-Radford, N.R., Eslinger, P.J., Damasio, H., and Kassell, N. (1985). Amnesia following basal forebrain lesions. *Archives of Neurology,* **42**, 263–271.

Dalla Barba, G. (1993). Confabulation: Knowledge and recollective experience. *Cognitive Neuropsychology,* **10**, 1–20.

DeLuca, J. (2000). A cognitive Neuroscience perspective on confabulation. *Neuropsychoanalysis,* **2**(2), 119–132.

DeLuca, J. and Cicerone, K.D. (1991). Confabulation following aneurysm of the anterior communicating artery. *Cortex,* **27**, 417–423.

DeLuca, J. (1992). Rehabilitation of confabulation: The issue of unawareness of the deficit. *NeuroRehabilitation*, **2**, 23–30.

DeLuca, J. (1993). Predicting neurobehavioral patterns following anterior communicating artery aneurysm. *Cortex*, **29**, 639–647.

DeLuca, J. and Diamond, B.J. (1995). Aneurysm of the anterior communicating artery: Aa review of neuroanatomical and neuropsychological sequelae. *Journal Clinical Experimental Neuropsychology*, **17**, 100–121.

DeLuca, J. and Locker, R. (1996). Cognitive rehabilitation following anterior communicating artery aneurysm bleeding: A case report. *Disability and Rehabilitation*. **18**, 265–272.

Dombovy, M., Drew-Cates, J., and Serdans, R. (1998). Recovery and rehabilitation following subarachnoid haemorrhage: Part II. Long-term follow-up. *Brain Injury*, **12**, 887–894.

Fotopoulou, A., Conwat, M., Griffiths, P., Birchall, D., and Tyrer, S. (2007). Self-enhancing confabulation: Revisiting the motivational hypothesis. *Neurocase*, **13**, 6–15.

Fischer, R.S., Alexander, M.P., D'Esposito, M., and Otto, R. (1995). Neuropsychological and neuroanatomical correlates of confabulation. *Journal of Clinical and Experimental Neuropsychology*, **17**(1), 20–28.

Gade A. (1982). Amnesia after operations on aneurysms of the anterior communicating artery. *Surgical Neurology*, **18**(1), 46–49.

Gilboa, A., Alain, C., Stuss, D.T., Melo, B., Miller, S., and Moscovitch, M. (2006). Mechanisms of spontaneous confabulations: A strategic retrieval account. *Brain*, **129**, 1399–1414.

Hirstein, W. (2005). *Brain Fiction*. Cambridge: MIT Press.

Hori, S. and Suzuki, J. (1979). Early and late results of intracranial direct surgery of anterior communicating artery aneurysms. *Journal of Neurosurgery*, **50**(4), 433–440.

Johnson, M.K. (1991). Reality monitoring: Evidence from confabulation in organic brain disease patients. In *Awareness of Deficit after Brain Injury: Clinical and Theoretical Issues* (eds. G.P. Prigatano and D.L. Schacter), pp. 176–197. New York, Oxford University Press.

Johnson, M.K., Hashtroudi, S., and Lindsay, D.S. (1993). Source monitoring. *Psychological Bulletin*, **114**, 3–28.

Kapur, N. and Coughlan, A.K. (1980). Confabulation and frontal lobe dysfunction. *Journal of Neurology, Neurosurgery and Psychiatry*, **43**, 461–463.

Kopelman, M.D. (1987). Two types of confabulation. *Journal of Neurology, Neurosurgery and Psychiatry*, **50**(11), 1482–1487.

Korsakoff, S.S. (1955). Psychic disorder in conjunction with peripheral neuritis (trans. M. Victor and P.I. Yakovlev). *Neurology*, **5**, 394–406. (Original work published in 1889).

Kraepelin, E. (1904). Lectures on clinical psychiatry (trans. T. Johnstone). London, Bailliere, Tindall, and Cox.

Kraepelin, E. (1907). Clinical psychiatry: A textbook for students and physicians (trans. A.R. Diefendorf). New York, Macmillan.

Kraepelin, E. (1919). Dementia praecox and paraphrenia (trans. R.M. Barclay). Edinburgh, UK, E. and S. Livingstone.

Luria A.R. (1973). The Working Brain. NY, Basic Books.

Luria A.R. (1980). Higher Cortical Functions in Man. NY, Basic Books.

Ljunggren, B., Sonesson, B., Saveland, H., and Brandt, L. (1985). Cognitive impairment and adjustment in patients without neurological deficits after aneurysmal SAH and early operation. *Journal of Neurosurgery, 62*(5), 673–679.

Mentis, M., Weinstein, E.A., Murphy, D.G.M., Mcintosh, A.R., and Pietrini, P. (1995). Abnormal brain glucose metabolism in the delusional misidentification syndromes. *Biological Psychiatry, 38*, 438–439.

Meyers, C.E., Bryant, D., DeLuca, J., and Gluck, M.A. (2002). Dissociating basal forebrain and medial temporal amnesic syndromes: Insights from classical conditioning. *Integrative Physiological and Behavioral Science, 37*(2), 85–102.

McCormick, W.F. (1984). Pathology and pathogenesis of intracranial saccular aneurysms. *Seminars in Neurology, 4*(3), 291–303.

Morris, M.D., Bowers, D., Chatterjee, A., and Heilman, K.M. (1993). Amnesia following a discrete basal forebrain lesion. *Brain, 115*, 1827–1847.

Moscovitch, M. (1989). Confabulation and the frontal systems: Strategic versus associative retrieval in neuropsychological theories of memory. In *Varieties of Memory and Consciousness: Essays in Honor of Endel Tulving* (eds. H.L. Roediger, III and F.I.M. Craik), pp. 133–160. Hillsdale, NJ, Lawrence Erlbaum Associates.

Moscovitch, M. and Melo, B. (1997). Strategic retrieval and the frontal lobes: Evidence from confabulation and amnesia. *Neuropsychologia, 35*(7), 1017–1034.

Nys, G.M., van Zandvoort, M.J., Roks, G., Kappelle, L.J., and de Haan, E.H. (2004). The role of executive functioning in spontaneous confabulation. *Cognitive and Behavioral Neurology, 17*, 213–218.

Okawa, M., Maeda, S., Nukui, H., and Kawafuchi, J. (1980). Psychiatric symptoms in ruptured anterior communicating aneurysms: Social prognosis. *Acta Psychiatrica Scandinavica, 61*(4), 306–312.

Papagno, C. and Baddeley, A. (1997). Confabulation in a dysexecutive patient: Implication for models or retrieval. *Cortex, 33*, 743–752.

Parkin, A.J. (1984). Amnesic syndrome: A lesion-specific disorder. *Cortex, 20*, 479–503.

Phillips, S., Sangalang, V., and Sterns, G. (1987). Basal forebrain infarction: A clinicopathologic correlation. *Archives of Neurology, 44*, 1134–1138.

Pihan, H., Gutbrod, K., Baas, U., and Schnider, A. (2004). Dopamine inhibition and the adaption of behavior to ongoing reality. *NeuroReport, 15*, 709–712.

Ptak, R and Schnider, A. (1999). Spontaneous confabulation after orbtitofrontal damage: The role of temporal context confusion and self-monitoring. *Neurocase, 5*, 243–250.

Rapcsak, S.Z., Kaszniak, A.W., Reminger, S.L., Glisky, M.L., Glisky, E.L., and Comer, J.F. (1998). Dissociation between verbal and autonomic measures of memory following frontal lobe damage. *Neurology, 50*, 1259–1265.

Rinkel, G., Djibuti, M., Algra, A., and van Gijn, J. (1998). Prevalence and risk of rupture of intracranial aneurysms: A systematic review. *Stroke, 29*, 251–256.

Schacter, D.L. (1987). Memory, amnesia, and frontal lobe dysfunction. *Psychobiology, 15*, 21–36.

Schnider, A. (2008). The confabulating mind: How the brain creates reality. Oxford, Oxford University Press.

Schnider, A. and Ptak, R. (1999). Spontaneous confabulators fail to suppress currently irrelevant memory traces. *Nature Neuroscience, 2*(7), 677–681.

Schnider, A., Ptak, R., von Daniken, C., and Remonda, L. (2000). Recovery from spontaneous confabulations parallels recovery of temporal confusion in memory. *Neurology, 55*, 74–83.

Schnider, A., von Daniken, C., and Gutbrod, K. (1996). The mechanisms of spontaneous and provoked confabulations. *Brain, 119*, 1365–1375.

Shapiro, B.E., Alexander, M.P., Gardner, H., and Mercer, B. (1981). Mechanisms of confabulation. *Neurology, 31*, 1070–1076.

Sonesson, B., Ljunggren, B., Saveland, H., and Brandt, L. (1987). Cognition and adjustment after late and early operation for ruptured aneurysm. *Neurosurgery, 21*(3), 279–287.

Stenhouse, L.M., Knight, R.G., Longmore, B.E., and Bishara, S.N. (1991). Long-term cognitive deficits in patients after surgery on aneurysms of the anterior communicating artery. *Journal of Neurology, Neurosurgery and Psychiatry, 54*(10), 909–914.

Stuss, D.T., Alexander, M.F., Lieberman, A., and Levine, H. (1978). An extraordinary form of confabulation. *Neurology, 28*, 1166–1172.

Tatu, L., Moulin, T., Bogousslavsky, J., and Duvernoy, H. (1998). Arterial territories of the human brain: Cerebral hemispheres. *Neurology, 50*(6), 1699–1708.

Talland, G.A. (1965). *Deranged Memory.* New York, Academic Press. pp. 41–57.

Teissier du Cros, J. and Lhermitte, F. (1984). Neuropsychological analysis of ruptured saccular aneurysms of the anterior communicating artery after radical therapy (32 cases). *Surgical Neurology, 22*(4), 353–359.

Turnbull, O.H., Jenkins, S., and Rowley, M.L. (2004). The pleasantness of false beliefs: An emotion-based account of confabulation. *Neuro-Psychoanalysis, 6*(1), 5–16.

Vilkki, J., Holst, P., Ohman, J., Servo, A., et al. (1990). Social outcome related to cognitive performance and computed tomographic findings after surgery for a ruptured intracranial aneurysm. *Neurosurgery, 26*(4), 579–584.

Victor, M. & Ropper, A.H. (2001). Cerebrovascular diseases. In *Principles of Neurology* . (eds. Adams and M. Victor), pp. 821–924. New York, McGraw-Hill.

Vilkki, J. (1985). Amnesic syndromes after surgery of anterior communicating artery aneurysm. *Cortex, 21*, 431–444.

Von Cramon, D.Y., Markowitsch, H.J., and Schuri, U. (1993). The possible contribution of the septal region to memory. *Neuropsychologia, 31*, 1159–1180.

Weinstein, E.A. (1996). Symbolic aspects of confabulation following brain injury: Influence of premorbid personality. *Bulletin of the Menninger Clinic, 60*(3), 331–350.

Weinstein, E.A. and Kahn, R.L. (1955). *Denial of Illness.* Springfield, IL, Charles C. Thomas.

Weinstein, E.A. and Lyerly, O.G. (1968). Confabulation following brain injury: Its analogues and sequelae. *Archives of General Psychiatry, 18*, 348–354.

Wheatly, J. and McGrath, J. (1997). Co-occurrence of executive impairment and amnestic syndrome following subarachnoid haemorrhage: A case study. *Cortex, 33*, 711–721.

Whitlock, F.A. (1981). Some observations on the meaning of confabulation. *British Journal of Medical Psychology, 54*, 213–218.

Chapter 2

False memories: A kind of confabulation in non-clinical subjects

Lauren French, Maryanne Garry, and Elizabeth Loftus

Confabulation means different things depending upon who is talking about it. It encompasses different definitions and ideas in terms of content, awareness, spontaneity, plausibility, and bizarreness. But most definitions have some common components; confabulations are generally considered to be the result of a belief or memory that has no basis in reality – yet confabulators believe that their claims are accurate (Hirstein, 2005; Johnson, 2000; Johnson et al., 2000; Schnider, 2003). A major focus of confabulation research tends to be on brain-damaged patients, yet this group is by no means the only one to experience confabulations (Johnson et al., 2000). In this chapter, we discuss research that shows how normal everyday people can come to produce confabulations. We deviate slightly from Hirstein's (2005) definition of confabulation, saying instead that a confabulation occurs when someone claims and confidently believes that something happened even though it never actually did.

False memories

False memories are one subset of confabulations. When people have false memories, not only do they believe that something happened even though it did not, but also they come to remember specific – but false – details about it. False memories can concern events that never happened or they may be distorted memories of events that actually did happen; either way the result is that people claim that something happened and they believe – and remember – that it happened, despite the fact that their belief is wrong and the thing never really occurred, or at least not in the way they claim. In short, a confabulation might occur because someone has a false memory and as a result claims to remember something that never actually happened.

Our focus here is on false memories in non-clinical subjects – everyday ordinary people. We argue that such confabulations are a byproduct of normally functioning memory processes and mechanisms, rather than the result of pathological conditions. False memories are completely normal and frequent in everyday life. To illustrate, we discuss research showing the myriad ways in which false memories can and do occur. Examining how this kind of confabulation occurs can provide insight into how confabulations more generally might come about in normal everyday situations. Of course, knowing that non-clinical subjects experience confabulations does not rule out a role for brain damage in confabulation – brain damage may work to exacerbate normal tendencies that lead to false memory creation. According to Johnson et al. (2000), experiences of confabulation in brain-damaged patients are probably a more extreme version of what non-brain damaged people experience; understanding the factors that contribute to both the more and less extreme manifestations might help us to understand the other.

To reiterate, our main focus is on one subset of confabulations: false memories. We discuss research on false memories and show how false memories result from normal memory processes. We also consider how deliberate fabrication can actually lead to the creation of false memories.

How normal is confabulation?

Alien abduction memories

Some people believe that aliens exist and that aliens abduct humans. In one survey, 27% of respondents reported believing that aliens had been to earth and 14% reported actually seeing a UFO (Gallup and Newport, 1991). In another survey, 54% of respondents reported believing that aliens abduct humans and 1% believed that they personally had been on a spaceship (Chequers et al., 1997). Some of these people don't merely believe in alien abduction – they actually 'remember' the experience of being abducted and being the subject of alien experimentation (Clancy, 2005; Mack, 1994). For instance, Mack describes several case studies of people who have vivid memories of being taken to spaceships by aliens, some on multiple occasions; these people can remember details such as having their clothing removed by the aliens, being examined and experimented on with specific tools, having their eggs and sperm harvested, and communicating with the aliens telepathically.

Carlos, a 55-year-old fine arts professor, is one example. Carlos is married and has three adult children. According to Mack (1994; chapter 14), Carlos is intelligent and does not suffer from any psychological disorder. As well as teaching popular classes at his college, he volunteers his time to work with prisoners, the elderly and people with handicaps and mental disorders. In all,

Carlos seems like a successful and grounded person. Through the use of hypnosis, Carlos remembers multiple abduction experiences – although he prefers to call them 'encounters' and he thinks of himself as a willing participant rather than a victim. Specifically, Carlos recalls in vivid detail the appearance of the different types of aliens he has seen, and the structure of the different rooms and ceilings in the spaceship. He remembers being taken out of his body to fly around with the aliens and being beamed up to the space ship via light. He remembers the extreme fear, pain, and nausea he felt when being examined by the insect-like 'reptilian machine'. He recalls lying on a table where a crystal instrument probed his organs, muscles, and body openings with a laser light that felt like a needle. To top it off, Carlos also remembers the aliens using the same instruments to examine his children.

Despite these extremely detailed memories, there is no scientific evidence that aliens exist, let alone that they come to earth and kidnap people (Clancy, 2005). Carlos, and other people who can recall being abducted by aliens do not appear to be lying; 'abductees' seem to genuinely believe their abduction memories. In fact, research shows that people's physiological responses to their abduction memories are similar to those of people who suffer from post-traumatic stress disorder (McNally et al., 2004).

Abductees' memories provide clear evidence that people can come to believe and remember entirely false experiences. Carlos is not alone. Many people remember being abducted by aliens, and many more people falsely remember things that are much less out of this world.

Distorted memories

False memories don't have to be extraordinary – in fact it is probably more likely that people will have distorted memories for events that really did happen, rather than create entirely false memories for events that never happened. One recent example is Rudy Giuliani's memory for his actions following the attacks on the World Trade Center (WTC; Buettner, 2007).

After the September 11, 2001 attacks on New York City, former New York City mayor Giuliani made a large number of trips to Ground Zero and buildings in the vicinity (Buettner, 2007). Since then, he has cultivated a persona that draws heavily on his post-attack experiences. In 2007, Giuliani spent much of his time campaigning to be the Republican presidential candidate and spoke often – some say too often – about the time he spent at Ground Zero lending a helping hand (Buettner, 2007).

The problem is that Giuliani seems to remember spending far more time at Ground Zero than the records suggest. Although he publicly compared the hours he put in to those of the rescue and cleanup workers and even claimed that he would be as likely as the rescue workers to suffer from the health consequences that have been linked to the clean up work, according to one analysis the records suggest a different story (Buettner, 2007).

About 30,000 volunteers and 10,000 firefighters worked cleaning up Ground Zero (Levin et al., 2004). We do not have records of the hours these workers spent at the site, but we do know that for the eight and a half months between September 11th 2001 and the end of May 2002 – when the clean up was officially over – a sample of 1,138 volunteers each spent between 24 and 4,080 hours working at the site, or a median 966 hours (Smith et al., 2004). Of course not everyone in this sample would have worked at the site for the entire duration, but taking a conservative approach – if they did work for the whole eight and a half months, based on the median duration, that would easily result in an average of over 100 hours per month. As for Giuliani's time, if we exclude the first 6 days after the attacks because there are no official records, we learn that he spent 29 hours over the following 3 months at Ground Zero (Buettner, 2007). Put another way, Giuliani spent more like 10 hours per month for the first 3 months – approximately one-tenth of the time spent by the average volunteer or firefighter.

Was Giuliani lying to an unsuspecting public in order to win votes? We think not. To lie about his involvement in the clean up would be far too risky and unnecessary given his reputation for having taken a big role in the aftermath. One possibility is that Giuliani simply underestimated the amount of time that rescuers spent working at the site. Another possibility is that Giuliani misremembers his own involvement. Records show that he did spend a substantial amount of time at Ground Zero; more than likely it would have been an extremely unpleasant experience for him. We suspect that not only would Giuliani have repeatedly thought about the experiences to himself, he also would have shared his experiences with other people, explaining to them what it was like at Ground Zero; perhaps he would also have listened to other people share their experiences with him. Furthermore, during the post-attack cleanup efforts, information about the rescue attempts and cleanup work was a very popular topic in the media. Taking all these factors into consideration, it is not surprising that Giuliani's memory might be compromised. In this chapter, we discuss research that shows how these factors may contribute to the development of a false memory.

Giuliani is not the only presidential contender to have his campaign claims questioned, nor the only person whose 9/11 memories have come under scrutiny. Fellow Republican presidential contender Mitt Romney was forced to recant a number of his claims, including one that he saw his father marching with Martin Luther King Junior (Johnson, 2007). In a slightly less political situation, the former president of the 9/11 Survivors' Network, Tania Head, was recently removed from her position after being unable to verify stories about her presence and rescue from the 78th floor of the South tower on September 11th (Dunlap and Kovaleski, 2007).

Flashbulb memories

Although he wasn't in New York during the WTC attacks, the President at the time – George W. Bush – has recalled on a number of different occasions how he heard about the attacks and how he reacted. Interestingly, his different reports are not consistent with one another and contain some significant errors (see Greenberg, 2004). Bush's memory reports have come under the same high-level scrutiny as Giuliani's, Romney's, and Head's, and his inconsistencies have led various people to cry conspiracy and cover-up; however, another possibility is that the President misremembers how he learned about the WTC attacks (Greenberg, 2004). Before reading on, take a second to remember how you heard about the attacks. How confident are you that your memory is correct? Like the former President, most people can remember how they heard about the WTC attacks and many are absolutely sure that what they remember is correct. However, contrary to what our feelings may tell us, many of these memories are wrong.

In 1977, Brown and Kulik coined the term 'flashbulb memories,' to describe people's cognitive responses to culturally significant and surprising events. The idea was that something like the flash on a camera 'fired' in the brain – and, like the flash enabling the camera to capture and preserve more detail than usual, so would the flash in the brain enable people to capture and remember more detail than usual. Brown and Kulik based their notion of flashbulb memories on the intense, vivid, and detailed recollections that many Americans had for the assassination of John F. Kennedy 15 years earlier.

The problem with Brown and Kulik's (1977) conclusions was that these JFK memories were very hard to corroborate (and they apparently never tried). Thus, while Brown and Kulik had data that flashbulb memories were unusually vivid, detailed, and emotional, they could not say whether those memories were unusually accurate. In 1986, another culturally significant and surprising event allowed Neisser and Harsh (1992) to address the question of accuracy. Within 24 hours of the space shuttle Challenger explosion, Neisser and Harsh asked a large number of people how they found out about the disaster, what time it was, where they were, who they were with, what they were doing, how they felt when they found out about the explosion, and what they did afterward. Two and a half years later, the researchers found a subset of the original sample, asked them the same questions again, and asked them to rate their confidence that their answers were correct.

How well did these memory reports match the reports from two and a half years earlier? In short, not well at all. For a quarter of the people, not one detail was consistent between the two reports. On average, fewer than half of the details reported in the follow-up questionnaire matched those reported in the original questionnaire. Not one person was completely consistent. What is even more interesting is that two and a half years later, most people were highly confident about the accuracy of their memories.

Why were people so bad at remembering? According to Neisser (1982), flashbulb events are culturally important, and as such they are the kind of events that are rehearsed repeatedly. There is usually a great deal of coverage from the media, both initially and on anniversaries. Additionally, because of the huge impact of the event, people probably think about it to themselves, perhaps even imagining a different outcome or being more personally involved in it. Finally – just like the former President did with the WTC attacks – people relate to others by sharing their experiences of learning about the important event, and they tell others what they are like by explaining how they reacted. These different sources all contribute new information to people's knowledge, understanding and importantly their memory of the event, and provide the means for people to update and revise their 'flashbulb' memories.

There have since been many more studies on flashbulb memories, including studies examining people's memories for hearing about the WTC attacks (for example, see Greenberg, 2004; Talarico and Rubin, 2007; Schmidt, 2004). Despite methodological variations – especially with regard to how long researchers have waited between the event and the follow-up memory tests – these studies are generally consistent with Neisser and Harsh's (1992) findings of distorted recall. Taken together, studies of flashbulb memories suggest that even when it comes to a significant event, we do not capture and preserve information so much as we continually update and reconstruct it – the end result is that what people remember now probably doesn't match what they might have recalled immediately after the event.

So far we have shown that people's memories can be wrong – sometimes a little bit wrong, other times completely wrong. But the real questions are why and how our memories change. In fact, research shows that memory can be distorted and compromised in very simple ways, but it actually benefits us that our memories are flexible rather than set in stone.

How do people's memories become inaccurate?

Exposure to post-event information

In real life, we do not let go of one moment as soon as the next moment arrives. Instead, we look back to the past, both at a personal level and at a societal level. We learn about significant events by watching the news or picking up a newspaper or gossip magazine; we listen to our friends and family members tell us about what they did or saw or heard; we read emails, letters, and cards with the same information; other people ask us about what we did or saw or heard, we give them answers and share our own memories; sometimes we simply remember to ourselves – thinking about what happened, perhaps even imagining what might have been if only we had done something differently. Remembering the past, sharing our experiences with others, and reminiscing together are all common human activities. However, because people undoubtedly experience things differently and remember different things about the same events, as a matter of course, they will also be exposed to new information about events after those events have happened. How does this new information affect people's memories of those events?

The misinformation effect

The misinformation effect paradigm was designed to address exactly that question (for example, see Belli, 1989; Lindsay, 1990; Loftus, 1991; Loftus et al., 1978; Loftus and Palmer, 1974; Loftus and Zanni, 1975; McCloskey and Zaragoza, 1985). In the typical misinformation effect experiment, researchers show people an event, usually a crime or traffic accident. Afterward, the researchers provide subjects with some misleading information about the event they just saw. In some studies, the misleading details are embedded in a post-event narrative description that subjects read or listen to, in others the misinformation is slipped into a leading question about the event. In some more recent studies, subjects discuss the critical event with another person and in doing so they expose each other to misinformation (for example, Gabbert et al., 2003; Garry et al., 2008). Typically, people end up reporting information that they only saw (or heard) after the event; sometimes people's memories are transformed so that they misremember details of the event and other times they add completely new details to their memory reports.

Adding details

A number of studies have shown that people can come to report non-existent details, objects, and even behaviors. For example, in one of the early misinformation effect studies, Loftus and Zanni (1975) led subjects to misreport that they had seen a broken headlight, simply by asking them if they had seen it. These subjects watched a slide sequence of a motor vehicle accident; afterward, half were asked if they had seen *the* broken headlight, and the other half if they had seen *a* broken headlight. The 'the headlight' subjects were significantly more likely to report having seen one, despite the fact that there was no broken headlight in the slide sequence.

In other studies, the non-existent details are embedded in a post-event narrative or post-event questions, or are mentioned in a post-event discussion or during post-event shared recall. Using these methods, people have come to falsely remember details as diverse as non-existent shrubs, non-existent buildings, non-existent people, and non-existent household items (Dodd and Bradshaw, 1980; Loftus, 1975; Roediger et al., 2001; Wright et al., 2000). Additionally, people have come to remember seeing characters do things that they actually did not do – for example, putting a hat on, stealing money from a wallet, throwing a note in the bin, stealing a cell phone, and knocking computer disks to the ground (Gabbert et al., 2003; Gabbert et al., 2006). In sum, when people are given new information after an event has occurred, they can add new details – both big and small – to their memory of that event.

Changing details

More commonly, in misinformation effect studies, people misremember the details: even though they see a detail in certain way, they later report seeing it in a different way.

Evaluating details

In one such study, subjects watched films of several car accidents, and afterward estimated how fast the cars were traveling (Loftus and Palmer, 1974). Critically, each variation of the question differed by only one word, giving subjects a different impression about how fast the cars were traveling when they contacted, hit, bumped, collided or smashed into each other. Even though all subjects saw the same films, their speed estimates depended on the verb used in the question. Estimates were lowest for 'contacted' and increased in the order listed above, producing the highest speed estimates for 'smashed.' Thus, information subtly embedded in a question can influence people's memory reports.

Contradictory details

Another way that people's memories can be transformed by misinformation is when they are given misleading information that contradicts what they actually saw. For example, subjects might watch someone trying on a blue hat but later read that he tried on a black hat (Loftus et al., 1978; McCloskey and Zaragoza, 1985; Takarangi et al., 2006). This method enables researchers to counterbalance critical items and compare memory for baseline information (control items, where subjects are not exposed to any misinformation) with memory for misled items (where subjects are exposed to the misinformation).

In these experiments, people have misremembered the color of objects such as a hat or a cup; they have incorrectly remembered the brand of certain products such as a drink or a magazine; they have misremembered what an object actually was, confusing a hammer with a screwdriver, or a yield sign with a stop sign; and they have even incorrectly remembered a target character's actions, misremembering someone stealing a wallet instead of putting the wallet on a bench, or spiking a drink instead of squeezing lemon into it (see for example, French et al., 2008; Loftus et al., 1978; McCloskey and Zaragoza, 1985; Takarangi et al., 2006).

Misinformation effect research provides a huge body of evidence that people's memories can be manipulated in subtle and not so subtle ways. Being exposed to new information after an event can change what people remember about that event. Perhaps this mechanism is generally beneficial, offering people a means to add information and to update meaning and consequences as they become clearer. However, this same process also creates the potential to contaminate memories, making them less accurate than before. Of course, either way, when people come to remember 'new' information, their memory is no longer accurate, regardless of whether that 'new' information itself is accurate. The result is that many memories are probably at least partially false, consisting both of facts and reconstructions.

Susceptibility to misinformation

However, the news isn't all bad. Just because people are exposed to misinformation doesn't necessarily mean that it will make its way into their memories. There are a number of factors that affect susceptibility to misinformation.

Memory quality

The better a person's memory for the original information, the less susceptible that person should be to misinformation (Loftus et al., 1978). In other words, factors that work to improve memory should also work to protect people from the influence of misleading information. When it comes to remembering an event, those factors include how involved the person was in the event, what the person paid attention to during the event, how stressed the person was during the event, how long the event was, the conditions of the event itself (for example, whether it was day or night), and how soon after the event the person tried to remember what happened. When people have a better memory they are better able to notice that any misleading information does not fit with their memory – thus, they can reject the misinformation as incorrect, and their memory will not be influenced. In sum, anything that helps people notice that the misinformation does not fit with the event should help protect them from being misled.

Misinformation messenger

Another factor that determines whether misleading information has any influence on people's memories is what they think about the source of the misinformation.

For example, does the 'misinformation messenger' seem reliable? In most misinformation studies, the experimenter is the misinformation messenger, transmitting misleading post-event suggestions by asking people leading questions, or providing them with a summary of the witnessed event. It is likely that subjects will see the experimenter – and thus the source of the misinformation – as authoritative, an expert about the event's details. Thus, some scientists have wondered if such a situation might inflate the impact of those misleading suggestions (Smith and Ellsworth, 1987).

Indeed, research shows that the source of the information is crucial to the outcome. For example, Dodd and Bradshaw (1980) ran a typical misinformation effect study, asking people first to watch a simulated motor vehicle accident before reading a narrative description. The twist was that one third of the subjects were told that the post-event narrative was the description provided to police by the faulty driver; another third were told that it was the description provided to police by an innocent bystander; and a final third – the control condition – were also told that the narrative came from an innocent bystander, but these subjects were given a narrative with no misinformation in it. Subjects who thought the narrative came from the innocent bystander incorrectly reported seeing the misinformation, but subjects who thought it came from the faulty driver did not report misinformation any more than the control group did. Why? Dodd and Bradshaw reasoned that because the faulty driver had a vested interest in not telling the truth, subjects would see him as a less credible source and resist the misleading information.

Since Dodd and Bradshaw's (1980) research, a number of studies have produced similar patterns of results. Vornik et al. (2003) found that subjects' perceptions of the speaker's power and social attractiveness determined how much they were influenced by the speaker's misleading suggestions. Echterhoff et al. (2005b) showed that subjects could discount misleading information – even after the fact – when they learned that the source of that information was either untrustworthy or incompetent.

Additionally, people are more likely to be influenced by misinformation if a romantic partner or a friend tells them about it, rather than if someone they have only just met tells them the same information (French et al., 2008b; Hope et al., 2008). Furthermore, in studies where people were led to believe that their discussion partners were less able than themselves to see and remember the critical information, they were less likely to be influenced by what those people said (French et al., 2009; Gabbert et al., 2007).

Taken together, these studies show that people's memories are easily distorted by information they come across after an event. Still, these studies also show that the amount of memory distortion can vary. The conditions of the event itself, a person's memory of the event, and perceptions of the source of any new information all contribute to how much that person's memory is eventually affected by the new information. In the course of everyday life, people probably use new information to update their memories. The end result is that what people remember about the past may have as much to do with what has happened since a particular event as it does with the event itself. In short, memory is a reconstruction, not a concrete record of what actually happened.

So far, the studies we have discussed focus on what happens when someone else transmits misleading post-event information. Yet memory distortion is not limited to those situations. In fact, people recalling the past can actually mislead themselves through deliberate fabrication and confabulation; in these situations, even though people might initially be aware that they are distorting the truth, telling tall stories can actually change their memories (Echterhoff et al., 2005a; Marsh, 2007; Marsh et al., 2005; McCann et al., 1991; Tversky and Marsh, 2000).

Deliberate fabrication

Sometimes people knowingly confabulate. This kind of confabulation is probably best described as a fabrication and in and of itself does not constitute a false belief or false memory. However, research shows that deliberate confabulation can lead to false memories.

Talking about the past

When people talk about the past, they often have goals other than accuracy – thus they talk about the past in a way that does not accurately reflect their memory (Marsh and Tversky, 2004). For example, an eyewitness to a violent crime may have completely different goals and speak about the event in a completely different way when explaining the details to the police than when explaining to a friend (Marsh et al., 2005).

People know that they deliberately exaggerate, minimize, fabricate, and omit details when they talk to other people about the past (Marsh and Tversky, 2004). For example, Marsh and Tversky (2004) examined how people talked about the past and found that people themselves reported 42% of their retellings to be inaccurate. Interestingly, these subjects admitted distorting information in 61% of their retellings – the discrepancy between these figures shows that storytellers did not equate distortion with inaccuracy. Given the large proportion of retellings that were distorted, perhaps people simply considered distortion to be a normal part of describing their memories, and as such did not consider their retellings to be inaccurate (Marsh and Tversky, 2004). This idea fits with research showing that accuracy is not the primary function of autobiographical memory (Hyman and Faries, 1992, see also Hyman and Loftus, 1998; Neisser, 1988).

Yet even when people know that they are deliberately altering the truth, doing so can lead to memory distortion. For example, when people wrote positive or negative letters about a character in a story, they later remembered that character in line with their biased letter writing (Tversky and Marsh, 2000). For instance, after writing a letter to recommend the character for fraternity membership, subjects recalled more of the character's positive behaviors, yet only as many annoying behaviors as they recalled for a control character. This same result was found regardless of whether subjects' letters included specific behaviors or more general evaluations about the character. Tversky and Marsh argued that writing a biased letter created a schema about the character, and subjects later used that schema to recall the character; as a result, they correctly recalled more schema consistent information, but they were also more likely to make memory errors consistent with the schema (see also Marsh et al., 2005).

Audience tuning

One common goal people have in telling others about the past is to identify with their audience. Thus, not only do people exaggerate, minimize, or even fabricate to make the story better – they also tell the story in a way that fits with what they know about the audience and tailor their message to suit the audience (Tversky and Marsh, 2000; Manis et al., 1974; Higgins, 1981; Echterhoff et al., 2005a). It makes perfect sense to change the message based on the needs of the audience and their prior knowledge. Naturally, teaching first year undergraduates about confabulation calls for a different message (and different level of detail) than teaching graduate students about confabulation. When people can adapt material to match the needs and abilities of the audience they can communicate effectively (Echterhoff et al., 2005a; Higgins, 1981).

However, people tailor messages not only to suit the audience's needs and knowledge, but also to suit the audience's perceived attitudes and opinions. This behavior may arise in part from not wanting to upset the audience or give them any cause to blame the messenger for the message (Manis et al., 1974). And just as when people change the details of their stories to suit their goals (to entertain their friends, to gain sympathy), tailoring the message to suit the audience can also affect what people remember later (Higgins, 1981; Echterhoff et al., 2005a; Higgins et al., 1982; McCann et al., 1991; Higgins and Rholes, 1978).

For example, subjects who read a story and then described a target character to another person – who either liked or did not like the character – tailored their descriptions to the audience's attitude, emphasizing positive traits for those who liked the character, and emphasizing negative traits for those who did not (Higgins and McCann, 1984). Importantly, this bias remained for subjects' later recall of the story. Those subjects whose audience liked the character remembered the character more favorably than subjects whose audience did not like the character. In other words, when people deliberately appeal to the perceived attitude of the audience, it can affect their own memories of the information communicated (Higgins and McCann, 1984).

Creating a shared reality

Why do people confuse what they said with what they read? Higgins (1981) suggested that two factors contribute to audience tuning effects. First, when people remember what they previously said, they don't think about the context that they said it in. As a result, they attribute the source of the message they conveyed to the original information, rather than to the biased audience and the tailoring of the message to suit that audience. Second, when people communicate about the past, what they say to each other and agree upon becomes a shared truth: people create a shared reality together, and as such, they perceive their agreed-upon truth as an objective and verified truth about what really happened. Higgins argues that when people later recall what they told the audience, they see the message as an objective truth simply because it was communicated and shared with the audience. Put another way, the message is seen to accurately reflect the past, and as a result, the communicator attributes the information to the original story, rather to his or her story-telling bias.

One important function of establishing shared reality is to provide a means for people to create and sustain social relationships; people are most likely to establish shared reality with people like them and people they like and trust (Echterhoff et al., 2005a). To test Higgins's (1981) suggestion that creating a shared reality was an important contributor to audience tuning effects, Echterhoff et al. manipulated this characteristic feature to create a situation where some subjects experienced a shared reality with their audience and others did not. Specifically, Echterhoff et al. told subjects that the audience was either an in-group member (university student) or an out-group member (hairdresser trainee). Subjects described a target character that their audience either liked or disliked. Regardless of whether the audience was an in-group or out-group member, subjects tailored their message to suit the audience's attitudes (more positive for liking, more negative for disliking). However, this tailoring only translated into later memory effects for those subjects who thought their audience was an in-group member. These results provide evidence that creating a shared reality plays an important role in audience tuning effects: when people tailor their messages to other people's likes and dislikes and when their messages are incorporated into a shared reality, the spin of those messages can influence what the communicator remembers at a later stage.

In the interests of good communication, when people interact with each other, they naturally adjust the details of the information they convey; in doing so they may fulfill goals to dramatize and entertain, to gain sympathy, support, or respect, or they may simply get onside with the audience by appealing to the audience's views and opinions. Whatever the reason, this alteration can lead to memory distortion when the material is remembered again at a later time.

Forced fabrication

What happens when someone fabricates a story, not to gain social approval, but because they are forced to do so? Consider the situation of a police officer interviewing a suspect – the suspect claims not to know anything about the crime. One technique that might be used is to ask the suspect what might have happened. In other words, the suspect knowingly fabricates a story that explains the crime. Does this kind of forced confabulation have any consequences for memory?

Zaragoza and colleagues have studied exactly this question (Ackil and Zaragoza, 1998; Zaragoza et al., 2001; see also Frost et al., 2006). Ackil and Zaragoza (1998) showed subjects a movie with parts missing from it and then interviewed them about the movie. During the interview, subjects were asked questions that they could not know the answer to because the relevant information was missing from the movie. Subjects were required to provide an answer for every question, so were forced to confabulate or fabricate answers. One week later, subjects took a memory test led by a different interviewer – and importantly they were warned that the first interviewer got some questions wrong and asked about things that didn't actually happen in the movie. Despite the warning, subjects falsely remembered details that they had deliberately fabricated a week earlier, and children were even more likely than college students to do so. Additionally, Zaragoza et al. (2001) found that forced confabulation was even more likely to lead to later false memories when it was followed by a confirmatory feedback by the interviewer.

In sum, when people remember the past, there are a number of ways that they might be exposed to new information about past events. They might read about some detail in the news, overhear people talking, or even talk about their own experiences in a way that doesn't match their memories. Whatever the source of this new information, it has the potential to contaminate people's memories. Of course, incorrectly remembering the details of an event is a far cry from remembering something that never actually happened at all.

How, then, do we explain such a phenomenon? As we shall see, there is a growing body of evidence showing that people can remember entire false experiences.

Wholly false memories

Remember Carlos, who vividly remembers experiences with aliens, including being beamed through light and leaving his body to fly around the atmosphere. Most of us would readily conclude that these events never happened. Yet Carlos appears not to be deliberately lying: rather, he seems to truly believe and remember the events. How is it that someone can come to remember whole events – even bizarre events – that never really took place?

Lost in the mall

Loftus and Pickrell (1995) first investigated whether people could come to remember completely fabricated events. They asked subjects to recall four childhood events, based on short descriptions provided by a family member. Although three of the event descriptions were based on events that really did happen during the subject's childhood, the remaining event was fabricated. Every subject attempted to recall the same false event – being lost in a shopping mall. Each subject's family member confirmed that the event had never actually happened and helped to personalize the fake description by adding details that fitted with the subject's life. Specifically, the family member provided other family members' names and suggested a probable location for the event to have occurred. Subjects attempted to recall the four events on three separate occasions; by the final interview, 25% of the subjects remembered something about the false event. The subjects in this study did not have any special characteristics that would predispose them to remembering wholly false experiences. Instead, they were simply normal people who came to remember details about an experience that they never had.

Since Loftus and Pickrell's (1995) study, other researchers have adapted the basic procedure, discovering that people can come to remember a wide range of experiences, such as going up in a hot air balloon, being rescued by a lifeguard, creating chaos at a wedding, playing a prank on a teacher, and being attacked by an animal (Garry and Wade, 2005; Heaps and Nash, 2001; Hyman et al., 1995; Lindsay et al., 2004; Porter et al., 1999). These studies show that all kinds of events – bizarre, emotional, incredibly specific – can be the stuff of completely false memories.

False photographs

Of course, in the real world, we rarely read narrative descriptions of events from our childhood. More often, when we reminisce about the past, we use photographs to cue our memories. Wade et al. (2002) investigated whether false photographs could lead people to develop false memories in the same way that false narrative could.

Just as Loftus and Pickrell (1995) had done in their 'lost-in-the mall' study, Wade et al. (2002) recruited subjects to recall four childhood events. However, they showed subjects photographs rather than event descriptions. Three of the photographs were real childhood photos, but the other photo was a fake – it depicted the subject and one or more family members taking a hot air balloon ride. A family member provided photos of the real events and also some extra photos from which images of the subject and family members could be taken and added to the prototype hot air balloon photo. After attempting to remember the events three times and following guided imagery instructions when they had difficulty in remembering, 50% of subjects came to remember something about the false event.

In Wade et al.'s (2002) study, when subjects were first presented with the fake photo, they would have had no memory of the event. Although in real life people are very unlikely to come across fake photos of their past, it is still possible that they may be presented with photos for which they have very little or no memory. Contrary to popular belief, memory tends to decay over time; forgetting the past is normal (Ebbinghaus, 1913). As a result, it is likely that people will not remember the events surrounding at least some of their childhood photographs. So, although people are not likely to be presented with a fake photo or a fake narrative and be asked to recall everything they can about the surrounding events, they may see a true photo and fail to remember the details of the surrounding events. Wade et al.'s (2002) study shows us what might happen in this situation. People may search their memories for related details; they may imagine what might have happened and who was likely to have been there at the time. As a result they may create a whole new memory based on the photo.

True photographs

To see how true childhood photographs might work to fuel false memories, Lindsay et al. (2004) used a modification of the false narrative method. This time subjects were presented with three narratives describing childhood events, two true and one false. The false narrative described the subject and a friend sneaking Slime – a children's toy made from a gooey sticky green substance – into their teacher's desk and later being punished for their actions. Half of the subjects in the study were given only narratives to cue their memories, but the other half were given the narratives and a copy of their class photo from the year corresponding to each event.

The results were striking. Of the subjects who used only the narratives as a memory cue, 45% reported something about the fake event by their third recall; of the subjects who saw both the narrative and the photo, 78% reported something about the event by their third recall, despite the fact that the event never really happened. This study provides clear evidence that true photos can be fuel for the fire – the additional information in the photo helped subjects to create false memories. The photo might have fueled false memories by providing perceptual information, by adding authority to the stories, and by helping subjects to speculate about the details (Lindsay et al., 2004).

Taken together, these studies show that trying to remember something that didn't happen can lead people to believe that it did happen and can lead some of them to go further and remember specific details about it. When people struggle to remember something from their pasts, they may imagine details, they may confuse these imagined details along with details from other memories, and as a result they create a whole false memory. In other words, one pathway to confabulation is through trying to remember.

Distinguishing true and false memories

The fact that people develop false memories in and of itself would not be such a big concern if the false memories were in some way distinguishable from true memories, if people could easily decide that a memory was false. Research examining many dimensions of true and false memories shows that they are often not easy to separate.

In some false memory studies, after being told that one of the events was false, subjects are asked if they can pick out the false event. In fact, subjects are not always able to do so. For example, in Loftus and Pickrell's (1995) study, 5 of the 24 subjects (21%) picked one of the true events as being false. Additionally, some of the subjects who correctly picked the false event did so through the process of elimination rather than because they truly believed it was false. Similarly, most of the subjects in Lindsay et al.'s (2004) study correctly picked out the Slime event as being false (42 of 45; 93%); yet rather than truly believing that the event was false, many subjects were surprised when they were told the event they picked actually was false. Perhaps these subjects also used a process of elimination and considered the initial difficulty they had in remembering the event and the focus on this event during the study as cues to figure out that the event was the false one (Lindsay et al., 2004). In another false memory study, 69 subjects of 75 picked out the false event (92%), yet beforehand 30% of the subjects said they would be prepared to bet money that the false event really happened (Porter et al., 1999). Even though people cannot always tell that false events are false, perhaps there are features of their memory reports that can be used to distinguish true from false memories.

One dimension that has been examined is the length of people's memory reports. Loftus and Pickrell (1995) found that subjects' descriptions of their false lost in the mall memories were significantly shorter than descriptions of their true memories. But just because a description was short did not mean it was false – false reports tended to be shorter, but some true memories were also very short. Instead of looking at the number of words used, Porter et al. (1999) looked at the number of details reported for true and false memories and found that there was no significant difference.

Another way we might distinguish true and false memories is by their per-ceived qualities, that is, how they feel when remembered. For example, people may judge their false memories to be less clear than true memories. Loftus and Pickrell (1995) found exactly that: subjects rated the clarity of their true memories as better than the clarity of their false memories. Similarly, subjects have been found to give higher ratings for true than false memories on a wide range of subjective memory qualities, such as their feelings of reliving the event (for example, see Garry and Wade, 2005; Lindsay et al., 2004; Porter et al., 1999). Despite these group differences, false memories sometimes get very high ratings and true memories sometimes get very low ratings; in other words, people's ratings of their subjective experiences cannot be used to dis-tinguish true memories from false memories. Similarly, research using multi-ple measures of the emotional content of true and false memories has shown that people tend to rate their true memories as more emotional than their false memories; however, emotions themselves are not diagnostic of authen-ticity; sometimes people rate their false memories as very emotional (Laney and Loftus, 2008). In contrast to the group differences in these studies, Hyman and Pentland (1996) found that subjects who originally did not recall their true events, but came to remember them over time gave similar ratings about the subjective qualities of their true and false memories (such as the emo-tional content and clarity).

As well as asking subjects how their memories feel, another approach has been to ask subjects how confident they are – perhaps people might not be as confident in their false memories. Subjects have rated their confidence that events really happened as higher for true than false events (Garry and Wade, 2005; Lindsay et al., 2004; Porter et al., 1999; Wade et al., 2004); yet despite these group differences, people are sometimes very confident that false events occurred (for example, Porter et al., 1999). Additionally, in other studies, subjects have rated themselves as just as confident in their true memories remembered over successive interviews as they are in their false memories remembered in the same way (Hyman and Billings, 1998; Hyman and Pentland, 1996). Although people's confidence may provide valuable information to distinguish true from false memories, there is some evidence to suggest that people might be just as confident in their true and false memories. The way people rate their memory experiences cannot be used to distinguish true memories from false memories, but it is possible that people's false memories still feel different from their true memories in some other way and that this difference simply did not show up on the rating measures described above. Perhaps there are differences that can be measured in other ways.

Taking a different tack, McNally et al. (2004) sought to determine whether people experience their false memories differently from their true memories. They asked people who remembered being abducted by aliens to describe several autobiographical experiences. As well as describing alien abduction experiences, subjects also described a stressful life experience, a positive life experience, and a neutral life experience. The researchers created audio files of these reports and played them to the subjects (as well as to matched controls who did not remember being abducted by aliens) who were asked to listen to and imagine the described events. While listening to the tapes, subjects' physiological responses (for example, heart rate, skin conductance) were measured. After listening to (and imagining) the events described, subjects rated their emotional responses. A major finding was that 'abductees' responses to their alien abduction scripts were comparable to the reactions of patients suffering from post-traumatic stress disorder when they think about their traumatic memories. McNally et al.'s results suggest that people experience true and false memories in similar ways, and thus even physiological measures don't reveal information that can help to identify the veracity of a given memory.

Despite many attempts to distinguish true and false memories, we still have no reliable method to do so. We cannot yet sort true memories from false memories on the basis of emotions, length, or the confidence with which they are held. In some studies, when people rate their memories, they experience true and false memories differently on average, but not so differently that we can create a diagnostic criterion. In other studies, people experience their false memories in a very similar way to their true memories.

One reason that people may not be able to distinguish their true memories from their false memories is that the memories are constructed in the same way, and as a result people then experience their memories in a similar way (Hyman and Pentland, 1996; McNally et al., 2004). How do people construct false memories? One important process in remembering and reconstructing the past is deciding where different information comes from.

Creating false memories

Source monitoring

Unfortunately, when we store information in our memory, it is not tidily filed away with a label stating its origin, like a sweatshirt would be (Johnson et al., 1993; Mitchell and Johnson, 2000; Lindsay, 2008). For example, when Mollie remembers being given a bicycle for her birthday, it doesn't pop out of her memory with a label telling her the date that the memory was created. Instead, she uses her knowledge and the characteristics of her memory to discern where and when the remembered event actually happened. For instance, the perceptual details of her memory might not be very vivid – so she might decide the event happened a long time ago. Mollie might be able to recall several instances in which she rode to school when she was 10 years old, but cannot recall any instance of doing so when she was 9 years old. And she knows that her birthday is in April and the year that she was born. As a result she can infer that she was given the bike on her tenth birthday, and the precise date and year that it happened.

Of course, this kind of process is prone to errors, especially with events that are not tied as tightly to well-known dates the way that birthdays are. Perhaps for example, Mollie didn't ride to school when she was 9 years old, not because she didn't have a bike yet, but because she wasn't allowed to cross the road by herself. As a result, what Mollie had attributed to being a memory of her tenth birthday wasn't really her tenth birthday at all.

As well as confusing external events with each other, people also make source monitoring errors by confusing something internal (that they only thought about or imagined) with something that really happened. Maybe Mollie never had a bike, but wished she did, and spent time imagining being given one and riding it to school; 20 years later, Mollie might have attributed the source of those thoughts and images not to her imagination, but to her memory of a real experience.

This situation is not very serious – it doesn't really matter whether Mollie was given the bike when she turned 9 or 10, or whether she even had a bike at all. However, these same kinds of source monitoring errors can lead to much more serious consequences in other situations. In the criminal justice system for instance, people could remember being attacked by a person that they only saw in a police line up. Or, they might remember the clothes their attacker was wearing because they saw the description in the newspaper afterward, an image came to mind, and then they later confused that image with their original memory. The criminal justice system relies on people to accurately reconstruct their memories – the idea that memory is highly malleable and highly susceptible to distortion should be a huge concern for all involved in the administration of justice.

Whatever the consequence of the eventual memory – the processes involved in misattributing the source of a memory should be the same. When people try to figure out where and when a memory was created, they have the potential to make a source monitoring error. This potential paves the path for false memory creation. However, there are other factors that contribute to false memory creation. For instance, to remember a false event, people must first believe that the event is plausible.

Plausibility

In order to lead subjects to create false memories, researchers use plausible false events. Yet this requirement can backfire: a possible criticism of false memory research is that people are asked to remember mundane, everyday, plausible events. Perhaps, this line of criticism goes, people would not so easily remember less plausible false events. The implication, of course, is that false memory research has only limited real-world implications. Indeed, Pezdek and colleagues have made just these claims (Pezdek et al., 2006; Pezdek et al., 1997; Pezdek and Hodge, 1999). For example, Pezdek et al. (1997) showed that while some subjects in their study did come to remember the plausible false experience of being lost in a mall, no subjects came to remember the less plausible false experience of having a rectal enema, despite using a similar method to try to implant the two types of false memories. But the problem is that people do come to remember implausible, even frankly bizarre experiences – such as having been in a satanic cult, or being abducted by aliens, experiences that many people would consider to be highly implausible. Thus, people who do remember these experiences must themselves have come to see them as plausible, even if society in general does not.

These kinds of memories led Mazzoni et al. (2001) to wonder just how plausibility is related to false memory formation, and furthermore, to wonder if plausibility can change over time. To address these questions, they recruited subjects who reported that they had never witnessed a demonic possession and believed that doing so was highly implausible. Months later, these subjects came to the laboratory with the impression that they were taking part in an unrelated study. There they read a number of short articles, including three on the issue of demonic possession. These articles provided subjects with information that demonic possessions were quite a common occurrence in their culture. Additionally, the articles included descriptions from people who claimed to have witnessed a possession and explained what their experiences were like. After another week, subjects again rated how plausible they thought witnessing a demonic possession was and how likely they thought it was that they had personally witnessed a demonic possession; ratings of both increased significantly after subjects read the articles. In other words, reading fake articles with descriptions of people's first hand accounts of watching a demonic possession and being told that demonic possession was common, led subjects to believe that demonic possessions were more plausible than they previously thought and to believe that they were more likely to have personally witnessed a demonic possession than they previously thought.

Even though people probably need to believe that an event is plausible before they will develop a false memory of it, these results show that people's perceptions of plausibility can change: people can come to see even highly implausible events as plausible. Mazzoni et al. (2001) suggested three steps that are necessary for someone to develop a false memory; first, they must believe that the specific event could plausibly have happened; second, they must develop a belief that the event actually happened to them; finally, they must make a source monitoring error and incorrectly decide that details they remember about the event must have come from a real experience.

Importantly, this study showed that simply exposing people to information about an event can lead them to find it more plausible and change their beliefs about their past – the first two steps to creating a false memory. Recall the example above of Carlos, the fine arts professor who remembers being abducted by aliens (Mack, 1994). Chances are someone like Carlos might be familiar with details of other abductees' reports of their experiences, might read a lot about alien abduction phenomena, watch alien abduction movies, and perhaps even dream about them afterward. All of these sources of information may work like the articles in Mazzoni et al.'s (2001) study, leading Carlos to see the experience (being abducted by aliens) as more plausible and more personally likely.

Beliefs about the past

Changing plausibility is only one route to changing people's autobiographies. Another route is changing people's beliefs about the experiences they have had in the past. One way to change people's autobiographical beliefs is to change the feelings that they experience when they think about a certain event – these feelings can be used to make source-monitoring decisions. For instance, when something comes to mind with relative ease, people might misattribute that feeling of fluency to familiarity, and as a result, believe that they had previously experienced that thing (Whittlesea and Williams, 2001a, 2001b).

For example, Bernstein et al. (2002) showed subjects statements describing childhood events, and for each one asked them to rate how confident they were that the event had happened to them. To manipulate the fluency that subjects experienced when they read each statement, half of the statements were presented with one of the key words scrambled (for example, 'broke a dwniwo playing ball') while for the other half the words were all spelled in the correct way. The idea was that when subjects saw a scrambled word, they would expect it to be difficult to unscramble; then, when they unscrambled it easily (due to contextual cues in the sentence), they would experience a surprising feeling of fluency, and then misattribute this feeling of fluency to familiarity – thinking that the event felt familiar because it really did happen to them (Whittlesea and Williams, 2001a, 2001b). In fact, the results showed exactly that: when subjects had to unscramble a word before making their confidence judgment, they became more confident that the event had actually happened during their childhood, providing evidence that people's subjective experiences are important in source-monitoring decisions (see also Bernstein et al., 2004). Importantly, when people were not given any additional cues to solve the anagrams, they were just as confident when they successfully unscrambled anagrams and when they saw the words intact. These results suggest that successfully solving the anagrams does not boost people's confidence, but successfully solving the anagrams with less difficulty than expected does boost people's confidence (Bernstein et al., 2002). In short, people's expectations and their subjective experience both play an important role in source monitoring.

Imagination inflation

Even a seemingly harmless everyday activity such as imagination can change autobiographical beliefs. Garry et al. (1996) asked people how confident they were that a list of different childhood events had happened to them (for example, 'Had a lifeguard pull you out of the water'). Subjects briefly imagined some of those events, but not others, and then rated their confidence again using the same list of childhood events. When subjects imagined the events, they were more likely to show increased confidence that the events had actually happened in their childhood, a result that Garry et al. called 'imagination inflation'. In other words, simply imagining being pulled out of the water by a lifeguard led people to be more confident that they actually had been. In real life, people day dream and imagine all the time – perhaps in doing so they are changing the beliefs they hold about what happened in the past.

Imagination may have increased subjects' confidence by increasing the ease with which the target events came to mind and by making those events feel more familiar. Research has since shown that doing something besides imagining can produce effects like imagination inflation. For example, Sharman et al. (2004) found that when subjects paraphrased event descriptions they became more confident that those events had happened (relative to events that they did not paraphrase). Additionally Sharman et al. (2005) found that when subjects explained how an event could have happened, that led them to be more confident that the event actually did happen (relative to events that they did not explain). This research supports the idea that increasing the fluency that people experience when they think about an event can lead them to become more confident that an event actually did happen in the past.

One criticism to be leveled at imagination inflation research is that elaboration and imagination could simply lead subjects to remember previously forgotten experiences – instead of leading to creation of a false belief, imagination might work to remind them of something that really did happen. To address these concerns, other studies examined imagination inflation for experiences that the experimenters knew for sure did or did not happen. One way to establish that an event did or did not happen is to control people's experiences. Goff and Roediger (1998) did exactly that by asking subjects to take part in three separate sessions of an experiment (see also Thomas et al., 2003). In the first session, subjects listened to a series of statements describing simple actions (for example, 'break the toothpick'). For some statements subjects simply listened to the description, and for others they either imagined performing or actually performed the actions. In the second session, subjects were asked to imagine performing some of the actions, up to a maximum of five times. Finally, in a third session, subjects were presented with a list of action statements and were asked to report which ones they had performed during the first session of the study.

Goff and Roediger (1998) found that people falsely remembered performing actions and they were more likely to do so the more times they imagined that action. In other words, imagining a false action can lead people to believe that they actually performed it, a finding suggesting that imagination inflation for childhood events is not simply the result of people remembering true experiences from their past.

Of course, many real-life confabulations are more unusual than being rescued by a lifeguard, or breaking a toothpick. How could we study the effects of imagining unusual experiences, yet still know for sure whether or not those imagined experiences really happened? Seamon et al. (2006) developed a clever way to solve this puzzle. They asked people to take a long walk with the experimenter around their university campus, one at a time. During the walk, they stopped at specific points, during which the experimenter read a statement describing an action. These actions were either familiar (for example, 'Check the Pepsi machine for change') or bizarre (for example, 'Get down on one knee and propose to the Pepsi machine'). People performed half the actions and imagined performing the other half. On a second campus walk, everyone visited some of these same locations again as well as some new locations; at each location they were asked to imagine the associated action.

Finally, 2 weeks later, subjects were asked to remember back to the original campus walk and report which actions they had performed. Seamon et al.'s results were right in line with other imagination inflation research: people falsely remembered performing actions that they had only imagined. What is more, imagination inflation occurred for both familiar and bizarre actions. Taken together, these studies demonstrate that imagination can lead people to believe that they performed actions that they did not perform, both within the laboratory and in a more real world setting.

Impossible events

Mazzoni and Memon (2003) took imagination inflation research one step further, showing that imagination can also lead to false memories. They asked people in the UK to imagine a childhood medical procedure whereby a nurse removed a skin sample from their pinky finger. The twist was that the event never happened: it was a medical procedure that was never practiced in the UK. After people imagined this false childhood event, they rated their confidence that it happened and described any details that they could remember about it. Mazzoni and Memon (2003) found that not only did imagination inflate people's confidence that the phony pinky test was real, but also created false memories in approximately 20% of their sample. In short, imagining fictitious experiences not only leads to increased autobiographical beliefs, but it can also lead to false memories.

Taken together, these studies show that deliberately imagining false experiences can lead to confabulation. Are we safe, then, if we avoid people who ask us to spend a minute imagining a different past? Perhaps not. Advertisers have long known of the power of imagination and encourage us – in subtle ways – to use our imagination. In one study, Braun et al. (2002) showed people fake advertisements that included a description of meeting Bugs Bunny at Disneyland. Subjects were asked to imagine the experience as it was described and to write about how it made them feel. Importantly, Bugs Bunny is a Warner Brothers character and would never have been seen at Disneyland; thus it would be impossible for subjects to have actually had the target experience. People who saw the Bugs Bunny advertisement became more confident that they had met Bugs at Disneyland during their childhood. Put another way, false advertising can lead people to believe they have had experiences that they never actually had.

Considered as a whole, these studies have obvious implications for confabulation because they suggest that imagination may lead people to believe that they have had experiences that they did not have. As a result, people may begin to remember the specific details of those experiences. One question that remains is whether it matters if people develop a false belief or memory? The accuracy of people's memories might be much less important than the other functions that memory plays (Hyman and Faries, 1992; Hyman and Loftus, 1998; Neisser, 1988). Yet perhaps having a false belief (or memory) might influence the decisions people make and the way that they behave.

Behavioral consequences

Some researchers set out to answer that question by targeting people's beliefs about their previous experiences with food (Bernstein et al., 2005). People first rated their liking for a list of foods (for example, spinach, watermelon, fish) and rated their confidence that they had experienced a number of different events related to food (for example, 'baked a pie with your mother'). Next, they were given some false feedback; the feedback suggested that sometime during childhood, they had been ill after eating either a dill pickle spear or a hard-boiled egg. Just as in the imagination inflation studies, people in this study rated their confidence that the different food events had happened a second time following the feedback, and they also rated the likelihood that they would choose to eat each of a long list of foods at a barbeque. The false feedback led people to be more confident that they had been sick (either from an egg or a dill pickle). Additionally, following the false feedback, people were less likely to choose the target food (egg or pickle) at the barbeque. In other words, the false feedback affected what people believed they had experienced in the past, and importantly, it also affected their preferences, decisions, and future behavior.

In sum, people can very easily be led to believe that something happened to them even though it did not. These false beliefs are sometimes accompanied by memory for details of the false events and can lead to behavioral consequences: falsely believing or remembering that they had a certain experience can lead people to act differently than they otherwise would.

Individual differences in false memories

Are we all equally susceptible to confabulation or are some people more disposed than others? Despite the fact that people are generally misled in misinformation effect studies and the fact that some subjects develop rich false memories in memory implantation studies, another portion of people never develop false memories. Many researchers have attempted to establish who will be most and least susceptible to confabulation. These efforts have yielded mixed results.

Some studies have examined various personality factors, to see whether they are related to false memories, or conversely, whether they might protect people from developing false memories. For example, we know that people who have dissociative tendencies might have difficulty distinguishing fantasy from reality. Thus, it seems likely that dissociative tendencies may also be related to false memory susceptibility. Although a number of studies have shown that dissociation is related to false memory susceptibility (for example, Candel et al., 2003; Hyman and Billings, 1998; Merckelbach et al., 2007; Ost et al., 2005; Porter et al., 2000; Wilson and French, 2006), another group of studies have found no such relationship (for example, Horselenberg et al. 2004; Platt et al. 1998).

Another personality characteristic that has been associated with false memory creation is how introverted or extraverted people are. People who are more introverted tend to be shy and avoid socializing with large groups of people whereas people who are more extraverted tend to be more outgoing and sociable. Some research shows that more introverted people are more likely to create false memories (for example, Porter et al., 2000) yet other research shows that more extraverted people are more likely to create false memories (for example, Frost et al., 2006).

A number of other factors have found to be related to false memory creation in a number of different paradigms. For instance, people who tend to make decisions on an emotional rather than a logical basis – as measured by the Myer–Briggs Type Indicator – also tend to produce more false memories (Frost et al., 2006); people who tend to put effort and time into thinking, rather than avoiding cognitive effort, tend to produce more false memories (Graham, 2007); people who believe in paranormal experiences (for example, extrasensory perception, life after death) and report having had paranormal experiences and abilities tend to produce more false memories (Wilson and French, 2006); people who remember being abducted by aliens tend to produce more false memories (Clancy et al., 2002); and people who can create vivid mental images tend to produce more false memories (Hyman and Billings, 1998).

Is confabulation associated only with people who suffer brain damage? The answer is no: instead, the research suggests that normal people in the normal processes of reconstructing the past are likely to create memories about their pasts – memories of things that did not happen at all, or at least that did not happen in the way remembered. Indeed, focusing on confabulating patients is a valuable avenue for researching confabulation – it may be that brain damage works to amplify the limitations of normal memory processes, increasing manifestations of confabulation in clinical patients relative to non-brain damaged people (Johnson et al., 2000).

These studies on individual differences in developing false memories have used many and varied methods, so it may be that some personality factors are important for memory distortion in some situations but not in others. Clearly, much work remains to be done in this area before we can begin to establish who might be more susceptible and less susceptible to memory distortion, and why. For now, we know there is no 'stand out' characteristic that distinguishes people who create false memories from those who do not. In sum, there may be tendencies for people with certain characteristics, or with certain mindsets to be more or less likely to create a false memory, but it certainly is not a case of black and white, but rather many more shades of gray.

Summary

In this chapter, we argued that false memories can be considered to be a subset of the phenomena of confabulation: people confidently claim to have had certain experiences that they never had. We described research showing that false memories are an inevitable by-product of the completely normal way that memory works. As such, virtually everyone is susceptible to memory distortion and confabulation. When people remember the past, they reconstruct it; when people reconstruct the past, they might introduce errors from both external and internal sources, and they might confuse the sources of that information. Some people do not develop false memories, but so far, we do not know who those people are, or what protects them from developing false memories. The research we have presented suggests that virtually all of us are susceptible to memory distortion and regardless of the content, the pathway to false beliefs and false memories is the same.

References

Ackil, J.K. and Zaragoza, M.S. (1998). Memorial consequences of forced confabulation: Age differences in susceptibility to false memories. *Developmental Psychology*, **34**, 1358–1372.

Belli, R.F. (1989). Influences of misleading postevent information: Misinformation interference and acceptance. *Journal of Experimental Psychology: General*, **118**, 72–85.

Bernstein, D.M., Godfrey, R.D., Davison, A., and Loftus, E.F. (2004). Conditions affecting the revelation effect for autobiographical memory. *Memory and Cognition*, **32**, 455–462.

Bernstein, D.M., Laney, C., Morris, E.K., and Loftus, E.F. (2005). False memories about food can lead to food avoidance. *Social Cognition*, **23**, 11–34.

Bernstein, D.M., Whittlesea, B.W., and Loftus, E.F. (2002). Increasing confidence in remote autobiographical memory and general knowledge: Extensions of the revelation effect. *Memory and Cognition*, **30**, 432–438.

Braun, K.A., Ellis, R., and Loftus, E.F. (2002). Make my memory: How advertising can change our memories of the past. *Psychology and Marketing*, **19**, 1–23.

Brown, R.R. and Kulik, J. (1977). Flashbulb memories. *Cognition*, **5**, 73–99.

Buettner, R. (2007). For Giuliani, Ground Zero as Linchpin and Thorn. *New York Times.* (Retrieved December 21, 2007). Available on line at http://www.nytimes.com/2007/08/17/us/politics/17giuliani.html?ref=us

Candel, I., Merckelbach, H., and Kuijpers, M. (2003). Dissociative experiences are related to commission errors in emotional memory. *Behaviour Research & Therapy,* **41**, 719–725.

Chequers, J., Joseph, S., and Diduca, D. (1997). Belief in extraterrestrial life, UFO-related beliefs, and schizotypal personality. *Personality and Individual Differences,* **23**, 519–521.

Clancy, S.A. (2005). *Abducted: How people come to believe they were kidnapped by aliens.* Cambridge, Harvard University Press.

Clancy, S.A., McNally, R.J., Schacter, D.L., Lenzenweger, M.F., and Pitman, R.K. (2002). Memory distortions in people reporting abduction by aliens. *Journal of Abnormal Psychology,* **111**, 455–461.

Dodd, D.H. and Bradshaw, J.M. (1980). Leading questions and memory: Pragmatic constraints. *Journal of Verbal Learning and Verbal Behaviour,* **19**, 695–704.

Dunlap, D.W. and Kovaleski, S.F. (2007). In a 9/11 survival tale, the pieces just don't fit. *New York Times.* (Retrieved December 21, 2007). Available on line at http://www.nytimes.com/2007/09/27/nyregion/27survivor.html

Ebbinghaus, H. (1913). *Memory: A contribution to experimental psychology.* New York, Teachers College, Columbia University. (Original work published in 1885).

Echterhoff, G., Higgins, E.T., and Groll, S. (2005a). Audience-tuning effects on memory: The role of shared reality. *Journal of Personality and Social Psychology,* **89**, 257–276.

Echterhoff, G., Hirst, W., and Hussy, W. (2005b). How eyewitnesses resist misinformation: Social postwarnings and the monitoring of memory characteristics. *Memory and Cognition,* **33**, 770–782.

French, L., Garry, M., and Mori, K. (2008). You say tomato? Collaborative remembering between intimate couples leads to more false memories than collaborative remembering between strangers. *Memory,* **16**, 262–273.

French, L., Garry, M., and Mori, K. (2009). *Expect the Best: Expectations Can Protect People from Memory Distortion in Social Interactions.* Manuscript under review.

Frost, P., Sparrow, S., and Barry, J. (2006). Personality characteristics associated with susceptibility to false memories. *American Journal of Psychology,* **119**, 193–204.

Gabbert, F., Memon, A., and Allan, K. (2003). Memory conformity: Can eyewitnesses influence each other's memories for an event? *Applied Cognitive Psychology,* **17**, 533–543.

Gabbert, F., Memon, A., and Wright, D.B. (2006). Memory conformity: Disentangling the steps towards influence during a discussion. *Psychonomic Bulletin and Review,* **13**, 480–485.

Gabbert, F., Memon, A., and Wright, D.B. (2007). I saw it for longer than you: The relationship between perceived encoding duration and memory conformity. *Acta Psychologica,* **124**, 319–331.

Gallup, G.H., Jr., and Newport, F. (1991). Belief in paranormal phenomena among adult Americans. *The Skeptical Inquirer,* **15**, 137–146.

Garry, M., French, L.Y., Kinzett, T., and Mori, K. (2008). Eyewitness Memory Following Discussion: Using the MORI Technique with a Western Sample. *Applied Cognitive Psychology,* **22**, 431–439.

Garry, M., Manning, C.G., Loftus, E.F., and Sherman, S.J. (1996). Imagination Inflation: Imagining a childhood event inflates confidence that it occurred. *Psychonomic Bulletin and Review*, 3, 208–214.

Garry, M. and Wade, K.A. (2005). Actually, a picture is worth less than 45 words: Narratives produce more false memories than photographs. *Psychonomic Bulletin and Review* 12, 359–366.

Goff, L.M. and Roediger, H.L. III (1998). Imagination inflation for action events: Repeated imaginings lead to illusory recollections. *Memory and Cognition*, 26, 20–33.

Graham, L.M. (2007). Need for cognition in the Deese-Roediger-McDermott paradigm. *Personality and Individual Differences*, 42, 409–418.

Greenberg, D.L. (2004). President Bush's false 'flashbulb' memory of 9/11/01. *Applied Cognitive Psychology*, 18, 363–370.

Heaps, C.M. and Nash, M. (2001). Comparing recollective experience in true and false autobiographical memories. *Journal of Experimental Psychology: Learning, Memory and Cognition*, 27, 920–930.

Higgins, E.T. (1981). The "communication game": Implications for social cognition and persuasion. In *Social Cognition: The Ontario Symposium of Personality and Social Psychology: Vol 1.* (eds. E.T. Higgins, C.T. Herman, and M.P. Zanna), pp. 343–392 Hillsdale, NJ. Erlbaum.

Higgins, E.T. and McCann, C.D. (1984). Social encoding and subsequent attitudes, impressions and memory: "Context-driven" and motivational aspects of processing. *Journal of Personality and Social Psychology*, 47, 26–39.

Higgins, E.T., McCann, C.D., and Fondacaro, R. (1982). The "communication game": Goal-directed encoding and cognitive consequences. *Social Cognition*, 1, 21–37.

Higgins, E.T. and Rholes, W.S. (1978). "Saying is Believing": Effects of message modification on memory and liking for the person described. *Journal of Experimental Social Psychology*, 14, 363–378.

Hirstein, W. (2005). *Brain Fiction: Self-Deception and the Riddle of Confabulation.* Cambridge, MIT Press.

Hope, L., Ost, J., Gabbert, F., Healey, S., and Lenton, E. (2008). "With a little help from my friends…": The role of co-witness relationship in susceptibility to misinformation. *Acta Psychologica*, 127, 476–484.

Horselenberg, R., Merckelbach, H., van Breukelen, G., and Wessel, I. (2004). Individual differences in the accuracy of autobiographical memory. *Clinical Psychology and Psychotherapy*, 11, 168–176.

Hyman, I.E., Jr. and Billings, F.J. (1998). Individual differences and the creation of false childhood memories. *Memory*, 6, 1–20.

Hyman, I.E., Jr. and Faries, J.M. (1992). The functions of autobiographical memory. In *Theoretical Perspectives on Autobiographical Memory* (eds. M.A. Conway, D.C. Rubin, H. Spinnler, and W.A. Wagenaar), pp. 207–221. Netherlands, Kluwer Academic Publishers.

Hyman, I.E., Jr., Husband, T.H., and Billings, F.J. (1995). False memories of childhood experiences. *Applied Cognitive Psychology*, 9, 181–197.

Hyman, I.E., Jr. and Loftus, E.F. (1998). Errors in autobiographical memory. *Clinical Psychology Review*, 18, 933–947.

Hyman, I.E., Jr. and Pentland, J. (1996). The role of mental imagery in the creation of false childhood memories. *Journal of Memory and Language [Special Issue: Illusions of Memory]*, **35**, 101–117.

Johnson, G. (2007). Romney backpedals on statements – again. *The Associated Press*. (Retrieved January 8, 2008). Available on line at http://ap.google.com/article/ALeqM5gqm5iBQgdTIHSsDf2AuvI5I-4QPgD8TLNGS80

Johnson, M.K. (2000). Comments on DeLuca. .(2000). A cognitive neuroscience perspective on confabulation. *Neuro-Psychoanalysis*, **2**, 150–158.

Johnson, M.K., Hashtroudi, S., and Lindsay, D.S. (1993). Source monitoring. *Psychological Bulletin*, **114**, 3–28.

Johnson, M.K., Hayes, S.M., D'Esposito, M., and Raye, C.L. (2000). Confabulation. In *Handbook of Neuropsychology: Vol 2. Memory and its Disorders*. (2nd edition.) (ed. L.S. Cermak), pp. 383–407. Amsterdam, Netherlands, Elsevier Science Publishers B.V.

Laney, C. and Loftus, E.F. (2008). Emotional content of true and false memories. *Memory*, **16**, 500–516.

Levin, S.M., Herbert, R., Moline, J.M., et al., (2004). Physical health status of World Trade Center rescue and recovery workers and volunteers—New York City, July 2002 – August 2004. *Morbidity and Mortality Weekly Report*, **53**, 807–812.

Lindsay, D.S. (1990). Misleading suggestions can impair eyewitnesses' ability to remember event details. *Journal of Experimental Psychology: Learning, Memory and Cognition*, **16**, 1077–1083.

Lindsay, D.S. (2008). Source monitoring. In *Cognitive Psychology of Memory. Vol. 2. Learning and Memory: A Comprehensive Reference*. (ed. H.L. Roediger, III). Oxford, Elsevier.

Lindsay, D.S., Hagen, L., Read, J.D., Wade, K.A., and Garry, M. (2004). True photographs and false memories. *Psychological Science*, **15**, 149–154.

Loftus, E.F. (1975). Leading questions and the eyewitness report. *Cognitive Psychology*, **7**, 560–572.

Loftus, E.F. (1991). Made in memory: Distortions in recollection after misleading information. In *The Psychology of Learning and Motivation: Advances in Research and Theory* (pp. 187–215) (ed. G.H. Bower), pp. 187–215. San Diego, CA, Academic Press.

Loftus, E.F., Miller, D.G., and Burns, H.J. (1978). Semantic integration of verbal information into visual memory. *Journal of Experimental Psychology: Human Learning and Memory*, **4**, 19–31.

Loftus, E.F. and Palmer, J.C. (1974). Reconstruction of automobile deconstruction: An example of the interaction between language and memory. *Journal of Verbal Learning and Verbal Behavior*, **13**, 585–589.

Loftus, E.F. and Pickrell, J.E. (1995). The formation of false memories. *Psychiatric Annals*, **25**, 720–725.

Loftus, E.F. and Zanni, G. (1975). Eyewitness testimony: The influence of the wording of a question. *Bulletin of the Psychonomic Society*, **5**, 86–88.

Mack, J.E. (1994). *Abduction: Human Encounters with Aliens*. New York, Macmillan.

Manis, M., Cornell, S.D., and Moore, J.C. (1974). Transmission of attitude relevant information through a communication chain. *Journal of Personality and Social Psychology*, **30**, 81–94.

Marsh, E.J. (2007). Retelling is not the same as recalling: Implications for memory. *Current Directions in Psychological Science,* **16,** 16–20.

Marsh, E.J. and Tversky, B. (2004). Spinning the stories of our lives. *Applied Cognitive Psychology,* **18,** 491–503.

Marsh, E.J., Tversky, B., and Hutson, M. (2005). How eyewitnesses talk about events: Implications for memory. *Applied Cognitive Psychology,* **19,** 531–544.

Mazzoni, G.A.L., Loftus, E.F., and Kirsch, I. (2001). Changing beliefs about implausible events: A little plausibility goes a long way. *Journal of Experimental Psychology: Applied,* **7,** 51–59.

Mazzoni, G.A.L. and Memon, A. (2003). Imagination can create false autobiographical memories. *Psychological Science,* **14,** 186–188.

McCann, C.D., Higgins, E.T., and Fondacaro, R.A. (1991). Primacy and recency in communication and self-persuasion: How successive audiences and multiple encodings influence subsequent evaluative judgments. *Social Cognition [Special Issue: Social cognition and communication: Human judgment in its social context],* **9,** 47–66.

McCloskey, M. and Zaragoza, M. (1985). Misleading postevent information and memory for events: Arguments and evidence against memory impairment hypotheses. *Journal of Experimental Psychology: General,* **114,** 1–16.

McNally, R.J., Lasko, N.B., Clancy, S.A., Macklin, M.L., Pitman, R.K., and Orr, S.P. (2004). Psychophysiological responding during script driven imagery in people reporting abduction by space aliens. *Psychological Science,* **15,** 493–497.

Merckelbach, H., Zeles, G., van Bergen, S., and Giesbrecht, T. (2007). Trait dissociation and commission errors in memory reports of emotional events. *American Journal of Psychology,* **120,** 1–14.

Mitchell, K.J. and Johnson, M.K. (2000). Source monitoring: Attributing mental experiences. In *The Oxford Handbook of Memory* (eds. E. Tulving and F.I.M. Craik), pp. 179–195.. New York, Oxford University Press.

Neisser, U. (1982) Snapshots or benchmarks? In *Memory Observed: Remembering in Natural Contexts* (ed. U. Neisser), pp. 43–48. San Francisco, W.H. Freeman & Co.

Neisser, U. (1988). Five kinds of self-knowledge. *Philosophical Psychology,* **1,** 35–59.

Neisser, U. and Harsh, N. (1992). Phantom flashbulbs: False recollections of hearing the news about Challenger. In *Affect and Accuracy in Recall: Studies of "Flashbulb" Memories. Emory Symposia in Cognition, Vol 4.* (eds. E. Winograd and U. Neisser), pp. 9–31. New York, Cambridge University Press.

Ost, J., Foster, S., Costall, A., and Bull, R. (2005). False reports of childhood events in appropriate interviews. *Memory,* **13,** 700–710.

Pezdek, K., Blandon-Gitlin, I., and Gabbay, P. (2006). Imagination and memory: Does imagining implausible events lead to false autobiographical memories? *Psychonomic Bulletin & Review,* **13,** 764–769.

Pezdek, K., Finger, K., and Hodge, D. (1997). Planting false childhood memories: The role of event plausibility. *Psychological Science,* **8,** 437–441.

Pezdek, K. and Hodge, D. (1999). Planting false childhood memories in children: The role of event plausibility. *Child Development,* **70,** 887–895.

Platt, R.D., Lacey, S.C., Iobst, A.D., and Finkelman, D. (1998). Absorption, dissociation, fantasy-proneness as predictors of memory distortion in autobiographical and laboratory-generated memories. *Applied Cognitive Psychology,* **12,** 77–89.

Porter, S., Birt, A.R., Yuille J.C., and Lehman, D.R. (2000). Negotiating false memories: Interviewer and rememberer characteristics relate to memory distortion. *Psychological Science*, **11**, 507–510.

Porter, S., Yuille, J.C., and Lehman, D.R. (1999). The nature of real, implanted, and fabricated memories for emotional childhood events: Implications for the recovered memory debate. *Law and Human Behavior*. **23**, 517—537.

Roediger, H.L., III, Meade, M.L., and Bergman, E.T. (2001). Social contagion of memory. *Psychonomic Bulletin and Review*, **8**, 365–371.

Schmidt, S.R. (2004). Autobiographical memories for the September 11th attacks: Reconstructive errors and emotional impairment of memory. *Memory and Cognition*, **32**, 443–454.

Schnider, A. (2003). Spontaneous confabulation and the adaptation of thought to ongoing reality. *Nature Reviews: Neuroscience*, **4**, 662–671.

Seamon, J.G., Philbin, M.M., and Harrison, L.G. (2006). Do you remember proposing to the Pepsi machine? False recollections from a campus walk. *Psychonomic Bulletin and Review*, *13*, 752–756.

Sharman, S.J., Garry, M., and Beuke, C.J. (2004). Imagination or exposure causes imagination inflation. *American Journal of Psychology*, **117**, 157–168.

Sharman, S.J., Manning, C.G., and Garry, M. (2005). Explain this: Explaining childhood events inflates confidence for those events. *Applied Cognitive Psychology*, **19**, 67–74.

Smith, R.P., Katz, C.L., Holmes, A., et al. (2004). Mental health status of the World Trade Center rescue and recovery workers and volunteers—New York City, July 2002 – August 2004. *Morbidity and Mortality Weekly Report*, **53**, 812–815.

Smith, V.L. and Ellsworth, P.C. (1987). The social psychology of eyewitness accuracy: Misleading questions and communicator expertise. *Journal of Applied Psychology*, **72**, 294–300.

Takarangi, M.K.T., Parker, S.L., and Garry, M. (2006). Modernizing the misinformation effect: The development of a new stimulus set. *Applied Cognitive Psychology*, **20**, 1–8.

Talarico, J.M. and Rubin, D.C. (2007). Flashbulb memories are special after all: In phenomenology not accuracy. *Applied Cognitive Psychology*, **21**, 557–578.

Thomas, A.K., Bulevich, J.B., and Loftus, E.F. (2003). Exploring the role of repetition and sensory elaboration in the imagination inflation effect. *Memory and Cognition*, **31**, 630–640.

Tversky, B. and Marsh, E.J. (2000). Biased retellings of events yield biased memories. *Cognitive Psychology*, **40**, 1–38.

Vornik, L.A., Sharman, S.J., and Garry, M. (2003). The power of the spoken word: Sociolinguistic cues influence the misinformation effect. *Memory*, **11**, 101–109.

Wade, K.A., Garry, M., Read, J.D., and Lindsay, D.S. (2002). A picture is worth a thousand lies: Using false photographs to create false childhood memories. *Psychonomic Bulletin and Review*, **9**, 597–603.

Whittlesea, B.W.A. and Williams, L.D. (2001a). The discrepancy-attribution hypothesis: I. The heuristic basis of feelings and familiarity. *Journal of Experimental Psychology: Learning, Memory, and Cognition*, **27**, 3–13.

Whittlesea, B.W.A. and Williams, L.D. (2001b). The discrepancy-attribution hypothesis: II. Expectation, uncertainty, surprise and feelings of familiarity. *Journal of Experimental Psychology: Learning , Memory, and Cognition*, **27**, 14–33.

Wilson, K. and French, C.C. (2006). The relationship between susceptibility to false memories, dissociativity, and paranormal belief and experience. *Personality and Individual Differences,* **41**, 1493–1502.

Wright, D.B., Self, G., and Justice, C. (2000). Memory conformity: Exploring misinformation effects when presented by another person. *British Journal of Psychology,* **91**, 189–202.

Zaragoza, M.S., Payment, K.E., Ackil, J.K., Drivdahl, S.B., and Beck, M. (2001). Interviewing witnesses: Forced confabulation and confirmatory feedback increase false memories. *Psychological Science,* **12**, 473–477.

Chapter 3

The cognitive consequences of forced fabrication: Evidence from studies of eyewitness suggestibility

Quin M. Chrobak and Maria S. Zaragoza

Introduction

One of the most striking features of confabulations produced by clinical patients is the confidence and conviction with which these sometimes fantastical state-ments and false memories can be held. Even when directly confronted with evidence that refutes the validity of their confabulations, they sometimes cling to their stories (Schnider et al., 1996a, 1996b; Schnider and Ptak, 1999; Burgess and McNeil, 1999; Schnider, 2001), producing secondary confabulations in an attempt to reconcile their flagrantly false claims with reality (Kopelman, 1987; Moscovitch, 1989, 1995).

Importantly, however, the phenomenon of confidently held false memories is not limited to clinical patients. Scientific research has amply demonstrated that normal memory processes are reconstructive rather than reproductive in nature and susceptible to a variety of errors and distortions. Moreover, these memory distortions are sometimes held with the same confidence and convic-tion as accurate memories (see Lindsay, 2008; Zaragoza et al., 2007) for reviews). In general, what differentiates clinical confabulation from the false memory errors seen in normal populations is that, in clinical cases, the patients' confabulations are more readily identified as false memories because they are more often implausible and inconsistent with reality. In the case of non-impaired participants, the opposite tends to be the case; as false memory errors are often credible and consistent with reality, they typically cannot be identi-fied as false on the basis of criteria such as plausibility or coherence alone. It is only in well-controlled memory experiments, where the original to-be-remembered information and the participants' memory reports can be systematically compared, that the nature and extent of people's propensity toward memory distortion becomes clear.

In laboratory studies of false memory development in normal populations, we have been studying a false memory phenomenon that we refer to as the 'forced fabrication effect[1].' An important similarity between the memory errors obtained in studies of forced fabrication and those observed in clinical confabulation is that in both cases, people develop false memories for information that they, themselves, invented. Unlike clinical confabulation, however, participants in our experiments start out *fully aware* that the events they have fabricated are mere inventions – they fabricate these fictitious events only because an interviewer coerces them into doing so. However, over time, some participants come to develop highly confident false memories of the fictitious events that they had been forced to fabricate knowingly at an earlier point in time. Hence, the forced fabrication effect provides a platform for understanding how, in non-impaired individuals, an accurate memory of having invented a falsehood evolves into a confidently held false memory. In the present chapter, we review the existing research and theory on the forced fabrication effect, with an eye toward extracting the implications of this research for understanding clinical confabulation.

The forced fabrication effect

Research on the forced fabrication effect has been conducted in the broader context of research on eyewitness suggestibility. The study of eyewitness suggestibility has a long tradition in experimental psychology, and a great deal of research has been conducted using an experimental paradigm developed by E. Loftus in 1970s (e.g. Loftus et al., 1978). In this paradigm, all participants (1) witness the same 'eyewitness event' (either live or videotaped and are then) (2) exposed to a post-event suggestive interview phase, where new, misleading false information is introduced, and (3) after a retention interval, are tested on their memories of the originally witnessed event. Many studies conducted with this paradigm have shown that participants will readily develop false memories for fictitious items and events that were only suggested to them during the post-event interview.

---

[1] In previous publications, we have referred to this phenomenon as the forced 'confabulation' effect. However, in order to differentiate this phenomenon from the clinical neuropsychological syndrome, the term "fabrication" has been used in more recent publications (e.g. Chrobak & Zaragoza, 2008) and will be used throughout this chapter.

Our work on forced fabrication stems from the observation that in real-world forensic investigations, suggestive interviews are not restricted to situations where an interviewer *provides* or implants some piece of false information (e.g. suggesting that a suspect carried a weapon when he did not). Rather, in some forensic interviews, the interviewer attempts to *elicit* from the witness testimony about events that the witness does not remember, did not see, or did not actually take place. In such cases, interviewers may press witnesses to go beyond their actual memory, pressuring them to speculate or even fabricate information about events that never happened. In such highly coercive interview contexts, witness may succumb to this pressure in an attempt to satisfy the interviewer and knowingly provide a fabricated account. The question of interest is whether participants might come to develop false memories for such knowingly fabricated events.

To answer this question, we have used a modified version of the traditional laboratory paradigm (an overview of the forced fabrication paradigm is provided in Figure 3.1.). As in the typical eyewitness suggestibility study, in our studies, all participants view an eyewitness event, are subsequently exposed to a suggestive interview, and are later tested on their memories for the witnessed event. The forced fabrication paradigm differs from the traditional paradigm in the nature of the suggestive interview. In the traditional paradigm, the interviewer *provides* some piece of false or misleading information, typically by presupposing its existence in an interview question. For example, an interviewer might suggest that a thief had a gun (when he did not) by asking the question, 'After the thief put his hand on the gun at his waist, did he go out the front door or the back door?' In the forced fabrication paradigm, by contrast, rather than being told some falsehood, the witness is forced to describe some blatantly false object or event. In contrast to the previous

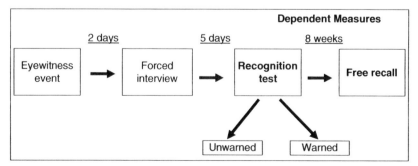

Figure 3.1. Methodology of a representative forced fabrication study (Chrobak and Zaragoza, 2008)

example, someone forced to fabricate information might be asked to *describe* the fictitious weapon carried by the thief (e.g. 'The thief had a weapon. What was it?'). Hence, in the forced fabrication paradigm, witnesses *generate* the false information themselves. Importantly, the participant/witness is not permitted to evade the interviewer's request to provide an answer to the false-event questions. Rather, participants are informed ahead of time that they must respond to all questions, even if they have to guess. Although participants vehemently resist answering these false-event questions, the interviewer 'forces' them to comply by repeatedly insisting that they just 'give their best guess' until participants eventually acquiesce by providing a relevant response.

To illustrate the coercive nature of these interviews and participants' resistance to answering these false-event questions, we provide below a portion of an interview with a participant from one of our studies (Chrobak and Zaragoza, 2008). In the example below, the participant had earlier witnessed a video clip from a movie involving two brothers at a summer camp. In one of the scenes that the participant actually witnessed, a camp counselor named Delaney stands up to make an announcement in the dining hall when he inexplicably loses his balance and, arms flailing, falls to the floor knocking platters of food off the table. This scene was used as the basis for a false-event question that forced participants to describe a fictitious practical joke that the experimenter claimed had caused him to fall. The interchange between the experimenter (E) and the participant (P) appears below:

> E: The next scene takes place in the dining hall. Delaney is asked to stand up and give an announcement. A practical joke is pulled on him that causes him to fall and end up on the ground. What was it?
>
> P: Uhh, I'm not sure what the practical joke was, ehh . . .I know that he fell, I thought he did it on purpose though.
>
> E: Just give your best guess about the practical joke.
>
> P: Umm uh no one was paying attention to him, and then I guess he slipped. I don't know. Yeah I really don't, like I thought like he did it on purpose to get everyone's attention. I didn't know there was a practical joke going on.
>
> E: Just give your best guess.
>
> P: Umm, let's see, I really don't remember, like I don't.
>
> E: Well, what did he slip on?
>
> P: A piece of food?
>
> E: Ok what was the practical joke that they pulled?
>
> P: Umm, like what do you mean like?
>
> E: How did it get there?
>
> P: I guess someone put it there.

E: Who might have put it there?

P: Probably, umm, not his little brother but what's that other guy that's causing trouble in the beginning?

E: Ratface?

P: Yeah probably Ratface.

E: And what food did he put there?

P: Uhh may be a banana? I don't know.

E: And how might he have put it there?

P: Uh, sneaking up there.

E: How did he sneak up there?

P: (laughs) I don't remember. Umm…

E: just give your best guess.

P: Umm he just was, doing it when no one was looking.

E: Ok so your answer was: Delaney slipped on some food, it was a banana that Ratface put there, and he might have sneaked it up there when no one was looking. Is there anything else you remember about the practical joke played on Delaney?

P: No, uhh yeah there was that lady that yelled at him and said that his foolishness isn't going to help them get donations from those ladies that were visiting.

The above transcript illustrates several characteristic features of forced fabrication interviews. First, in order to comply with the experimenter's demands participants have to make-up or fabricate a response to the false-event questions (in this case, the participant had to invent the practical joke because no practical joke was actually depicted in the video clip). Second, participants' resistance to answering such false-event questions clearly indicates their awareness that they do not know the answer. In the above example, the participant repeatedly states that he does not remember a prank, and in fact, the participant directly questions whether there was a prank at all. Moreover, as is typically the case, the resistance is so strong that it takes several conversational turns before the interviewer is able to elicit any information relevant to the question. In addition, it often takes a number of additional conversational turns before the interviewer is able to elicit an account from the participant that contains the desired level of detail and specificity. Clearly, this participant would have never generated this fictitious prank event had he not been forced to do so.

The main objective of forced fabrication studies is to assess whether participants might come to develop false memories of having witnessed the events they had knowingly confabulated earlier. The consistent finding across a number of studies is that people do sometimes develop false memories for their forced fabrications and that these false memories are often held with very high confidence. To assess false memory development, participants are given delayed tests of memory for the witnessed event. In some cases, this means probing participants for the specific information that they had earlier fabricated For example, 5 days after the interview described above, the above-mentioned participant returned to the lab and a different experimenter asked him, 'When you watched the video, did you see Ratface put a banana on the floor by Delaney when all of the ladies and boys were in the dining hall?'. Although, this participant correctly rejected the forcibly fabricated event as not witnessed on this initial test, the findings were quite different when he was tested again 8 weeks later (we note, however, that other participants did falsely assent to their forced fabrications at the 1-week recognition test). Specifically, 8 weeks after viewing the video event, this participant returned to the lab for a surprise free recall test and was instructed to recall the events witnessed in the video as completely and accurately as possible – as if providing testimony in a court of law. Aside from this general instruction, participants were not given any additional prompts or cues and were free to provide as much or as little information as they wished (see Chrobak and Zaragoza, 2008). During this surprise free recall test, this participant freely provided the following account of the dining hall scene:

> And I think what happens next is they are in the cafeteria and Delaney is um, supposed to get everyone's attention, some reason. But he is um, like I think I think Ratface pulls a trick on him with a banana peel or something, he slips and he falls and he is, gets in trouble by the chief and says that's the wrong way to get attention from the crowd.

As evidenced by this transcript, the very same participant who had correctly and publicly rejected the forced fabrication as false on the 5-day recognition test, nevertheless incorporated a detailed version of his fabricated event into the testimony freely provided 2 months later. Indeed, in this study, almost half of the participants who correctly rejected their forced fabrications on a 1-week recognition test freely incorporated their forced fabrications into their testimony 8 weeks later.

The finding that forced fabrication can result in false eyewitness memories has now been demonstrated in a number of studies involving both children (Ackil and Zaragoza, 1998; Zaragoza et al., 2001b) and adults (Chrobak and Zaragoza, 2008; Frost et al., 2003; Hanba and Zaragoza, 2007; Pezdek et al., 2007; Zaragoza et al., 2001a), on 1-week recognition tests and long-term free recall tests, and for forced fabrications that range from isolated items or details (Frost et al., 2003; Hanba and Zaragoza, 2007; Pezdek et al., 2007; Zaragoza et al., 2001a) to fabricated accounts that are broad in scope and extended in time

(Chrobak and Zaragoza, 2008; see example provided above), and even forced fabrications that can falsely incriminate someone (Zaragoza et al., 2001b).

Do people develop genuine false memories for forcibly fabricated information?

Of course, the finding that participants report their forced fabrications on a test of the witnessed event does not, in and of itself, provide evidence of false memory development. Given the social demands of an interview situation, there are a number of reasons why participants might report their forced fabrications even if they are well aware that they do not remember witnessing these fabricated events. For example, participants might feel pressure to respond consistently across test sessions because they may find it unflattering to admit that their responses during the initial interview were mere fabrications. Alternatively, they may feel that the demands of the experimental situation are such that they are expected to report the events they were earlier forced to fabricate. Researchers who have studied the effects of forced fabrication on memory have been sensitive to these potential influences on participants' memory reports and, for this reason, have taken care to design studies in such a way that these social demands are eliminated (or at least minimized). In particular, in all studies of the forced fabrication effect reviewed here, the experimenter who tested participants' memory on the delayed tests was different from the one who carried out the forced fabrication interview, thus minimizing any perceived pressure to respond consistently across test sessions. More importantly, virtually all studies have used a warning that explicitly informs participants before taking the memory test that the person who had interviewed them initially had asked them some questions about events that never actually happened. They are further instructed that their task is to differentiate between those events they specifically remember witnessing in the video and information they may have encountered during the interviews. Importantly, several studies have shown that in spite of the explicit warning that they had been misled, many participants will endorse their forced fabrications on memory tests of the witnessed event (e.g. Ackil and Zaragoza, 1998; Hanba and Zaragoza, 2007; Zaragoza et al., 2001a), even though they have been instructed to discriminate between those events they witnessed first-hand and information encountered in subsequent interviews. Indeed, participants will frequently make these endorsements with a high level of confidence despite the presence of a pre-test warning (e.g. Zaragoza et al., 2001a).

Additional evidence that participants develop genuine false memories of their forced fabrications comes from studies investigating the phenomenological experience associated with these false memories. One method that has been used to assess the phenomenological experience of false memories is Tulving's (1985) remember/know procedure. Following recall or recognition of a test item, participants are asked to indicate whether they *remember* seeing it during the original event or if they just *know* that it occurred, but cannot actually recollect the specific episode. Frost et al., (2003) showed that participants frequently indicated that they 'remember' witnessing details that they had previously been forced to fabricate and did so more often than control participants who had not initially fabricated the critical items. Collectively, then, the evidence suggests that participants do sometimes develop genuine false memories for their forced fabrications.

A theoretical framework

Why might people be prone to confusing their forced fabrications for actually perceived events? Research and theory on source monitoring have shown that source confusions arise when the information that is retrieved from memory about an item's source is ambiguous or incomplete, and/or when less than optimal judgment processes are used to evaluate an item's source (see Johnson et al., 1993; Lindsay, 2008, for reviews). According to the source monitoring framework (SMF), source monitoring is not a single ability, but involves a variety of interrelated cognitive processes including encoding, retrieval, and decision-making/reasoning processes. By this account, identification of sources does not involve the recollection of a 'tag' that specifies the source of a memory. Rather, the attribution of a memory to a source is a complex judgment that typically involves assessing the characteristics of a memory in the light of a current task or agenda. These judgments are typically made relatively automatically and with little introspective awareness (i.e. the outcome 'pops' into mind), although more deliberate source judgments are possible. From this view, errors in source monitoring arise either because people fail to encode or activate the memory characteristics necessary to support accurate source monitoring, or because they fail to engage in the extensive and complex decision-making processes that accurate source monitoring requires.

As predicted by the SMF, a consistent finding in the source monitoring literature is that source misattributions are most likely to be observed when people attempt to discriminate between sources that are very similar, or overlap, on a variety of dimensions. For example, there is considerable evidence that visual imagery can serve as a potent catalyst to false memory creation (Goff and Roediger, 1998; Hyman and Pentland, 1996) because imagining suggested events imbues the memory representation of the suggested event with sensory and perceptual details similar to those of perceived events (see Drivdahl and Zaragoza, 2001; Thomas et al., 2003).

In the eyewitness suggestibility paradigm, there are multiple sources of overlap between the witnessed event itself and the post-event interview about that event, and it is easy to see why participants might have difficulty in discriminating between these two sources of information. Specifically, the forensic interview is about the very same people and events the participants witnessed, resulting in a great deal of overlap in semantic content. Moreover, attempts to answer these questions at the time of the interview (whether participants knew the answer or not) were likely accompanied by active rehearsal and mental reconstruction of the witnessed event. Reflecting on the events of the video while attempting to answer the questions serves to increase the overlap between the two sources even further. A final consequence of pressing witnesses to describe a poorly remembered or fictitious event is that it forces the witness to create a concrete, perceptually detailed, and well-specified version of the fictitious event. Creating a fictitious event with characteristics typical of witnessed events renders the fabricated event highly confusable for a memory of something that actually took place.

In spite of this extensive overlap, the finding that participants develop false memories for events they were knowingly forced to fabricate is quite surprising. One might expect participants' memories of the confabulated details to be associated with memories of having resisted the experimenter's requests. This association should have protected them from misremembering the source of their fabrications later on. Although it is probably the case that all situations involving exposure to misinformation produce some degree of uneasiness, interview situations where participants are forced to fabricate responses are likely to produce much greater levels of discomfort. Indeed, across our studies, the vast majority of participants resist responding to the false-event questions (e.g. by remaining quiet; or by overtly expressing lack of knowledge) and have to be encouraged to guess. In fact, most participants had to be probed at least twice by the experimenter before they provided a response to the false-event questions. We interpret the finding that people develop false memories for their forced fabrications as evidence that, over time, they become less likely to remember/retrieve that they had been forced to fabricate these events.

In recent years, our program of research has begun to uncover some of the mechanisms that appear to underlie the development of false memories for forcibly fabricated events. In the following section, we review these mechanisms with an eye toward articulating their possible implications for understanding clinical confabulation.

Mechanisms of false memory development for forcibly fabricated events

I. The role of uncertainty monitoring

As mentioned in the foregoing discussion, one cognitive vulnerability that contributes to false memory development in the forced fabrication paradigm is people's failure to retrieve/remember that they were forced to make up their fabricated accounts. However, because the fabrications are self-generated (see the next section on self-generation) people appear to have very strong and enduring memories for the content of their forced fabrications, as evidenced by the fact that they freely incorporate their fabrications into their testimony even months after the interview (Chrobak and Zaragoza, 2008). The combined influence of a strong memory for the fabricated account, without the attendant knowledge that it was forcibly fabricated, appears to predispose participants to these false memory errors. In what follows, we use the umbrella term 'uncertainty monitoring' to describe people's ability to detect, remember, and use feelings of uncertainty to guide their cognitive processing. Research has shown that factors that improve uncertainty monitoring tend to reduce false memory for forced fabrications, and, similarly, factors that discourage uncertainty monitoring tend to increase false memory development.

A. Factors that improve attention to encoding and retrieval of uncertainty reduce false memory development

We have shown in several studies that overt verbal resistance to answering false-event questions (e.g. blunt refusals to respond, verbal responses such as 'that didn't happen', or 'I don't remember that') is associated with reductions in false memory development 1 week later. Importantly, however, more passive forms of resistance (such as remaining quiet and refusing to respond) do not reduce false memory rates reliably (Zaragoza et al., 2001a). We interpret these findings as evidence that publicly expressing resistance (as opposed to keeping such thoughts internal) enhances memory for the resistance and for having fabricated the response, thus reducing the development of false memories.

In our studies of the forced fabrication effect on children, we have found that young children (ages 5–6) are disproportionately susceptible to developing false memories for forcibly fabricated events when compared to older children and adults (e.g. Ackil and Zaragoza, 1998). One factor that likely contributes to children's greater susceptibility to false memory for their forced fabrications is their failure to attend to and use feelings of uncertainty to guide their cognitive processing (e.g. Schwanenflugel et al., 1996). Rather, young children evidence an over-reliance on familiarity as a basis for judging what was seen. There is considerable evidence that information about an item's familiarity is accessed quickly and relatively automatically, whereas retrieval of the contextual features that can specify an item's source (in this case, retrieving that the item was knowingly fabricated) is more effortful and time-consuming (see, e.g. Johnson et al., 1993).

We (Zaragoza et al., 2003) hypothesized that it would be possible to improve children's ability to distinguish between false memories based on fabrications and true memories based on witnessed events if we could improve their memory for having fabricated the false information. To this end, we had 1st and 3rd grade children who overtly indicate their confidence in their confabulated answers at the time they generated them (see, e.g. Wells and Bradfield, 1988) for evidence that such a manipulation improves retrospective memory for confidence in adults). The children were asked to indicate their confidence in each answer they generated during the post-event interview by choosing one of two photographs. One photo, depicting a child with a confused, pensive look represented 'not sure' and the other photo, depicting a child with a pleased and satisfied look represented 'sure' (see Lu et al., 1997), for use of a related technique with a clinical population). The goal of the intervention was to induce children to think more explicitly and deeply about their low confidence in their fabricated answers and to provide them a means of representing their lack of confidence in a concrete, visible way so as to increase the likelihood that they would remember their lack of confidence in their fabricated answers over the long term.

Of course, such a manipulation can work only if young children can accurately discriminate between answers they 'know' and answers that are mere guesses. The results confirmed that they were capable of such a task, as even 5- and 6-year old children were remarkably accurate in identifying their answers to true-event questions as things they were sure about and their confabulated answers to false-event questions as things they were 'unsure' about. The key finding, however, occurred 1 week later. First- and third-grade children who made overt confidence judgments about their confabulated responses immediately after generating them were much less likely to endorse the confabulated events as 'witnessed' than children who had not been asked to make confidence judgments. In a second experiment, Zaragoza et al. (2003) showed that the benefit of this intervention lasted at least 2 weeks for third-grade children, but only one week for the first-grade children, thus, showing that even with the help of this intervention, information about the uncertainty associated with one's knowledge is highly susceptible to forgetting. In sum, the results show that, even in young children, manipulations that improve participants' memory for the uncertainty associated with their forced fabrications reduce false memory development.

Another variable that has been shown to improve uncertainty monitoring is a retroactive warning, provided before the memory test, correctly informing participants that they had earlier been interviewed about fictitious events that never actually happened. In one study involving fabrication of entire fictitious events (Chrobak and Zaragoza, 2008), we showed that such a warning provided before a 1-week delayed recognition test eliminated false memory for fabrications, even though it had no effect of the base rate of errors (i.e. the warning increased sensitivity and did not merely induce a more conservative response bias). In contrast, participants who did not receive the warning claimed to remember witnessing their forced fabrications (We note, however, that in several studies involving forced fabrications of more limited scope, participants evidenced significant false memory effects on a 1-week delayed test even when given a warning, e.g. Hanba and Zaragoza, 2007; Zaragoza et al., 2001a). The finding that false memory is reduced following a warning suggests that in some cases, information about the uncertainty associated with fabricated information may be available, but participants fail to access and/or use it. Presumably, the warning encourages participants to engage in a more effortful search for source relevant information in memory and a more careful evaluation of the information they retrieve, resulting in fewer misattribution errors.

B. Factors that encourage forgetting or discounting of uncertainty increase false memory development

If the development of false memories for knowingly fabricated events results from failures in uncertainty monitoring, then factors that promote poor uncertainty monitoring should be associated with increases in false memory development. The available research is consistent with this prediction. For example, one factor that is strongly associated with increased false memory development is length of the retention interval. Memory of having been forced to make up the fabricated information appears to be especially susceptible to forgetting. We have shown, for example, that the benefits of overt resistance and even retroactive warnings are relatively short-lived. For example, Chrobak and Zaragoza (2008) showed that although a warning reduced false memory development on a 1-week recognition test, after an 8-week retention interval, the warned participants freely reported their forced fabrications as often as the unwarned participants. In the same study, we found that although overt verbal resistance to answering the false-event questions offered some protection against false memory development on a 1-week test, after 2 months having overtly resisted was not associated with lower false memory development. In contrast, participants freely reported their fabricated responses at a high rate even after several months delay, thus showing that memory for the content of their fabrications remained strong.

Another factor that can lead participants/witnesses to discount their uncertainty in their fabricated responses is receiving feedback that their fabricated response is correct. In several studies, we have shown that *confirmatory interviewer feedback* provided immediately after the participant is forced to fabricate the response (e.g. 'That's right, _____ is the correct answer'; Wells and Bradfield, 1998) is a potent catalyst to false memory development. Several studies have shown that, relative to neutral interviewer feedback (' _____, OK'), confirmatory interviewer feedback provided after the fabricated response led to significant increases in the incidence of false memories, increased confidence in those false memories, and an increased likelihood that participants would incorporate their forced fabrications into their accounts of the event on tests of long-term free recall (Hanba and Zaragoza, 2007; Zaragoza, et al., 2001a). Importantly, these increases in false memory occurred even among participants who did not remember receiving the feedback. We have hypothesized that one mechanism through which confirmatory feedback increases false memory is by leading participants to discount their uncertainty in their confabulated responses and embrace them as 'truth'. By discounting uncertainty, we mean that the confirmatory feedback encourages participants to ignore, suppress, or disregard as unimportant the fact that they were unsure in their confabulated responses, thus promoting forgetting of the uncertainty that had been associated with their forced fabrications. Upon receiving feedback that their forced guesses were in fact 'correct', participants may have been motivated to disregard those aspects of the false-event questioning episode that threatened their positive self-image (i.e. knowledge that they did not know the answer to the question or gave in to the demand to make up a response) and preferentially attended to those aspects of the questioning episode that bolstered their self-image (knowledge that the answer they provided was correct).

Several lines of evidence support the proposal that confirmatory feedback encourages participants to discount their uncertainty in their confabulated responses. First, confirmatory feedback eliminates the advantage normally associated with overt verbal resistance. That is, following confirmatory interviewer feedback, it is no longer the case that forced fabrications accompanied by overt verbal resistance show lower false memory development (Zaragoza et al., 2001a). Second, there is evidence that confirmatory interviewer feedback greatly increases the confidence with which false memories for knowingly fabricated events are held. In a study assessing the effects of interviewer feedback in repeated forced fabrication interviews (where feedback was provided in the first interview only), Hanba and Zaragoza (2007) showed that, relative to neutral feedback, confirmatory feedback provided after a forcibly confabulated response greatly increased the likelihood that participants would provide the same confabulated response when re-interviewed 2 days later, led participants to report these repeated confabulations with greater speed and fewer expressions of doubt, and increased the prevalence of false memories on a delayed test. Moreover, regardless of accuracy, responses that had earlier been reinforced with confirmatory feedback were much more likely to be judged by others as credible. Later studies showed that these effects of confirmatory feedback are not 'undone' by a retroactive warning that the feedback they received was completely unreliable and should be ignored. Hence, it appears that the confidence inflation that results from confirmatory feedback is robust and difficult to reverse.

Relative to neutral feedback, confirmatory feedback also increases the speed with which participants later endorse their false memories as 'truth'. Whereas participants generally endorse their accurate memories with greater speed than their false confabulated memories, following confirmatory feedback, participants endorse their false memories as quickly as their accurate memories (Hanba and Zaragoza, 2007). We interpret this as evidence that, in the absence of confirmatory feedback, participants sometimes retrieve some information about their uncertainty.

II. The role of self-generation

One way in which confabulation differs from other kinds of suggestive influences is that the false information is self-generated. Indeed, the fact that the participant has 'created' the fictitious event may make it especially confusable for a 'real' memory later on. Self-generated information will be better remembered than information that is not (Hirshman and Bjork, 1988; Slamecka and Graf, 1978), thus rendering confabulations more familiar than other information in memory. Moreover, there are reasons to expect that the act of generating these confabulations will likely bind them to their representation of the witnessed event (see Burns, 1990; Hirshman and Bjork, 1988; and McDaniel et al., 1988), for evidence that generation improves encoding of the characteristics shared by the cue and the target word, as well as the relationships between the items on the list). Finally, because a self-generated fictitious event will be constructed within the constraints of a person's idiosyncratic knowledge and beliefs, the content of the made-up account may later be perceived by them as especially plausible and real.

To assess whether self-generation promotes false memory creation, Ackil and Zaragoza (2007) conducted a controlled study that directly compared false memory rates resulting from forced fabrication, where the participant is forced to self-generate the fictitious information (GENERATE-fabrication condition), to situations where the same participants simply read forcibly fabricated information generated by another participant (READ-fabrication condition). As in the typical study, participants were asked a series of true and false-event questions. To implement the generate versus read manipulation, participants were given an answer sheet that listed answers for some of the false-event questions (READ condition) but provided no answers for other false-event questions (GENERATE condition). In those cases where an answer was provided (READ condition), participants were instructed to simply read the answer aloud; however, in those cases where no answer was provided (GENERATE condition), participants were instructed to provide a response to the question aloud, even if they had to guess (as is done in the typical forced fabrication study). As in previous studies, participants greatly resisted generating responses to the false-event questions (either by verbally protesting or by refusing to respond until they were pressed to do so). In contrast, participants never resisted when asked to read aloud the fictitious answers provided on the answer sheet. Two weeks later, participants returned to the lab and were greeted by a new experimenter who accurately warned them that they had earlier read and generated answers to questions about fictitious events that never happened. They were then given a cued recall test of their memory for the witnessed event. In spite of the overt verbal resistance that accompanied the self-generated fabrications, the clear finding was that participants were significantly more likely to recall fabricated information that they had self-generated as compared to fabricated information that they had read. This finding suggests that false information that is self-generated may be particularly likely to develop into a false memory (cf., Lane and Zaragoza, 2007).

III. The role of causal relations and narrative coherence

As in clinical cases involving confabulation, the events that witnesses are pressed to fabricate during a forensic investigation are not isolated incidents, but rather, bear some relation to a broader context (e.g. a larger, more complex series of events they witnessed). Our research suggests that the causal and logical relationship between the forcibly fabricated information and other knowledge or events in memory may play a critical role in false memory development. Specifically, it appears that participants are especially likely to develop false memories of their forced fabrications if incorporating their fabrications can lead to a more complete, coherent account of the events they actually witnessed.

In most forensic investigations, the role of the eyewitness is to provide detailed information about the people and events that caused an outcome that

Table 3.1 Summary of manipulation and results for Chrobak and Zaragoza (2007)

Group	Viewed antecedent	Forced fabrication	Viewed next scene	Delayed free recall of forced fabrication
'Consequence'	Counselors sneaking out in a canoe	Where did they go and what did they do when the snuck out at night? (e.g. *drinking with the girls' camp*)	Delaney gets in serious trouble with the camp director	0.27
'No consequence'	Counselors sneaking out in a canoe	Where did they go and what did they do when the snuck out at night? (e.g. *drinking with the girls' camp*)	Delaney tries riding a horse and rides through camp	0.10

is well-established (e.g. a crime or an accident). The situation we have sought to mimic in our studies of forced fabrication are those where the witness never saw or does not remember some of the key events that caused the outcome, and they are pressed to provide an account based on nothing more than guesses and speculations. A very recent and as yet unpublished discovery in our laboratory (Chrobak and Zaragoza, 2007) is that participants are more likely to develop false memories for knowingly fabricated events when the events we have forced them to make up help explain events that they actually witnessed, as compared to situations when their forced fabrications do not provide a causal explanation for observed events.

A summary of the method and results of the Chrobak and Zaragoza (2007) study is provided in Table 3.1. In this study, all participants viewed the movie clip described earlier. In the critical scene, two male counselors named Delaney and Moe sneak out of their cabins at night and are depicted getting into canoes. The movie clip then cuts to the next day. The groups differed only in the information depicted in the immediately ensuing scene (i.e. all of the scenes leading up to and including the critical scene, and all scenes after the ensuing scene were identical). For participants in the Consequence group, the ensuing scene depicts Delaney getting in serious trouble with the director of the camp the next day, who is shocked and disappointed by his behavior. For participants in the No Consequence group, the ensuing scene is an unrelated scene that depicts Delaney trying to ride a horse. During the post-event interview 2 days later, participants in both groups were asked to fabricate the same fictitious event, namely, they were asked to describe what the counselors did after they snuck out in canoes, including where they went and who they were with. Again, the answers that participants were forced to provide were complete fabrications, as the clip that participants witnessed provided no information about where Delaney and Moe went or what they did after getting in the canoe.

In sum, what we sought to manipulate in this study was the strength of the causal relationship between the events participants were forced to fabricate and the subsequent events they had actually witnessed. In the Consequence group, the fabricated event that participants were forced to provide helps to better explain the events that were actually witnessed (the counselors getting in serious trouble). Although it is plausible that the two counselors got in trouble for simply sneaking off on the canoe (which was what actually transpired), a fabricated event that involves, for example, the counselors going to a girls camp and getting drunk with some girls provides additional rationale for stealing the canoes and better justification for the severe reprimand Delaney received. In contrast, for the No Consequence group, the relation of the fabricated event to the subsequent witnessed events is quite different. Although for both groups there is a plausible antecedent that precedes the event they were forced to fabricate (e.g. the counselors sneaking out at night), for participants in the No Consequence group, the fabricated event (such as going to the girls camp) is not linked to an observed consequence. Hence, in the No Consequence group, the fabricated event does not serve the same explanatory function.

Six weeks later participants returned to the lab and were instructed to freely recall the events of the movie clip as completely and accurately as possible. As shown in Table 3.1, the results were quite striking: Participants in the Consequence group were much more likely to freely report their forcibly fabricated events than participants in the No Consequence group, even though the events participants were forced to fabricate were identical. We interpret this finding as evidence that participants were more likely to develop false memories for their forced fabrications when incorporating this information into their memories helped to provide a more complete, coherent explanation of the events they observed.

There is considerable empirical evidence that in perceiving, comprehending, and remembering events, people are highly motivated to construct a coherent representation of the world around them (e.g. Schank and Abelson, 1977). To this end, people seek to understand the underlying causes of things they experience (e.g. the reasons for people's behavior) and to infer the causal relations between events that comprise the episodes they experience (e.g. Weiner, 1985). Moreover, studies of text comprehension have shown that memory representations preserve the causal relations between events (van den Broek and Lorch, 1993), and that those parts of a story that are central to its causal structure are especially likely to be recalled (Trabasso et al., 1984; Trabasso and Sperry, 1985; van den Broek, 1988; Van den Broek and Trabasso, 1986). Hence, our finding that participants are more likely to develop false memories for fabricated events that provide a causal explanation for witnessed events is consistent with the broader finding in the cognitive literature that people are naturally predisposed to inferring and remembering the causal relationships among the events they experience.

Implications for clinical confabulation

The preceding section outlined several mechanisms related to the development of false memories for forcibly fabricated information and events in non-impaired individuals. In particular, we have described how the ability to monitor uncertainty, the unique mnemonic properties associated with self-generated information, and the causal relations between fabricated and observed events play a role in false memory development. In what follows we elaborate on the potential implications of these findings for understanding clinical confabulation.

Research on the forced fabrication effect has amply documented that people can be poor at monitoring uncertainty associated with information in memory. Even when forced to fabricate information against their wills, people appear to forget very quickly that they were forced to generate these fabrications and often come to embrace their forced fabrications as truth. However, manipulations such as warnings can improve uncertainty monitoring, thus showing that these monitoring processes are both effortful and demanding, and that people do not always monitor uncertainty to the best of their ability. Finally, the research on confirmatory feedback suggests that failures to monitor uncertainty might also reflect a motivational component – perhaps it is more comfortable to be confident in one's knowledge than to come to terms with the fact that one is uncertain about one's past.

How does 'uncertainty monitoring' relate to clinical confabulation? At first glance it may not appear particularly relevant to clinical confabulators – who appear to produce such false statements without *any* uncertainty as to the veridicality of their statements. However, it is important to note that simply because clinical confabulators produce such statements freely (e.g. without resistance) this does not necessarily imply the complete absence of uncertainty when blatantly implausible information is confabulated. Some of the false statements produced by clinical confabulators appear to be associated with at least a fleeting recognition (e.g. a laugh or a hesitation) of the inaccuracy of their statements. Consider, for example, patient HW described in Moscovitch (1989). After indicating that he has been married for 4 months, HW is asked how many children he has. With a laugh, he indicates that he has 4 children and that is pretty good for only being married months. His response seems to indicate that he has at least a momentary awareness of the contradictory nature of his statements. In other words, there is evidence that he has at least some transitory uncertainty in his response.

What, then, is the fate of any such uncertainty? Given that confabulating patients show deficits in source monitoring relative to normal populations (e.g. Dalla Barba et al., 1997; Johnson et al., 1997), it is possible that patients tend to ignore information regarding their confabulations' uncertainty, or simply do not have the cognitive resources required to accurately monitor uncertainty. Thus, poor attention to, encoding and monitoring of uncertainty may partially explain those situations in which clinical confabulators defend their sometimes fantastical statements so vehemently.

Also relevant to clinical confabulation is the finding that false information that is self-generated is particularly likely to result in false memories. An important parallel between both clinical confabulators and the false memory errors seen in the forced fabrication participants is that in both cases the false information is self-generated by the individual and not provided by some external source. Where clinical confabulators differ from normal participants is in their resistance to generating these fabrications. As our studies have shown, non-impaired participants vehemently resist speculating about events that they do not remember or did not witness, thus increasing the likelihood that participants will accurately remember that they, themselves, fabricated the information later on. In contrast, clinical confabulators freely engage in such fabrication, often with very little prompting from an interviewer, thus making it much less likely that they will recognize or remember that the confabulated information was self-generated. That confabulations are self-generated so freely may in part explain why confabulators will sometimes vehemently assert their faulty claims, despite seemingly overwhelming external evidence to the contrary. One characteristic of self-generated information is that it is very well-remembered, readily available, and comes to mind fluently. As such, it is more likely to be deemed reliable and accurate. Self-generated information is also likely to be particularly plausible to the confabulator, as it is constrained by his/her idiosyncratic knowledge base. Overall then, an over-reliance on familiarity coupled with poor source monitoring may explain why many confabulations contain accurate information that is temporally displaced (Deluca, 2000; Ptak and Schnider, 1999; Schnider et al., 1996a; Schnider et al., 1996b; Talland, 1965).

Finally, our research on forced fabrication has highlighted the importance of understanding the function that the fabricated information serves in memory. Specifically, in our research we have shown that participants are more likely to develop false memories for fabricated events that provide a causally consistent and coherent account of the events that were actually observed. When fabricated information does not serve this explanatory function, participants are much less likely to develop false memories.

We propose that in attempting to understand clinical confabulation, it is also important to understand the function these confabulations serve for the patient. It is of course true that the confabulated accounts provided by clinical patients are not always coherent or internally consistent (Moscovitch, 1995) when evaluated against verifiable reality. Nevertheless, it is still the case that the confabulations may appear coherent to the confabulator. This notion is articulated in a recent account of clinical confabulation proposed by Orulv and Hyden (2006). According to this account, the narratives produced by confabulators are attempts to make sense of their current reality and should not be viewed in terms of objectively true and false statements. Rather, the authors claim, their confabulations follow a *narrative logic* that 'does not concern the world as it is, but the world *as it makes sense*' (Orulv and Hyden, 2006, p. 670) to the individual.

Indeed, one of the challenges that faces the confabulator is the need to relate themselves to their current environment and their personal history in a meaningful way. This is done by looking for connections between events and actions, and finding links between outcomes and the events that caused them. Presumably, the dysfunctional mental landscape of the confabulator, caused by amnesia, frontal damage, a combination of both, or some other deficit, may actually further necessitate this need for organization. If the confabulated accounts reported by clinical populations follow a narrative organization, albeit a distorted one, then they should be influenced by the same causal relationships that structure recollection in the normal system. Indeed, the responses that clinical confabulators provide in response to specific questions regarding 'how' and 'why' an event occurred appear to at least minimally fulfill this causal role – albeit in sometimes implausible ways. To that end, the types of confabulations produced by clinical populations can be viewed as the result of a meaning-making process gone awry, resulting in the communication of faulty information.

In this regard, it is interesting to consider the origin of the word *confabulate*. As several researchers have pointed out (e.g. Berrios, 1998; Hirstein, 2005), the word dates back as early as 1450, and in its original usage, meant: *to talk familiarly together, converse, chat* (Oxford English Dictionary, 2nd Edition). Although this definition has since changed, the original meaning of the word conveys an important concept relevant to our understanding of clinical confabulation: the purposeful attempt to convey information about the self to an audience. Although the false statements produced by confabulators may not be true according to an objective reality, they do represent the confabulators attempt to relate themselves to the outside world in terms of their own perceived reality. To that end, their attempts at organizing and relating information to others is, as in non-impaired individuals, motivated by an attempt to achieve narrative coherence.

Summary and conclusions

Our research on the forced fabrication effect provides insight into the workings of a cognitive system that, although usually accurate, is capable of producing confidently held memories of fictitious events. We believe the false memory errors that result from forced fabrication are especially relevant to understanding clinical confabulation, because in both cases, the individual comes to have a false belief in fictitious events that they have created. In this chapter, we have identified several mechanisms that contribute to the development of false memories in the forced fabrication paradigm and have reviewed the research supporting our claims. In addition, we have attempted to show how these same mechanisms may contribute to the erroneous confabulations that clinical patients sometimes produce.

References

Ackil, J.K. and Zaragoza, M.S. (2007). *Is Forced Confabulation More Dangerous Than False Memory Implantation?* Poster Presented at the Annual Meeting of the Psychonomic Society. CA, Long Beach.

Ackil, J.K. and Zaragoza, M.S. (1998). Memorial consequences of forced confabulation: Age differences in susceptibility to false memories. *Developmental Psychology*, **34**(6), 1358–1372.

Berrios, G.E. (1998). Confabulations: A conceptual history. *Journal of the History of the Neurosciences*, **7**(3), 225–241.

Burgess, P.W. and McNeil, J.E. (1999). Content-specific confabulation. *Cortex*, **35**, 163–182.

Burns, D.J. (1990). The generation effect: A test between single-and multifactor theories. *Journal of Experimental Psychology: Learning, Memory, and Cognition*, **16**(6), 1060–1067.

Chrobak, Q.M. and Zaragoza, M.S. (2007, July). *Forced Confabulation of Entire Events: The Role of Observed Consequences in the Development of False Memories.* Paper presented at the Society for Applied Research in Memory and Cognition. Lewiston, Maine.

Chrobak, Q.M. and Zaragoza, M.S. (2008). Inventing stories: Forcing witnesses to fabricate entire fictitious events leads to freely reported false memories. *Psychonomic Bulletin & Review*, **15**(6), 1190–1195.

Dalla Barba, G., Cappelletti, J.Y., Signorini, M., and Denes, G. (1997). Confabulation: Remembering 'another past,' planning 'another' future. *Neurocase*, **3**, 425–436.

DeLuca, J. (2000). A cognitive neuroscience perspective on confabulation. *Neuro-Psychoanalysis*, **2**(2), 119–132.

Drivdahl, S.B. and Zaragoza, M.S. (2001). The role of perceptual elaboration and individual differences in the creation of false memories for suggested events. *Applied Cognitive Psychology*, **15**(3), 265–281.

Frost, P., Lacroix, D., and Sanborn, N. (2003). Increasing false recognition rates with confirmatory feedback: A phenomenological analysis. *American Journal of Psychology*, **116**, 515–525

Goff, L.M. and Roediger, L. (1998). Imagination inflation for action events: Repeated imaginings lead to illusory recollections. *Memory & Cognition*, **26**(1), 20–33.

Hanba, J.M. and Zaragoza, M.S. (2007). Interviewer feedback in repeated interviews involving forced confabulation. *Applied Cognitive Psychology*, **21**, 433–455.

Hirshman, E. and Bjork, A. (1988). The generation effect: Support for a two-factor theory. *Journal of Experimental Psychology: Learning, Memory, and Cognition*, **14**(3), 484–494.

Hirstein, W. (2005). *Brain Fiction: Self-Deception and the Riddle of Confabulation*. Cambridge, MA, MIT Press.

Hyman, I.E. and Pentland, J. (1996). The role of mental imagery in the creation of false childhood memories. *Journal of Memory and Language*, **35**, 101–117.

Johnson, M.K., Hashtroudi, S., and Lindsay, D.S. (1993). Source monitoring. *Psychological bulletin*, **114**, 3–28.

Johnson, M.K., O'Connor, M., and Cantor, J. (1997). Confabulation, memory deficits, and frontal dysfunction. *Brain and Cognition*, **34**(2), 189–206.

Kopelman, M.D. (1987). Two types of confabulation. *Journal of Neurology, Neurosurgery & Psychiatry*, **50**(11), 1482–1487.

Lane, S.M. and Zaragoza, S. (2007). A little elaboration goes a long way: The role of generation in eyewitness suggestibility. *Memory & Cognition*, **35**(6), 1255–1266.

Lindsay, D.S. (2008). Source monitoring. In *Learning and Memory: A Comprehensive Reference: Vol. 2. Cognitive Psychology of Memory* (Series ed. J. Byrne & Vol. ed. H.L. Roediger III), pp. 325–348. Oxford, Elsevier.

Loftus, E.F., Miller, D.G., and Burns, H.J. (1978). Semantic integration of verbal information into a visual memory. *Journal of Experimental Psychology: Human Learning & Memory*, **4**, 19–31.

Lu, L., Barret, A.M., Schwartz, R.L. et al. (1997). Anosognosia and confabulation during the Wada test. *Neurology*, **49**, 1316–1322.

McDaniel, M.A., Waddill, P.J., and Einstein, G.O. (1988). A contextual account of the generation effect: A three-factor theory. *Journal of Memory and Language*, **27**(5), 521–536.

Moscovitch, M. (1989). Confabulation and the frontal systems: Strategic versus associative retrieval in neuropsychological theories of memory. In *Varieties of Memory & Consciousness* (eds. H.L. Roediger III and F.I.M. Craik), pp. 133–160. Hillsdale, NJ, Erlbaum.

Moscovitch, M. (1995). Confabulation. In *Memory Distortions: How Minds, Brains, and Societies Reconstruct the Past* (ed. D.L. Schacter), pp. 226–251. Cambridge, MA, Harvard University Press.

Orulv, L. Hyden, L. (2006). Confabulation: Sense-making, self-making and world-making in dementia. *Discourse Studies*, **8**(5), 647–673.

Oxford English Dictionary. (1992). (2nd edition). Oxford, Oxford University Press.

Pezdek, K., Sperry, K., and Owen, S.M. (2007). Interviewing witnesses: The effect of forced confabulation on event memory. *Law and Human Behavior*, **31**, 463–478.

Ptak, R. and Schnider, A. (1999). Spontaneous confabulations after orbitofrontal damage: The role of temporal context confusion and self-monitoring. *Neurocase*, **5**(3), 243–250.

Schank, R.C. and Abelson, R.P. (1977). *Scripts, plans, goals, and understanding: An inquiry into human knowledge structures.* Hillsdale, NJ, Erlbaum.

Schnider, A., Gutbrod, K., Hess, C.W., and Schroth, G. (1996a). Memory without context: Amnesia with confabulations after infarction of the right capsular genu. *Journal of Neurology, Neurosurgery & Psychiatry*, **61**(2), 186–193.

Schnider, A., von Däniken, K., and Gutbrod, K. (1996b). The mechanisms of spontaneous and provoked confabulations. *Brain,* **119**, 1365–1375.

Schnider, A. and Ptak, R. (1999). Spontaneous confabulators fail to suppress currently irrelevant memory traces. *Nature Neuroscience*, **2**(7), 677–681.

Schnider, A. (2001). Spontaneous confabulation, reality monitoring, and the limbic system: a review. *Brain Research Reviews*, **36**, 150–160.

Schwanenflugel, P.J., Fabricius, W.V., and Noyes, C.R. (1996). Developing organization of mental verbs: Evidence for the development of a constructivist theory of mind in middle childhood. *Cognitive Development,* **11**, 265–294.

Slamecka, N.J. and Graf, P. (1978). The generation effect: Delineation of a phenomenon. *Journal of Experimental Psychology: Human Learning and Memory*, **4**(6), 592–604.

Talland, G.A. (1965). Deranged memory. New York, Academic Press.

Thomas, A.K., Bulevich, J.B., and Loftus, E.F. (2003). Exploring the role of repetition and sensory elaboration in the imagination inflation effect. *Memory & Cognition*, **31**(4), 630–640.

Trabasso, T., Secco, T., and Van den Broek, P. (1984). In *Casual Cohesion and Story Coherence* (eds. H. Mandl, N.L. Stein, and T. Trabasso), pp. 83–111. Learning and comprehension of text. Hillsdae, NJ, Erlbaum.

Trabasso, T. and Sperry, L. (1985). Causal relatedness and importance of story events. *Journal of Memory and Language*, **24**(5), 595–611.

Tulving, E. (1985). Memory and consciousness. *Canadian Psychology,* **26**, 1–12.

Van den Broek, P. and Lorch, F. (1993). Network representations of causal relations in memory for narrative texts: Evidence from primed recognition. *Discourse Processes*, **16**(1–2), 75–98.

Van den Broek, P. and Trabasso, T. (1986). Causal networks versus goal hierarchies in summarizing text. *Discourse Processes*, **9**(1), 1–15.

Van den Broek, P. (1988). The effects of causal relations and hierarchical position on the importance of story statements. *Journal of Memory and Language*, **27**(1), 1–22.

Weiner, B. (1985). "Spontaneous" causal thinking. *Psychological Bulletin*, **97**(1), 74–84.

Wells, G.L. and Bradfield, L. (1998). Good, you identified the suspect: Feedback to eyewitnesses distorts their reports of the witnessing experience. *Journal of Applied Psychology*, **83**(3), 360–376.

Zaragoza, M.S., Belli, R.F., and Payment, K.E. (2007). Misinformation effects and the suggestibility of eyewitness memory. In *Do Justice and Let the Sky Fall: Elizabeth Loftus and Her Contributions to Science, Law, and Academic Freedom* (eds.M. Garry and H. Hayne), pp. 35–63. Maywah, NJ, Erlbaum.

Zaragoza, M.S., Payment, K., Kichler, J., Stines, L., and Drivdahl, S. (2001b). Forced confabulation and false memory in child witnesses. In *Developmental Changes in False Memory Formation: Errors as By-products of a Functional System.* Symposium conducted at the biennial meeting of *the Society for Research in Child Development,* (eds. Chairs S. Ghetti and J. Schaff), Minneapolis, MN.

Zaragoza, M.S., Payment, K., Weimer, B., and Cain, E. (2003). An intervention reduces false memories following forced confabulation. Paper presented at the *Biennial Meeting of the Society for Research in Child Development.* Tampa, FL.

Zaragoza, M.S., Payment, K.E., Ackil, J.K., Drivdahl, S.B., and Beck, M. (2001a). Interviewing witnesses: Forced confabulation and confirmatory feedback increase false memories. *Psychological Science,* **12**, 473–477.

Chapter 4

Confabulation, the self, and ego functions: The ego dysequilibrium theory

Todd E. Feinberg

A *confabulation* has been broadly defined as an erroneous statement that is made without a conscious effort to deceive (Berlyne, 1972) or alternatively 'statements or actions that involve unintentional but obvious distortions' (Moscovitch and Melo, 1997; see also DeLuca 2000; Hirstein 2005). Early observations of confabulation were made by Korsakoff (1892; Victor and Yakovlev, 1955) who observed that patients with what is now known as Wernicke-Korsakoff syndrome demonstrated both amnesia and *pseudoreminiscences*, an observation that was subsequently confirmed by later investigators (Bonhoeffer, 1901, 1904; Van der Horst, 1932; Williams and Rupp, 1938; Talland, 1961, 1965). Subsequently, many varieties of confabulation have been noted to occur in a wide range of types and clinical settings (for reviews see DeLuca 2000; Feinberg 1997; Feinberg and Giacino 2003; Johnson et al. 2000).

Subtypes of confabulation

Due to the diversity of forms it takes, confabulation is most appropriately thought of as a syndrome, not a single disorder. Several investigators have offered dichotomous schemes in an effort to organize these different varieties into meaningful subgroups. Initially, Kraepelin (1904, 1907, 1919) distinguished two subtypes of confabulation, *simple confabulation* that he suggested was caused in part by errors in the temporal ordering of real memories and *fantastic confabulations* that he observed were more likely to be bizarre and patently impossible statements that were not or could be derived from veridical memories. Later, Berlyne (1972) affirmed the validity of this distinction and further noted that momentary confabulation typically was provoked by questions from the examiner and that the content of such confabulations usually consisted of actual memories that were temporally displaced. Van der Horst (1932) and Williams and Rupp (1938) also noted that many confabulations were derived from preserved past memories, observations that support the viewpoint that confabulation results from *temporal context confusion* due to frontal-executive dysfunction (Schnider et al.,1996a, 1996b; Schnider and Ptak, 1999; Schnider et al., 2000). Kopelman (1980) reframed the two major catagories of confabulation while retaining the essential characteristics of the two types described by Berlyne. He described *provoked confabulations* that were elicited specifically in response to questions that probed the patient's memory and *spontaneous confabulations* that were more grandiose, florid, and occurred without provocation.

Schnider (2008) has recently proposed that the forms of confabulation can be organized within four subtypes: *intrusions* or *simple provoked confabulations* that appear during memory testing, *momentary confabulations* that occur during conversations or questions, *fantastic confabulations* that are imaginative creations that are not based in reality and may be bizarre, and *behaviorally spontaneous confabulations* that reflect an abnormal 'adaptation of thought to ongoing reality' that results from a failure to suppress currently irrelevant memories to ongoing experience. Schnider also makes the point that not all confabulations are based upon memory impairment, and he distinguished *mnestic confabulation* in patients whose confabulation is based primarily upon memory failure from *non-mnestic confabulations* that derive from false perceptions of the body and the world.

'Negative' versus 'positive' theories

Cognitively based theories of confabulation that invoke particular neuropsychological deficits help to explain some of the *negative* features of confabulation. For instance, confusion in the temporal context or disturbed memory retrieval (Moscovitch, 1989, 1995; Moscovitch and Melo, 1997) could cause a confusion between old memories and recent memories. However, these explanations are incomplete when attempting to address the *positive* features reported in confabulation.

For example, theories of confabulation that emphasize memory deficits or deficient retrieval strategies do not adequately account for the observation that in certain patients, particularly those who produce spontaneous, bizarre, or 'fantastic' confabulations that are not based upon veridical memory, the confabulatory beliefs persist in spite of corrective feedback. Several authors have emphasized the delusional quality of these varieties of confabulation. Weinstein (1996) noted that patients with *reduplicative paramnesia* frequently maintained an incorrect orientation in spite of correction and referred to this variety of disorientation as 'symbolic or delusional environmental disorientation'. Burgess and co-workers (1996) in a broader context, referred to a variety of delusional confabulation as 'delusional paramnesic misidentification' or 'delusion with paramnesia' to emphasize the link of these delusional confabulations to memory disorders.

Neutral and personal confabulation

In an effort to distinguish those cases of confabulation that were more directly and exclusively related to cognitive and perceptual defects and those that are more intimately dependent upon personality, motivation , and other significant personal issues, we proposed another dichotomy within the broader group of confabulatory patients (Feinberg, 1997; Feinberg and Roane, 1997). In this theory, we posited that there are two broad varieties of confabulations. One form is called *neutral confabulation* (Table 4.1). Neutral confabulation may occur in any sensory or cognitive domain, for instance in the memory or visual domain, and in this sense may be mnestic or non-mnestic. However, the sphere of the confabulation is usually confined to that domain. The content of neutral confabulations is non-delusional, and when the error is pointed out to the patient, in our experience, the confabulation can be corrected. Neutral confabulation does not entail the creation of fantastic or imaginary persons, places, or events. Hence, the designation *neutral*. Common examples of neutral confabulation include visual completion/confabulation in hemianopic, split-brain, and neglect patients (Feinberg et al., 1994; Feinberg, 1997; Feinberg and Roane, 1997) and confabulatory (illusory) limb movements in patients with hemispatial neglect and anosognosia for hemipleplegia (Feinberg et al., 2000).

Provoked confabulations in amnesic patients are often of the neutral type. The following patient demonstrates neutral confabulation within the memory domain. This patient, O.G. is a man in his 50s who sustained bilateral frontal damage secondary to a traumatic brain injury with resulting profound anterograde and retrograde amnesia. He was previously employed as a manager in a large company involved in employee training and planning, although when asked he could not actually recall what kind of work he did, his home address, and he gave the ages of his children approximately 10 years younger than their actual ages. The patient produced confabulations that were a combination of his past work experience and his current experience in the rehabilitation facility in which he was currently an inpatient. The following interview was obtained by neuropsychologist Dr. Joseph Giacino:

> EXAMINER: *And so where are you living now?*
> O.E.: *I'm staying right here in the hotel I came from.*

EXAMINER: *And why are you in a hotel at this point?*

O.E.: *I'm staying there for my company there to try to help with my situation.*

EXAMINER: *And what do you do at the hotel?*

S.C.: *I'm responsible for the training situation right now.*

EXAMINER: *Who else is there?*

O.E.: *My wife is there and there is a whole set of people. Their operations, procedures, do the stuff for them that they can't do.*

EXAMINER: *What do you do there specifically?*

O.E.: *Involved with serving and eating...I set procedures to handle the daily one per day. So anyone we send through the training in the morning we have to have breakfast for, then we have to have lunch for, then we have to have dinner for...so we write that what everyone has to go through what the procedures are.*

EXAMINER: *And these people who you direct procedures for, why are they there?*

O.E.: *They are there because that's what we want them to do. We want them to handle these operations in order to handle our products.*

In our experience, many people who were employed prior to their brain injury when they are confabulatory in open interviews, produce neutral confabulations that are temporally displaced memories about their employment. Thus, patients will often claim they are at a work site, at the office, on a construction job, etc. Many of these neutral confabulations are banal, changing from moment to moment and day to day, and contain no unbelievable or bizarre elements. They are most often a condensation of their premorbid memories with some aspect of their current ongoing experience.

Neutral confabulations stand in contrast to *personal confabulation* (Table 4.2; Feinberg, 1997; Feinberg and Roane, 1997). In personal confabulation, the patient misconstrues an actual event in his or her life or creates a wholly fictitious and distorted narrative about themselves or persons close to them. Patients who display personal confabulation represent themselves, their personal experiences, and their problems and preoccupations in a story. The story is a narrative of events that ostensibly but not actually has occurred to the patient in the past, or it is a false account of the patient's current experiences. The narrative may involve real or fictitious places or persons; the events described in the confabulation may rather be commonplace, but are often

Table 4.1 Examples of neutral forms of confabulation in neurological patients

Confabulation in a neglected hemispace (Young et al., 1992; Feinberg et al., 1994)
Confabulatory limb movements in anosognosia for hemiplegia (Feinberg et al., 2000)
Confabulations in corpus callosotomy patients (Gazzaniga, 1985, 2000)

Table 4.2 The 'neutral versus personal' continuum of confabulation

Neutral confabulation	Personal delusional confabulation*
Unimodal	Multimodal
Impersonal	Self-referential and autobiographical
Motivation not essential	Motivationally driven
Personality type not essential	Personality may be important
Non-symbolic	May be symbolic and metaphorical
Non-delusional and correctable	Delusional and impervious to correction
Inconsistent/variable	Repeated and long lasting

* In our earlier descriptions of this dichotomy we referred to all delusional forms as personal confabulation. Now, we use the terms *personal confabulation*, *delusional confabulation* or *personal delusional confabulation* somewhat interchangeably. This variety most closely corresponds to 'fantastic' confabulation in traditional dichotomies.

quite fantastic in nature. The themes within the story often involve the patient's neurological problems, but they may also be about any traumatic event or circumstance of a personal nature. Unlike neutral confabulations, personal confabulations are much more delusional, fixed, and particular details may be stated with every retelling.

I wish to note that in our earlier descriptions of this dichotomy, we referred to all delusional forms of confabulation as personal confabulation. In more recent papers, we have also used the term *delusional confabulation* or *personal delusional confabulation* for essentially the same subtype of confabulation. The advantage of the more general term 'personal confabulation' is that there are more features implied by this term than delusions alone (Table 4.2) but I believe that the delusional aspect is indeed the most salient and important feature of personal confabulation. With regard to the traditional criteria outlined above, this form of confabulation most closely corresponds to 'fantastic' confabulation.

A personal delusional confabulation was produced by patient J.K, a man in his 20s with a lesion of the right hemisphere that required surgical excision that left him with left hemispatial neglect and left hemiplegia. He was originally from Asia, but he was living and currently hospitalized in New York City. He spoke of his loneliness and his desire to be reunited with his loved ones, desires that were expressed in his misidentification of his left arm as actually being his 'brother's arm'. He produced the following responses to my questions:

T.E.F.: *What is this?* [I held up his left arm for him to see].

J.K.: *It's supposed to be my arm, but I think it's my brother's arm. I tell that to everyone but they don't believe me. My brother was on the wrong track for a while, and he got involved with some gangsters. They chopped off his arms and threw them in the river.* [touching the left arm] *I found this in my coffin. Some people thought I was dead and it was there*

T.E.F.: *Now what about, you mentioned something about being in...you found it in your coffin. Tell me about that.*

J.K.: *I don't know why I was in a coffin....after I was carried to the hospital...I was in a coffin...that's what I remember...I was laying next to this arm* [pointing to left arm]...*I was in a coffin.*

T.E.F.: *And that's how you found it?*

J.K.: *Yeah that's how I found it...*

T.E.F.: *Were you alive?*

J.K.: *I was alive...I didn't die...I found the arm in the coffin.*

In a subsequent interview, we continued to discuss J.K.'s problems:

T.E.F.: *What's wrong? Why are you here?*

J.K.: *I had some type of brain injury. Not exactly sure what happened.*

T.E.F.: *Do you have any weakness anywhere?*

J.K.: *Yes. I can't move my left arm. I can feel things there but I can't move it.* [touching his left hand]

T.E.F.: *You have told me that all your family is overseas, and that you miss them very much. How does it feel to have your brother's arm here?*

J.K.: [Patient begins to cry profusely. He holds his left arm in his right hand.] *It makes me happy. It makes me very happy. It makes me feel closer to my brother. Emotionally it makes me happy.* [He remains very tearful] *I feel sad to not be able to see my friends and family. I have to wait for them to come see me. I am learning so much. This is a sort of rebirth. It was so sad. But now I'm not sad, because I can now correct my mistakes.* [Crying]

T.E.F.: *How did it make you feel that it was your brother's?*

J.K.: *I thought it was a little funny...like a little gross.*

T.E.F.: *A little funny and a little gross? But you also said...*

J.K.: *But now it makes me a little comforted.*

T.E.F.: *A little what?*

J.K.: *Comforted...because I have my brother here* [Pointing to left arm, begins to cry]. *Its a little comfort for me now....*

T.E.F.: *A little comforting for you?*

J.K.: *But now it makes me a little comforted.*

T.E.F.: *OK so why? You said it kept you company?*

J.K.: *Yes.*

T.E.F.: *How did it make you feel emotionally?*

J.K.: *I felt stronger….*

T.E.F. *Because…you missed your family?*

J.K.: *Yeah…I missed my brother.*

[I lifted it toward his right side and asked him how he felt about it.]

J.K.: *I feel good. I feel good about this…Its feels good. I don't know. Just because.*

T.E.F.: [I lifted his right hand.] *How about this?*

J.K.: *This is my hand…my right hand.*

T.E.F.: *How do you feel about this?*

J.K.: *This is OK….*

T.E.F.: *This one is OK…You just feel OK about this one?*

J.K.: *This one doesn't have a story like this one (pointing to his left hand)…it has a story. Like the one I told you…this hand has a background that makes me feel closer to my brother.*

J.K.'s narrative displays all the features of personal delusional confabulation. It is multimodal so that the left arm is misidentified whether it is seen, touched, or reflected upon in memory. The references to the arm being 'chopped off' and found in a 'coffin' are self-referential and metaphorical references to his personal feelings about its 'lifeless' nature and his concerns about his own health. The beliefs were delusional, fixed, and reported with the same details intact. There was a motivational and wish-fulfilling aspect to them, in that it was a comfort to him that the arm belonged to his brother.

Hemispheric asymmetries and personal delusional confabulation

In a recent survey (Feinberg et al., 2005), we attempted to determine the anatomical correlates of these personal and delusional confabulations. The criteria for inclusion in our series were patients who displayed stable and delusional confabulatory misidentification(s), reduplication(s), or other varieties of delusional confabulation. In order to be included in the analysis, all cases had to have focal brain pathology that was adequately characterized in the report. Based upon these criteria, we identified in 27 patients a total of 29 instances of delusional misidentification, reduplication, or confabulation.

In terms of the hemisphere involved, there was a strong tendency for the right hemisphere to be affected, and all observations and all patients (100%) displayed some degree of right hemisphere damage. In contrast, only 15 (51.72%)

had left hemisphere damage ($p < 0.05$). When we considered cases with unilateral damage, there were 14 (48.28%) observations with right hemisphere damage only while there were no (0%) cases with left hemisphere damage only ($p < 0.001$). Taken together, these findings indicate a strong right hemisphere bias in terms of side of damage.

Regarding the location of the lesion, 10 (34.48%) cases had exclusively frontal damage, and perhaps most significantly, we found that in 28 out of 29 observations (96.6%), right frontal damage was present ($p < 0.001$). There were no cases of any other brain region exclusively leading to delusional confabulation ($p < 0.01$). These data suggest that the frontal cortex, especially the right frontal sector, is highly related to delusional confabulation.

The overall finding of a right hemisphere bias in these cases is consistent with prior studies that found that right hemisphere dysfunction is particularly common in delusional misidentification of places and persons (Alexander et al., 1979; Feinberg and Shapiro, 1989). Feinberg and Shapiro (1989) found that in reported cases of misidentification or reduplication, where cerebral dysfunction was unilateral, there was a highly significant right-hemispheric predominance in reduplication. This finding has been subsequently confirmed by others (Förstl et al., 1991; Fleminger and Burns, 1993; Burgess et al., 1996).

However, it is worth noting that the right hemisphere and strong right frontal bias we observed is not found in confabulatory patients in general. Johnson and co-workers (2000) did a careful and extensive analysis of the anatomical features of confabulatory patients. However, in their analysis, these authors *specifically eliminated* cases which showed evidence of misidentification, reduplicative paramnesia, Anton's syndrome, or confabulation associated with anosognosia for hemiplegia. In other words, conveniently for present purposes, these authors specifically *excluded* all the types of subjects who were the subjects of our survey, and thus can serve as the perfect comparison group. In the Johnson et al. study, within the ACoA (anterior communicating artery aneurysm) group, the largest group, there were approximately equal numbers of left (14) and right (15) hemisphere cases and marginally more unilateral (29) than bilateral (22) cases. Therefore, in contrast to patients with delusional confabulations, there is no evidence to suggest laterality effects in confabulatory patients when considered as a group.

Toward a theory of personal delusional confabulations

I suggest that at the extremes, there is ample evidence that the neutral and personal forms can be distinguished. However, I doubt that these forms are entirely dissociable. Rather, clinical experience suggests that there is a continuum of confabulatory patients, ranging from cases that are neutral and non-delusional to those patients who are motivated to produce delusional confabulations that are autobiographical, self-referential, refractory to correction, may be wishful, and depend to a greater extent on the patient's premorbid personality. We therefore need an explanation of these personal delusional forms. Additionally, we would want the explanation to account for the high incidence of right hemisphere lesions in these cases, and we want the theory to be as parsimonious as possible.

'Reality monitoring' defect

Johnson and co-workers (1991, 2000) suggest a reality monitoring framework or a source monitoring framework to explain some aspects of confabulation (for review see Johnson et al. (2000)). According to the reality monitoring framework (Johnson, 1991), confabulations result from the failure to discriminate between memories and internally derived thoughts. According to the source monitoring framework, disturbances in the 'encoding, retrieval, and evaluation' of perceptions and memories lead us to a failure to distinguish veridical memory from self-generated confabulations. Confabulation in this view results from a failure of judgment processes that determine whether the perceptual information in a memory represents a true memory or imagination, and additional judgments about whether this information conforms to previously acquired knowledge (Johnson et al., 2000).

A failure of reality monitoring could help explain why some confabulations appear to be 'wish-fulfilling' but it does not explain why confabulations may become delusional in some patients and not others, and why delusional patients, in contrast to patients with confabulation in general, have right frontal lesions. It also does not explain why the misidentifications in these cases are so selective or why patients do not have a generalized impairment in reality testing.

Geschwind's disconnection hypothesis and Gazzaniga's 'interpreter'

Norman Geschwind (1965) proposed that some confabulatory responses were based upon a disconnection of perceptual regions from the language areas of the verbal (left) hemisphere:

> One most important implication is that the 'introspections' of the patient as to his disability may be of little or no use to the examiner. The patient cannot 'introspect' about the activities of a piece of brain which had no connexion to the speech area. What he tells you is of little value in elucidating the mechanism and may indeed be actively misleading. Indeed, it becomes clear that many of the patient's responses can

only be described as confabulatory, i.e. they are attempts to fill gaps in the information available to his speech area; phrased in more conventional terms they are attempts to explain what the patient cannot understand.

(Geschwind, 1965, p. 590)

In the case of the patient with a right hemisphere lesion who was unaware of his paralysis (the anosognosic response), Geschwind reasoned that since the verbal hemisphere lacks the requisite knowledge regarding the left-side hemispace and the left side of the body, the patient fills in the information by the process of perceptual completion. Here, the patient uses the information accurately available from the intact side to fill in the 'gap' on the impaired side.

The left side of the body and of space is then 'lost'. The patient will then respond in many instances by using the technique of confabulatory completion that I have discussed above.

(Geschwind, 1965, p. 600)

Geschwind's theory that confabulations occur as a result of disconnection from the language areas is a plausible account of the presence of some confabulations in patients with right hemisphere lesions who display neutral confabulations about the left side of space and the left arm.

Michael Gazzaniga offers a very similar explanation for the same forms of confabulation, but this time based upon split-brain research (see for example Gazzaniga, 1985, 2000). Gazzaniga presents the view that the verbal left hemisphere is the final arbiter of individual's consciousness and serves as an 'interpreter' that enables the individual to 'construct theories about the relationship between perceived events, actions, and feelings' (Gazzaniga, 2000, p. 1293). A typical example of the left (verbal) hemisphere's interpreter function is a response given by the split-brain patient P.S. In the split-brain condition a stimulus can be presented independently to one hemisphere without the opposite hemisphere being fully aware of the nature of the stimulus. In the case of P.S. when this subject was presented with simultaneous yet different visual stimuli to each hemisphere, he could perform correct yet different responses with each hand simultaneously. Gazzaniga and LeDoux describe the behavior of P.S. under these conditions:

What is of particular interest, however, is the way the subject verbally interpreted these double-field responses. When a snow scene was presented to the right hemisphere and a chicken claw was presented to the left, P.S. quickly and dutifully responded correctly by choosing a picture of a chicken from a series of four cards with his right hand and a picture of a shovel from a series of four cards with his left hand. The subject was then asked, 'What did you see?' 'I saw a claw and I picked the chicken, and you have to clean out the chicken shed with a shovel'.

> In trial after trial, we saw this kind of response. The left hemisphere could easily and accurately identify why it had picked the answer, and then subsequently, and without batting an eye, it would incorporate the right hemisphere's response into the framework. While we knew exactly why the right hemisphere had made its choice, the left hemisphere could merely guess. Yet, the left did not offer its suggestion in a guessing vein but rather as a statement of fact as to why that card had been picked.
>
> (Gazzaniga and LeDoux, 1978, p. 148–9)

Gazzaniga notes that the one effect of the disconnection of the right hemisphere from the left in these cases is to give the left (verbal) hemisphere free reign in interpreting – and in this instance misinterpreting – the patient's actions. Like Geschwind, Gazzaniga argues that when the left hemisphere is faced with incomplete information, it tends to construct elaborate and false interpretation of events in an effort to make sense of actions or perceptions whose content or cause is actually unknown to the patient. Gazzaniga adds that in contrast to the left hemisphere, the right hemisphere maintains a more veridical construct of the person's actions and perceptions, and is less likely to fill in missing data or construct false beliefs. Gazzaniga (2000) also interprets anosognosia and asomatognosia as the result of the disconnection or destruction of the right hemisphere from the verbal left hemisphere:

> When a neurologist holds a patient's left hand up to the patient's face, the patient gives a reasonable response: 'That's not my hand'. The interpreter, which is intact and working, cannot get news from the parietal lobe since the flow of information has been disrupted by the lesion. For the interpreter, the left hand simply does not exist any more, just as seeing behind the head is not something the interpreter is supposed to worry about. It is true, then, that the hand held in front of him cannot be his. In this light, the claims of the patient are more reasonable.
>
> (Gazziniga, p. 1319)

According to these accounts, it is quite plausible that some of the *positive* aspects of confabulation could arise from the interpreter function, an idea that is consistent with theories that invoke the 'gap filling' functions of neutral confabulations as demonstrated by some amnestic patients (Bonhoeffer, 1901, 1904). However, the Geschwind-Gazzaniga account fails to explain the personal delusional varieties of confabulation on a number of accounts.

(1) In many cases of personal delusional confabulation, there is no sensory disconnection from the language areas. In the delusional varieties of confabulation, the lesions are frontal, or right frontal, and do not necessarily entail or require a disconnection of sensory representations from language areas (Feinberg et al., 2005). Further, a 'filling in', disconnectionist, or

'interpreter' account fails to explain those cases of personal delusional confabulation – for example delusions about imaginary children – in which the confabulations are wholly fictitious and do not rely on any mis-perception on the patient's part.

(2) The confabulations in personal delusional forms are case selective, in that only specific and emotionally significant aspects of the patient's personal world are the topic of the confabulation, reduplication, or misidentifica-tion. In the split-brain patient, or in some patients with hemineglect, *any information* that emanates from the left hemispace, whether it is personally significant or not, may be the subject of a confabulation.

(3) The confabulations in the split-brain cases are simple, rather facile and often *logical*. The confabulations in the personal delusional forms cases are often bizarre or at least improbable, wish fulfilling, or metaphorical.

(4) If callosal disconnection were sufficient to produce unawareness or non-recognition of the left limb, why don't any split-brain patients demon-strate asomatognosia of the left limb? Even in alien hand cases that occur after sectioning of the corpus callosum, the actions of the alien hand are perceived as unwanted and unwilled, and the patient does not confabulate that there is a rational purpose for the action. Therefore, not all instances of callosal disconnection result in even neutral confabulation, and other factors must be at work.

Feinberg's ego dysequilibrium theory of personal delusional confabulation

For these reasons, we have suggested (Feinberg, 1997; Feinberg and Roane, 1997; Feinberg, 2001; Feinberg et al., 2005) that a disturbance in *ego boundaries* and *ego functions* plays a significant role in the production of the personal delu-sional varieties of confabulation. For instance, in delusional asomatognosia cases such as J.K. described earlier, the plegic left arm is not simply misidentified, it is psychologically projected onto another person who in the case of J.K. is close to the patient. Indeed, in many instances of personal delu-sional confabulation, the patients' own disabilities may be attributed to an external fictitious or reduplicated persons (Feinberg, 2001). Thus, these cases demonstrate the potential role of psychological *projection* that constitutes a disturbance of self and self-related functions. This could also help explain why the delusional confabulations and misidentifications are almost universally selective with reference to aspects of the self or others of personal significance, and why the delusional misidentifications are consistently within this domain.

According to the *ego dysequilibrium theory*, the right frontal damage creates a *two-way disturbance* between the self and the environment specifically with regard to personal relatedness that could lead to disorders of *both* under- and over-relatedness to the environment. Without the mediation of right frontal regions that subserve certain self- and ego-related functions, patterns of personally significant incoming information may be disconnected from a feeling of familiarity (Alexander et al., 1979; Feinberg and Shapiro, 1989) or personal relatedness (Feinberg, 1997, 2001). On the other hand, in the presence of an internally derived motive, such as the desire to be home or to be physically well, without the appropriate mediation of the ego functions of the right frontal regions, the wish may appear in the patient's mind as an externalized reality. In a similar fashion, in delusional asomatognosia, when the right frontal regions fail to establish the appropriate ego boundaries, the feelings of alienation from the arm result in the unmediated projection of the arm directly into the environment.

It is within the domain of these positive features that individual differences in motivation, personality, and adaptation may come into play that help explain why only a minority of patients with right frontal injury develop these disorders. There is some evidence from our survey (Feinberg et al., 2005) that many of the patients who develop delusional confabulation after brain injury were already predisposed to abnormal ego functions prior to their brain injury. For example, in one classic case that was reported by Alexander et al. (1979), the delusional ideation of a patient with Capgras syndrome was attributed to the presence of bilateral frontal deficits that created the inability to resolve conflicting or competing information. However, in the Alexander et al. case (1979), the patient suffered from 'grandiose and paranoid delusions, and had auditory hallucinations' *prior* to the brain injury that led to his Capgras delusions. This raises the possibility that in some cases pre-morbid personality features or psychopathology, especially paranoia, perhaps subserved by brain areas left undamaged by the cortical lesions played a positive role in the production of these symptoms. One of the striking features in our review was that 5/6 cases of Capgras form of delusional misidentification involving persons had either prior or current paranoia, suspiciousness or depression. Three of seven cases with Frégoli syndrome for persons had paranoia or other delusions, so the same association with psychopathology was present in this group, but not to the extent seen in patients who displayed Capgras for persons.

This point of view is supported by the finding that delusions in general have been reported to occur with increased frequency in the presence of right hemisphere pathology (Levine and Grek, 1984). Malloy and Richardson (1994) in a literature review of a wide variety of content-specific delusions, including delusional misidentification, sexual delusions, and somatic delusions, found a high incidence of lesions of the frontal lobes and right hemisphere, and Kumral and Özturk (2004) found delusional ideation in 15 of 360 stroke patients that was associated with right posterior temporoparietal lesions.

Conclusions

In summary, I propose that there is a continuum of confabulation along a neutral-personal dimension that is determined by the degree that the confabulation is delusional, motivated, and distorted by the individual's emotional needs and influenced by pre-morbid personality. The personal and delusional forms are significantly associated with right hemisphere and especially right frontal functions. An *ego dysequilibrium theory* of personal confabulation is proposed in which the right hemisphere plays a critical role in determining the personal relatedness of the self to the world. However, it must also be the case that since personal confabulation is a verbal behavior, left hemisphere functions will always play a central role in their creation.

Finally, the cases we have described as demonstrating personal delusional forms of confabulation were actually nicely described in another context by Sigmund Freud over seventy years ago:

> Pathology has made us acquainted with a great number of states in which the boundary lines between the ego and the external world become uncertain or in which they are actually drawn incorrectly. There are cases in which parts of a person's own body, even portions of his mental life – his perceptions, thoughts and feelings – appear alien to him and as not belonging to his ego; there are other cases in which he ascribes to the external world things that clearly originate in his own ego and that ought to be acknowledged by it. Thus, even the feeling of our own ego is subject to disturbances and the boundaries of the ego are not constant.

(Freud, 1930, p. 66)

Freud in his day dreamed of a time when the functions of the psyche could be framed in neurobiological terms. I believe the study of the personal delusional confabulatory patient will help neuroscience achieve that goal.

References

Alexander, M.P., Stuss, D.T., and Benson, D.F. (1979). Capgras syndrome: A reduplicative phenomenon. *Neurology, 29*, 334–339.

Berlyne, N. (1972). Confabulation. *British Journal of Psychiatry, 120*, 31–39.

Bonhoeffer, K. (1901). *Die akuten Geisteskrankheiten der Gewohnheitstrinker.* Gustav Fischer, Jena.

Bonhoeffer, K. (1904). Der Korsakowsche Symptomenkomplex in seinen Beziehungen zu den verschiedenen Krankheitsformen. *Allgemeine Zoologie Psychiatry*, **61**, 744–752.

Burgess, P.W., Baxter, D., Martyn, R., and Alderman, N. (1996). Delusional paramnesic misidentification. In *Method in Madness: Case Studies in Cognitive Neuropsychiatry* (eds. P.W. Halligan and J.C. Marshall), pp. 51–78. East Sussex, UK. Psychology Press.

DeLuca, J.A. (2000). Cognitive neuroscience perspective on confabulation. *Neuro-Psychoanalysis*, **2**, 119–132.

Feinberg, T.E. (1997). Anosognosia and confabulation. In *Behavioral Neurology and Neuropsychology* (1st Edition) (eds. T.E. Feinberg and M.J. Farah), pp. 369–390. New York, McGraw-Hill.

Feinberg, T.E. (2001). *Altered egos: How the Brain Creates the Self.* New York, Oxford University Press.

Feinberg, T.E., DeLuca, J., Giacino, J.T., Roane, D.M., and Solms, M. (2005). Right hemisphere pathology and the self: Delusional Misidentification and Reduplication. In *The Lost Self: Pathologies of the Brain and Identity* (eds. T.E. Feinberg and J.P. Keenan), pp. 100–130. New York, Oxford.

Feinberg, T.E. and Giacino, J. (2003). Confabulation. In *Behavioral Neurology and Neuropsychology*, (2nd Edition) (eds. T.E. Feinberg and M. Farah.), pp. 363–372. New York, McGraw-Hill.

Feinberg, T.E. and Keenan, J.P. (2005). Where in the brain is the self? *Consciousness and Cognition*, **14**, 661–678.

Feinberg, T.E. and Roane, D.M. (1997). Anosognosia, completion and confabulation: The neutral-personal dichotomy. *Neurocase*, **3**, 73–85.

Feinberg, T.E., Roane, D.M., and Ali, J. (2000). Illusory limb movements in anosognosia for hemiplegia. *Journal of Neurology, Neurosurgery, and Psychiatry*, **68**, 511–513.

Feinberg, T.E., Roane, D., Schindler, R.J., Kwan, P.C., and Haber, L.D. (1994). Anosognosia and visuoverbal confabulation. *Archives of Neurology*, **5**, 468–473.

Feinberg, T.E. and Shapiro, R.M. (1989). Misidentification-reduplication and the right hemisphere. *Neuropsychiatry, Neuropsychology, and Behavioral Neurology*, **2**, 39–48.

Fleminger, S. and Burns, A. (1993). The delusional misidentification syndromes in patients with and without evidence of organic cerebral disorder: A structured review of case reports. *Biological Psychiatry*, **33**, 22–32.

Förstl, H., Almeida, O.P., Owen, A.M., Burns, A., and Howard, R. (1991). Psychiatric, neurological and medical aspects of misidentification syndromes: A review of 260 cases. *Psychological Medicine*, **21**, 905–950.

Gazzaniga, M.S. (1985) *The Social Brain*. New York, Basic books.

Gazzaniga, M.S. (2000). Cerebral specialization and interhemispheric communication: Does the corpus callosum enable the human condition? *Brain*, **123**, 1293–1326.

Gazzaniga, M.S. and LeDoux, J.E. (1978). *The Integrated Mind*. New York, Plenum.

Geschwind, N. (1965). Disconnexion syndromes in animals and man. *Brain*, **88**, 585–644.

Hirstein, W. (2005). *Brain Fiction: Self-Deception and the Riddle of Confabulation*. Cambridge, MA, MIT Press.

Johnson, M.K. (1991). Reality monitoring: Evidence from confabulation in organic brain disease patients. In *Awareness of Deficit after Brain Injury: Clinical and Theoretical Issues* (eds. G.P. Prigatano and G.L. Schacter), pp. 176–197. New York, Oxford University Press.

Johnson, M.K., Hayes, S.M., D'Esposito, M., and Raye, C.L. (2000). Confabulation. In *Handbook of Neuropsychology* (2nd Edition) (eds. J. Grafman and F. Boller), pp. 383–407. Amsterdam, The Netherlands, Elsevier Science.

Kopelman, M.D. (1980). Two types of confabulation. *Neurology, Neurosurgery, and Psychiatry*, 43: 461–463.

Korsakoff, S.S. (1955). Psychic disorder in conjunction with peripheral neuritis (trans. M. Victor and P.I. Yakovlev). *Neurology*, 5, 394–406. (Original work published in 1889).

Kraepelin, E. (1904). *Lectures on ClinicalPsychiatry*. (trans. T. Johnstone). London, Bailliere, Tindall, and Cox.

Kraepelin, E. (1907). *Clinical Psychiatry: A Textbook for Students and Physicians*. (trans. by A.R. Diefendorf). New York, MacMillan.

Kraepelin, E. (1919). *Dementia Praecox and Paraphrenia*. (trans. R.M. Barclay). Edinburgh, UK, E and S. Livingstone.

Kumral, E. and Özturk, Ö. (2004). Delusional state following acute stroke. *Neurology*, 62, 110–113.

Levine, D.N. and Grek, A. (1984). The anatomic basis for delusions after right cerebral infarction. *Neurology*, 34, 577–582.

Malloy, P.F. and Richardson, E.D. (1994). The frontal lobes and content-specific delusions. *The Journal of Neuropsychiatry and Clinical Neurosciences*, 6, 455–466.

Moscovitch, M. (1989). Confabulation and the frontal systems: Strategic vs. associative retrieval in neuropsychological theories of memory. In *Varieties of Memory and Consciousness: Essays in Honour of Endel Tulving* (eds. H.L. Roediger and F.M. Craik), pp. 133–160. Hillsdale, NJ, Lawrence Erlbaum.

Moscovitch, M. (1995). Confabulation. In *Memory Distortion: How Minds, Brains and Societies Reconstruct the Past* (ed. D.L. Schacter), pp. 226–251. Cambridge, MA, Harvard University Press.

Moscovitch, M. and Melo, B. (1997). Strategic retrieval and the frontal lobes: Evidence from confabulation and amnesia. *Neuropsychologia*, 35, 1017–1034.

Schnider, A. (2008). *The Confabulating Mind: How the Brain Creates Reality*. New York, Oxford.

Schnider, A., von Daniken, C., and Gutbrod, K. (1996a). Disorientation in amnesia. A confusion of memory traces. *Brain*, 119, 1627–1632.

Schnider, A., Gutbrod, K., Hess, C.W., and Schroth, G. (1996b). Memory without context: Amnesia with confabulations after infarction of the right capsular genu. *Journal of Neurology, Neurosurgery, and Psychiary*, 61, 186–193.

Schnider, A. and Ptak, R. (1999). Spontaneous confabulators fail to suppress currently irrelevant memory traces. *Nature neuroscience*, 2, 677–681.

Schnider, A., Ptak, R., von Daniken, C., and Remonda, L. (2000). Recovery from spontaneous confabulations parallels recovery of temporal confusion in memory. *Neurology*, 55, 74–83.

Talland, G.A. (1961). Confabulation in the Wernicke-Korsakoff syndrome. *Journal of Nervous and Mental Diseases*, 132, 361–381.

Talland, G.A. (1965). *Deranged Memory*. New York, Academic Press.

Van Der Horst, L. (1932). Uber die Psychologie des Korsakowsyndroms. *Monatschr Psychiatry and Neurology,* **83**, 65–84.

Weinstein, E.A. (1996). Symbolic aspects of confabulation following brain injury: Influence of premorbid personality. *Bulletin of the Menninger Clinic,* **60**, 331–350.

Williams, H.W. and Rupp, C. (1938). Observations on confabulation. *American Journal of Psychiatry,* **95**, 395–405.

Young, A.W., Hellawell, O.J., and Welch, J. (1992). Neglect and visual recognition. *Brain,* **115**, 51–71.

Chapter 5

He is not my father, and that is not my arm: Accounting for misidentifications of people and limbs

William Hirstein and V. S. Ramachandran

Through the early part of the 20th century it was assumed that a confabulation was simply a false memory report – or more precisely a false claim alleged to be a memory report – and the term was restricted to these uses. But there was something more contained in the initial concept of confabulation that enticed people to apply it to more than just memory reports. During the remainder of the 20th century, the use of 'confabulation' was gradually expanded to cover claims made by other types of patients, including patients who deny that they are injured, or paralyzed, or even blind. Split-brain patients who make false claims about why they did certain things were also said to confabulate, as well as patients with misidentification disorders, who make false claims about the identities of people. More recently, it has been found that children up to a certain age will tend to confabulate when asked to recall events, and some writers have argued that even normal people will confabulate in certain contexts.

Several contemporary writers attempting to construct a broader definition of 'confabulation' have despaired of the fact that some of the syndromes involve memory disorders (Korsakoff's, and aneurysm of the anterior communicating artery), whereas others involve problems of perception (denial of paralysis or blindness, split-brain syndrome, misidentification disorders) (e.g. Johnson et al., 2000). Since both memory and perception are knowledge domains, however, perhaps there is a broader sense of 'confabulation' that applies to knowledge itself, or more specifically, to the making of knowledge claims. According to this approach, to confabulate is to unintentionally make an ill-grounded (and hence probably false) claim that one should know is ill-grounded (Hirstein, 2005).

According to two-phase theories of confabulation, they are the result of two different phases of error. The first occurs in one of the brain's epistemic systems, either mnemonic or perceptual. This produces an ill-grounded memory or perception. These malfunctioning perceptual or mnemonic processes tend to be located in the back half of the brain's cortex, in the temporal or parietal lobes. Second, even with plenty of time to examine the situation and with urging from doctors and relatives, the patient fails to realize that the response is flawed, due to a malfunction of higher level brain processes located toward the front of the brain, in the prefrontal lobes. Nonconfabulating brains sometimes create flawed responses, but we are able to correct them, using these different prefrontal processes. If I ask you whether you have ever seen the Eiffel Tower, for instance, your brain is happy to provide an image of the Tower, even if you've never been near it. But you are able to reject this as a real memory. You catch the mistake at the second phase. Thus, the typical etiology of confabulation involves damage in the posterior of the brain to some perceptual or mnemonic process, causing the first error stage, coupled with damage to some prefrontal process, causing the second error stage. The two events of damage need not occur at the same time; there are numerous cases in the literature in which patients with an existing site of brain damage began confabulating after damage to a second site.

Capgras' syndrome, one of the misidentification syndromes in which patients claim that people close to them have been replaced by impostors, and *asomatognosia*, in which patients deny ownership of their own limbs, are the two oddest members of the family of confabulation syndromes and the most difficult to assimilate to what is known about the others. A comprehensive theory of confabulation that encompasses these syndromes as well as the other confabulation syndromes could shed a great deal of light on some extremely puzzling human responses to brain injury. Neurologist Todd Feinberg has recently proposed an account designed to encompass both the misidentification syndromes and asomatognosia (Feinberg, 2001), according to which they are disorders of the patient's sense of personal relatedness to other people and to his own body. According to another view, the two syndromes are to be explained by the patient's attempt to interpret a missing sense of familiarity when he looks at the person or limb. Perhaps because the patient's ability to reason is also compromised, he accepts the odd interpretation that someone else's limb dangles from his shoulder and someone else lives in his house. Aside from showing that these two syndromes fit the suggested definition of 'confabulation,' our point in this paper is that we can understand why people have these strange beliefs if we understand the nature of the representation systems that, when damaged, produce them.

If we understand confabulation as an epistemic problem, the confabulation syndromes can be categorized as disorders of the brain's knowledge domains:

(1) Knowledge of the body and its surroundings: denial of paralysis.

(2) Knowledge of past events involving oneself, i.e. autobiographical memories: Korsakoff's syndrome; anterior communicating artery syndrome.

(3) Knowledge of other people: the misidentification syndromes.

(4) Knowledge of our minds: split-brain syndrome, brain stimulation cases.

(5) Knowledge derived from visual perception: Anton's syndrome.

Put in terms of individually testable criteria, the recommended definition of 'confabulation' is:

S confabulates (that *p*) if and only if:

(1) S claims that *p*;

(2) S believes that *p*;

(3) S's thought that *p* is ill-grounded;

(4) S does not know that her thought that *p* is ill-grounded;

(5) S should know that her thought that *p* is ill-grounded;

(6) S is confident about that *p*.

The concept of *claiming* (rather than, for instance, *saying* or *asserting*) is broad enough to cover a wide variety of responses by subjects and patients, including non-verbal responses, such as drawing and pointing. The second criterion captures the sincerity of confabulators. If explicitly asked, 'Do you believe that *p*?,' they will answer yes. The third criterion refers to the problem that caused the flawed response to be generated: processes within the relevant knowledge domain were not operating correctly. Criterion number four refers to a cognitive failure at a second phase, the failure to check and reject the flawed response. The fifth criterion captures a normative element in our concept of confabulation: if the confabulator's brain were functioning properly, she would realize that the claim is ill-grounded. The claims made are about things any normal person would easily get right. The sixth and last criterion refers to another important characteristic of confabulators observed in the clinic: the serene certainty they have in their claims, even in the face of obvious disbelief by their listeners, or obvious contradictions in what they claim. This epistemic approach eliminates a problem with the falsity criterion in the original definition, according to which confabulations are false memory reports: a patient might answer correctly, but out of luck. The problem is not so much the falsity of the patients' claims but rather their ill-groundedness and consequent unreliability. In short then, in this epistemic view, to confabulate is to confidently make an ill-grounded claim that one should know, but does not know, is ill-grounded.

Anosognosia and Asomatognosia

'Anosognosia,' means lack of knowledge, or unawareness, of illness. First described in detail by Babinski (1914), this unawareness can accompany certain types of paralysis caused by damage to the right inferior parietal cortex and seems to play a role in causing an intriguing response known as *denial* in some patients. When asked about their disabilities, they will calmly and firmly deny that they are paralyzed or weakened. The typical denial patient, interviewed as he rests in bed after a stroke that has paralyzed his left arm, will claim that both arms are fine. When asked to touch the doctor's nose with his left arm, the patient will move his torso slightly and then stop. When asked whether they touched the doctor's nose, some patients will say that they did, while others will admit that they didn't, but confabulate a reason why, such as that they are tired, don't feel like following commands right now, always had a weak left arm, and so on. These patients are said to suffer from *neglect* – they neglect their arms as well as the space on their left, by never attending to that space, or initiating actions with that arm.

While there is evidence that some anosognosic patients have some types of somatosensation, typically important higher level somatosensory areas are damaged. These posterior areas of damage, especially in the inferior parietal cortex, create the first malfunction needed for confabulation, but until very recently no clear pattern of frontal damage had emerged in the study of anosognosia. In 2005, however, Berti et al. showed that patients who denied paralysis differed from those with paralysis but no denial in that the denial patients had additional damage in the frontal portions of a large brain network involved in the planning of motor actions. These frontal areas are directly connected to the damaged inferior parietal areas. Apparently, the frontal areas are capable of monitoring intended actions. As Berti and her colleagues say, 'monitoring systems may be implemented within the same cortical network that is responsible for the primary function that has to be monitored' (Berti et al., 2005, p. 488).

Capgras' syndrome

Neurological patients with Capgras' syndrome claim that people close to them, typically spouses, parents, or children, have been replaced by similar-looking impostors. When asked how they can tell that the person is an impostor, Capgras' patients may confabulate. One patient claimed that she could tell her husband had been replaced because the new person tied his shoelaces differently, while another patient said that the impostor of her son 'had different-colored eyes, was not as big and brawny, and that her real son would not kiss her' (Frazer and Roberts, 1994, p. 557). The patient's attitude toward the alleged impostor can vary. The majority of Capgras' patients are suspicious of the target person, and many are paranoid about the 'impostor,' and attribute ill-will to him, but there are also cases where the patient's attitude is positive.

Capgras' syndrome patients thus misidentify people, including themselves (as seen in photos or even in a mirror). Capgras' syndrome fits the pattern of damage seen in the memory syndromes: damage to some knowledge system, in this case a perceptual one, paired with frontal damage. Several writers have hypothesized that the first damaged process is one that normally produces an emotion at the sight of a familiar person. One candidate for the second damaged process is one that detects conflicts among mental states and alerts other parts of the brain that initiate a resolution of the conflict. Confabulators in the clinic do seem bad at detecting and resolving conflicts in their claims. They are not bothered when the doctor points out that they are contradicting themselves, for instance.

Another type of misidentification syndrome is in one way the opposite of Capgras' syndrome. Patients with Fregoli's syndrome will claim that certain people they know are capable of manifesting different physical appearances, so that the patients might complain that a certain person is following them or spying on them while taking on the outward appearance of different people. Hence, they are claiming that someone unfamiliar is actually familiar, whereas the Capgras' patients are claiming that someone familiar is actually unfamiliar.

Three accounts

In the cases of both Capgras' syndrome and asomatognosia, the familiar is claimed to be unfamiliar; something very close, a loved one or a body part, is claimed to be distant from self. Just as some patients with asomatognosia will claim that the arm they see is someone else's arm, the Capgras' patient will claim that people who should be very familiar to him have actually been replaced by strangers. The French neurologist Jacques Vié (1930) was the first to explicitly mention this similarity. In this section, we will examine three candidate explanations for the misidentification syndromes and asomatognosia:

The emotional account

According to the emotional account of Capgras' syndrome, the patient fails to experience the normal emotional reaction to the sight of a familiar person, and this causes him to form the belief that the person is an impostor. This account seems to originate with Capgras' and Reboul-Lachaux's seminal article, in which they write that 'the delusion of doubles is not ... really a sensory delusion, but rather the conclusion of an emotional judgment' (Capgras & Reboul-Lachaux, 1923/1994, p. 128). Many subsequent writers have argued that in Capgras' syndrome, there is a disconnection between the representation of a face and what Ellis and Young refer to as 'the evocation of affective memories' (Ellis & Young, 1990, p. 243) (see also Staton et al., 1982; Bauer, 1986; Hirstein & Ramachandran, 1997). The patients recognize a face, but do not feel the expected emotions, and confabulate to explain this: 'When patients find themselves in such a conflict (that is, receiving some information which indicates the face in front of them belongs to X, but not receiving confirmation of this), they may adopt some sort of rationalization strategy in which the individual before them is deemed to be an impostor, a dummy, a robot, or whatever extant technology may suggest' (Ellis and Young, 1990, p. 244).

The weak link in the emotional account is the connection between the absence of an emotion and the creation of the impostor story. Why doesn't the patient merely say that people seem strange or unfamiliar to him? Stone and Young (1997, p. 344) add another ingredient, the patient's prior personality, suggesting that once the patient loses the normal affective reactions to faces, 'because of a co-existing suspicious mood, or maybe a premorbid disposition, the person arrives at the idea that the source of these strange experiences must lie in a change in the external world, and the possibility of some kind of a trick, perhaps involving a substitution presents itself.' But why would so many different patients with different personalities, and different premorbid dispositions arrive at the same highly unlikely story about the same trick? The emotional account also seems not to be a good candidate for expansion into a more comprehensive account that could also be applied to asomatognosia. When applied to asomatognosia, the emotional account would generate the claim that we normally experience an emotional reaction at the sight of our arms, then confabulate that the arm is not our own in order to explain the absence of this emotion, which seems extravagant.

The personal relatedness account

The patient who says, 'That's not my father,' and the one who says, 'That's not my arm,' have the same basic problem, according to Feinberg and his colleagues (Feinberg and Roane, 1997). 'Asomatognosia can be understood as a Capgras syndrome for the arm in which the personal relationship with the body part is lost' (Feinberg et al., 2005, p. 103). The Capgras' patient has lost his sense of personal relatedness to his father, while the asomatognosic has lost his sense of personal relatedness to his arm. Feinberg then sets up a fascinating comparison between Capgras' and asomatognosia on one hand, and Fregoli's syndrome: both Capgras' patients and asomatognosic patients claim that someone or something personally related to them is unfamiliar. In contrast, the patient with Fregoli's syndrome sees unfamiliar people as familiar, or more broadly, falsely sees people as being personally related to him. Feinberg argues that this distinction, between seeing something as personally related and seeing something as distant and foreign, is of use in forming a taxonomy of the misidentification disorders. As he puts it, 'the essential dichotomization of these various disorders is on the basis of an alteration in personal relatedness or significance' (Feinberg and Roane, 1997, p. 80). Syndromes such as Capgras' and asomatognosia which involve a decreased sense of relatedness in the patient 'should be thought of as a disavowal, estrangement, or alienation from persons, objects, or experiences'. Syndromes such as Fregoli's are on the 'the opposite side of the spectrum' and 'are manifestations of an over-relatedness with persons, objects, or experiences' (Feinberg and Roane, 1997, p. 80).

Feinberg and his colleagues acknowledge that not all patients can be described as claiming either under- or over-relatedness to people and things. Some of them do both at the same time, with the same person. 'Many of the important misidentifications seen in neurological patients actually represent a *co-occurrence* of both Capgras and Fregoli types of misidentifications' (Feinberg and Roane, 1997, p. 80). Many confabulations by asomatognosics do not involve the patient claiming that the arm or person is completely unrelated to him. One patient of Feinberg's said that her hands were not hers but her husband's, saying that 'He left them . . . just like he left his clothes' (Feinberg, 2006, p. 3). Because of this third, mixed type, Feinberg and his colleagues phrase their hypothesis in its final form as follows: syndromes such as Capgras', Fregoli's, and asomatognosia 'represent either an increase, a decrease, or simultaneous increase and decrease in the patient's personal relatedness to objects, persons, places, or events in the patient's environment' (Feinberg and Roane, 1997, p. 80).

A representational account

Personal relatedness is an extremely broad concept, perhaps too broad to be of explanatory value in this context. A very high percentage of the representations in our brains are of things personally related to us, for obvious reasons. The entirety of episodic-autobiographical memory, for instance, contains representations of events that are personally related to us. In addition to episodic memory, we use somatotopic maps to represent several different properties of our bodies, and our semantic memories contain a self-concept that knits together all sorts of biographical information about us and is immediately connected to our concepts of people and things of significance to us. A second criticism of the personal relatedness account arises from the presence of 'mixed' patients, who show both an increase and a decrease in their senses of personal relatedness for an object or person. This indicates that the patients do not line up neatly on a single personal relatedness continuum.

The following account offers a more specific explanation of Capgras' syndrome, Fregoli's syndrome, asomatognosia, and other disorders of person and limb recognition that fits the two-phase approach that has been taken to the other confabulation syndromes. It provides an alternative account for why these syndromes exhibit the interesting variations in personal relatedness that Feinberg and his colleagues observed. It is also much more specific than the emotional account, in that it is able to explain the content of the patients' delusions. Our brains represent people both allocentrically and egocentrically. Allocentric representations of people are viewpoint-independent representations of their external bodily features. Our representations of peoples' faces are a paradigmatic example of allocentric representations. One sign that they are viewpoint-independent is that we can recognize people from many different angles. Egocentric representations encode the positions of things and spaces relative to a central 'ego'. Our representations of the spaces we inhabit are usually egocentric; they represent the distance of objects from us, the trajectories of objects with regard to our location, and so on. Egocentric representations contain an intrinsic point of view, while allocentric representations are viewpoint independent. Egocentric representations give the ego a privileged place in the representations system, while a person's allocentric system can represent him as one person among many. Among the faces we are able to visually recognize is our own, usually seen in a mirror, but the same allocentric visual recognition processes are used whether we are looking at ourselves or at our friends.

The egocentric system is responsible for part of our normal sense that we are embodied minds, moving about an environment. I am aware of having a mind, with its ongoing mental life. This mind is represented as being inside my body. And my body is represented as being inside an environment. There is truly an ego at the center of this system, in the sense of 'ego' that means mind. This egocentric system does not always represent us, however. It has two modes of functioning which we will call self-mode and other mode. In self-mode, this system represents my mind, situated in my body, situated in my environment. When this system functions in other mode it represents other people as minds situated in bodies, situated in environments. We represent people egocentrically and suggest, by simulating their current experiences from their points of view. When I represent you from my perspective, I am representing you allocentrically. When I represent you from your perspective, I am typically representing you egocentrically. In either mode, the system is egocentric; but different individuals can occupy the ego position in the system. In self-mode, I am the ego at the center of this system, in other mode the egocentric system represents or simulates the egocentric system of a person of interest. Interestingly, the entire egocentric system functions as a representation in other mode, but only the body and space portions of the egocentric system function as representations in self-mode since the mental part of the egocentric system literally is part of our minds, rather than being a representation of them in self-mode.

The (visual) allocentric system represents people from the outside, including detailed facial representations, as well as representations of entire bodies, characteristic modes of dress, or ways of behaving (some people can be recognized by their walks, for instance). The skin seems to mark the boundary of what the allocentric system represents, while the mental component of the egocentric system represents events occurring inside the skin, as experienced from the point of view of that body's owner. Egocentric representations involve somatosensory representations, but also involve our awareness of our conscious perceptions, thoughts, and emotions. Allocentric representations are primarily visual, but also involve auditory representations, as well as representations generated by other sensory systems. The egocentric system may well have other modes, including what we might call an alternative self-mode, which we use to imagine ourselves in other locations, or future situations.

Representations of minds and representations of bodies

We employ or own egocentric representation system in other mode, or as a simulation, to understand the actions of other people. This is a variety of simulation theory (Goldman, 2006) in which an egocentric representation system is employed as an analog model of that same system in another person. We perceive personality by representing moods, emotions, and character. We read several different features of minds using several different brain processes, one of which, we suggest, is the egocentric mind-reading system described here. The problem of the misidentification patients according to this account is the failure of their brains to activate the correct egocentric representation of the person they are looking at. Once we get to know a person well, we develop an individualized egocentric representation of her mind. We create egocentric concepts of others. We will argue below that we also possess generic egocentric representations that can be applied to people we do not yet know well. These generic representations show themselves in our psychologies as character stereotypes. We observe a person for a few moments, then conclude, 'Ah, he's one of *those* kinds of people', calling the appropriate generic egocentric representation into play in our attempt to understand him.

One piece of data that is at least consistent with the claim that malfunction exists in a system that is involved in representing both ourselves and others is the regular occurrence of self-misidentifications along with misidentifications of others. The misidentification syndromes can be understood as caused by damage to the mind-representing part of this large egocentric representation system. Analogously, asomatognosia can be understood as due to damage in the body-representing part of the egocentric representation system. According to this hypothesis, both Capgras' and Fregoli's syndromes are mind-reading disorders, due to failures of one of our mind-reading systems (Hirstein, 2005), a set of brain processes we use to understand and predict the behavior of others. Capgras' syndrome occurs when egocentric representations of a particular person are damaged or inaccessible and are replaced by other, incorrect egocentric representations, perhaps generic ones.

The representational account of misidentification takes what the patients say seriously, unlike the other approaches, which dismiss it as a convenient creation. There is nothing specific about the absence of a sense of personal relatedness or of emotional arousal that would lead someone to posit an impostor. But the experience of an unfamiliar mind situated within a familiar body, with a familiar face, is exactly what would lead to the assertions about impostors. According to Feinberg's account, the Capgras' patient experiences a lack of personal relatedness, and this causes him to claim that the person he sees is an impostor. But the patient does not merely see someone familiar as unfamiliar, he perceives that person as having a *different identity* from the person he knows. The patient does not merely treat the 'impostors' as less related than before, but as no longer having the same mind, the same motives, moods, and emotions (e.g. paranoid Capgras' patients attribute evil intentions to the impostors).

According to the representational account, the Capgras' patient perceives his father as having a foreign mind, and this makes him claim that he is an impostor. To claim that someone is not your father, but rather some stranger pretending to be your father is to make a claim about the identity of that person, and also to disavow the personal relatedness of that person. Logically, the identity of someone is independent of that person's degree of personal relatedness to us, but in practicality, when the identity of loved ones is at stake, alterations in perceived identity will also involve alterations in perceived personal relatedness. Conversely, alterations in the patient's sense of personal relatedness need not also involve alternations in perceived identity. One might experience a loss in the sense of personal relatedness to a person, yet not doubt the identity of that person, even if that person is one's father, so that the person might say, 'Dad seems like a stranger to me', but be speaking metaphorically, not literally as the Capgras' patient does. If I perceive my wife as having an alien mind that alters my sense of her personal relatedness to me, but if she seems strange to me, this need not alter my perception of her identity. Thus, an alteration in one's sense of personal relatedness alone is not sufficient to produce a misidentification patient.

The personal relatedness factor one sees in the misidentification syndromes may be due to the way that the egocentric system is typically used to represent people, objects, and events of personal significance. Rather than explaining the patient's beliefs by way of a malfunction in her person-representation systems, Feinberg attributes them partly to emotional/motivational factors. The tendency of patients to cling strongly to the delusional belief, according to Feinberg, 'suggests that there is an impediment or resistance to the truth' (Feinberg et al., 2005, p. 115). Feinberg posits various motivational factors to explain this tenacity, but another explanation for the patients' insistence on their beliefs is that they are experiencing a pronounced perception of an unfamiliar mind in a familiar body. This perception comes from a normally trustworthy source, and the patients lack the ability to critically assess its groundedness.

The way we know what to expect from a person is to create a simulation of him or her. But how do we represent the personalities of the people we know? As we watch the angry person, we don't just understand his angry actions, but we understand how the anger was generated. We know how our own anger generates angry actions because we experience this causation directly. We can also understand why someone does not act. When we understand someone's pain, we understand how the pain restricts her actions and depresses her moods. Representations of personalities also include representations of that person's characteristic emotions and moods.

We use this system to construct full-blown representations of the minds of people close to us. In order to produce an accurate simulation of another person, we need an extensive and detailed representation. We need to build a complete scale model of an airplane in order to test it in a wind tunnel, for example, because of the holistic way in which changes in one property of the airplane affect others. If we change the airflow over one part of the plane, we have then changed the airflow over the parts of plane behind this part. Similarly, we need a full model of a minded, embodied person in an environment in order to perform effective simulations of people in alternative situations.

Some types of simulations of minds can be thought of as functions from perceptions to actions. Two different people will respond differently to the same perceptions. One person may do what another person merely considers then inhibits, in the same situation, because of differences in the way that prefrontal executive processes 'filter' contemplated actions. There are also cases where a perception causes a certain emotion which in turn causes an action. In order to represent these personalities, these functions, we would also need to simulate these emotions. Knowing someone means knowing what makes her happy and what makes her angry, as well as how she behaves when she's angry or happy. We are not normally aware of our mind representations as representations because we simply see ourselves as perceiving people with emotions and personalities and characters. We do not realize that we are not actually seeing their emotions, intentions, or motives, but we are reproducing them within ourselves.

We normally represent our limbs as the business end of our bodies, the executors of our wills in the world. We represent animate limbs with additional types of representations that we do not employ when we look at dead limbs. We also represent the arms of others as executors of actions. Sometimes when we know that arms will be acting toward us, we focus our attention on them, as do boxers, for instance (the attention, not the eyes, which are typically directed at the opponent's head). But even in these cases, we do not represent the arms as the real initiators of the actions. We also track the mental states of the owner of those arms, and we represent the actions of the arms as caused by his mental states.

Is this representational view extravagant? It posits an entire type of representation, egocentric representations of others, in addition to the known allocentric representations. One general defense we would make of this runs as follows: we should not be surprised that a species whose success is so tied to its social nature has representation systems this elaborate for perceiving and understanding others. Social factors have been more important to an individual's survival and flourishing than the mere pragmatics of obtaining food and shelter for some time now. The average contemporary person supports herself not by knowledge of how to grow food and weave clothes, but by knowledge of other people, and how and when to interact with them. Given that the view that we represent the minds of others in real time has become broadly accepted, why would our brains throw away these instances of representation and miss the chance to accumulate them in memory into representations of minds?

Executive processes

According to the two-phase theory of confabulation we are working within here, once a person or limb is misidentified (phase one), the brain of the patient fails to employ executive processes to correct the error (phase two).

What exactly are executive processes, though? Cognition requires both representations and processes for manipulating those representations – these latter are executive processes. Executive processes perform many different operations on representations. One clear illustration of executive processes at work managing representations occurs when we recall some past event from our lives. Your memory itself is just a huge collection of representations; executive processes must control the search and reconstruction processes that take place when we remember. Executive processes control mental activity by allowing us to shift our focus from perception to memory or back, or to rearrange items held in working memory (e.g. in the digit span task, where a sequence of numbers is read out loud to the subject, who must then report the sequence in reverse order) (Shimamura, 2002).

Johnson's theory of memory confabulations is that they are caused by a deficit in a general executive function that she calls 'reality monitoring', – the ability to distinguish real from imagined events (Johnson, 1991). Real memories can often be distinguished from mere imaginings by the amount of perceptual detail they contain, as well as by the use of supporting memories. Normal people are able to differentiate real from spurious information at high success rates, employing executive processes. This seems to be a learned, or at least a developed ability. Small children often have trouble drawing the line between the real and the merely imagined until their frontal lobes develop. When the relevant executive processes are damaged, mere imaginings can be mistaken for actual visual experiences. In the early days of psychosurgery, Whitty and Lewin (1957) described a condition which they called 'vivid daydreaming' that appeared in 8 of 10 patients who had undergone an anterior cingulectomy (removal of a portion of cortex from the medial prefrontal lobes) in an attempt to control severe obsessive compulsive disorder. The patients would claim odd things happened to them in the hospital – a man said his wife had stopped by for tea, and a woman claimed she saw the nurses putting pins in her food – then admit that they could not tell whether they had imagined them or whether the events had really happened.

A great deal of what we normally call thinking, deciding, planning, and remembering is accomplished primarily by the brain's executive processes. One introspectively accessible measure of the amount of executive activity is our sense of mental effort. Increased mental effort correlates with the increased usage of oxygen by executive areas, which is detectable by brain imaging. In such studies, tasks are devised that require the intervention of executive functions, and then brain activity is monitored as the subject attempts the task. Most executive processes reside in the prefrontal lobes, including the dorsolateral frontal lobes on the side of the brain, the ventrolateral frontal lobes below them, and the orbitofrontal lobes located on the brain's undersurface just above the eye sockets (Moscovitch and Winocur, 2002). One area that is frequently active during effortful processing is the aforementioned anterior cingulate. The anterior cingulate is thought to play a role in resolving conflicts between routine actions that are not relevant to the present task and novel actions that are relevant. It also activates strongly when the subject detects an error in his response (Carter et al., 1999).

It is important to note that the executive processes can participate in the act of recognition itself, in that they have the power to overrule our initial perceptual identifications. We all experience strange perceptions at times, but we are able to correct them using executive processes. As Rapcsak et al. (1994) note, 'the frontal lobes are also likely to be responsible for detecting and resolving potential ambiguities arising in connection with the operations of perceptual recognition systems' (Rapcsak et al., 1994, p. 577). I believe that I see my friend during a trip to Tibet, but then I realize how improbable that is – this friend never travels, has no interest in Tibet, etc. – so I do not allow myself to recognize that person as my friend. When a person encounters an object, what she identifies it as is a product of three dissociable factors: the state of the allocentric representation system, the state of the egocentric representation system, and the state of the person's executive processes. When we first become aware of a person's presence, two different streams of processing commence their work. Failure of either the allocentric stream or the egocentric stream, coupled with the relevant executive failure, should produce a confabulation if the patient is asked the right question, which in the case of Capgras' syndrome is simply a question about the identities of the people standing at his bedside.

Anomalies of limb recognition

The decision must be made at the executive level as to whether the presence in consciousness of a given representation truly means that the represented object is there. For example, the existence of phantom limbs involves (we will argue below) an active egocentric representation of the missing limb, but at the executive level that activity is not taken as a veridical representation (mainly because the allocentric system strongly confirms the absence of the limb). Conversely, severing of the nerve to an arm can produce the impression that the arm is not there, due to the removal of somatosensation, which is part of the egocentric system. But executive processes are able to let the continued correctness of the external, allocentric representations of the arm overrule this impression: The arm is still there, merely numb. The executive systems apparently have the ability to let either the allocentric system or the egocentric system win out over the other, in the event of discord between their represen-tations of the object confronting one.

Feinberg and his colleagues tested 12 patients with right hemisphere stroke damage for asomatognosia, by holding up the patient's left hand so that it was visible to him and asking 'What is this?' (Feinberg et al., 1990). The most com-mon response was to call the limb 'your [the doctor's] hand' or 'your arm'. One patient referred to the limb as 'a breast' and a 'deodorant'. One patient called it 'my mother-in-law's' hand (Feinberg et al., 1990, p. 1391). Asomatognosics may claim that the arm 'belongs to a fellow patient previously transported by ambulance, or that it had been forgotten in bed by a previous patient' (Bisiach and Geminiani, 1991). One of Feinberg's other patients called his left arm 'a useless piece of machinery' (Feinberg, 2001). As the tone of some of these responses implies, patients may display dislike or even hatred of the paralyzed limb, a condition known as *misoplegia*. Another patient called his arm a piece of 'dead wood' (Weinstein, 1991); yet another called his arm 'a piece of dead meat' (Critchley, 1974). 'The theme of the arm as being "dead" in some sense, literally or figuratively, is common in asomatognosic patients' according to Feinberg (2006, p. 4). Some patients claim that their flesh is rotting away (Fine, 2006, p. 52). Patients tend not to bother to elaborate these claims into more coherent stories about how exactly a limb came to be left in bed, for instance. The arm involved is almost always the left arm, and asomatognosia also occurs at a high frequency among patients whose right hemisphere is temporarily anesthetized.

If Capgras' syndrome is the opposite of Fregoli's syndrome, then what is the opposite of asomatognosia? The vast majority of people who undergo amputa-tion of a limb have a clear sensation that the limb is still there – a phantom limb. So vivid is this impression that many patients, upon regaining con-sciousness after the operation, do not realize that the limb is gone until they lift the covers and see. Their experience of the limb seems to be the same as before; they experience it as being in a certain position, as being hot or cold, as being in pain, as being paralyzed, and sometimes even as moving in response to their intentions, for instance as reaching out to shake hands with someone (Ramachandran and Hirstein, 1998).

Mild variants of the clinical syndromes

The problem in asomatognosic patients is that they have lost the capacity to represent the arm as something that they can accomplish tasks with. We accom-plish tasks with tools, but we move them from the outside, whereas we move our arms and legs from the inside. Our limbs respond not to our actions, as tools do, but to our wills. In the asomatognosic patient the amputation, performed by nature itself, is a sort of inner amputation. For humans, the arms are the primary executors of the will. In them a portion of the will's domain has been cut off. The asomatognosic's arm is there, but it seems to him that it is not; the phantom limb patient's arm is not there, but it seems to him that it is. The arms of phantom limb patients feel the same from the inside, as it were, but obviously do not look the same on the outside. Asomatognosia is just the opposite: the patient's limb looks the same externally but lacks certain internal sensations.

If the representational account proposed here is correct, asomatognosia is due to two factors, destruction of an egocentric representation of the limb involved together with damage to executive processes capable of correcting the impression that the limb is not their own. Patients who suffer only the first type of damage while possessing intact executive processes might experience the strong impression that the affected limb is not their own but be able to correct it. The writer Oliver Sacks suffered a bad fall while hiking in the mountains of Norway, breaking his leg at the femur. The break almost severed a nerve in his leg, causing a complete loss of somatosensation together with paralysis of the leg for several weeks. He describes his impressions as he sat in bed looking down at his leg in its cast:

> It was utterly strange, not-mine, unfamiliar. I gazed upon it with absolute non-recognition. I have had—we all have had—sudden odd moments of non-recognition, jamais vu; they are uncanny while they last, but they pass very soon, and we are back in the known and familiar world. But this did not pass—it grew deeper and deeper—and stronger, and stronger.
>
> The more I gazed at that cylinder of chalk, the more alien and incomprehensible it seemed to me. I could no longer feel it as "mine," as part of me. It seemed to bear no relation whatever to me. It was absolutely not-me—and yet, impossibly, it was attached to me—and even more impossibly, "continuous" with me.

> (Sacks, 1984, p. 72)

This may be the sort of experience that could lead a person without intact executive functioning to simply accept it on face value: this thing is not my leg. Alternatively, the phantom limb patient with intact executive processes also still has these egocentric processes operating. This allows her to maintain a rational attitude toward her predicament and overrule the sense that her arm is still there. The soundness of the egocentric representation system is an important factor in the success of prosthetic devices: the patient comes to accept the device as part of her because the egocentric representation of her former arm successfully inhabits it.

Apotemnophilia and asomatognosia

Apotemnophilia is a curious disorder in which a person has a strong desire to amputate a healthy limb that they typically describe as being overpresent or intrusive. We can gain a better understanding of this syndrome by applying our account to it. Apotemnophilia is often regarded as being 'merely psychological' or the product of some sort of attention-getting strategy, although why it should take this strange form is never explained. There are several pieces of evidence that indicate that there is a specific neurological problem at work. First, the condition usually begins in early childhood. Second, the subject usually has no other psychological problems of any consequence. Third, the subject can point to a specific line, e.g. two centimeters above the elbow, along which he or she desires amputation; i.e. it isn't simply a vague desire to eliminate a limb as one would expect from a psychological account. Fourth, in more than two-thirds of cases the left limb is involved. Just as with asomatognosia, the left arm is much more frequently involved than the right.

Information from touch as well as muscle and joint sense initially gets sent – after thalamic relay – to the primary (S1) and secondary (S2) somatosensory cortices in the postcentral gyrus within which there are systematic topographically organized maps of bodily sensations (including the skin surface). After that processing moves to the superior parietal lobule (SPL), within which (together with visual feedback about limb position and vestibular feedback) one's body image is created. Crucially, the body image receives input from multiple modalities (especially vision, proprioception, and 'reafference' signals from motor commands) and is constantly updated in response to feedback from the environment or from one's own body – including visceral and vestibular input.

We observed that skin-conductance responses to touching the affected limb were abnormally high in three apotemnophilics (Brang et al., 2008). The abnormal responsiveness was seen only below the line of desired amputation and only in the affected limb. In preliminary brain imaging (MEG) studies on two subjects, we found that touching the affected limb showed abnormal activation in the ipsilateral hemisphere and reduced activity in the contralateral superior parietal lobule (Ramachandran et al., 2008). Based on these considerations, we suggest that there is a genetically hardwired image – possibly a topographically organized representation – of one's body in the right superior parietal lobule, but also encompassing regions of the inferior parietal cortex as well as the polysensory TPO (temporo-parieto-occipital) junction cortex. This is the body representing portion of the egocentric representation system. Partial evidence for the idea of a congenital body image comes from previous case reports of patients with congenitally missing arms reporting phantoms. We suggest that if a particular body part fails to be represented in this body image, the result may be a desire to have it removed.

Yet if this were true why wouldn't the patient remain simply indifferent to the arm, as in asomatognosia? Why the claim that it is 'overpresent and intrusive' (sometimes mildly aversive)? After all, patients with brachial avulsion or arm numbness and paralysis caused by stroke do not desire the arm to be amputated. Oliver Sacks in the example above claims that his temporarily paralyzed leg was alien to him, but he did not want it to be cut off. The key difference, we suspect, is that in apotemnophilia there is normal sensory input from the limb to S1 (primary somatosensory cortex) but no representation of the arm in the polysensory body image representation in SPL or in the inferior parietal cortex. This discrepancy is crucial for creating the feeling of 'overpresence' and mild aversiveness of the limb and the accompanying desire for amputation. Conversely, after avulsion or hemiparesis the input to S1 itself is lost; so there is, if anything, an indifference rather than an 'overpresence' (although at an intellectual or cognitive level the patient 'knows' the arm is paralyzed). This discrepancy between S1 and the egocentric polymodal body image may also explain the heightened skin conductance responses to touching the limb and the essentially ineffable and verbally non-communicable nature of the experience ('It is overpresent and intrusive yet it is still part of me and that's why I want to be rid of it', etc.).

In an asomatognosic patient, there is input missing to both S1 (as a result of deafferentation) and a portion of the body image is damaged by stroke and this leads to an indifference – sometimes an outright denial ('This isn't my limb doctor') rather than a desire for amputation. On the other hand, if there is differential damage to sensory input to S1 and to the body image, then that would create a discrepancy that leads to feelings of actual aversion ('this arm is a communist,' said one patient) and paranoia rather than mere alienation. The same logic applies to asomatognosia, but in some cases there may be some sparing of S1 but no corresponding recipient zone in SPL resulting in a discrepancy that (in accordance with our postulate) leads to aversion or abhorrence in addition to alienation and denial, i.e. misoplegia.

In summary, it is known that patients with arms missing from birth sometimes experience vivid phantoms, suggesting that there is a genetically laid down scaffolding for ones body image in SPL (which probably also receives reafference signals from motor commands originating in the premotor cortex). We postulate that in some individuals, this scaffolding is incomplete and missing a representation of the arm. Hence, the sense of alienation – often from early childhood – accompanied by a desire for amputation. But if this scheme is correct how does one explain the fact that patients with brachial plexus avulsion – who also have complete sensory deafferentation from the arm to both S1 and SPL – do not experience the desire for amputation even if the arm is painful? The answer, we suggest, is that in avulsion the input to S1/2 itself is missing and it fails to get relayed to SPL so no neurons get activated in either S1 or SPL. Consequently, there is no discrepancy. But in apotemnophilia the input to S1 and output to SPL are normal but there is no corresponding 'body image' zone in SPL to receive the signal. The net result is a discrepancy that leads to the strange aversive feeling (if that is the right word) and desire for amputation.

Anomalies of person recognition

Neurological patients with *prosopagnosia* can no longer visually recognize the people they know, but continue to attribute the same personalities and other mental traits to them once they recognize them via some other means, such as by voice. Sometimes a prosopagnosic may succeed in a certain type of effortful visual recognition by depending on specific clues, such as a person's distinctive nose or eyes, or even the type of glasses or tie he typically wears, as opposed to normal face perception which is done quickly and holistically rather than in such piecemeal fashion. The prosopagnosic cannot easily recognize his friends and family by their external appearances, as their faces are not familiar. But once the patient hears his mother speak, he recognizes her, and will treat her as his mother. For the prosopagnosic, the familiar face is not present, but the person is.

For the Capgras' patient, the familiar face is present, but the person is not. The Capgras' patient's relevant executive processes are malfunctioning, and this prevents him from realizing how implausible the impostor claim is and rejecting it. The typical prosopagnosic does not have executive damage, but according to the account described here, a prosopagnosic with executive damage should confabulate when asked to identify people. The two patients of Rapcsak et al. (1994) seem to fit this profile. Both of them were unable to recognize familiar faces, and when asked to identify faces in photographs, they employed the style typically seen in prosopagnosics of attempting to identify faces by focusing on features. The use of this strategy, together with executive failure, caused the patients to confabulate that unfamiliar people were familiar because the unfamiliar person shared some facial feature with the familiar person. One of the patients pointed to a fellow patient on the ward, for example, and exclaimed, 'There's my father! I'd recognize that hooked nose anywhere!' (Rapcsak et al., 1994, p. 569). Both patients had suffered massive right hemisphere strokes that produced 'fronto–temporal–parietal' areas of damage that were perhaps extensive enough to produce the required damage to both the face perception system and a related prefrontal executive area. The authors support the idea of frontal executive damage by noting that 'the dysfunction of the decision making process in our patients was evidenced by the fact that they rarely if ever attempted to verify the correctness of their initial impressions regarding a person's identity. Instead, they seemed to accept the output generated by the impaired face recognition system unconditionally' (Rapcsak et al., 1994, p. 576). We might call this syndrome *dysexecutive prosopagnosia.* It causes misidentifications based on superficial similarities of facial features that patients lack the executive processes to correct. There is an analogy here with dysexecutive prosopagnosia in the realm of limbs. Amputee patients with phantom limbs have not normally also sustained brain damage, but if a person lost a limb *and* damaged the relevant frontal processes, would he actually deny that his limb was gone? The Capgras' patient D.S. described in Hirstein and Ramachandran (1997) was such a person. D. S.'s right arm was amputated just below the elbow and at several points after his car accident that resulted in both the amputation and brain damage, he denied that his arm was gone.

The analogy, prosopagnosia is to Capgras' what phantom limb is to asomatognosia, is not perfect. There is a significant difference between the sort of representation failure that occurs with phantom limbs and the failure in prosopagnosia. In the prosopagnosic, (allocentric) face representations are damaged or inaccessible, whereas in the phantom limb patients, (allocentric) representations of the missing limb are presumably intact, but not satisfied. Perhaps then, an even closer analog of phantom limb applied to the person is a case in which the interior, the mind, of a person is somehow there, without a body. Claims about ghosts, imaginary friends, and anthropomorphic conceptions of gods and spirits may be cases of this.

The patient with Cotard's syndrome says that he and/or others are dead, hollow, or empty beings. These patients perceive bodies and faces well enough, but see no persons at home in them, rather like a dense neurological version of the psychiatric notion of depersonalization. Cotard himself reported that his patient said that she had 'no brain, nerves, chest, or entrails, and was just skin and bone' (Berrios and Luque, 1995, p. 185). One Cotard's patient described 'feeling nothing inside' (Wright et al., 1993); another patient 'felt that her brain was dead' (Young et al., 1994). In 1788, Charles Bonnet described a patient who, after what appears to have been a stroke, 'demanded that the women should dress her in a shroud and place her in a coffin since she was in fact already dead' (Förstl and Beats, 1992). According to the representational account, Cotard's syndrome is caused by destruction of the mind-representing part of the egocentric representation system. Patients with Cotard's and Capgras' syndromes recognize familiar people externally, but attribute either no mind at all to them, and hence speak of them as 'dead' or 'robots' (Cotard's), or they perceive them to have strange, unknown minds, and hence speak of them as 'impostors' (Capgras').

The Fregoli's syndrome patient sees a certain significant person as somehow inhabiting several different bodies. According to the representational account, what happens in Fregoli's syndrome is that the patient's egocentric representation of a familiar person is paired with allocentric representations of unfamiliar faces and bodies. This produces in the patient the impression of a single person disguising herself as a succession of strangers. Intermetamorphosis is an especially odd misidentification syndrome in which the patient perceives someone as changing from one identity to another, including changes in that person's face. People sometimes appear to metamorphose into other people right before their eyes. Courbon and Tusques' (1932) original patient was a woman who said that her husband's face could change to look exactly like that of a neighbor, and that many other people took on the appearance of her son. Intermetamorphosis apparently involves activation of both the allocentric and egocentric components of incorrect person representations.

Neuroscientific findings

Theories of the crucial neural locus for asomatognosia have focused on the inferior parietal lobes, particularly on the right side. The inferior parietal lobes are constituted by two gyri, the supramarginal gyrus (Brodmann's area 40) and the angular gyrus (Brodmann's area 39) Nielsen (1938) was the first to argue, in 1938, that the crucial site of damage leading to asomatognosia is the right supramarginal gyrus or its connections to subcortical areas. The study mentioned earlier by Feinberg et al. (1990) involving 12 asomatognosic patients supported this localization.

In 2003, Rizzolatti and Mattelli argued that the traditional division of visual streams leaving the occipital lobe into a ventral and a dorsal one (Ungerleider and Mishkin, 1982) is inadequate and that the dorsal stream of visual processing should be divided into two separate streams, one which they call the dorso–dorsal stream and another they call the ventro–dorsal stream. The dorso–dorsal stream has all of the characteristics traditionally attributed to the dorsal stream: it involves the superior parietal lobe and functions to provide information required to execute actions involving, e.g. reaching for nearby objects. The idea of a ventro–dorsal stream is a new concept, however, and the stream has been found to have some interesting characteristics. Area PF in the rhesus monkey, which corresponds to the supramarginal gyrus in humans, is the primary recipient of visual input for this stream. The inferior parietal lobe receives input from the superior temporal polysensory area, an area that merges input from several different sense modalities (Desimone and Gross, 1979). Area PF is now known to contain mirror neurons, neurons that respond when the subject executes a particular, e.g. arm action, or when the subject sees another person execute that same action (Rizzolatti and Craighero, 2004). In our earlier terminology, PF is able to operate in both self-mode and other mode.

The crucial posterior damage site for misidentification syndromes (in addition to frontal damage causing executive failures) may be a cortical area just inferior to the supramarginal gyrus, the temporo-parietal junction (TPJ). Two Cotard's patients studied by Young and his colleagues (Young et al., 1992; Young et al., 1994) had temporo-parietal contusions along with bilateral frontal damage. The Capgras' patient of Staton et al. (1982) showed 'moderate atrophy ... at the temporo-parietal junction.' Similarly, a Capgras' patient seen by Johnson and Raye (1998) had a right temporo-parietal hematoma. A Fregoli's patient described by Feinberg et al. (1999) also had damage at the temporo-parietal junction. The temporo-parietal junction has been found to be active during several 'theory of mind' tasks, in which subjects need to understand the actions and motives of others. Saxe has recently undertaken a series of fMRI studies designed to clarify the role played by the right temporo-parietal junction in understanding the minds of others. In a typical task, the brain of a subject is scanned as she observes people performing certain actions, or displaying certain emotions. Saxe describes the TPJ as an 'area for representing mental states' (Saxe, 2006, p. 235) that responds selectively to 'the attribution of mental states' (Saxe and Wexler, 2005) and plays a role in developing an 'integrated impression' of people. This may be the sort of area that when damaged affects our representations of the minds of other people, producing (along with executive failure) the misidentification disorders. We also postulated above that these separate events of representing peoples' minds are accumulated in episodic memory – biographical memories. There is evidence of a TPJ link to the autobiographical memory system (Maguire, 2001), and Fink et al. (1996) found TPJ activity during a task in which subjects recalled emotional autobiographical events from their pasts.

Damage to this complex of areas should produce problems in the patient's egocentric representation of himself, as well as in his egocentric representations of others. Adolphs et al. (1996) found activity in the right parietal cortex during a task in which subjects attributed mental states to others. They suggest in a subsequent work that, 'in addition to retrieval of visual and somatic records, the difficulty of the particular task we used may make it necessary for subjects to construct a somatosensory representation by internal *simulation*. Such an internally constructed somatic activity pattern – which could be either covert or overt – would simulate components of the emotional state depicted by the target face. In essence, the brain would reconstruct a state akin to that of the person shown in the stimulus' (Adolphs et al., 2001). Representations of emotional states would be part of the egocentric representation system; they are a way of representing the mind of the person of interest.

Mirrors and mirrors neurons

In the early 1990s, Rizzolatti and his colleagues recorded the firing rates of individual neurons in the frontal motor cortex (ventral area 6) of rhesus monkeys as they performed hand actions, such as taking an almond out of a cup (Rizzolatti et al., 1996). When one of the researchers returned from lunch, he licked his ice cream cone in the monkey's view, causing the neurons to fire, to the researchers' great surprise. Rizzolatti and his colleagues went on to discover these 'mirror neurons' in several brain areas. Mirror neurons are most effectively activated by the sight of simple hand and arm actions, such as picking up an object. They receive both visual input, from a ventral visual stream, and somatosensory input, and they are found in both motor areas and somatosensory areas. Apparently the brain uses its own body representations to understand the actions of others. In effect they allow you to put yourself in the other's shoes, viewing the world from the other's perspective, not just physically, but mentally as well. Such an ability would be necessary for imitation of skills and in reading another's mental states to infer what he intends to do, which is vital for social interactions. The proportion of cells that represent mirror neurons in humans is somewhat in dispute – partly because of limitations in fMRI techniques – but that they exist is beyond doubt. Just as mirror neurons exist for motor commands there are what might be loosely called 'emotional mirror neurons' and 'pain mirror neurons' that fire when you are hurt with a needle or when you merely watch someone else being hurt.

There are, as we shall see, even touch mirror neurons (in the parietal lobes) that fire whether you are touched or merely watch your friend being touched. Such neurons dissolve the barrier between 'Me' and 'others.' We recently observed a phantom limb patient who could actually feel touch sensations when he merely watched stimuli delivered to *another* person, a student assistant (Ramachandran and Rogers-Ramachandran, 2008). On one occasion we 'poked' the student with a needle as the subject watched. Even though the poke was gentle the patient couldn't have known this because we had asked the student to wince, withdraw her hand, and shout. This time the patient screamed and withdrew his phantom claiming to actually feel the pain. The pain lasted for several minutes until the subject once again watched the student's hand being massaged.

Consider what happens when a non-amputee is touched. Touch receptors from your skin send signals to somatosensory cortices and eventually to the superior parietal lobule where inputs from different sense modalities (and reafference from motor commands) are combined. This generates your sense of a coherent body image that endures through time and space. As we noted, many of these – the 'touch mirror neurons' – fire not only when you are being touched but also when you watch someone being touched. But if so, how do they know the difference? Why don't you literally feel touch sensations when merely watching someone being touched, given that your mirror neurons are firing away?

The answer might be that when you watch someone touched, even though your 'touch mirror neurons' are activated, the receptors in your skin are not stimulated and this lack of activity (the 'null signal') informs your normal touch neurons (i.e. non-mirror touch neurons) that your hand is *not* being touched. They in turn veto the output of mirror touch neurons at some later stage so you don't actually experience touch sensations; you merely empathize. They would not, of course, inhibit the mirror neuron system itself for that would defeat the purpose in having mirror neurons. Instead they only block the output that leads to conscious experience without inhibiting the empathy component. This would explain the otherwise inexplicable observation that an amputee – as noted above – can actually feel the touch signals in his phantom arm when he watches someone else being touched. The amputation had removed the null signal from the skin causing his mirror neuron output to be experienced directly as conscious touch sensations. Indeed, watching the student's hand being massaged produced pain relief in his own hand. The important lesson is that feeling 'touch' involves far more than sensing the activation of touch receptors from your hand; it results from complex neural networks interacting with each other and sometimes with other brains.

Mirrors themselves are of great interest here since they produce something brand new in our evolutionary story, the ability to see ourselves. The person looking in a mirror is aware of himself in his normal way but is also now using mirror neurons to represent *himself*, as opposed to their normal function in representing others. One phenomenon that is capable of yielding more clues about how to unite our understandings of asomatognosia and the misidentification syndromes such as Capgras' and Cotard's is called 'mirror agnosia.' We discovered that certain anosognosic patients have lost their ability to interpret mirror images. The test is simple: a mirror is held in front of the patient so that he can see himself from the torso up. As he watches, an assistant holds a pen just above the patients' left shoulder, so that the pen is visible to him only in the mirror. The patient is then told to grab the pen with his right hand. Amazingly, some patients will repeatedly bump their hands into the mirror, or try to reach behind it rather than simply reaching back toward their left to grasp the pen (Ramachandran et al., 1997).

Some Capgras' patients experience the impostor delusion when they look at themselves in a mirror. The patient of Silva et al. 'developed the delusion that his facial reflection in mirrors and other glass surfaces was no longer his own face but the work of an autonomous evil being. The image of his face was identical to his own face except that the image appeared to be very sinister and aggressive' (Silva et al., 1992, pp. 574–575). Breen et al. (2000) describe a patient with right hemisphere dysfunction who came to believe that his mirror image was actually another person. He did not believe that the person in the mirror wanted to hurt him, though, and when asked what the man in the mirror thought, the patient answered that he hadn't been able to get him to talk. The patient was not shocked by these events and impassively noted that the man shaved when he shaved and dressed as he dressed. When Breen and her colleagues tested the patient for mirror agnosia, he repeatedly bumped his hand against the mirror. Breen et al. (2004) also report a second patient who misidentified himself in mirrors and had temporo-parietal damage.

Understanding how to interpret mirrors requires knowledge of how to move from the default origin of the egocentric representation system, our own minds, out into the world, reflected at the appropriate angle off the mirror. We also need to shift the origin of the egocentric representation system when we observe other people, from our own minds to that of the person of interest. Damage to the egocentric representation system compromises both of these abilities. Saxe notes that 'the TPJ region is also selectively recruited for determining how the spatial relations between two objects would appear from a character's point of view versus the subject's own position' (Saxe, 2006, p. 236). Blanke and his colleagues have found that one can produce a vivid out-of-body experience involving what they refer to as an 'abnormal egocentric visuospatial perspective' (Blanke et al., 2005) by electrically stimulating the temporo-parietal junction (Blanke and Arzy, 2005), something that again is consistent with its use to represent not only our own location in space, but also locations that we are not currently in. This suggests that Blanke is able to produce out-of-body experiences by stimulating the right TPJ not because we evolved a brain area that let us have such experiences, but because Blanke and his colleagues are stimulating an area that is capable of representing non-actual egocentric situations, primarily so that it can function in other mode to simulate other people.

The areas in and around the TPJ are participating in several diverse and fascinating mental functions, and just as in the case of the prefrontal lobes, we are still in the process of developing conceptual schemes that adequately classify and describe both the functions and the systems responsible for them. Aichhorn et al. (2006) recommend that the TPJ be divided into two areas, arguing that its dorsal portion is 'responsible for representing perspective differences and making behavioral predictions,' while its ventral part – along with the medial prefrontal cortex – region is responsible for 'predicting behavioral consequences' of another person's mental states. The brain's right hemisphere appears to contain areas, such as the inferior parietal cortex and the temporo-parietal junction (TPJ) just below it, that serve the dual function of representing ourselves on certain occasions, and other people on other occasions. We suggest that areas such as the supramarginal gyrus and the TPJ, working in concert with interconnected areas in the temporal and prefrontal lobes, are responsible for the sense of oneself as an embodied being with a mind situated in an environment. Out-of-body experiences, for instance, contain representations of what one's phenomenology, one's mental life, would be like, as well the changes in one's body and its environment. We represent our minds as directing intentional activity into this spatial milieu via the body. Alternatively, when we understand the intentional actions of others, this area serves as an egocentric representation of them.

Conclusion

The account here, if correct, brings the misidentification syndromes and asomatognosia into line with the rest of the confabulation syndromes by showing how they also fall under the two-factor theory. Confabulation is caused by two events: (1) damage to some perceptual or mnemonic process in the posterior of the brain, typically the cortex, and (2) damage to some prefrontal process that monitors and can manipulate and/or correct the output of that perceptual or mnemonic process. In the case of neglect and asomatognosia, the posterior lesion tends to occur in the inferior parietal lobe, often in the supramarginal gyrus. The lesion that produces misidentifications seems to be just below that one, in the temporo-parietal junction. Damage to these egocentric representation systems alters, sometimes quite subtly, the way that the person perceives herself and her body, as well as other people and their bodies. But instead of saying that her limb doesn't feel the same, or that something is different about her father, the patient with damage to these structures, as well as to their allied prefrontal structures, will claim that the limb is not her limb and that the man at her bedside is not her father. When the patient's executive processes are intact, however, she can overrule mere appearances: even though it feels as if my arm is still there, it isn't (phantom limb), even though that person seems like a stranger, he isn't (prosopagnosia).

If the approach described here is right, we build large, detailed representations of the minds of those close to us. These representations are exquisitely sensitive to changes in the beliefs or personalities of the people they are directed at. We create these representations so automatically, and they operate so subtly, that when they are damaged we have trouble understanding what has happened.

The damage leads in some minds to the creation of confabulations about who these people are. If this approach is right, these syndromes, as well as asomatognosia and other allied syndromes, can be understood as responses to damage of certain types to a representational system with a certain structure. The personal element in the misidentification syndromes observed by Feinberg and his colleagues is a by-product of the operation of the egocentric representation system. This system either represents me, or things and people of interest to me. The change in personal relatedness does not offer a very specific explanation of the contents of the confabulations, however. It is not just that the person seems to the Capgras' patient not to be personally related to him (or that the sight of the person fails to produce an emotional response, as in the emotional account). The representational account described above provides an account that explains what the patients explicitly say.

References

Adolphs, R., Damasio, H., Tranel, D., and Damasio, A.R. (1996). Cortical systems for the recognition of emotion in facial expression. *Journal of Neuroscience*, **16**, 7678–7687.

Adolphs, R., Tranel, D., and Damasio, A.R. (2001). Neural systems subserving emotion: Lesion studies of the amygdala, somatosensory cortices, and ventromedial prefrontal cortices. In *Handbook of Neurophysiology* (ed G. Gainotti). New York, Elsevier.

Aichhorn, M., Perner, J. Kronbichler, M., Staffen, W., and Ladurner, G. (2006). Do visual perspective tasks need theory of mind? *Neuroimage*, **30**, 1059–1068.

Babinski, J. (1914). Contribution a l'etude des troubles mentaux dans l'hemiplegie organique cerebrale (anosognosie). *Revue Neurologique*, (Paris) **27**, 845–848.

Bauer, R.M. (1986). The cognitive psychophysiology of prosopagnosia. In *Aspects of Face Processing* (eds. H. Ellis). Dordrecht, Nijhoff.

Berrios, G.E., and Luque, R. (1995). Cotard's syndrome: Analysis of 100 cases. *Acta Psychiatrica Scandia*, **91**, 185–188.

Berti, A., Bottini, G., Gandola, M., et al.(2005). Shared cortical anatomy for motor awareness and motor control. *Science*, **309**, 488–491.

Bisiach, E. and Geminiani, G. (1991). Anosognosia related to hemiplegia and hemianopia. In *Awareness of Deficit After Brain Injury: Clinical and Theoretical Issues* (eds. G.P. Prigatano and D.L. Schacter). Oxford, Oxford University Press.

Blanke, O. and Arzy, S. (2005). The out-of-body experience: Disturbed self-processing at the temporo-parietal junction. *Neuroscientist*, **11**, 16–24.

Blanke, O., Mohr, C., Michel, C.M., et al. (2005). Linking out-of-body experience and self-processing to mental own-body imagery at the temporoparietal junction. *The Journal of Neuroscience*, **25**, 550–557.

Brang, D., Mc Geoch, P.D., and Ramachandran, V.S. (2008). Apotemnophilia: A neurological disorder. *Neuro Report*, **19** (13), 1305–1306.

Breen, N., Caine, D., Coltheart, M., Hendy, J., and Roberts, C. (2000). Towards an understanding of delusions of misidentification: Four case studies. In *Pathologies of Belief* (eds. M. Coltheart and M. Davies). Oxford, Blackwell.

Breen, N., Caine, D., and Coltheart, M. (2004). Mirrored-self misidentification: Two cases of focal onset dementia. *Neurocase*, 7, 239–254.

Capgras, J. and Reboul-Lachaux, J. (1923). L'illusion des 'sosies' dans un délire systématisé chronique. *Bulletin de la Société Clinique de Médecine Mentale*, 11, 6–16. Reprinted In Delusional misidentifications: The three original papers on the Capgras, Fregoli and intermetamorphosis delusions (eds. H.D. Ellis, J. Whitley and J.P. Luauté) (1994). *History of Psychiatry*, 5, 117–146.

Carter, C.S., Botvinick, M.M., and Cohen, J.D. (1999). The contribution of the anterior cingulate cortex to executive processes in cognition. *Reviews in the Neurosciences*, 10, 49–57.

Courbon, P. and Tusques, J. (1932). *L'illusion d'intermetamorphose et de charme*. *Annals of Medical Psychology*, 90, 401–406.

Critchley, M. (1974). Misoplegia or hatred of hemiplegia. *Mt. Sinai Journal of Medicine*, 41, 82–87.

Desimone R. and Gross, C.G. (1979). Visual areas in the temporal cortex of the macaque monkey. *Brain Research*, 178, 363–380.

Ellis, H.D. and Young, A.W. (1990). Accounting for delusional misidentifications. *British Journal of Psychiatry*, 157, 239–248.

Feinberg, T.E., Haber, L.D., and Leeds, N.E. (1990). Verbal asomatognosia. *Neurology*, 40, 1391–1394.

Feinberg, T.E. and Roane, D.M. (1997). Anosognosia, completion and confabulation: The neutral-personal dichotomy. *Neurocase*, 3, 73–85.

Feinberg, T.E., Eaton, L.A., Roane, D.M., and Giacino, J.T. (1999). Multiple Fregoli delusions after brain injury. *Cortex*, 35, 373–387.

Feinberg, T.E. (2001). *Altered Egos: How the Brain Creates the Self*. Oxford, Oxford University Press.

Feinberg, T.E., DeLuca, J., Giacino, J.T., Roane, D.M., and Solms, M. (2005). Right hemisphere pathology and the self: Delusional misidentification and reduplication. In *The Lost Self: Pathologies of Brain and Identity* (eds. T.E. Feinberg and J.P. Keenan) Oxford, Oxford University Press.

Feinberg, T.E. (2006). Our brains, our selves. *Daedalus*, Fall, 1–9.

Fine, C. (2006). *A Mind of its Own. How your Brain Distorts and Deceives*. New York, W.W. Norton and Co.

Fink, G.R., Markowitsch, H.J., Reinkemeier, M., Bruckbauer, T., Kessler, J., and Heiss, W.D. (1996). Cerebral representation of one's own past: Neural networks involved in autobiographical memory. *Journal of Neuroscience*, 16, 4275–4282.

Förstl, H. and Beats, B. (1992). Charles Bonnet's description of Cotard's delusion and reduplicative paramnesia in an elderly patient (1788). *British Journal of Psychiatry*, 160, 416–418.

Frazer, S.J. and Roberts, J.M. (1994). Three cases of Capgras' syndrome. *British Journal of Psychiatry*, 164, 557–559.

Goldman, A. (2006). *Simulating Minds: The Philosophy, Psychology, and Neuroscience of Mindreading*. Oxford, Oxford University Press.

Hirstein, W. and Ramachandran, V.S. (1997). Capgras syndrome: A novel probe for understanding the neural representation of the identity and familiarity of persons. *Proceedings of the Royal Society of London, Series B* **264**, 437–444.

Hirstein, W. (2005). *Brain Fiction: Self-Deception and the Riddle of Confabulation*. Cambridge, MA, MIT Press.

Johnson, M.K. (1991). Reality monitoring: Evidence from confabulation in organic brain disease patients. In *Awareness of Deficit After Brain Injury: Clinical and Theoretical Issues* (eds. G.P. Prigatano and D.L. Schacter). Oxford, Oxford University Press.

Johnson, M.K. and Raye, C.L. (1998). False memories and confabulation. *Trends in Cognitive Sciences*, **2**, 137–145.

Johnson, M.K., Hayes, S.M., D'Esposito, M.D., and Raye, C.L. (2000). Confabulation. In *Handbook of Neuropsychology* (eds. J. Grafman and F. Boller). New York, Elsevier.

Maguire, E.A. (2001). Neuroimaging studies of autobiographical memory. In *Episodic Memory: New Directions in Research* (eds. A. Baddeley, J. Aggleton, and M.A. Conway). Oxford, Oxford University Press.

Moscovitch, M. and Winocur, G. (2002). The frontal cortex and working with memory. In *Principles of Frontal Lobe Functions* (eds. D.T. Stuss and R.T. Knight). Oxford, Oxford University Press.

Nielsen, J.M. (1938). Gerstmann syndrome; finger agnosia, agraphia, confusion of right and left, acalculia; comparison of this syndrome with disturbances of body scheme resulting from lesions of right side of brain. *Archives of Neurological Psychiatry*, **39**, 536–560.

Ramachandran, V.S., Altschuler, E.L., and Hillyer, S. (1997). Mirror agnosia. *Proceedings of the Royal Society of London, Series B* **264**, 645–647.

Ramachandran, V.S. and Hirstein, W. (1998). The perception of phantom limbs: The D.O. Hebb lecture. *Brain*, **121**, 1603–1630.

Ramachandran, V.S., McGeoch, P.D., and Brang, D. (2008). Apotemnophilia: A neurological disorder with somatotopic alterations in SCR and MEG activation. Society for Neuroscience Meeting, Washington DC.

Ramachandran, V.S. and Rogers-Ramachandran, D. (2008). Sensations referred to a patient's phantom arm from another subjects intact arm: Perceptual correlates of mirror neurons. *Medical Hypotheses*, **70**, 1233–1234.

Rapcsak, S.E., Polster, M.R., Comer, J.F., and Rubens, A.B. (1994). False recognition and misidentification of faces following right hemisphere damage. *Cortex*, **30**, 565–583.

Rizzolatti, G. and Craighero, L. (2004). The mirror neuron system. *Annual Reviews of Neuroscience*, **27**, 169–192.

Rizzolatti, G., Fadiga, L., Gallese, V., and Fogassi, L. (1996). Premotor cortex and the recognition of motor actions. *Cognitive Brain Research*, **3**, 131–141.

Rizzolatti, G. and Mattelli, M. (2003). Two different streams form the dorsal visual system: Anatomy and function. *Experimental Brain Research*, **153**, 146–157.

Sacks, O. (1984). *A Leg to Stand On*. New York, Summit Books.

Saxe, R. (2005). Against simulation: The argument from error. *Trends in Cognitive Sciences*, **9**, 174–179.

Saxe, R. (2006). Uniquely human social cognition. *Current Opinion in Neurobiology*, **16**, 235–239.

Saxe, R. and Wexler, A. (2005). Making sense of another mind: The role of the right temporo-parietal junction. *Neuropsychologia*, **43**, 1391–1399.

Shimamura, A.P. (2002). Memory retrieval and executive control processes. In *Principles of Frontal Lobe Functions* (eds. D.T Stuss and R.T. Knight). Oxford, Oxford University Press.

Silva, J.A., Leong, G.B., Wine, D.B., and Saab, S. (1992). Evolving misidentification syndrome and facial recognition deficits. *Canadian Journal of Psychiatry*, **37**, 239–241.

Staton R.D., Brumback R.A., and Wilson, H. (1982). Reduplicative paramnesia: A disconnection syndrome of memory. *Cortex*, **18**, 23–36.

Stone, T. and Young, A.W. (1997). Delusions and brain injury: The philosophy and psychology of belief. *Mind and Language*, **12**, 327–364.

Ungerleider, L.G. and Mishkin, M. (1982). Two visual streams. In *Analysis of Visual Behavior* (eds. D.J. Ingle, M.A. Goodale and R.J.W. Mansfield). Cambridge, MA, MIT Press.

Vié, J. (1930). Un trouble de l'identification des personnes: l'illusion des sosies. *Annals of Medical Psychology*, **88**, 214–237.

Weinstein, E.A. (1991). Anosognosia and denial of illness. In *Awareness of Deficit After Brain Injury: Clinical and Theoretical Issues* (eds. G.P. Prigatano and D.L. Schacter). Oxford, Oxford University Press.

Whitty, C.W. and Lewin, W. (1957). Vivid day-dreaming: An unusual form of confusion following anterior cingulectomy in man. *Brain*, **80**, 72–76.

Wright, S., Young, A.W., and Hellawell, D.J. (1993). Sequential Cotard and Capgras delusions. *British Journal of Clinical Psychology*, **32**, 345–349.

Young, A.W., Robertson, L.H., Hellawell, D.J., de Pauw, K.W., and Pentland, B. (1992). Cotard delusion after brain injury. *Psychological Medicine*, **22**, 799–804.

Young, A.W., Leafhead, K.M., and Szulecka, T.K. (1994). Capgras and cotard delusions. *Psychopathology*, **27**, 226–231.

Chapter 6

Delusional confabulations and self-deception

Alfred R. Mele

How is confabulation related to self-deception? Obviously, that depends on what confabulation and self-deception are. In the first main section, I sketch a position that I have developed elsewhere on self-deception. I turn to confabulation in the second main section. Confabulation in general is more than I can take on in this chapter. I focus on confabulations associated with a trio of delusions.

Self-deception

According to a traditional view, self-deception is an intrapersonal analog of stereotypical interpersonal deception.[1] In the latter case, deceivers intentionally deceive others into believing something, p, and there is a time at which the deceivers believe that p is false while their victims falsely believe that p is true. If self-deception is properly understood on this model, self-deceivers intentionally deceive themselves into believing something, p, and there is a time at which they believe that p is false while also believing that p is true.

In Mele (2001) (and in earlier work, beginning with Mele (1983)), I criticize this view and defend an alternative, deflationary view, according to which self-deception does not entail any of the following: intentionally deceiving oneself; intending (or trying) to deceive oneself; intending (or trying) to make it easier for oneself to believe something; concurrently believing each of two explicitly contradictory propositions. I also argue that, in fact, ordinary instances of self-deception do not include any of these things. My data include widespread agreement that various vignettes count as cases of self-deception. I argue that explaining how the protagonists come to believe what they do in these vignettes does not require appealing to any of the items in the preceding list and that an

---

[1] For citations of this tradition in philosophy, psychology, psychiatry, and biology, see Mele (2001) p. 125, n. 1. *Stereotypical* interpersonal deception does not exhaust interpersonal deception.

alternative style of explanation is more plausible and much more firmly grounded in relevant empirical work.

Obviously, falsely believing that p in the absence of deception by anyone else is not sufficient for self-deception. If it were, we would be self-deceived whenever we make, for example, unmotivated arithmetical mistakes. That is why motivation figures prominently in the literature on self-deception.

Elsewhere, I have distinguished between what I call *straight* and *twisted* cases of self-deception (Mele, 1999, 2001). In straight cases, which have dominated the literature, people are self-deceived in believing something that they want to be true – for example, that their children are not using illegal drugs. In twisted cases, people are self-deceived in believing something that they want to be false (and do not also want to be true). For example, an insecure, jealous husband may believe that his wife is having an affair despite having only thin evidence of infidelity and despite his wanting it to be false that she is so engaged (and not also wanting it to be true that she is). In cases of both kinds, as I have explained in Mele (2001) and briefly explain below, self-deceivers have motivationally biased beliefs.

Some illustrations of ways in which our desiring that p can contribute to our believing that p in instances of straight self-deception will be useful (see Mele, 2001, pp. 26–27). Often, two or more of the phenomena I describe are involved in an instance of self-deception.

(1) *Negative misinterpretation.* Our desiring that p may lead us to misinterpret as not counting (or not counting strongly) against p data that we would easily recognize to count (or count strongly) against p in the desire's absence. For example, Rex just received a rejection notice on a journal submission. He hopes that the rejection was unwarranted, and he reads through the referees' comments. Rex decides that the referees misunderstood two important but complex points and that their objections consequently do not justify the rejection. However, the referees' criticisms were correct, and a few days later, when Rex rereads his paper and the comments in a more impartial frame of mind, it is clear to him that this is so.

(2) *Positive misinterpretation.* Our desiring that p may lead us to interpret as *supporting p* data that we would easily recognize to count against p in the desire's absence. For example, Sid is very fond of Roz, a college classmate with whom he often studies. Because he wants it to be true that Roz loves him, he may interpret her declining his invitations to various social events and reminding him that she has a steady boyfriend as an effort on her part to 'play hard to get' in order to encourage Sid to continue to pursue her and prove that his love for her approximates hers for him. As Sid interprets

Roz's behavior, not only does it fail to count against the hypothesis that she loves him, but also it is evidence that she does love him. This contributes to his believing, falsely, that Roz loves him.

(3) *Selective focusing/attending.* Our desiring that *p* may lead us to fail to focus attention on evidence that counts against *p* and to focus instead on evidence suggestive of *p*. Beth is a 12-year old whose father died recently. Owing partly to her desire that she was her father's favorite, she finds it comforting to attend to memories and photographs that place her in the spotlight of her father's affection and unpleasant to attend to memories and photographs that place a sibling in that spotlight. Accordingly, she focuses her attention on the former and is inattentive to the latter. This contributes to Beth's coming to believe – falsely – that she was her father's favorite child. In fact, Beth's father much preferred the company of her brothers, a fact that the family photo albums amply substantiate.

(4) *Selective evidence gathering.* Our desiring that *p* may lead us both to overlook easily obtainable evidence for ~*p* (not -*p*) and to find evidence for *p* that is much less accessible. For example, Betty, a political campaign staffer who thinks the world of her candidate, has heard rumors from the opposition that he is sexist, but she hopes he is not. That hope motivates her to scour his past voting record for evidence of his political correctness on gender issues and to consult people in her own campaign office about his personal behavior. Betty may miss some obvious, weighty evidence that her boss is sexist – which he in fact is – even though she succeeds in finding less obvious and less weighty evidence for her favored view. As a result, she may come to believe that her boss is not sexist. Selective evidence-gathering may be analyzed as a combination of hyper-sensitivity to evidence (and sources of evidence) for the desired state of affairs and blindness – of which there are, of course, degrees – to contrary evidence (and sources thereof).

In none of these examples does the person hold the true belief that ~*p*, and then intentionally bring it about that he or she believes that *p*. Yet, assuming that these people acquire relevant false, unwarranted beliefs in the ways described, these are garden-variety instances of self-deception (or so I claim).[2]

---

[2] If, in the way I described, Betty acquires or retains the false belief that her boss is not sexist, it is natural to count her as self-deceived. This is so even if, owing to her motivationally biased evidence-gathering, the evidence that she actually has does not weigh more heavily in support of the proposition that her boss is sexist than against it.

Rex is self-deceived in believing that his article was wrongly rejected, Sid is self-deceived in believing certain things about Roz, and so on.

We can understand why, owing to her desire that her father loved her most, Beth finds it pleasant to attend to photographs and memories featuring her as the object of her father's affection and painful to attend to photographs and memories that put others in the place she prizes. But how do desires that *p* trigger and sustain the two kinds of misinterpretation and selective evidence-gathering? It is not as though these activities are intrinsically pleasant, as attending to pleasant memories, for example, is intrinsically pleasant.

Attention to some sources of *unmotivated* biased belief sheds light on this issue. Several such sources have been identified (see Mele, 2001, pp. 28–31), including the following two:

(1) *Vividness of information.* A datum's vividness for us often is a function of such things as its concreteness and its sensory, temporal, or spatial proximity. Vivid data are more likely to be recognized, attended to, and recalled than pallid data. Consequently, vivid data tend to have a disproportional influence on the formation and retention of beliefs.

(2) *The confirmation bias.* People testing a hypothesis tend to search (in memory and the world) more often for confirming than for disconfirming instances and to recognize the former more readily (Baron, 1988, pp. 259–265). This is true even when the hypothesis is only a tentative one (and not a belief one has). People also tend to interpret relatively neutral data as supporting a hypothesis they are testing (Trope et al., 1997, p. 115).

Although sources of biased belief apparently can function independently of motivation, they also may be triggered and sustained by desires in the production of *motivationally* biased beliefs.[3] For example, desires can enhance the vividness or salience of data. Data that count in favor of the truth of a proposition that one hopes is true may be rendered more vivid or salient by one's awareness that they so count. Similarly, desires can influence which hypotheses occur to one and affect the salience of available hypotheses, thereby setting the stage for the confirmation bias.[4] Owing to a desire that *p*, one may test the hypothesis that *p* is true rather than the contrary hypothesis. In these ways and others, desires that *p* may help produce unwarranted beliefs that *p*.

---

[3] I develop this idea in Mele (1987) ch. 10 and 2001. Kunda (1990) develops the same theme, concentrating on evidence that motivation sometimes primes the confirmation bias. Also see Kunda (1999) ch. 6.

[4] For motivational interpretations of the confirmation bias, see Friedrich (1993) and Trope and Liberman (1996) pp. 252–65.

An interesting recent theory of lay hypothesis testing is designed, in part, to accommodate self-deception. I explore it in Mele (2001), where I offer grounds for caution and moderation and argue that a qualified version is plausible.[5] I call it the *FTL theory*, after the authors of the two articles on which I primarily drew, Friedrich (1993) and Trope and Liberman (1996). Here, I offer a thumbnail sketch.

The basic idea of the FTL theory is that a concern to minimize costly errors drives lay hypothesis testing. The *errors* on which the theory focuses are false beliefs. The *cost* of a false belief is the cost, including missed opportunities for gains, that it would be reasonable for the person to expect the belief – if false – to have, given his desires and beliefs, if he were to have expectations about such things. A central element of the FTL theory is a 'confidence threshold' – or a 'threshold', for short. The lower the threshold, the thinner the evidence sufficient for reaching it. Two thresholds are relevant to each hypothesis: 'The acceptance threshold is the minimum confidence in the truth of a hypothesis', p, sufficient for acquiring a belief that p 'rather than continuing to test [the hypothesis], and the rejection threshold is the minimum confidence in the untruth of a hypothesis,' p, sufficient for acquiring a belief that $\sim p$ 'and discontinuing the test' (Trope and Liberman, 1996, p. 253). The two thresholds often are not equally demanding, and acceptance and rejection thresholds, respectively, depend 'primarily' on 'the cost of false acceptance relative to the cost of information' and 'the cost of false rejection relative to the cost of information'. The 'cost of information' is simply the 'resources and effort' required for gathering and processing 'hypothesis-relevant information' (p. 252).

Confidence thresholds are determined by the strength of aversions to specific costly errors together with information costs. Setting aside the latter, the stronger one's aversion to falsely believing that p, the higher one's threshold for belief that p. These aversions influence belief in a pair of related ways. First, because other things being equal, lower thresholds are easier to reach than higher ones, belief that $\sim p$ is a more likely outcome than belief that p, other things being equal, in a hypothesis tester who has a higher acceptance threshold for p than for $\sim p$. Second, the aversions influence *how* we test hypotheses – for example, whether we exhibit the confirmation bias – and *when we stop* testing them (owing to our having reached a relevant threshold).[6]

---

[5] See Mele (2001) pp. 31–49, 63–70, 90–91, 96–98, 112–18.

[6] Whether and to what extent subjects display the confirmation bias depends on such factors as whether they are given a neutral perspective on a hypothesis or, instead, the perspective of someone whose job it is to detect cheaters. See Gigerenzer and Hug (1992).

Friedrich claims that desires to avoid specific errors can trigger and sustain 'automatic test strategies' (p. 313), which supposedly happens in roughly the nonintentional way in which a desire that p results in the enhanced vividness of evidence for p. In Mele (2001, pp. 41–49, 61–67), I argue that a person's being more strongly averse to falsely believing that $\sim p$ than to falsely believing that p may have the effect that he primarily seeks evidence for p, is more attentive to such evidence than to evidence for $\sim p$, and interprets relatively neutral data as supporting p, without this effect's being mediated by a belief that such behavior is conducive to avoiding the former error. The stronger aversion may simply frame the topic in a way that triggers and sustains these manifestations of the confirmation bias without the assistance of a belief that behavior of this kind is a means of avoiding particular errors. Similarly, having a stronger aversion that runs in the opposite direction may result in a skeptical approach to hypothesis testing that in no way depends on a belief to the effect that an approach of this kind will increase the probability of avoiding the costlier error. Given the aversion, skeptical testing is predictable independent of the agent's believing that a particular testing style will decrease the probability of making a certain error.

The FTL theory applies straightforwardly to both straight and twisted self-deception. Friedrich writes:

> a prime candidate for primary error of concern is believing as true something that leads [one] to mistakenly criticize [oneself] or lower [one's] self-esteem. Such costs are generally highly salient and are paid for immediately in terms of psychological discomfort. When there are few costs associated with errors of self-deception (incorrectly preserving or enhancing one's self-image), mistakenly revising one's self-image downward or failing to boost it appropriately should be the focal error.
>
> (Friedrich, 1993, p. 314)

Here, he plainly has straight self-deception in mind, but he should not stop there. Whereas for many people it may be more important to avoid acquiring the false belief that their spouses are having affairs than to avoid acquiring the false belief that they are not so engaged, the converse may well be true of some insecure, jealous people. The belief that one's spouse is unfaithful tends to cause significant psychological discomfort. Even so, avoiding falsely believing that their spouses are faithful may be so important to some people that they test relevant hypotheses in ways that, other things being equal, are less likely to lead to a false belief in their spouses' fidelity than to a false belief in their spouses' infidelity. Furthermore, data suggestive of infidelity may be especially salient for these people and contrary data quite pallid by comparison. Don Sharpsteen and Lee Kirkpatrick observe that 'the jealousy complex' – that is, 'the thoughts, feelings, and behavior typically associated with jealousy episodes' – is interpretable as a mechanism 'for maintaining close relationships' and appears to be 'triggered by separation, or the threat of separation, from attachment figures' (Sharpsteen and Kirkpatrick, 1997, p. 627). It certainly is conceivable that, given a certain psychological profile, a strong desire to maintain one's relationship with one's spouse plays a role in rendering the potential error of falsely believing one's spouse to be innocent of infidelity a 'costly' error, in the FTL sense, and more costly than the error of falsely believing one's spouse to be guilty. After all, the former error may reduce the probability that one takes steps to protect the relationship against an intruder. The FTL theory thus provides a basis for an account of both straight and twisted self-deception (Mele, 2001, ch. 5).

I have concentrated on roles for motivation in self-deception. Roles for affect also merit attention (see Mele, 2003). It is often held that emotions have desires as constituents. Even if that is so, might emotions contribute to some instances of self-deception in ways that do not involve a constituent desire's making a contribution? Suppose that Art is angry at Bill for a recent slight. His anger may prime the confirmation bias by suggesting an emotion-congruent hypothesis about Bill's current behavior – for example, that he is behaving badly again – and it may increase the salience of data that seem to support that hypothesis.[7] There is evidence that anger tends to focus attention selectively on explanations in terms of 'agency,' as opposed to situational factors (Keltner et al., 1993). Perhaps Art's anger leads him to view Bill's behavior as more purposeful and more indicative of a hostile intention than he otherwise would. If anger has a desire as a constituent, it is, roughly, a desire to lash out against the target of one's anger. Possibly, anger can play the biasing roles just mentioned without any constituent desire's playing them.

If an emotion can do this, perhaps an emotion may contribute to an instance of self-deception that involves *no* desires at all as significant biasing causes. It is conceivable, perhaps, that Art enters self-deception in acquiring the belief that Bill is behaving badly now, that the process that results in this belief features his anger's playing the biasing roles just described, and that no desires of his have a biasing effect in this case. If it is assumed that Art believes that Bill is behaving badly despite having stronger evidence for the falsity of that hypothesis than for its truth, an FTL theorist will find it plausible that Art had a lower threshold for acceptance of that hypothesis than for rejection of it, that the difference in thresholds is explained at least partly in terms of relevant desires, and that this difference helps to explain Art's acquiring the belief he does. But this position on Art's case is debatable, and I leave the matter open.

---

7 There is evidence that 'emotional states facilitate the processing of congruent stimuli' and that 'attentional processes are involved in [this] effect' (Derryberry, 1988, pp. 36, 38). Gordon Bower and Joseph Forgas review evidence that emotions make 'emotionally congruent interpretations of ambiguous stimuli more available' (2000, p. 106).

Although I have never offered a conceptual analysis of self-deception, I have suggested the following proto-analysis: people enter self-deception in acquiring a belief that p if and only if p is false and they acquire the belief in *a suitably biased way* (Mele, 2001, p. 120)[8]. The suitability at issue is a matter of kind of bias, degree of bias, and the nature of causal connections between biasing processes (or events) and the acquisition of the belief that p. My suggestion is that someone interested in constructing a conceptual analysis of entering self-deception in acquiring a belief that p can start here and try to tease out an account of suitable bias. For guidance on this, see Mele (2001), ch. 6 and 2009.

In Mele (2006), I suggest that, as self-deception is commonly conceived, something along the following lines is a test for a level of motivational or emotional bias appropriate to a person's being self-deceived in acquiring a belief that p: Given that S acquires a belief that p and D is the collection of relevant data readily available to S during the process of belief acquisition, if D were made readily available to S's impartial cognitive peers and they were to engage in at least as much reflection on the issue as S does and at least a moderate amount of reflection, those who conclude that p is false would significantly outnumber those who conclude that p is true. Call this *the impartial observer test*. It is a test for a person's satisfying the suitable bias condition on self-deception. A person's passing the test is evidence of bias suitable for self-deception.

I close this section with some comments on this test. By 'cognitive peers,' I mean people who are very similar to the person being tested in such things as education and intelligence. Cognitive peers who share certain relevant desires with the subject – as one's spouse may share one's desire that one's child is not seriously ill – may often acquire the same unwarranted belief that the subject does, given the same data. But the relevant cognitive peers, for present purposes, are *impartial* observers. At least a minimal requirement for impartiality

---

[8] Some readers will object to the requirement that p be false. As I see it, the requirement captures a purely lexical point. A person is, by definition, *deceived in* believing that p only if p is *false*; the same is true of being *self-deceived in* believing that p. The condition in no way implies that the falsity of p has special importance for the *dynamics* of self-deception. Motivationally biased treatment of data may sometimes result in someone's believing an improbable proposition, p, that, as it happens, is *true*. There may be self-deception in such a case, but the person is not self-deceived in believing that p nor in acquiring the belief that p. As I understand the pertinent expressions, people may be deceived *into* believing something that they are not deceived *in* believing (see Mele, 1987, pp. 127–28). A might execute a tricky plan for deceiving B into believing something that, unbeknownst to A, is true. And A might thereby cause B to believe this proposition, p. Since p is true, B is not deceived *in* believing it. Even so, it is plausible that A deceived B *into* believing it, if A caused B to believe that p partly by deceiving him into believing some false propositions suggestive of p.

in the present context is that one neither shares the subject's desire that p nor has a desire that $\sim p$. Another plausible requirement is that one not prefer avoidance of either of the following errors over the other: falsely believing that p and falsely believing that $\sim p$. A third is that one not have an emotional stake in p's truth or falsity. The test is a test for a level of motivational or emotional bias appropriate to self-deception. I take the suitability of the impartial observer test – or something similar, at least – to be implicit in the conceptual framework that informs common-sense judgments about what is and is not plausibly counted as an instance of self-deception.[9]

Some delusional confabulations

Some confabulations are associated with delusions. Confabulations of this kind are my concern here. DSM-IV offers the following gloss on 'delusion':

> A false belief based on incorrect inference about external reality that is firmly sustained despite what almost everyone else believes and despite what constitutes incontrovertible and obvious proof or evidence to the contrary. The belief is not one ordinarily accepted by other members of the person's culture or subculture (e.g. it is not an article of religious faith). When a false belief involves a value judgment, it is regarded as a delusion only when the judgment is so extreme as to defy credibility. Delusional conviction occurs on a continuum and can sometimes be inferred from an individual's behavior. It is often difficult to distinguish between a delusion and an overvalued idea (in which case the individual has an unreasonable belief or idea but does not hold it as firmly as is the case with a delusion).

> (DSM-IV, 1994, p. 765)

Two points merit emphasis. As delusions are understood in DSM-IV, they are exceptionally resistant to contrary evidence and the contrary evidence is very strong. Both points are reinforced elsewhere in DSM-IV: 'The distinction between a delusion and a strongly held idea . . . depends on the degree of conviction with which the belief is held despite clear contradictory evidence' (DSM-IV, 1994, p. 275). I take it that 'degree of conviction' (or firmness of belief) here is at least partly a matter of how strong the contrary evidence would need to be to undermine the belief.[10]

---

[9] I say 'or something similar' because, for reasons that emerge shortly, the test, as formulated, may not be reliable in unusual cases of certain kinds.

[10] The idea that all delusions are 'based on incorrect inference about external reality' is dispensable. A person might have the delusion that he lacks certain internal organs (Davies et al., 2001, p. 136). Presumably, such a delusion need not be based on an inference about external reality. With this exception, I follow the quoted gloss.

William Hirstein writes, 'It would be wrong to classify even spontaneous confabulation as a type of delusion, since delusions are, minimally, false or ill-grounded beliefs . . . whereas confabulations are false (or ill-grounded) claims' (Hirstein, 2005, p. 18; my emphasis). Even so, some confabulations may *express* delusional beliefs. As Hirstein puts the point, 'A delusion might give rise to a confabulation', as in 'the case of Capgras' syndrome' (Hirstein, 2005, p. 19).

One way to approach the connection between self-deception and confabulations that express delusional beliefs – 'delusional confabulations,' for short – features intuitions about cases. Another approach features an investigation of the causes, in these spheres, of the pertinent beliefs. I opt for the latter. In this section, I consider three delusions: the Capgras delusion, delusional jealousy (or the Othello syndrome), and the reverse Othello syndrome.

The Capgras delusion

Bob believes that his wife has been 'replaced by an exact replica or impostor' (Stone and Young, 1997, p. 327). This is an instance of the Capgras delusion. Part of the cause in Bob's case, apparently, is a brain injury that deprives him of his normal affective response to his wife's face (Stone and Young, 1997, p. 337). Various views have been advanced about additional causal factors. I will discuss one such view for illustrative purposes.

Martin Davies and his coauthors motivate an interesting suggestion about a pair of factors (Davies et al., 2001). Bob experiences his wife as someone who looks just like her but is not really her, and he 'accepts this perceptual experience as veridical' (Davies et al., 2001, p. 153). The first factor is this experience, which includes the impostor idea as part of its content, as opposed, for example to the idea's being a hypothesis that is separate from and prompted by the experience. The second factor is a problem that accounts for Bob's accepting the experience as veridical rather than rejecting it as not veridical. The main proposal Davies et al. offer about the form this problem takes is intriguing. As they observe, 'Normal subjects are . . . able to suspend their unreflective acceptance of veridicality and make a more detached and critical assessment of the credentials of their perceptual experiences' (Davies et al., 2001, p. 153). Their proposal is that Capgras patients have a deficit in this connection. If this is 'the nature of the second factor in the etiology of delusions', then hypotheses that are included in 'the patients' own perceptual experience [are] resistant to being critically assessed and recognized as implausible, but hypotheses generated by someone else [are] assessed in the normal way' (Davies et al., 2001, p. 153).

Davies et al. recognize that their proposal generates the prediction that people with this deficit will be led to have false beliefs by their visual illusions in general, and they are clearly uncomfortable about this (Davies et al., 2001, p. 153). My own immediate concern is with the bearing of their proposal on the impartial observer test. As Davies et al. observe, 'At least some delusional patients show considerable appreciation of the implausibility of their delusional beliefs' (Davies et al., 2001, p. 149). Andrew Young writes, 'Capgras delusion patients can be . . . able to appreciate that they are making an extraordinary claim. If you ask "what would you think if I told you my wife had been replaced by an impostor", you will often get answers to the effect that it would be unbelievable, absurd, an indication that you had gone mad' (Young, 1998, p. 37). Even many delusional patients on the panel of impartial observers might judge that Bob's wife was not replaced by an impostor. And a higher percentage of panel members with similar experiences but no delusions might make that judgment. Suppose the overwhelming majority of panelists deem Bob's belief false. Would that constitute good evidence that Bob's treatment of data is motivationally or emotionally biased?

The basic question behind the impartial observer test, of course, is whether something in the motivation/emotion category biased the subject's treatment of data in the process that produced the belief at issue and whether, if this happened, the biasing was robust enough to be appropriate for self-deception. The idea is to strip away the potential motivational and emotional sources of bias while holding the evidence fixed and to see what happens. If the subject's belief is reached by the great majority in the absence of those sources, that is evidence that they did not play the biasing role at issue in the subject. If the converse belief is reached by the great majority, that is evidence that motivation or emotion did play this biasing role in the subject, and the relative size of the majority is evidence of the robustness of the role. But, of course, some nonmotivational and nonemotional factor might be present in the subject in the latter case and absent in the panel, and it might be doing a lot of causal or explanatory work. This is exactly the situation with Capgras patients if what Davies et al. propose is correct. That is, what would account for the difference in belief is a certain *cognitive* deficit that is outside the categories of motivation and emotion. And even if it were insisted that people must have that deficit in order to count as *cognitive* peers of the target person, that would make no difference if Davies et al. are right; for the proposed deficit shows up only in responses to one's own experiences.[11]

---

[11] Recall my assertion that 'a person's passing the [impartial observer] test is evidence of bias suitable for self-deception'. One moral of the paragraph to which this note is appended is that if a special cognitive deficit of the kind at issue is doing the causal or explanatory work, that fact undermines the evidence.

If what produces the Capgras delusion is a weird experience together with the removal or disabling of a cognitive mechanism that, in special cases, inhibits a kind of default transition from experience to corresponding belief, the delusion seems to lie well beyond the sphere of self-deception. And independent of the proposal by Davies et al., if we lack good reason to believe that motivation or emotion biases the Capgras patient's treatment of data, thereby contributing to the delusional belief, we lack good reason to believe that the delusion is an instance of self-deception. Note that accepting that the Capgras delusion is explained partly by emotional factors does not commit one to accepting that emotion biases the person's treatment of data. For example, we apparently should accept that a major emotional change – a certain loss of affect – plays an important role in producing the delusion. But this loss is a *cause* of relevant experiential data: *causing* data is one thing and *biasing* a person's treatment of data is another.

Young reports on a 'person who experienced both the Cotard and Capgras delusions in sequence' (Young, 1999, p. 577). People with the former delusion believe that they are dead. Young writes:

> This curious association of two unusual delusions has been reported in other cases too, and the key factor seems to be the patients' moods – when in a suspicious mood, they think that other people are impostors, when depressed they think they are dead. There is an obvious parallel here to . . . findings that people with persecutory delusions tend to make external attributions and depressed people internal attributions as to the causes of negative events.
>
> (Young, 1999, p. 577)

What might Davies et al. say about this? Perhaps, that just as the Capgras patient's experience includes the impostor idea as part of its content, the Cotard patient's experience includes the idea that the subject is dead as part of its content. Perhaps in people with both delusions at different times, their feelings of suspicion are part of the cause of their having an experience that includes the impostor content, and their depression is part of the cause of their having an experience that includes the 'I am dead' content. If so, affective states – depression and feelings of suspicion – would help to explain the delusions. But again they would do so by helping to cause experiential data – these experiences with strange content – rather than by biasing the person's treatment of data. My question is whether the Capgras patient's treatment of relevant data is motivationally or emotionally biased. The evidence and theorizing that I have seen does not support an affirmative answer.

Delusional jealousy

Next on the agenda is delusional jealousy, one of the types of delusion identified in DSM-IV's gloss on delusion. It is defined there as 'The delusion that one's sexual partner is unfaithful' (DSM-IV, 1994, p. 765). David Enoch asserts that it is difficult to differentiate 'between normal and excessive, excessive and neurotic, and neurotic and psychotic [jealousies]. The various types overlap and the boundaries are blurred' (Enoch, 1991, p. 52). Earlier, I offered a scenario featuring a jealous husband as an illustration of twisted self-deception. Enoch's assertion suggests that, in the sphere of jealousy, one might be able to locate self-deception on a continuum that includes delusional jealousy and that being self-deceived in believing that one's sexual partner is unfaithful might at least overlap with delusional jealousy. This suggestion is consistent with DSM-IV's description of the 'jealous type' of delusional disorder: 'This subtype applies when the central theme of the person's delusion is that his or her spouse or lover is unfaithful. This belief is arrived at without due cause and is based on incorrect inference supported by small bits of "evidence" (e.g. disarrayed clothing or spots on the sheets), which are collected and used to justify the delusion' (DSM-IV, 1994, p. 297).

There are also grounds for pessimism about the suggestion at issue. Michael Soyka observes that 'Delusions of jealousy are a frequent symptom in various psychiatric disorders. . . . Most . . . patients with delusions of infidelity are schizophrenics' (Soyka, 1995, p. 118). Barbara Breitner and David Anderson report that 'Three large studies found 30–50% of the morbidly jealous suffered from psychosis, a similar proportion neurosis or personality disorder, 5–7% alcoholism and the remainder miscellaneous conditions, most commonly organic disorders' (Breitner & Anderson, 1994, p. 703). Silva et al. assert that 'delusional jealousy rarely exists as the only prominent symptom but is usually found in conjunction with other symptoms, including other delusions and psychotic symptoms' (Silva et al., 1998, p. 616). In a study of 20 people with delusional jealousy, half had directly relevant auditory hallucinations (some of which were commands to attack the partner) and two had relevant visual hallucinations (Silva et al., 1998, pp. 615–616). In a study of 133 demented patients, 'All patients with delusional jealousy . . . had at least one other psychotic symptom', as compared with '70.5% of patients without delusional jealousy' (Tsai et al., 1997, p. 492).

One possibility is that, although jealous people who are self-deceived in believing that their partners are unfaithful and people with delusional jealousy believe the same thing, the causes of that belief in the two groups are so different that the groups do not overlap. Consider people with delusional jealousy who have auditory hallucinations informing them that their partners are unfaithful or visual hallucinations of their partners being unfaithful. A proposal like the one Davies et al. make about Capgras patients may be made about them. Perhaps, owing to a cognitive deficit, they accept the 'experience as veridical'. In those without such hallucinations, one needs to look elsewhere for causes. Tsai et al. found in their study of 133 demented patients that 'The frequency of delusions of theft [and] persecutory delusions . . . was significantly higher in the delusional jealousy group' (Tsai et al., 1997, p. 492).[12] When delusions show up in pairs or larger groups, one is inclined to look for a common cause, especially when the delusions are thematically related. Infidelity may be viewed as encompassing both theft (by the new romantic partner or partners) and persecution. To the extent that one is inclined to see delusions of theft and persecution as falling outside the sphere of self-deception and as being explained in part by a cognitive deficit, one should have the same inclination toward delusions of infidelity in people who have one or both of the other delusions.

Another possibility merits attention: namely, that the FTL model applies straightforwardly to some people with delusional jealousy, perhaps especially those in whom this is 'the only prominent symptom'. The hypothesis is that the error costs for some people with this problem are such that they have an extremely high threshold for accepting the fidelity proposition. It is extremely important to them not to believe that their partners are faithful if, in fact, they are unfaithful. Adequate support for this hypothesis would require a plausible account of why it is that they have these extreme error costs. Such an account would provide grounds for belief that motivation is playing a major biasing role and that these delusionally jealous people are self-deceived.

Reverse Othello syndrome

Reverse Othello syndrome is 'delusional belief in the fidelity of a romantic partner' (Butler, 2000, p. 85). As in ordinary straight self-deception, the person believes something that he wants to be true. Indeed, a stock example of straight self-deception is the person who believes in the fidelity of his or her spouse despite strong evidence to the contrary – evidence that would lead the great majority of impartial cognitive peers to believe in infidelity. Accordingly, the prospects for an important biasing role for motivation in this syndrome might look bright.

Peter Butler (2000) examines the case of a middle-aged man, B. X., who suffered a severe head injury in a high-speed car accident. His romantic partner, N, ended their relationship five months later, which B. X. acknowledged. Despite the absence of contact with her, he subsequently 'developed an intense delusional belief that [she] remained sexually faithful and continued as his lover and life partner' (Butler, 2000, p. 86). He even came to believe that he married

---

[12] They also mention visual hallucinations and the Capgras syndrome in this sentence.

N while he was a patient (Butler, 2000, p. 87). Doctors tested B. X. for other delusions and found no unrelated ones (Butler, 2000, p. 88). After some months, 'his delusional system began to break up'. A few months later he accepted the truth.

One important difference between B. X. and his self-deceived counterpart in the stock example I mentioned is B. X.'s belief that he married N. If there is any experiential basis for his belief in the marriage, it is something on the order of dreams or hallucinations. B. X. reported that the wedding 'occurred at the Central Synagogue in front of several hundred guests' (Butler, 2000, p. 88). He might have dreamed or hallucinated that. Suppose he did. And suppose the dream or hallucination – possibly a repeated one – was a cause of his belief and was caused in part by a wish to be married to N or some wish of that kind. Then, motivation played a role in B. X.'s belief in his marriage. But its playing this particular role would highlight a role for a serious cognitive deficit. When a dream or hallucination is radically out of line with obvious reality, people without a serious cognitive deficit do not regard the experience as veridical after they awake or exit the hallucination.

Butler reports that 'When questioned about the absence of photographs of the ceremony or corroboration from his family [B. X.] remained adamant the marriage had occurred and set his communicator to repeat the words "just because"' (Butler, 2000, p. 88). Seemingly, B. X. wants not to think about these absences. He may understandably be motivated to focus his attention on the imagined marriage and to ignore considerations that point to its being a fantasy. The belief that he is married to N obviously gives B. X. pleasure, and entertaining challenges to that belief is unpleasant for him. Selective focusing or attending, which is at work in some ordinary cases of self-deception, may also be at work in B. X. Even if he does not enter self-deception in acquiring the belief that he is married to N, he may be self-deceived in continuing to believe this.

The Capgras delusion again

Might people with the Capgras delusion be self-deceived in persisting in believing that a loved one has been replaced by an imposter? Recall the assertion by Davies et al. that 'Normal subjects are . . . able to suspend their unreflective acceptance of veridicality and make a more detached and critical assessment of the credentials of their perceptual experiences' (Davies et al., 2001, p. 153). Suppose that people with the Capgras delusion are literally *unable* to do this. Then even if, like B. X., they refuse to reflect on challenges to their beliefs raised in conversation, this is not a cause of the persistence of their delusional beliefs. For even if they were to reflect on the challenges, no change of belief would result; they are, by hypothesis, unable to shed the beliefs. Whether these people are self-deceived in retaining their delusional beliefs depends on the causes of their retention of them. If selective focusing is present here but is not a cause of belief retention, the observation that it is present does not warrant a diagnosis of self-deception.

Suppose that the pertinent cognitive deficit in some Capgras patients does not render them unable 'to suspend their unreflective acceptance of veridicality' and instead makes it extremely difficult for them to do this. Then, processes like selective focusing might do some work in sustaining the delusional belief. But the causal contribution may be so small that we may be disinclined to count the Capgras patient as self-deceived.

Delusional confabulations and self-deception

In all of the specific examples of delusional beliefs discussed above, the beliefs were *expressed* by the believer. If sincere expression of a delusional belief is sufficient for confabulation, all of these people were confabulating. Obviously, given my uncertainty about whether those who suffer from the delusions I discussed are self-deceived either in acquiring or in retaining their delusional beliefs, I am uncertain about whether their confabulations on these topics – specifically, confabulations expressing their delusional beliefs – express beliefs that they are self-deceived in acquiring or retaining. The source of my uncertainty in this connection is my uncertainty about whether motivation/emotion helps either to produce or to sustain these beliefs in these people *by biasing their treatment of data*, and, if it does, how robust the effect is.

Hirstein writes, 'The problem in both confabulation and self-deception is the failure of frontal processes to discard ill-grounded beliefs' (Hirstein, 2005, p. 216); 'both are due to a failure of the brain's belief checking and improving processes' (Hirstein, 2005, p. 236). Suppose that 'the problem' Hirstein mentions is at least *an* important problem in both spheres and that both confabulation and self-deception are due at least partly to the failure of the identified processes. Then, as I understand self-deception, if we are interested in learning whether delusional confabulations of the sort I have discussed express beliefs that the believer is self-deceived either in acquiring or in retaining, we should try to ascertain whether and how motivation/emotion is linked to the problem and involved in the failure.

Hirstein contends that 'in the case of self-deception, some process is capable of keeping the checking processes away from the thought that needs to be checked' and that 'in confabulatory neurological patients, the checking processes themselves are damaged, or in some more permanent and concrete way kept from evaluating the candidate belief' (Hirstein, 2005, p. 214). In the same vein, he asserts that 'The confabulator has brain damage, while the self-deceived person's mind is in a suboptimal operating state from an epistemic point of view. We hold the self-deceived person more at fault than we do the confabulator . . . because there is reason to think the self-deceived person can use the processes needed to dislodge his belief' (Hirstein, 2005, p. 226). One implication is that, owing to brain damage of a certain kind or kinds, the confabulators at issue lack the capacity to dislodge the beliefs at issue (and to prevent themselves from acquiring them). If that is so, then motivation/emotion might not play a significant role in biasing their treatment of data. A cognitive deficit of the sort I have discussed may be at work in the absence of any motivationally or emotionally biased treatment of data, or in the presence of only very slight biasing of this kind. In that case, these people are self-deceived neither in acquiring nor in retaining the beliefs at issue, as I understand self-deception's etiology.

I briefly consider a delusion of another kind before wrapping things up. Hirstein (citing Ramachandran and Blakeslee 1998) writes:

> If patients who denied paralysis were given a nonthreatening reason for being paralyzed, the denial abated, as shown by an injection experiment. A doctor approaches the bedside of a patient denying left arm paralysis and says, "I'm going to give you an injection that will briefly cause your arm to be paralyzed. The paralysis will take effect right after the injection." After a fake injection, these patients admitted paralysis. The perfect comparison test for this is to conduct the same procedure with the other arm. When this was done, the patient typically tried to move her arm, succeeded, and said something such as, "I guess it didn't work".

> (Hirstein, 2005, p. 138)

Suppose that, before the experiment, these patients believed that their left arms were not paralyzed. Then, the experiment seems to show that it is false that they had a cognitive deficit at the time of such a kind that no experience could disabuse them of a belief of this kind at that time. And, of course, because the belief that one's arm is temporarily paralyzed owing to an injection is much more palatable than the belief that one has a paralyzed arm owing to persisting physical damage, there is some reason to believe that motivation did play a biasing role in producing and sustaining their earlier beliefs that the arm was not paralyzed. Then again, the present belief is that the arm is paralyzed *now*, and the patients may believe that while also believing that, usually, their left arms are not paralyzed and that they will regain use of the arm as soon as the injection wears off. A delusional belief about the usual condition of their left arms may persist in these patients, and its persistence may be the product of a cognitive deficit rather than of motivational or emotional biasing of relevant data.

In this chapter, I have focused on three specific kinds of delusional confabulation – confabulations associated with the Capgras syndrome, delusional jealousy (or the Othello syndrome), and the reverse Othello syndrome. My aim was to shed some light on what sorts of causes of belief-acquisition or belief-persistence would support or challenge the idea that beliefs expressed in delusional confabulations in general are beliefs the person is self-deceived in acquiring or retaining. In the case of the confabulations on which I focused, there are significant grounds for caution about the claim that self-deception is involved. But this is not to say that the same grounds for caution are present in all kinds of delusional confabulation. Whether that is so is a topic for another occasion.[13]

References

American Psychiatric Association. (1994). *Diagnostic and Statistical Manual of Mental Disorders* (4th edition). Washington, DC.

Baron, J. 1988. *Thinking and Deciding*. Cambridge, Cambridge University Press.

Bower, G. and Forgas, J. (2000). Affect, Memory, and Social Cognition. In *Cognition and Emotion* (eds E. Eich, J. Kihlstrom, G. Bower, J. Forgas, and P. Niedenthal). Oxford, Oxford University Press.

Breitner, B. and Anderson, D. (1994). The organic and psychological antecedents of delusional jealousy in old age. *International Journal of Geriatric Psychiatry*, **9**, 703–707.

Butler, P. (2000). Reverse othello syndrome subsequent to traumatic brain injury. *Psychiatry*, **63**, 85–92.

Davies, M., Langdon, R., and Breen, N. (2001). Monothematic delusions: Towards a two-factor account. *Philosophy, Psychiatry, and Psychology*, **8**, 133–158.

Derryberry, D. (1988). Emotional influences on evaluative judgments: Roles of arousal, attention, and spreading activation. *Motivation and Emotion*, **12**, 23–55.

Enoch, D. (1991). Delusional jealousy and awareness of reality. *British Journal of Psychiatry*, **159** (suppl. 14), 52–56.

Friedrich, J. (1993). Primary error detection and minimization PEDMIN strategies in social cognition: A reinterpretation of confirmation bias phenomena. *Psychological Review*, **100**, 298–319.

Gigerenzer, G. and Hug, K. (1992). Domain-specific reasoning: Social contracts, cheating, and perspective change. *Cognition*, **43**, 127–171.

Hirstein, W. (2005). *Brain fiction: Self-deception and the riddle of confabulation*. Cambridge, MA, MIT Press.

---

[13] A draft of this article was completed during my tenure of a 2007–08 NEH Fellowship. (Any views, findings, conclusions, or recommendations expressed in this article do not necessarily reflect those of the National Endowment for the Humanities.) Parts of this article derive partly from earlier work of mine – most proximally, my 2006 and 2009. I am grateful to William Hirstein for comments on a draft of this article.

Keltner, D., Ellsworth, P., and Edwards, K. (1993). Beyond simple pessimism: Effects of sadness and anger on social perception. *Journal of Personality and Social Psychology*, **64**, 740–752.

Kunda, Z. (1990). The case for motivated reasoning. *Psychological Bulletin*, **108**, 480–498.

Kunda, Z. (1999). *Social Cognition*. Cambridge, MA, MIT Press.

Mele, A. (1983). Self-Deception. *Philosophical Quarterly*, **33**, 365–377.

Mele, A. (1987). *Irrationality: An Essay on Akrasia, Self-Deception, and Self-Control.* New York, Oxford University Press.

Mele, A. (1999). Twisted Self-Deception. *Philosophical Psychology*, **12**, 117–137.

Mele, A. (2001). *Self-Deception Unmasked*. Princeton, Princeton University Press.

Mele, A. (2003). Emotion and Desire in Self-Deception. In *Philosophy and the Emotions*. (ed. A. Hatzimoysis) Cambridge, Cambridge University Press.

Mele, A. (2006). Self-Deception and Delusions. *European Journal of Analytic Philosophy*, **2**, 109–124.

Mele, A. (2009). Have I Unmasked Self-Deception or Am I Self-Deceived? In *The Philosophy of Deception*. (ed. C. Martin). New York, Oxford University Press.

Ramachandran, V. and Blakeslee, S. (1998). *Phantoms in the Brain*. New York, William Morrow.

Sharpsteen, D. and Kirkpatrick, L. (1997). Romantic jealousy and adult romantic attachment. *Journal of Personality and Social Psychology*, **72**, 627–640.

Silva, J., Ferrari, M., Leong, G., and Penny, G. (1998). The dangerousness of persons with delusional jealousy. *Journal of the American Academy of Psychiatry and the Law*, **26**, 607–623.

Soyka, M. (1995). Prevalence of delusional jealousy in schizophrenia. *Psychopathology*, **28**, 118–120.

Stone, T. and Young, A. (1997). Delusions and brain injury: The philosophy and psychology of belief. *Mind and Language*, **12**, 327–364.

Trope, Y., Gervey, B., and Liberman, N. (1997). Wishful Thinking from a Pragmatic Hypothesis-Testing Perspective. In *The Mythomanias: The Nature of Deception and Self-Deception* (ed. M. Myslobodsky). Mahwah, NJ, Lawrence Erlbaum.

Trope, Y. and Liberman, A. (1996). Social Hypothesis Testing: Cognitive and Motivational Mechanisms. In *Social Psychology: Handbook of Basic Principles* (eds. E. T. Higgins and A. Kruglanski). New York, Guilford Press.

Tsai, S., Hwang, J., Yang, C., and Liu, K. (1997). Delusional jealousy in dementia. *Journal of Clinical Psychiatry*, **58**, 492–494.

Young, A. (1998). *Face and Mind*. Oxford, Oxford University Press.

Young, A. (1999). Delusions. *The Monist*, **82**, 571–589.

Chapter 7

Confabulation as a psychiatric symptom

P. J. McKenna, E. Lorente-Rovira, and G. E. Berrios

In a recent book on confabulation, Schnider (2008) identified the famous psychiatrist Kraepelin along with Korsakoff as one of the two key figures in the early development of the concept of confabulation. It is true that Kraepelin (1886 – 1887) gave an early account of what would now be termed fantastic confabulation in patients with general paralysis and senile dementia. However, he made an arguably greater contribution in documenting the occurrence of something seemingly very similar in psychiatric patients, initially in the disorder he was later to call schizophrenia (Marková and Berrios, 2000), and then particularly in a closely related variant of this, paraphrenia (Berrios, 1998). Although this phenomenon was subsequently neglected throughout most of the twentieth century, it is now emerging as a non-trivial theme in current thinking and research on confabulation.

Kraepelin's confabulatory paraphrenia

Some-time after he delineated schizophrenia in 1896, Kraepelin (1913) felt obliged to draw attention to a small group of patients who deviated from the typical picture in significant ways. As in schizophrenia, these patients developed persistent and steadily worsening psychotic symptoms; however, they stood out by virtue of having a clinical picture which was dominated by delusions and hallucinations, with other symptoms such as thought disorder (incoherence of speech) and catatonic symptoms being far in the background. These patients also failed to develop the deterioration which for Kraepelin was the common denominator of the otherwise quite varied clinical presentations of schizophrenia: many remained able to work and, other than a certain superficiality of emotional expression, apathy and emotional flattening was the exception rather than the rule. Finally, the patients' age of onset was between 30 and

55 years of age, somewhat later than the typical commencement of schizophrenia in early adult life. Partly because of the marked delusional component, but almost certainly for other reasons as well, Kraepelin chose to resurrect an earlier psychiatrist's, Kahlbaum's, term 'paraphrenia' to describe these patients (Berrios, 2003)[1].

As he was wont to do, Kraepelin divided paraphrenia into a number of subgroups, although he considered that these were not sharply demarcated from one another. The largest group, which he termed *paraphrenia systematica*, was characterized by the insidious development of persecutory and referential delusions, with auditory hallucinations and other delusions appearing later. The remaining types were much less common. One was *paraphrenia expansiva*, where the delusions were grandiose rather than persecutory, and auditory and visual hallucinations appeared sooner than in paraphrenia systematica. The other two types he termed *paraphrenia confabulans* and *paraphrenia phantastica*. The characteristic feature of both of these was the production of a seemingly endless succession of extremely florid, fantastic, and constantly shifting delusions. In both, but especially in the former, the patients also voiced many false memories.

The false memories the patients described in *paraphrenia confabulans* and *paraphrenia phantastica* tended to have an adventurous, story-like quality, and the fictitious events would be related with complete conviction and precise details – one patient reported to the authorities that he had dug up a human arm, causing a police investigation. The false memories could be absolutely fixed and repeated again and again in almost exactly the same words, but more typically further details would be added on questioning and the stories would undergo a progressive embroidering:

> ...the patients bring forward with the most profound conviction an enormous number of extraordinary stories absolutely in the form of personal experiences. They can describe exactly every glance, every look of the persons concerned; they report every word, even though the events are referred back for decades.... Sometimes the often repeated descriptions fix themselves in the patients' minds in such a way that they are repeated almost in the same words. But, especially in the beginning, it is sometimes

---

[1] Kahlbaum introduced the term 'paraphrenia' not to denote any particular clinical entity, but merely to draw attention to the tendency of certain psychiatric disorders to develop at certain periods in life – in his scheme, for example, paraphrenia hebetica was the insanity of adolesence and paraphrenia senilis was the insanity of the elderly. It is also possible that Kraepelin was acknowledging a general indebtedness to Kahlbaum, who was a major formative influence on his views.

possible by questions to make the patients add fresh decorations, and they themselves continually produce additions which meantime have occurred to them.

For example, the patient who told the police that he had dug up the arm of a corpse went on to report over the next few days that his neighbor had buried something that smelt of corpses under a tree, that numerous individuals, including his mother, were disappearing from the village where he lived, that dogs were being fed human flesh, and that a woman had threatened him with a revolver and announced that it would be his turn in a week.

Delusional memory and delusional confabulation

Kraepelin's separation of paraphrenia from schizophrenia did not stand the test of time. A colleague carried out a follow-up of his patients (Mayer, 1921) and found that only around a third of them retained their characteristic features over time. In around half of the rest, the picture ultimately became one of schizophrenia. In the other half, the diagnosis was revised to another psychiatric category such as paranoia or manic-depressive psychosis, or dementia or some other form of organic brain disease supervened[2].

Nevertheless, the falsifications of memory that Kraepelin described and which were seen *par excellence* in confabulatory paraphrenia went on to enter the lexicon of psychiatric symptomatology as delusional memory and delusional confabulation. Two types of delusional memory have come to be recognized (Buchanan, 1991). In one, new and special significance is attributed to events that took place in the past. The classic example here is Fish's (Hamilton, 1984) description of a patient who realized he was of royal descent when he remembered that the fork he had used as a child had a crown on it. This type of delusional memory is simply an uncommon species of the delusion of reference or, in the words of Wernicke (1906), one of the authors who originally distinguished it, a retrospective delusional interpretation.

In the other type of delusional memory, the patient describes memories of events and experiences which never happened. For a complicated set of historical reasons, these false memories also came to be classified as delusions, although they could equally well have been considered to be hallucinations

---

[2] Nevertheless, 40 years later Roth and co-workers (Roth and Morrissey, 1952; Roth et al., 1995) resurrected the concept as 'late paraphrenia', to describe the development of schizophrenia-like illnesses in middle or late life. This is now a well-established clinical entity which, apart from the age of onset and the fact that it almost exclusively affects women, conforms closely to Kraepelin's description of paraphrenia systematica.

(in fact the term 'memory hallucination' can also be found in the twentieth century literature).

The most rigorous contemporary description of psychiatric symptoms is that of Wing et al. (1974), which was developed as a glossary to a structured psychiatric interview, the Present State Examination. This defines delusional memories as 'experiences of past events which clearly did not occur but which the subject equally clearly remembers, e.g. "I came down to earth on a silver star in 1964"'. In the same glossary, Wing et al. (1974) also give what appears to be the only contemporary acknowledgement of the phenomenon of delusional confabulation, which they characterized as the subject making up delusions on the spot:

> Delusional confabulations are beliefs which the subject can be led on to elaborate during the course of the interview. If the phenomenon is present, however, the symptom usually occurs spontaneously.

Wing et al. (1974) grouped delusional memories and delusional confabulation with fantastic delusions. This almost certainly reflected the clinical impression that the three symptoms tend to be seen in association with one another. Clinical experience also suggests that the three symptoms a share a fantastic quality, i.e. they are not just inherently unlikely or bizarre, but flout common sense at its most elementary. Patients with fantastic delusions report that they have two heads, have visited other planets, have given birth to thousands of children, remember members of the royal family being present when they were born, etc.

Nathaniel-James and Frith's provoked confabulations in schizophrenia

Wing et al. (1974) considered delusional confabulation to be a very rare symptom. However, recent work suggests that, in a less extravagant form, confabulation can be seen with considerably greater frequency in schizophrenia. This proposal originated in a study by Nathaniel-James and Frith (1996). They noted that cognitive impairment is nowadays accepted as frequently accompanying schizophrenia[3]. Since memory and executive impairment are prominent

---

[3] It is now accepted (e.g. see McKenna, 2007) that there is a variable degree of overall intellectual impairment in the disorder, which ranges from a minor lowering of IQ from estimated premorbid levels in many patients to what is to all intents and purposes a dementia in a minority of those with the most chronic, severe forms of illness. Many patients also show deficits in executive function and long-term memory which appear to be disproportionate to the overall level of intellectual impairment.

aspects of this, confabulation might be an expected consequence. They therefore attempted to elicit confabulations in a sample of 12 schizophrenic patients by reading them fables and asking them to repeat them back to the examiner. All of the patients included some information which was not present in the narrative, in contrast to only one of 12 control subjects. One of the five fables used was the following:

> A rich man took a valuable cargo on a voyage across dangerous seas. A storm soon blew up and the ship went down throwing the passengers into the sea. They all began to swim for their lives except the rich man who raised his arms to heaven and promised his God all kinds of riches if he was saved. The other passengers shouted to the praying man, 'Don't leave it for God to save you, swim for yourself'.

To which one patient responded:

> A rich man went on a swimming expedition* and he stopped swimming in the middle of the ocean*. In the middle of the ocean he decided that he would pray to our Lord God... he would pray to God*, our Lord... Jesus who would* .. um... Jesus our Lord, who would accept his prayer*,... answered prayer*. But he carried on praying as was his word* and he was hailed by people on a passing boat* who said, 'God won't help you, swim for yourself.' (Ideas which were not in the original story are marked by asterisks.)

Particularly noteworthy for Nathaniel-James and Frith (1996) was the way in which the patients confabulated. Thus, in the above example, the patient began by stating that a rich man went on 'a swimming expedition' and then went on to include statements about praying and being hailed by other passengers, material which was in the original story but represented a scrambled version of the events that took place. They contrasted this with the confabulations reported in a series of amnesic and Alzheimer patients by Kopelman (1987), where there were numerous examples of entirely new and unrelated material. For example, recalling a story from the Wechsler Memory Test in which a woman was robbed of £15, one of Kopelman's patients stated that the woman had got a job in a pub to make this amount of money and that her husband had left her, neither of which were present in the original story or could have been reconstructed from information in it.

Nathaniel-James and Frith (1996) also investigated the neuropsychological correlates of this form of schizophrenic confabulation. They found no relationship with overall intellectual impairment. There was an association with poor recall of the fables used to elicit confabulation, but not with performance on any of a range of other memory tests. With respect to executive function, confabulation was significantly associated with impairment on the Hayling Test (Burgess and Shallice, 1997), a task requiring inhibition of prepotent responses, but not with performance on two other tests, the Wisconsin Card Sorting Test and verbal fluency.

A handful of further studies have made it clear that memory impairment is neither necessary nor sufficient for confabulation in schizophrenia (Nathaniel-James et al., 1996; Kramer et al., 1998; Dab et al., 2004). While two studies found, like Nathaniel-James and Frith (1996), that confabulation was linked to impairment on executive tests requiring inhibition of prepotent responses (Dab et al., 2004; Salazar-Fraile et al., 2004), there has been no agreement about whether patients who confabulate show more impairment than those who do not on other tests of executive function (Nathaniel-James et al., 1996; Dab et al., 2004; Salazar-Fraile et al., 2004).

In an attempt to resolve some of these uncertainties, Lorente-Rovira et al. (2007) divided 34 schizophrenic patients into confabulators and non-confabulators, based on a split around the maximum number of confabulations produced by 17 normal controls. According to this criterion, there were 10 confabulators (>3 confabulations/5 fables) and 23 non-confabulators (≤2 confabulations/5 fables). As found by Nathaniel-James and Frith (1996), the confabulators performed significantly more poorly on recall of fables, but not on any of the four subtests of the Doors and People Test (Baddeley et al., 1994), a memory test covering verbal recall, verbal recognition, visual recall, and visual recognition. Among executive tests, there were no differences between the groups on the Hayling Test, the Brixton Test (Burgess and Shallice, 1997) (a test of set shifting conceptually similar to the Wisconsin Card Sorting Test) or verbal fluency. There was a marginal difference ($p = 0.05$) on the Cognitive Estimates Test (Shallice and Evans, 1978), in which subjects have to make guesses in response to questions they would be unlikely to know the precise answer to, such as, *How fast do racehorses gallop?* and *What is the age of oldest person alive in Britain today?*. The only tests on which the confabulators clearly performed more poorly than the non-confabulators were two semantic memory tasks: the Semantic Verification Task (Laws et al., 1995), where subjects have to respond true or false to 56 sentences, half of which are true (e.g. *Buses are driven*) and half false (e.g. *Geese have four legs*), and the Camel and Cactus Test (Bozeat et al., 2000) where subjects are shown a series of questions in which the name of an object (e.g. *camel*) is written and have to decide which of four other words (*tree, sunflower, cactus, or rose*) it is most closely related to.

LR, a patient with delusional confabulation

LR became ill at the age of 17 when he started expressing strange ideas and became increasingly withdrawn. Prior to becoming ill, he had been somewhat socially isolated and odd, but did averagely well at school and worked for a time. There was no history of alcohol abuse or neurological disease.

In hospital, he was noted to have bizarre hypochondriacal delusions and auditory hallucinations, and was also slow and showed catatonic symptoms. Accordingly a diagnosis of schizophrenia was made. He improved with treatment but relapsed and had further admissions. During these he was recorded as having a number of so-called first-rank symptoms, such as thought insertion and delusions of control, which are considered to have a reasonably high degree of diagnostic specificity for schizophrenia. As time passed, he developed obvious negative symptoms of schizophrenia, becoming apathetic and showing very poor self-care.

Eventually LR became chronically hospitalized. His clinical picture was stable for several years: from time to time he would allude to his previous ideas of having Alzheimer's disease but mostly seemed free of delusions. In contrast, he experienced continual auditory hallucinations and at times had visual hallucinations ('shapes') as well. Occasionally, he would become distressed by his symptoms, but most of the time he was calm and well-behaved, although he was at all times seriously lacking in motivation. Somewhat unusually for schizophrenia, he showed continuous mild catatonic symptoms including aprosodic speech – a flat, robotic intonation – and ambitendence – difficulty and hesitancy in everyday activities such as standing up and going through doors.

Over the years LR took part in a number of neuropsychological studies that were being carried out in the hospital. On one occasion, at the age of 33, a psychologist who was testing him became alarmed when he started talking about violent ideas. When questioned about these ideas he told the following story, which he recounted in a matter-of-fact way without any apparent distress. He continued to give much the same account over the next few days, during which he was videotaped.

> Q: The main thing I wanted to ask you about today about what you were telling me on Wednesday about the Carlton brothers. Can you tell me again?
>
> A: OK I'll tell you what happened. In 1978, I shot a man in the back of the head in a shop in Cambridge. I put one cartridge into him. My brother David put about eight into him. I shot a man in the leg called Conrad Carlton.
>
> Q: When was this?
>
> A: About 1978. I frogmarched him from St. Neots right into the Midlands with a shotgun pointed at him. It was an empty shotgun.
>
> Q: Was this on foot?
>
> A: Yeah. Right into the Midlands, about 80-odd miles

Q: Both walking?

A: Yeah, I did. I was on the television.

Q: How did you end up on television?

A: Because I had a shotgun pointed at him, you know. I was sort of notorious, you know we had a bit of fame – well the wrong sort of fame – but, you know, we got into a sort of contest and he could have lost his life. If I had aimed a few inches higher I could have killed him.

Q: Where did you shoot him?

A: I shot him in the leg.

Q: And you say this was a contest.

A: Yes [laughs]. Only he lost it. In 1979, Richard, Conrad Carlton, Reg Walters and, um, Davis, shot my father in the head with a shotgun in a removal van in Papworth Everard hospital grounds.

Q: What were the circumstances of that, then?

A: Well, the Walters, Richard and Reg Walters, and the Wilson brothers got together and they murdered my father in the back of a removal van in Papworth Everard hospital grounds. I think they shot him in the head with a shotgun and Reg and Richard smashed the back of his head with club hammers and axes. And Richard said bring the next one up and Conrad and Paul got hold of me and tried to get me in the back of the removal van, and I said you are not going to get me into that and do what you did to my father.

Q: Why were you around there?

A: To visit my father in hospital.

Q: What was the matter with him?

A: He had a lung disease. He had emphysema.

Q: Carry on from there.

A: Then I think Paul then – this was 1979 after me and my brother shot this man in Cambridge – and I think Richard shot me in the head with a shotgun and they couldn't get me into the back of the van, so Richard took me back home in his car. And during the night I was laying in bed and I could feel myself dying – yes, because of the shotgun wound to my head. I said I am not going to die, I am going to get out of this. I went to work the next morning, you know, and the foreman looked at me and said, 'You can't work like that you have got a hole in your head'.

Q: Where was this hole?

A: [indicates] I think it was on the left-hand or right-hand side of my head. The shotgun split my head open I had about an eight or nine inches split in my skull.

Q: You went to work like that?

A: I did, yeah.

Q: So the foreman said…

A: He said you can't work like that you've got a hole in your head. So he took me down the hospital in his car and they took the shot out of my head and patched me up.

LR continued to describe these events over the next few weeks when questioned about them, although with less detail. Several months later he still maintained that they had happened, but he could not be induced to elaborate. When asked about the events several years later he at first denied them but then indicated he had a very vague recollection of being involved with criminals a long time ago.

Like many patients with schizophrenia, LR shows a discrepancy between his premorbid IQ of 100, as estimated using the National Adult Reading Test (Nelson, 1991), and his current WAIS-R IQ of 86. However, he is unusual for patients with chronic, severe illness in that he shows little in the way of memory or executive impairment. As shown in Table 7.1, he scored in the normal range on all of a number of tests of visual and visuospatial function, and also on two language tests, a naming test and a test of syntactical comprehension, the Test for the Reception of Grammar (TROG). He scored in the 'poor memory' range on the Rivermead Behavioural Memory Test (RBMT) (Wilson et al., 1985), a test of 'everyday' memory impairment, i.e. in the low normal range. He was well above the 5th percentile for his age group on the two verbal memory subscales of the Doors and People Test, but was close to this cutoff on the two visual memory subscales.

On the Behavioural Assessment of the Dysexecutive Syndrome (BADS) (Wilson et al., 1996), a battery of six tests of executive impairment designed to be sensitive to executive failures in daily life, LR achieved an overall ('profile') score of 18 out of a maximum of 24, close to the normal 50th percentile. His scores on a range of other executive tests were also almost all in the normal range. The only exception was the Hotel Test (Manly et al., 2002), another 'ecologically valid' test designed to mimic the kinds of executive skills necessary for making decisions under conditions where there are multiple demands. Participants are required to carry out parts of five different hotel-related activities over a 15-minute period, such as compiling bills, sorting coins, and making-up conference labels. Explicit instructions are given that they should not attempt to carry out any of the tasks fully, which would be impossible in the allotted period. In addition, they have to remember to press a button to open and close garage doors at specified times. LR only managed to do parts of three of the five tasks, whereas all but one of a comparison group of normal adults scored the maximum of 5.

As mentioned above, LR's spontaneous confabulation was a transitory phenomenon. However, several years after it had come and gone, he took part in the above-mentioned study of confabulation designed to replicate and extend Nathaniel-James and Frith's (1996) findings. He was found to be a confabulator, giving five confabulated ideas across the five fables. Most of these were

Table 7.1 LR's performance on a range of neuropsychological tests

Test	Score	Normal 5th percentile cutoff/ other normative data
Visual/visuospatial function		
VOSP incomplete letters (max 20)	20	17
VOSP silhouettes (max 30)	24	16
VOSP position discrimination (max 20)	19	18
VOSP number location (max 10)	10	7
VOSP cube analysis (max 10)	10	6
Rey figure copy (max 36)	33	29
Language		
Graded Naming Test (max 30)	21	14
TROG (max 80)	78.5	75
Memory		
RBMT screening score (max 12)	8	Poor memory
Doors/people verbal recall (max 36)	34	21
Doors/people verbal recognition (max 24)	24	14
Door/s people visual recall (max 36)	28	26
Doors/people visual recognition (max 24)	16	15
Executive function		
BADS profile score	18	Average
Brixton Test (scaled score)	6	Average
Hayling Test (scaled score)	8	Good
Cognitive Estimates Test (error score)	2	13
Letter-number sequencing	9	8
Verbal fluency (letters/1 minute)	10	10
Verbal fluency (animals/1 minute)	19	14
Hotel Test (tasks achieved)	3	5*

*42/43 normal adults scored maximally on this test.
VOSP – Visual Object and Space Perception battery (Warrington and James, 1991).

.

concentrated in one of the stories, the so-called Donkey and the Salt story (his accounts of what happened in the other fables were mostly very brief). This story goes as follows:

> A donkey, loaded with salt, had to wade a stream. He fell down and for a few minutes lay comfortably in the cool water. When he got up, he felt relieved of a great part of his burden, because the salt had melted in the water. Long-ears noted this advantage and at once applied it the following day when, loaded with sponges, he again went through the same stream. This time he fell purposely but was grossly deceived. The sponges had soaked up the water and were considerably heavier than before. The burden was so great that he fell and could not go on.

LR gave the following recollection of this story:

> This man was trying to cross a deep stream on a donkey. He couldn't get across, so he went back – went about half way across. Got these sponges, put all these sponges on the donkey. Crossed the river again and the sponges soaked up water. And he fell off the donkey.

Conclusion

There is no doubt that the phenomenon of confabulation can be seen in schizophrenia. It is clear that it is very uncommon in a spontaneous form, and when it does occur it always seems to take the form of so-called fantastic confabulation. With the possible exception of general paralysis of the insane, this schizophrenic form of confabulation appears to go considerably beyond even the most adventurous and illogical forms of spontaneous confabulation encountered in neurological disease.

Simple, momentary, or provoked confabulations, on the other hand, appear to be commonplace, at least as elicited during story recall. These latter confabulations are not fantastic in form, but it remains an open question whether or not they differ from the corresponding neurological form of the symptom. On the one hand, Nathaniel-James and Frith have argued that they are due to re-organization and reconstruction of existing statements in the stories used to elicit them, rather than the invention of wholly fictitious events seen in amnesic and demented patients. On the other hand, Kopelman (1999) has pointed out that some of his patients with amnesia and dementia also showed re-organization of material in the stories which elicited their confabulations. In the study of Lorente-Rovira et al. (2007) both invented and re-organized confabulations were found, but it was clear that the former were less frequent than the latter.

It is uncertain whether confabulation is ever seen as a psychiatric phenomenon outside schizophrenia. In Kraepelin's original account (Kraepelin, 1886–1887, see also Marková and Berrios, 2000; Schnider, 2008), he stated that patients with mania could present with falsifications of memory 'resembling the ones observed in milder forms of general paralysis', but he did not give any examples. To the authors' knowledge, there are no convincing descriptions of confabulations, fantastic or otherwise in mania or psychotic depression in the contemporary literature. Additionally, Buchanan (1991) has argued on various phenomenological grounds that delusional memories should be considered a first-rank symptom, i.e. pathognomonic of schizophrenia. His arguments may or may not be convincing, but a restriction of delusional accounts of events that never happened to schizophrenia certainly accords with clinical experience.

Perhaps the most widely accepted explanation of confabulation in neurological disease is that a combination of memory impairment and impaired executive function are prerequisites for its occurrence (Kapur and Coughlan, 1980; Baddeley and Wilson, 1988; Moscovitch and Melo, 1997). The neuropsychological underpinnings of confabulation in schizophrenia appear to be different. Nathaniel-James and Frith's (1996) and subsequent studies of provoked confabulation make it clear that the phenomenon is not closely linked to either the memory or executive impairment seen in the disorder. If anything, the findings point to a relationship with semantic memory impairment. These results are clearly different from those, for example, of Moscovitch and Melo (1997) who found that amnesic patients with confabulation were significantly more impaired on executive tasks than those without. Similarly, our patient LR with fantastic confabulation showed no more than a minor memory impairment and he passed most executive tests without difficulty (although, his failure on the Hotel Test, designed to be more sensitive to executive problems than traditional tests provides an intriguing exception).

The gulf between the neuropsychology of psychiatric and neurological confabulation may not be quite as wide as it first appears, however. Even in neurological disorders it is clear that neither memory nor executive impairment are sufficient conditions for the appearance of confabulation, and what additional cognitive factors cause it to appear and then disappear in patients whose neuropsychological status sometimes remains unchanged remain unknown. It is also noteworthy that Schnider (2008) has argued that spontaneous confabulation may not be linked to executive impairment in the same way as provoked confabulation – in his and co-workers' studies, executive function neither predicted the occurrence of confabulation in a group of spontaneous confabulators nor paralleled it in the course it followed. Schizophrenic confabulation remains an enigma, but there are still grounds for believing that it will turn out to rest on mechanisms more similar than different to those underlying the neurological form of the symptom.

References

Baddeley, A. and Wilson, B. (1988). Frontal amnesia and the dysexecutive syndrome. *Brain and Cognition,* **7**, 212–230.

Baddeley, A.D., Emslie, H., and Nimmo-Smith, I. (1994). *Doors and People. A test of visual and verbal recall and recognition.* Bury St. Edmunds, UK, Thames Valley Test Company.

Berrios, G.E. (1998). Confabulations: A conceptual history. *Journal of Historical Neuroscience,* **7**, 225–241.

Berrios, G.E. (2000). Paramnesias and delusions of memory. In *Memory Disorders in Psychiatric Practice* (eds. G.E. Berrios y and J.R. Hodges), pp. 348–368. Cambridge, Cambridge University Press.

Berrios, G.E. (2003). The insanities of the third age: A conceptual history of paraphrenia. *Journal of Nutrition, Health and Aging,* **7**, 394–399.

Bozeat, S., Lambon Ralph, M.A., Patterson, K., Garrard, P., and Hodges J.R. (2000). Non-verbal semantic impairment in semantic dementia. *Neuropsychologia,* **38**, 1207–1215.

Buchanan, A. (1991). Delusional memories: First-rank symptoms? *British Journal of Psychiatry,* **159**, 472–474.

Burgess, P.W. and Shallice, T. (1997). *The Hayling and Brixton Tests.* Bury St Edmunds, UK, Thames Valley Company Limited.

Dab, S., Morais, J., and Frith, C. (2004). Comprehension, encoding, and monitoring in the production of confabulation in memory: A study with schizophrenic patients. *Cognitive Neuropsychiatry,* **9**, 153–182.

Hamilton, M. (1984). *Fish's Schizophrenia* (3rd Edition). Bristol, Wright.

Kapur, N. and Couglan, A.K. (1980). Confabulation and frontal lobe dysfunction. *Journal of Neurology, Neurosurgery and Psychiatry,* **43**, 461–463.

Kopelman, M.D. (1987). Two types of confabulation. *Journal of Neurology, Neurosurgery and Psychiatry,* **50**, 1482–1487.

Kopelman, M.D. (1999). Varieties of false memory. *Cognitive Neuropsychology,* **16**, 197–214.

Kraepelin, E. (1886–1887). Über Erinnerungsfälschungen. *Archiv für Psychiatrie und Nervenkrankheiten,* **17**, 830–843; **18**, 199–239, 395–436.

Kraepelin, E. (1913). *Dementia Praecox and Paraphrenia* (Trans. R.M. Barclay, 1919). Edinburgh, Livingstone.

Kramer, S., Bryan, K.L., and Frith, C.D. (1998). Confabulation in narrative discourse by schizophrenic patients. *International Journal of Language and Communication Disorders,* **33** (supplement), 202–207.

Laws, K.R., Humber, S.A., Ramsey, D.J.C., and McCarthy, R.A. (1995). Probing sensory and associative semantics for animals and objects in normal subjects. *Memory,* **3**, 397–408.

Lorente-Rovira, E., Pomarol-Clotet, E., McCarthy, R.A., Berrios, G.E., and McKenna, P.J. (2007). Confabulation in schizophrenia and its relationship to clinical and neuropsychological features of the disorder. *Psychological Medicine,* **37**, 1403–1412.

Manly, T., Hawkins, K., Evans, J., Woldt, K., and Robertson, I.H. (2002). Rehabilitation of executive function: Facilitation of effective goal management on complex tasks using periodic auditory alerts. *Neuropsychologia,* **40**, 271–281.

Marková, I.S. and Berrios, G.E. (2000). Insight into memory deficits. In *Memory Disorders in Psychiatric Practice* (eds. G.E. Berrios and J.R. Hodges), pp. 204–233. Cambridge, Cambridge University Press.

Mayer, W. (1921). Über paraphrene psychosen. *Zentralblatt für die gesamte Neurologie und Psychiatrie*, **26**, 78–80.

McKenna, P.J. (2007). *Schizophrenia and Related Syndromes* (2nd Edition). Hove, Psychology Press.

Moscovitch, M. and Melo, B. (1997). Strategic retrieval and the frontal lobes: Evidence from confabulation and amnesia. *Neuropsychologia*, **35**, 1017–1034.

Nathaniel-James, D.A. and Frith, C.D. (1996). Confabulation in schizophrenia: Evidence of a new form? *Psychological Medicine*, **26**, 391–399.

Nathaniel-James, D.A., Foong, J., and Frith, C.D. (1996). The mechanisms of confabulation in schizophrenia. *Neurocase*, **2**, 475–483.

Nelson, H. (1991). *National Adult Reading test (NART)* (2nd Edition). Windsor, UK, NFER-Nelson.

Salazar-Fraile, J., Tabarés-Seisdedos, R., Selva-Vera, G., et al. (2004). Recall and recognition confabulation in psychotic and bipolar disorders: Evidence for two different types without unitary mechanisms. *Comprehensive Psychiatry*, **45**, 281–288.

Schnider, A. (2008). *The Confabulating Mind: How the Brain Creates Reality*. Oxford, Oxford University Press.

Shallice, T. and Evans, M.E. (1978). The involvement of the frontal lobes in cognitive estimation. *Cortex*, **14**, 294–303.

Warrington, E.K. and James, M. (1991). *The Visual Object and Space Perception Battery*. Bury St. Edmunds, UK, Thames Valley Test Company.

Wernicke, K. (1906): *Grundriss der Psychiatrie* (2nd Edition). Leipzig, Thieme.

Wilson, B.A., Alderman, N., Burgess, P., Emslie, H., and Evans, J. (1996). *Behavioural Assessment of the Dysexecutive Syndrome*. Bury St Edmunds, England, Thames Valley Company Limited.

Wilson, B.A., Cockburn, J.M., and Baddeley, A.D. (1985). *The Rivermead Behavioural Memory Test*. Bury St Edmunds, UK, Thames Valley Test Company.

Wing, J.K., Cooper, J.E., and Sartorius, N. (1974). *The Measurement and Classification of Psychiatric Symptoms*. Cambridge, Cambridge University Press.

Chapter 8

Confabulation and delusion

Max Coltheart and Martha Turner

Confabulation and delusion are both conditions which involve distorted beliefs about the world. They have traditionally been treated separately in the literature, one as a disorder of memory, the other as a disorder of belief. However, in this chapter we will explore an intriguing similarity between confabulation and delusion, namely the tendency in both for people to seek to justify their unjustifiable false memories or false beliefs when these are challenged. We think that the combination of ideas from theoretical work on delusion and from theoretical work on confabulation may be especially instructive in understanding this phenomenon, so ideas from both fields will loom large in this chapter.

We begin with five examples. They are very different from each other; what unites them, we suggest, is that all are examples of confabulation, a view that we will defend after presenting the examples.

Five examples

Delusion

Sufferers from the Capgras delusion, a condition reviewed by Forstl et al. (1991) and by Edelstyn and Oyebode (1999), believe that one or more people very familiar or emotionally close to them, often a spouse, have been replaced by strangers. This delusional belief (which defines the Capgras condition) has several typical properties (which are also the properties of other kinds of delusional beliefs – see Coltheart, 2007):

(a) The belief is *usually held firmly* despite the existence of good evidence that it is false. Such evidence includes, for example, that the stranger looks exactly like the spouse (in those cases where it *is* the spouse), that the patient's family and friends and clinicians all urge that this person *is* the spouse, and that the 'stranger' can be shown to know things about the patient and the patient's past life that no stranger could possibly know.

(b) The belief is *rarely acted upon*, for example, the patient does not usually take any steps to discover the whereabouts of the spouse who is believed to be missing.

(c) The belief can be *the only unusual belief* the patient holds.

(d) The patient may appreciate that what he believes to be true is *a very unusual occurrence*, but that does not shake his confidence that this belief is true.

Many patients with this or other kinds of delusional belief are perfectly willing to discuss their beliefs and will even tolerate an interlocutor quizzing them about these beliefs if this is done diplomatically. They may even be willing to engage in conversations about the evidential basis of the delusional belief and even to offer evidence which they consider supports this belief, if they are asked for such evidence. Since such offers of evidence are central to the topic of our chapter, we will provide several examples from sufferers of Capgras delusion of responses made by them to the question: 'How do you know this is not X?' (where X is the person who is believed to have been replaced).

Case 2 of Frazer and Roberts (1994, p. 557) said that she could distinguish the stranger from her husband because the stranger tied his shoelaces slightly differently.

Case 3 of Frazer and Roberts (1994, p. 557), when asked how she could distinguish the stranger from her son, 'claimed that he had different-coloured eyes, was not as big and brawny, and that her real son would not kiss her. On one occasion she claimed "They're as different as chalk and cheese"'.

Case 1 of Todd et al. (1981, p. 320) stated that he could distinguish the stranger from his wife because the stranger 'looked older and had more grey hairs than his wife'.

Case 2 of Todd et al. (1981, p. 321), when asked how she could distinguish the stranger from her daughter, explained that 'the false one's teeth are funny and I could spot it'.

Case HL of Lewis et al. (2001, p. 227), whose Capgras delusion pertained to her son's *voice*, when asked how she knew it was a stranger talking to her and not her son, said 'He didn't come across as chirpy . . . or the person he was'.

Why did the patients respond in this way when asked for evidence that would support their delusional beliefs? With respect to Capgras delusion, Todd et al. (1981, p. 324) offered the following answer to this question: 'The minor differences between prototype and impersonator so often perceived by Capgras syndrome patients are doubtless produced by the process known as secondary rationalization'. But this answer is a suggestion about *how* the response was arrived at, not about why it was arrived at. The patients could, after all, have responded to the question 'How do you know this is not X?' by saying 'I don't know how, I just do'. *Why* instead do they respond by inventing fictitious differences between the 'stranger' and the replaced person?

This kind of response from delusional patients when asked questions of the form 'What makes you believe that?' is by no means confined to Capgras delusion. There are many examples of the same kind of thing with other forms of delusion. Indeed, there are even examples where delusional patients are specifically provided with evidence that clearly indicates the falsity of the delusional belief. A rational response here would be to abandon the delusional belief, or at the very least to acknowledge the inconsistency between it and the evidence just provided. Delusional patients typically don't do that; they instead make attempts, sometimes absurd ones, to explain away the evidence offered as a challenge to their delusional belief. Some examples are as follows:

Patient JK suffered from Cotard delusion. People with that delusion believe that they are dead, and she expressed that belief. Young and Leafhead (1996, p. 158) report the following conversation with her:

> We asked her during the period in which she claimed to be dead whether she could feel her heart beat, whether she could feel hot or cold and whether she could feel whether her bladder was full. JK said that, since she had such feelings even though she was dead, they clearly did not represent evidence that she was alive.

> (Young and Leafhead, 1996, p. 158)

An elderly in-patient lady with anosognosia for hemiplegia after a large right hemisphere stroke when being interviewed by one of us mentioned that her husband was a patient in the hospital too (though in fact he had died some years previously, and she had previously provided a detailed and accurate account of the circumstances of his death).

> Examiner: 'But didn't you tell me that he had died a while ago at home, in the lavatory one Sunday afternoon?'
>
> Patient: 'Yes'.
>
> Examiner: [looks at the patient with a puzzled expression]
>
> The patient shrugs and says 'Well, I'm not religious'.

In sum, then, it has frequently been reported that when patients are asked to explain what evidence they have for a false delusional belief, they will offer such evidence, no matter how skimpy or fictitious this 'evidence' is, and when they are provided with evidence that suggests that the belief they hold is false, they will discount it or seek to explain it away.

Amnesia

Next, we invite the reader to consider the following examples, all of which are from patients whose disorder was amnesia and not delusion.

An amnesic patient who had been married for 30 years and had four adult children was asked 'How long have you been married?' and responded 'Four months' (Moscovitch, 1999).

An amnesic patient who had been admitted to hospital because of a rupture of the anterior communicating artery was asked 'Why are you in hospital?' The answer provided was 'Because I was bitten by a rabbit' (M. Turner, patient GN).

A sufferer from Korsakoff's syndrome, who had been a businessman but was currently not employed, when asked what he had done that morning said 'I went to a business meeting' (Hirstein, 2005, p. 196).

A patient with profound amnesia after a head injury, when asked what he had eaten for lunch that day, said 'A couple of sandwiches, potato chips, and an apple' (Demery, Hanlon and Bauer, 2008, p. 296), a response which was completely incorrect, even though contextually appropriate.

Why do amnesic patients respond in this way when asked for memories which they cannot produce because of their amnesia? The patients could, after all, respond to such questions simply by saying 'I don't know' or 'I can't remember'. Instead, they respond by producing *false memories* about their past lives. These examples from amnesic patients seem to us closely analogous to the examples we have quoted from cases of people with delusions. Deluded people cannot give true answers to the question 'Why do you believe that?' because they don't know what has caused them to hold the delusional belief; nevertheless, they will offer answers to the question, rather than saying 'I don't know'. Amnesic patients cannot give true answers to questions about their pasts because of their amnesia; nevertheless, they will offer answers to such questions, rather than saying 'I don't know'.

Thus, the two types of patient have in common that they do not produce 'I don't know' responses when they should. Of course, what they *do* produce is very different. The deluded patients produce rationalizations; the amnesic patients produce false memories.

The split brain

Gazzaniga and LeDoux (1978, p. 148–149) described some behavior of the split-brain patient PS thus:

> When a snow scene was presented to the right hemisphere and a chicken claw was presented to the left, PS quickly and dutifully responded correctly by choosing a picture of a chicken from a series of four cards with his right hand and a picture of a shovel from a series of four cards with his left hand. The subject was then asked 'What did you see?' 'I saw a claw and I picked the chicken, and you have to clean out the chicken shed with a shovel'.

In trial after trial, we saw this kind of response. The left hemisphere could easily and accurately identify why it had picked the answer, and then subsequently, and without batting an eye, it would incorporate the right hemisphere's response into the framework. While we knew exactly why the right hemisphere had made its choice, the left hemisphere could merely guess. Yet, the left did not offer its suggestion in a guessing vein but rather as a statement of fact as to why that card had been picked.

(Gazzaniga and LeDoux, 1978, p. 148–149)

Split-brain patients cannot give true spoken answers to questions about why their left hand acted as it did because the hemisphere responsible for speech does not have access to the hemisphere that generates actions of the left hand; nevertheless, they will offer answers to such questions, rather than saying 'I don't know'.

Hypnosis

One can hypnotize people and suggest to them that, after they have been brought out of the hypnotic state, when they observe the hypnotist perform action A (e.g. saying 'Well, what did you think of that?'), they will perform action B (e.g. putting their hands behind their head). This is known as a post-hypnotic suggestion because it is a suggestion given during hypnosis about something that will happen after the hypnosis. Such experiments have been reported by Barnier and McConkey (1995). A second posthypnotic suggestion can be given during the hypnosis: that after having been brought out of the hypnotic state the hypnotized person will not remember being given the suggestion about actions A and B.

Then, after the person is brought out of hypnosis, during casual conversation the hypnotist says to subjects 'Well, what did you think of that?', and the subjects will put their hands behind their heads. Now the hypnotist can ask the subject: 'I noticed that you just put your hands behind your head. Why did you do that?' What will the subject say?

As far as we know, there is no hypnosis work of this kind in which just this kind of challenge has been employed. Relevant, though, is some work on hypnotically induced deafness. Zimbardo et al. (1981) hypnotized subjects and suggested to them that their hearing was poor. They were also given a posthypnotic amnesia suggestion: when they had been brought out of hypnosis they would not remember the deafness suggestion. Posthypnosis, they were exposed to a conversation between others, to which they listened. They reported that this conversation was hard to hear. After they had listened to this conversation, they were administered a questionnaire and an interview assessing paranoia, on which they scored more highly than control groups. This result is consistent with the idea that the experimental subjects attributed their experienced difficulties in hearing the conversation to malicious intent of the conversants, not to their own hardness of hearing. This rather implies that if these subjects had been asked 'Why was it that you found the conversation hard to hear?' they would produced answers attributing this difficulty to the speakers – answer such as 'They were speaking very quietly, they were whispering'.

So, though not quite the right kind of work has yet been done here, we believe that such work will yield another example of the general scenario we are considering here. These hypnotized subjects do not know why they are having the experience of finding it difficult to hear a conversation, so they cannot give true answers when asked why this is so. Nevertheless (we believe), if they are asked this question they will offer answers, rather than saying 'I don't know'.

Forcing people to explain their behaviors

An experiment by Wilson and Nisbett (1978) took place in a bargain store in a shopping mall. Each of 52 subjects was asked to choose which of four stockings hanging on a rack they thought was the best quality. The four stockings were identical. After subjects chose one of the four stockings, they were asked 'Could you tell me why you chose that one?'

A total of 80 different reasons for choice was proffered by the subjects. Most concerned the superior knit, weave, sheerness, elasticity or workmanship possessed by the chosen stocking in comparison with the other three. None of these variables could have been responsible for the choice, of course, since the four stockings were identical with respect to all five of these variables.

What *did* exert some control over stocking choice was position on the rack. The probability of choice as a function of position from left to right was 12%, 17%, 31%, and 40% ($p < 0.025$). But when subjects were explicitly asked whether position might have influenced their choice, 98% said this was not the case. Only 1 of the 52 subjects even mentioned position as a factor that might have affected her choice (though in fact she did not choose the stockings in the most commonly chosen position, the rightmost: she chose the second from the left), explaining that she had just been hearing about order effects in the psychology classes she was taking at the time.

Whatever the true reason for any subject's choice on any trial in this experiment, it was not to do with intrinsic properties of the four stockings presented, since the four were identical. Perhaps the subjects were truly guessing; perhaps some choices were controlled by position. But the subjects seemed not to know any of this since those were not the explanations for their choices that they came up with. Yet though they did not know the answer to the question 'Why did you choose this stocking?', they did provide answers, rather than saying 'I don't know'.

What do these five examples have in common?

In all five examples, people are asked questions the answers to which they do not know or cannot access. The scenarios, however, differ greatly with respect to why these answers cannot be accessed.

Capgras and other delusion: the true answer to the question of why the patient has the delusional belief is that specific forms of brain damage are present which suggest the belief and which prevent it from being rejected. But the patients do not know that they are suffering from such damage and even if they did they would not know why such damage would have the specific effect of generating a delusional belief. That is why they don't know the true answer to the question 'Why do you believe that?'

Amnesia: the reason that the true answers to the questions about past life events are not known to the amnesic patients is simply because these facts are not present in, or not retrievable from, the patients' memories.

Split brain: the right hemisphere knows the true answers to questions about the causes of left-hand actions, but the left hemisphere does not; and it is the left hemisphere that understands the question and would produce the answer if the answer were known to it.

Hypnosis: the true answer to questions about why the posthypnotically suggested action was carried out or why it was posthypnotically difficult to hear conversations is not accessible to the subjects because of the posthypnotic suggestion of amnesia for the hypnotic suggestions.

Explanation for choice behavior: assuming that there are no uncaused actions, each subjects' choice on each trial must have had a cause. Whatever these causes were, however, the subjects don't know them or don't have conscious access to them since if they did they would produce them when asked. They do not, producing instead putative causes which could not have been the causes of their actions.

Thus, the reason why people do not know or cannot access the answers to the relevant questions is not at all the same in these five scenarios. But what is common to all five scenarios is that not knowing, or being able to access, the answers to questions does not prevent people from offering answers to them rather than simply replying 'I don't know'.

Given that this behavior arises consistently across what is a highly diverse set of scenarios, the behavior would seem theoretically interesting and deserving of attempts to explain it. A term to describe the behavior is also needed. It might be called 'rationalization'. We'd like to call it 'confabulation'.

Within the literature on amnesia, the term 'confabulation' is frequently defined in a way that disallows its use in the other four situations described here. A definition that is widely cited and widely accepted within the amnesia literature is that of Berlyne (1972, p. 31), who defined confabulation as 'a falsification of memory occurring in clear consciousness in association with an organically derived amnesia'. Adherence to that definition rules out the use of the term in the delusional, hypnosis, split-brain, and stocking-choice examples.

On the other hand, rather more general usages of the term 'confabulation' are present in the literatures under conditions other than amnesia, usages that allow the term to be used in all five of the scenarios we have been discussing. For example, 'many of the patient's responses can only be described as confabulatory i.e. they are attempts to fill gaps in the information available to his speech area; phrased in more conventional terms they are attempts to explain what the patient cannot understand' (Geschwind, 1965, p. 590, referring to a patient with a disconnection between the left-hemisphere speech areas and the right hemisphere, not a patient with amnesia); Hirstein (2005) uses the term 'confabulation' when discussing patients who are delusional and not amnesic.

It seems to us that there is clearly a common theme to the five examples we have given, So we'd like to say that what's occurring in all five situations is that the persons concerned are confabulating. Our definition of the term 'confabulation' is thus as follows. When a person does not know or does not have access to the answer to a question addressed to that person (typically the question might be a request for explanation of why the person behaved in a certain way, or else a question asking why the person holds a particular belief), but when asked the question responds by offering an answer to it rather than saying 'I don't know', and if this is done with no intention to deceive the questioner, then that response counts as a confabulation.

Categories of confabulation

Within the literature on amnesia, though not outside it, a number of dichotomies of confabulation have been proposed. Perhaps the most significant of these is the distinction between spontaneous and provoked confabulations.

Spontaneous confabulations are 'untrue, sometimes bizarre statements that are readily evident in the patient's everyday conversation, which express false beliefs that they sometimes act on' (Zannino et al., 2008, p. 832). An example of a spontaneous confabulation is given by Stuss et al. (1978, p. 1168): 'During an early interview, he stood up without warning, walked to a window, gazed out on the surrounding buildings, returned to his seat and informed the examiner that his (the examiner's) boat had been stolen'.

Provoked confabulations are answers to questions to which the patient cannot give the correct answer because of his amnesia: all of the examples given above under the heading *Amnesia* are example of provoked confabulations.

Zannino et al. (2008, p. 832) express doubts about whether provoked and spontaneous confabulations are sufficiently similar for both to be called 'confabulations'. It is indeed hard to see what similarity there is between asking a patient what he did that morning and getting the response 'I went to a business meeting' when that was not so ('provoked confabulation') and the example of 'spontaneous confabulation' quoted above from Stuss et al. (1978). Unless one is unwilling to distinguish between confabulation and delusion, surely what we have in the Stuss et al. example is a delusional belief, not a confabulation? And the definition of spontaneous confabulation offered by Zannino et al. (2008) (see above) is identical to many definitions of delusion.

According to the definition of confabulation we are proposing, then, the kinds of behavior referred to in the amnesia literature as 'spontaneous confabulations' don't count as examples of confabulation; instead, for us they count as examples of delusional beliefs. In other words, our use of 'confabulation' corresponds to what is called 'provoked confabulation' in the amnesia literature.

A second distinction made in the amnesia literature is the distinction between primary and secondary confabulation proposed by Moscovitch (1989). Secondary confabulations are 'attempts to rationalize statements that the patient has already made' (Fireman et al., 2003, p. 73). Confabulators 'generally seem untroubled by the absence of causal coherence in their narratives; however, if their attention is called to their errors, they may engage in secondary confabulations in an attempt to restore this missing causal structure. Thus they may still be able to weave together a possible (if implausible and inaccurate) story from the discontinuous memories they have retrieved' (Fireman et al., 2003, p. 74). Similarly, 'When faced with the unrealistic content of his/her stories, the patient is surprised, struggles, and tries to make an acceptable explanation. While doing this they can use additional fabrications, which some authors refer to as secondary confabulation (Moscovitch, 1989). Patients do not intentionally mislead their doctors when telling these stories, do not have a gain by doing so[1], and are not consciously aware of what they are doing' (Gündoğar and Demirci, 2007, p. 3).

---

[1] The assumption that the patient has nothing to gain here is questionable. Might not the patients be seeking to conceal, from their doctors or even from themselves, the embarrassing or distressing fact that their memories are seriously defective?

How does this distinction between primary and secondary confabulation relate to the definition of confabulation that we adopt in this chapter? An example will help here. Mattioli et al. (1999, p. 417) report the following conversation with the profoundly amnesic patient AZ: '"What did you do yesterday?" "Yesterday I went to my office and then started a project of a new machine. In the afternoon I took a swim in the lake". It should be noted that it was January and AZ had not resumed work after the accident. Confronted with these objections he replied, "I still work, although I am sometimes a little tired", and "but this is an especially mild January"'.

As the terms are used in the amnesia literature, we have here two primary confabulations (the patient's reports about having gone to the office yesterday and about having swum in the lake later in the day) each being a response to a specific question probing memory. And we have two secondary confabulations (the patient's claims about still being employed and about the mildness of January), each a response to a challenge to one of the primary confabulations.

These two types of response do seem quite different. For example, one type (the secondary confabulation) is a response to a challenge to statements by the patient, and the other (the primary confabulation) is not. So this is a distinction one would not want to surrender. How, then, is it to be made if one uses the definition of confabulation we are adopting in this chapter?

In both the primary-confabulation and the secondary-confabulation examples here, the amnesic patient does not know or does not have access to the answer to questions addressed to him, but nevertheless responds by offering an answer to the question rather than saying 'I don't know', and apparently with no intention to deceive the questioner. So, both the primary confabulations and the secondary confabulations here count as confabulations by our definition.

Given this, and given that the distinction between primary and secondary confabulation as it is used in the amnesia literature does seem to refer to two genuinely different phenomena, we would like adopt this distinction as part of our conception of what confabulation is.

This immediately raises the question of how this primary/secondary distinction might apply outside the domain of amnesia. We accept the definition of secondary confabulations as responses by a person to challenges from others to statements made by that person. Given that, consider all the quotations from deluded people in the *Delusions* section above. We offered all of these as examples of confabulation: but are they primary or secondary confabulations? They must all be classified as secondary confabulations because all are responses to challenges to statements that the deluded person has made. In that case, what would count as a primary confabulation in a case of delusional belief? Do primary confabulations occur in cases of delusion? Do they occur in the other three scenarios we have discussed (split brain, hypnosis, stocking choice)?

We have reached the conclusion that the answer to this question is No. Every example of confabulation we gave earlier for all of the scenarios except amnesia consists of persons offering (unjustifiable) defenses to (justified) challenges to (unjustified) statements that they had previously made. So for all four of these scenarios, none of the confabulations that we mentioned were primary confabulations. However, that does not mean that we believe that primary confabulation occurs only in people suffering from amnesia (we return to this point below).

We elaborate the definition of confabulation we gave earlier by offering the following definitions of 'primary confabulation' and 'secondary confabulation'.

Primary confabulation: When a person does not know or does not have access in memory to the answer to a question addressed to that person, but when asked the question responds by offering an answer to it, rather than saying 'I don't know', and if this is done with no intention to deceive the questioner, then that response counts as a primary confabulation.

Secondary confabulation: When a person has made a statement whose truth cannot be adequately justified by appeal to facts or argument, and an interlocutor has challenged that statement by, for example, asking for it to be justified (when it cannot be) or offering something as evidence against it which is strong evidence, a response which offers patently inadequate justification, or which represents a patently unjustifiable refusal to accept the counter-evidence, counts as a secondary confabulation. It is secondary to whatever it is that caused the initial generation of the unjustifiable statement.

Why do people confabulate?

Nisbett and Schacter (1966) requested subjects (college undergraduates) to take a series of shocks of increasing intensity. Some had been given a placebo pill which they were told would produce heart palpitations, breathing irregularities, hand tremor, and butterflies in the stomach (which are in fact the physical symptoms evoked by electric shock). The subjects in the with-pill condition were willing to tolerate four times as much amperage as the nonpill subjects. The with-pill subjects were then asked 'I noticed that you took more shock than average. Why do you suppose you did?' We know the answer, of course: it was because of the pill – the responses to the shocks were being wrongly attributed to the pill. But 9 of the 12 subjects did not mention the pill in their answers. That presumably means that they did not know the answer to the question. And yet they did offer answers. 'Gee, I don't really know . . . well, I used to build radios and stuff when I was 13 or 14, and maybe I got used to electric shock' was what one subject said. These answers were primary confabulations, according to the definition of primary confabulation given above.

It must be acknowledged that the one example of an actual response offered by Nisbett and Schacter and cited above has something of the flavor of a speculation, beginning as it does with 'Gee, I don't really know . . .'. One really needs to inspect detailed transcripts of all subjects' answers to the question about why they tolerated higher than average shocks to reach a more than tentative conclusion here concerning whether primary confabulations were really occurring.

The same phenomenon was reported by Storms and Nisbett (1970). Insomniac subjects given a placebo pill which they were told would produce certain symptoms (which were in fact the symptoms of insomnia) got to sleep earlier than did a control group of insomniac subjects not given this placebo treatment (presumably because the former group attributed the symptoms to the effects of the pill and not to insomnia). But when the earlier getting-to-sleep was reported to the with-pill subjects and they were asked why this happened to them, they typically did not mention the pill; instead 'they typically replied that they usually found it easier to get to sleep later in the week, or that they had taken an exam that had worried them but had done well and could now relax, or that problems with a roommate or girlfriend seemed on their way to a resolution' (Nisbett and Wilson, 1977, p. 238). Again, these replies satisfy our definition of primary confabulation.

We can see no difference between what these college undergraduates did when asked to explain why their shock tolerances were unexpectedly high or why they got to sleep unexpectedly early, and what amnesic patients do when their primary confabulations are challenged, or what Capgras patients do when asked to explain why they believe that a person they are looking at is not their spouse but some stranger (or other delusional patients do when asked to justify their beliefs). The appropriate answer in all these cases is to say 'I don't know' and stop there. At least some college students and at least some brain-damaged patients eschew this answer, and instead offer a variety of answers that have no justification.

Where do these answers come from, if they are not correct reports of introspections? Nisbett and Wilson argue that

> 'It seems likely, in fact, that the subjects in the present studies, and ordinary people in their daily lives, do not even attempt to interrogate their memories about their cognitive processes when they are asked questions about them'.
>
> (Nisbett and Wilson, 1977, p. 249)

So they then pose the following question:

> 'while people usually appear stumped when asked about perceptual or memorial[2] processes, they are quite fluent about why they behaved as they did in some social

---

[2] The example they give here: 'If a person is asked "What is your mother's middle name?" the answer appears swiftly in consciousness. Then if the person is asked "How did you come up with that?", he is usually reduced to the inarticulate answer, "I don't know, it just came to me".' (Nisbett and Wilson, 1977, p. 232).

situation or why they like or dislike an object or another person. It would seem to be incumbent on one who takes a position that denies the possibility of introspective access to higher order processes to account for these reports by specifying their source. If it is not direct introspective access to a memory of the processes involved, what is the source of such verbal reports?'

(Nisbett and Wilson, 1977, p. 232)

And the answer to this question that they propose (Nisbett and Wilson, 1977, p. 248) is that 'When people are asked to report how a particular stimulus influenced a particular response, they do so not by consulting a memory of the mediating process, but by applying or generating causal theories about the effects of that type of stimulus on that type of response. They simply make judgments, in other words, about how plausible it is that the stimulus would have influenced the response. These plausibility judgments exist prior to, or at least independently of, any actual contact with the particular stimulus embedded in a particular complex stimulus configuration'. Specifically, 'If the stimulus psychologically implies the response in some way (Abelson, 1968) or seems "representative" of the sorts of stimuli that influence the response in question (Tversky and Kahneman, 1974), the stimulus is reported to have influenced the response' (Nisbett and Wilson, 1977, p. 233).

Stimulus dimensions highly representative for judging whether a person you are with is someone you know obviously include eye color, physique, willingness to kiss you, hair color, dental configuration, chirpiness of vocal communication – even style of shoelace-tying. All of those are dimensions reported by Capgras patients as having influenced their decisions that the person they were with was a stranger (even though the person was their spouse).

It is important to note here that there are two aspects to the Nisbett–Wilson account. The first is their view that subjects frequently don't know what caused them to behave in a certain way, e.g. to tolerate high levels of shock. Even the 3 subjects out of 12 who mentioned the pill might have had no more justification for offering this explanation than the subject who offered the radio-building explanation. All these subjects are casting around for explanations that are plausible, and three of them might by chance have chosen one that was actually true. But if that were all there was to the Nisbett–Wilson account, then confabulation would not be Moscovitch's 'honest lying' because confabulators would know that they didn't know the answer to the question they are being asked, and so any answer other than 'I don't know' would not be honest. The second aspect of the Nisbett–Wilson account is crucial here. It is that on their view not only do subjects frequently not know what caused them to behave in a certain way, but that also the subjects don't know that they don't know, and it is for this reason that they accept as true the accounts they come up with. So for this reason, the shocking and stocking subjects are not being dishonest.

For the same reason, neuropsychological patients who confabulate are not being dishonest.

We believe, then, that when we see confabulations occurring in people with delusional beliefs, amnesia, or callosal sections, the brain damage is not the cause – at least not the direct cause – of the confabulation. The normal response of human beings, when put into the situation of being asked for explanations of their behavior where they don't know what the explanation is and don't know that they don't know this, is to confabulate. Brain damage can put people into this situation. But so can hypnosis. And so can cognitive psychologists carrying out experiments such as those of Nisbett and his colleagues.

We are left wondering, though, why it is that only some amnesic patients produce primary confabulations when their memories are probed; other amnesic patients will say they don't know that answer to the probe question. What distinguishes those patients who produce primary confabulations from those who do not? And does the same question arise regarding the work by Nisbett and colleagues we discussed earlier, with college-student subjects: are there some who respond 'I don't know' to the same questioning that evokes secondary confabulations in others?

Acknowledgements

We thank Amanda Barnier. Emily Connaughton, Michael Connors, Rochelle Cox, William Hirstein, Robyn Langdon, Ryan McKay, Vince Polito, and Nerolie Wise for their criticisms of earlier drafts.

References

Abelson, R.P. (1968). Psychological implication. In *Theories of Cognitive Consistency: A Sourcebook* (eds. R.P. Abelson et al.). Chicago, Rand McNally.

Barnier, A.J. and McConkey, K.M. (1995). An experiential analysis of conflict resolution in hypnosis. In *Contemporary International Hypnosis* (eds. G.D. Burrows and R.O. Stanley), pp. 89–96. London, Wiley Publications.

Berlyne, N. (1972). Confabulation. *British Journal of Psychiatry,* **120**, 31–39.

Coltheart, M. (2007). The 33rd Bartlett lecture: Cognitive neuropsychiatry and delusional belief. *Quarterly Journal of Experimental Psychology,* **60**, 1041–1062.

Demery, J.A., Hanlon, R.E., and Bauer, R.M. (2008). Profound amnesia and confabulation following brain injury. *Neurocase,* **7**, 295–302.

Edelstyn, N.M.J., and Oyebode, F. (1999). A review of the phenomenology and cognitive neuropsychological origins of the Capgras syndrome. *International Journal of Geriatric Psychiatry,* **14**, 48–59.

Fireman, G.D., McVay, T.E., and Flanagan, O.J. (2003). *Narrative and Consciousness: Literature, Psychology and the Brain.* Oxford, Oxford University Press.

Forstl, H., Almeida, O.P., Owen, A.M., Burns, A., and Howard, R. (1991). Psychiatric, neurological and medical aspects of misidentification syndromes: A review of 260 cases. *Psychological Medicine,* **21**, 905–910.

Frazer, S.J. and Roberts, J.M. (1994). Three cases of Capgras' syndrome. *British Journal of Psychiatry,***164**, 557–559.

Gazzaniga, M.S. and LeDoux, J.E. (1978). *The Integrated Mind.* NY, Plenum Press.

Geschwind, N. (1965). Disconnexion syndromes in animals and man. *Brain,* **88**, 237–644.

Gündoğar, D. and Demirci, S. (2007). Confabulation: A symptom which is intriguing but not adequately known. *Turkish Journal of Psychiatry,* **18**, 172–178.

Hirstein, W. (2005). *Brain Fiction: Self-Deception and the Riddle of Confabulation.* Cambridge, MA. MIT Press.

Lewis, M.B., Sherwood, S., Moselhy, H.F., and Ellis, H.D. (2001). Autonomic responses to familiar faces without autonomic responses to familiar voices: Evidence for voice-specific Capgras delusion. *Cognitive Neuropsychiatry,* **6**, 217–228.

Mattioli, F., Miozzo, A., and Vignolo, L.A. (1999). Confabulation and delusional misidentification: A four year follow-up study. *Cortex,* **35**, 413–422.

Moscovitch, M. (1989). Confabulation and the frontal systems: Strategic versus associative retrieval in neuropsychological theories of memory. *Varieties of Memory and Consciousness: Essays in Honour of Endel Tulving* (eds Roediger, H.L. and Craik, F.I.M). Hillside, NJ, Lawrence Erlbaum Associates. pp. 133–160.

Nisbett, R.E. and Schachter, S. (1966). Cognitive manipulation of pain. *Journal of Experimental Social Psychology,* **2**, 227–236.

Nisbett, R.E. and Wilson, T.D. (1977). Telling more than we can know: Verbal reports on mental processes. *Psychological Review,* **84**, 231–259.

Storms, M.D. and Nisbett, R.E. (1970). Insomnia and the attribution process. *Journal of Personality and Social Psychology,* **2**, 319–328.

Stuss, D.T., Alexander, M.P., Lieberman, A., and Levine, H. (1978). An extraordinary form of confabulation. *Neurology,* **28**, 1166–1172.

Todd, J., Dewhurst, K., and Wallis, G. (1981). The syndrome of Capgras. *British Journal of Psychiatry,* **139**, 319–327.

Tversky, A. and Kahncman, D. (1974). Judgment under uncertainty: Heuristics and biases. *Science,* **184**, 1124–1131.

Wilson, T. de C. and Nisbett, R.E. (1978). The accuracy of verbal reports about the effects of stimuli on evaluations and behavior. *Social Psychology,* **41**, 118–131.

Young, A.W. and Leafhead, K.M. (1996). Betwixt life and death: Case studies of the Cotard delusion. In *Method in Madness: Case Studies in Cognitive Neuropsychiatry* (eds. Halligan, P.W. and Marshall, J.C.). Hove, UK. Psychology Press.

Zannino, G.D., Barban, F., Caltagirone, C., and Carlesimo, G.A. (2008). Do confabulators really try to remember when they confabulate? A case report. *Cognitive Neuropsychology,* **25**, 831–852.

Zimbardo, P.G. and Anderson, S.M. (1981). Induced hearing deficit generates experimental paranoia. *Science,* **212**, 1529–1531.

Chapter 9

Anosognosia for hemiplegia: A confabulatory state

Kenneth M. Heilman

The *Merriam-Webster* dictionary defines confabulation as 'to fill in gaps in memory…'. This definition might suggest that confabulation is an intentional behavior that is meant to deceive. In this review I will provide evidence that in many brain-damaged people confabulation is induced by retrieval failures as well as unawareness of their disabilities and in these patients confabulation is not intentional or a motivated attempt to deceive.

One of the most dramatic forms of confabulation is anosognosia. In spite of having a profound neurological deficit, patients with this disorder tell the examiner that they have no problems. In addition, when patients with anosognosia are asked questions about their abilities and disabilities their answers might be confabulatory. This essay will explore why patients with hemispheric dysfunction might be unaware of their disabilities such as weakness and confabulate.

Anosognosia for hemiplegia: definition

Patients with a severe hemiplegia from large cerebral lesions may be unaware of their profound weakness. Thus, when they are asked why they came to the hospital they might tell the examiner that it was for some other reason. When asked if they are weak in any part of their body they will often tell the examiner that they are not weak. If they are asked whether they can perform certain functions that depend upon normal strength of their contralesional limbs they will tell the examiner that they would have no trouble performing these functions. They even also tend to select tasks that would require that both hands be used (Ramachandran and Rogers-Ramachandran, 1996). Babinski (1914) called this lack of knowledge or awareness 'anosognosia'. This term derives from three morphemes a = without, noso = disease, and gnosis which means knowledge. In this chapter we will review some of the major theories that have been proposed to explain anosognosia for hemiplegia. We will also discuss some of the studies that appear to either support or refute these theories.

Psychological denial

Weinstein and Kahn (1955) in their book, *Denial of Illness*, suggested that patients with diseases that induced severe disabilities, such as hemiplegia, fail to admit their illness because their denial is a psychological defense mechanism which helps them reduce or attenuate the distress of this catastrophic event. To test this denial hypothesis, Weinstein and Kahn attempted to assess the pre-morbid personality of those individuals who demonstrated anosognosia for hemiplegia. They found that the patients who demonstrated anosognosia during their current illness were more likely to use this denial coping strategy before their current illness.

There is little question that recognizing that you have a devastating illness can cause severe anxiety and depression. To help avoid these psychologically painful conditions people often convince themselves that they are well or have some other less serious condition. Hence, psychological denial might help account for some of the patients' denial of hemiplegia. However, there are some factors that the denial theory cannot explain. For example, anosognosia for hemiplegia is associated more often with right than left hemisphere.

Strokes The psychological denial theory, however, cannot account for this asymmetry. However, according to Babinski's definition the unawareness or denial of hemiplegia had to be verbally explicit and many patients with left hemisphere disease are aphasic and, therefore, cannot explicitly verbally deny their hemiplegia.

The coping strategies that a person uses throughout their life should not be influenced by the side of the brain that is damaged by a stroke. Thus, if anosognosia of hemiplegia is found to be more frequently associated with right than left hemisphere dysfunction and this asymmetrical prevalence is not an artifact induced by the more frequent association of aphasia with left than right hemisphere dysfunction, this finding would not be compatible with the psychological denial hypothesis.

To test the hemispheric laterality hypothesis of anosognosia we studied patients who were undergoing selective hemispheric anesthesia in preparation for epilepsy surgery (the Wada procedure). During left hemisphere anesthesia, patients who are left-hemisphere dominant for language are often unable to communicate and thus we waited for our subjects to recover from both the left and right hemispheric anesthesia before we assessed them for anosognosia by asking them if their arm was weak (Gilmore et al., 1992). We found that after recovery of speech following the left-sided injection, most patients reported having right arm weakness. In contrast after right hemisphere anesthesia, most of these same people were unaware that they were weak on their left side.

During this Wada procedure, none of our patients lost consciousness when either hemisphere was put to sleep and at the time they were questioned, none of the patients were confused. Whereas Dywan (1995) did not replicate our findings, the reason for these different results have not been determined, but several other investigators including Carpenter et al. (1995) and Durkin et al. (1994) did replicate our findings.

In our study, first we anesthetized one hemisphere (e.g. the right) and after the recovery of this hemisphere from anesthesia we then anesthetized the other (e.g. left) hemisphere of the same participants. Most of these patients showed anosognosia with right but not left hemisphere anesthesia. Therefore, pre-morbid personality differences could not account for the asymmetries we found. By the time patients were asked questions about their hemiplegia, they were no longer hemiplegic and therefore, there was no reason for these sub-jects to have psychologically motivated denial as suggested by Weinstein and Kahn (1955). These observations, however, do not preclude the possibility that some patients might use psychological denial as a defense mechanism. In some of our Wada studies, we found that some patients while having left hemi-spheric anesthesia were aphasic and hemiparetic, but would be aware of only one of the deficits and not the other. If these patients were denying their hemi-plegia or aphasia, because of psychologically motivated denial, we would have expected them to deny both symptoms (Breier et al., 1995). The reason why some patients denied hemiplegia but not aphasia or vice versa remains unclear.

Confusional state

Mesulam and his colleagues (1976) demonstrated that acute confusional states can be associated with right parietal lesions, and Hecaen and Albert (1978) sug-gested that anosognosia may be related to confusion. Most of the patients with anosognosia from right hemisphere stroke do not appear to be in a confusional state when tested for memory and language and many patients with anosogno-sia for hemisplegia from stroke complain about other ailments. Thus, a confu-sional state could not fully account for anosognosia of hemiplegia ailments.

Deafferentation: Impaired sensory feedback

In order to know that something is not working a person needs feedback. If someone was driving your car and it broke down, unless that person called, you might not know that your car is broken. Levine and his co-workers (1991) proposed a similar explanation for anosognosia for hemiplegia, namely that patients with anosognosia for hemiplegia may be unaware of their hemiplegia because they do not get sensory feedback that the limb is weak. Patients with large right hemisphere infarctions might have injury to their primary somatosensory cortical areas and their sensory association areas as well as damage to the visual geniculo-calcarine system. However, if a person wanted to accomplish an act that required the use of the left upper limb or both limbs such as buttoning a blouse or shirt and the act could not be performed, that person should be aware that something is wrong. We, however, want to formally test this feedback hypothesis. In order to test this hypothesis we drew numbers on the left hand of our patients who were undergoing Wada testing and when their right hemisphere was anesthetized we moved their left hand into their right visual field. To make certain that they could see their left plegic hand they were asked to name the number written on their hand. After these patients named the number correctly, we asked if their arm and hand were weak. Although we did have some subjects who after seeing their left hand in the right visual field and being asked if that hand was weak, did admit that their hand was weak. Thus, we cannot rule out the possibility that a sensory deficit might have contributed to these subject's unawareness of their weakness, but there are other explanations of this discovery and the majority of patients who could read the number written on their left hand still denied the presence of weakness, suggesting that sensory feedback deficits cannot entirely explain anosognosia.

If patients had a contralesional hemianopia and a hemibody sensory loss, when asked if their arm-hand was weak they could have moved their eyes to the left or even explored their left hand arm with their right arm. The failure to explore the left side of egocentric hemispace is more likely to be associated with neglect than deafferentation. In addition, as will be discussed below in the feed-forward section, in those patients whose anosognosia did abate when their arm was moved to right hemispace, the recognition of their weakness might have been, in part, related to the examiner asking these patients if their hand arm was weak. Finally, in another study we wanted to learn whether during right hemisphere anesthesia, proprioception at the left shoulder, versus the fingers of their left hand, was spared because the shoulder was closer to the midline. We found that while there was a proprioceptive loss of finger movements, the movements of the shoulder joint were correctly perceived by our subjects (Lu et al., 1997a). Before we anesthetize one hemisphere we asked the patients to extend both arms at the shoulder joint. After the barbiturate anesthetic was injected into the carotid artery the arm fell down. Since our subjects were unaware that their left arm was no longer extended at the shoulder, their anosognosia cannot be explained by an isolated proprioceptive deficit.

Hemispatial neglect

In the prior section, we discussed the sensory feedback hypothesis of anosognosia. If someone had a defect limited to proprioception and/or a hemianopia, they might not have anosognosia because they could explore the contralesional side by moving their intact arm or their eyes to the contralesional limb and space. Thus, in the presence of an afferent defect, a failure to detect contralesional upper limb weakness might have to be associated with unawareness of contralesional space or deficits in exploration. If anosognosia or weakness, was at least in part, induced by failure to explore the contralesional hemispace and body, we would expect to see asymmetrical exploratory deficits in patients with hemispheric dysfunction. It has been well established that neglect, like anosognosia for hemisplegia is more commonly associated with right than left hemisphere dysfunction. In addition to having inattention to contralesional (left) hemispace, with patients neglect often have directional (contralesional) and hemispatial (contralesional) exploratory defects (see Heilman et al., 2003 for a review). It is possible that the during Wada testing, the patients who discovered that their hand was weak when it was brought from left to right hemispace, were also suffering from hemispatial neglect. Although we did not test the patients undergoing Wada testing for neglect, many of the patients who have anosognosia from right hemisphere injury also have left unilateral neglect. Thus, the patients who do not recognize their weakness might have neglect or a combination of neglect and deafferentation. However, only a small percentage of subjects undergoing selective right hemispheric anesthesia improved when their arm was moved into right egocentric hemispace. Thus, if hemispatial neglect accounted for these patients' unawareness of hemiplegia, this left-sided hemispatial inattention unawareness (neglect), together with an exploratory defect induced by left hemispatial and directional akinesia, would only explain anosognosia for hemiplegia in a small proportion of subjects.

Asomatognosia

Patients with right hemisphere dysfunction may not only demonstrate hemispatial neglect, but also may demonstrate personal neglect or asomatognosia. The patients who were able to name the number in their hand may have not been able to determine that their hand-arm was weak because they did not recognize that the hand with the number written on it was their own hand. To determine if patients undergoing right hemispheric anesthesia who had anosognosia had personal neglect or asomatognosia and if this disorder was related to their anosognosia, we performed another experiment (Adair et al., 1995). After barbiturate injection into the right carotid and the onset of hemiparesis, the examiner either moved the subject's hand into a restrictive viewing space where the patient could only see his/her own hand or moved the subject's hand to a position that was outside this viewing space where he/she could not see their hand. In this latter condition, however, the examiners placed their own hand into the subject's restricted viewing space. After the patient's hand was placed in the viewing space, the patients were asked if the hand that they are viewing is the examiner's hand or their own hand. While each person's hands are almost as unique as their faces, to help make the task more difficult we selected an examiner who was approximately the same age as the subject, and also the same sex and race.

We found a small group of subjects with anosognosia, associated with right hemisphere anesthesia, who were unable to discriminate between their own and the examiner's hands (Adair et al., 1997). The overwhelming majority of our subjects, however, in spite of being unaware of their hemiparesis, were able to recognize their own, versus the examiner's hands. These results suggest that although there are some subjects whose anosognosia may be related to personal neglect or asomatognosia, these self-recognition disorders cannot entirely account for the presence of anosognosia.

Imagined or phantom movements

People who have lost a part of their body often have the sensation that this body part is still present. When this hallucination is experienced after the loss of limb this phenomenon is called a phantom limb. Some people with phantom limbs also have phantom movements of these limbs. If a patient with a left hemiplegia has phantom movements, it is possible that this person would be unaware of their hemiparesis and confabulate about being able to move his/her paretic limbs. Therefore, we wanted to test the hypothesis that phantom movements could account for anosognosia of hemiplegia (Lu et al., 1997a) and again used the Wada procedure to test this hypothesis. We assessed for the presence of phantom movements by asking our blindfolded patients to attempt to lift their left (paralyzed) upper extremity and then to demonstrate the position of their left arm in relation to their body, by placing their right (un-paralyzed) upper extremity in the same position as their left. To learn if phantom movement was associated with a loss of proprioceptive feedback during right hemisphere anesthesia, we also tested proprioception of this left limb by lifting the paretic arm and having the blindfolded patients demonstrate the position of the left limb by raising their right upper extremity to the same position as the left limb. Using this procedure, we found only one subject with anosognosia who experienced phantom movement. There were other subjects who had phantom movements but these subjects were without anosognosia. The patient with the phantom movement and anosognosia also had impaired proprioception. However, the two other subjects with phantom movements appeared to have normal proprioception suggesting that a loss of position sense is not a necessary condition for experiencing phantom movements. Although our results suggest that phantom movements in the absence of visual and proprioceptive feedback may contribute to anosognosia, this mechanism would appear to play only a minor role.

Confabulatory state

Feinberg and colleagues (1994) wanted to learn if patients with anosognosia have a propensity to confabulate in other domains, a confabulatory state. To learn if patients with anosognosia have a confabulatory state, these investigators studied patients who either had or did not have anosognosia for hemiplegia. In order to assess for the presence of confabulation, they had these subjects attempt to identify rapidly presented stimuli in the ipsilesional and contralesional visual fields. These investigators found that when no stimuli were presented to the contralesional field, the patients with anosognosia were significantly more likely to provide confabulatory responses, by stating that they saw objects in this contralesional (e.g. left) visual field when there was no object present.

To further study the relationship between anosognosia and confabulation, we again studied patients who had intractable epilepsy and were undergoing selective hemispheric anesthesia, the Wada test (Lu et al., 1997b). During hemispheric anesthesia, when these patients had a contralateral hemiparesis we applied one of three different tactile stimuli to our patient's fingertips. During the time when the stimulus was being applied, the subjects were prevented from directly viewing these materials. In some trials, however, no stimuli were applied. After these patients either received or did not receive one of these tactile stimuli they were presented with a response card that contained the three different textured materials including one with which the subjects might have been touched. This response card also had a question mark to indicate if the patient was uncertain whether or not they had been touched. If the subject pointed to a texture when they were not touched, it was considered a confabulatory response. If they pointed to a blank or question mark when touched with the textured material or they pointed to the wrong texture, it was considered a perceptual error. On this test we found no significant relationships between anosognosia and confabulation in the tactile modality. There were subjects who were aware of the hemiparesis, but who provided confabulatory responses and there were other subjects with anosognosia who did not confabulate on this task. It is possible that confabulation might be modality specific and we tested only one modality. Although there were a few subjects who did have both anosognosia and confabulation, the reason these subjects confabulated is not known and their confabulation might have been related to a disconnection that is discussed in the next section.

Disconnection

According to Geschwind's (1965) disconnection hypothesis, lesions of the right hemisphere may not only destroy primary sensory areas as well as sensory association areas and polymodal areas, but these lesions might also injure the neurons that give rise to the association fibers that travel from the cortex of one hemisphere to the cortex of the other hemisphere. Thus, a lesion of the right hemisphere might disconnect association areas in the right hemisphere from the left hemisphere's language-speech centers. According to Geschwind's disconnection hypothesis for anosognosia, right hemisphere lesions disconnect the right hemisphere from the left (verbal) hemisphere. Studies of patients with callosal disconnection have revealed that when stimulation on the left side occurs and when they are asked the nature of this stimulus patients often confabulate a response. Thus, the proprioceptive information from the left arm, which would inform the cortex that the limb is not moving, cannot get access to the verbal left hemisphere. In the absence of this information, the left hemisphere might confabulate a verbal response. This disconnection postulate can also provide an explanation for why anosognosia is more frequently associated with right than left hemisphere lesions. To test the disconnection hypothesis using the Wada technique as mentioned we examined patients undergoing right hemisphere anesthesia by moving their left paretic hand into their right visual field, such that the left hemisphere could be made aware of the left arm. If the mechanism of anosognosia of hemiplegia is that the right hemisphere injury disconnects the left hemisphere from the right, then when the left hemisphere is able to directly view the left hemiplegic extremity, the anosognosia should abate. In our Wada studies, however, with right hemisphere anesthesia we found that only five of fifteen subjects were helped by this maneuver (Adair et al., 1997).

While less common, we have seen patients who with left hemisphere anesthesia developed a right hemiplegia and were unaware that their right arm was weak. An interhemispheric disconnection syndrome cannot account for these observations. In addition, the finding that a few subjects discovered left arm weakness when their left hand was brought into their right body space and visual field might have not been entirely related to this maneuver allowing them to bypass a hemispheric disconnection. As we also discussed, the discovery of weakness, when the arm is moved to the right, might have been related to sensory defects or hemispatial neglect.

Intentional or feed-forward hypothesis

When we tested the sensory-neglect and the disconnection hypotheses, we brought the left hand into the right body space-right and right visual field, but most of the patients who discovered that their left hand-arm was weak only discovered their weakness after they were asked if they could move their left hand and observed that they could not move it. Perhaps in this experiment the critical element in their discovery of left hand weakness was being asked if their hand was weak. It is possible that the patients who had anosognosia during right hemisphere anesthesia did not spontaneously test their left arm's ability to move, but only examined it when asked. This observation might suggest that in some patients' anosognosia for hemiplegia is related to a motor activation or an intentional feed-forward deficit (Heilman, 1991; Heilman et al., 1998).

This feed-forward theory of anosognosia deals with a person's expectations of movement. If a person has no expectation of movement and then does not detect a movement, that person might not learn that they are paralyzed. In order for this feed-forward hypothesis to be able to explain anosognosia for weakness, the brain would need to have a comparator such that when we plan or begin to make a movement we set this comparator. During and after the performance of this movement, sensory (proprioceptive or visual) information (feedback) comes into this comparator. If the feedback does not match the set or expectations, the subject is alerted that there might have been a performance failure. In the absence of anosognosia, when a patient is weak, this reduced ability to move a limb is detected when there is a mismatch between the expected of movement and the perception of movement. If, however, there is no expectancy, then there might be no detection and hence anosognosia for hemiplegia.

We often see patients with right hemisphere damage who have action-intentional deficits. These patients demonstrate little or no desire or intention to move and thus do not plan or prepare to move. If the patient has no intention to move and does not activate the motor system the person will not move. The loss of an intention to move, with a failure to move is called akinesia. Patients with limb akinesia (motor neglect) might or might not also have motor weakness. In either of these conditions, the person with akinesia will not set their comparator and therefore will not develop the expectation of movement. If there is no expectation of movement and then there is a failure of movement, no mismatch is generated and without this mismatch there is no recognition of disability, or dysfunction.

When a person attempts to perform a very strenuous motor task, even if he/she is primarily using one hand, he/she will activate some of their upper trunk muscles on both sides of the body. Thus, if a patient has anosognosia of hemiplegia when they attempt to make a movement of the paretic extremity he/she might not activate their proximal muscles because they are not attempting to initiate the movement. To test this action-expectancy model, we measured the activation of the pectoralis muscles, using electromyogram (EMG) in brain-damaged and control subjects during the time they squeezed a dynamometer with their right and left hands (Gold et al., 1994). We found that when normal people and patients with a severe left hemiplegia, and even with spatial neglect, but without anosognosia attempt to squeeze a dynamometer, as hard as they possibly can, they contract both pectoralis muscles. When a patient with anosognosia for left hemiplegia squeezed the dynamometer with his normal (ipsilesional) right hand, the pectoralis muscles on the left and right sides contracted. In contrast, when this patient with anosognosia was asked to squeeze with the contralesional paretic hand, there appeared to be little evidence for contraction of either pectoralis muscle. These observations suggest that this patient with anosognosia for hemiplegia did not attempt to initiate a grasping action with his left hand, a loss of motor intention. In the absence of an intention to move, there was no expectancy to move or to receive feedback that the hand moved, and therefore, this patient had no mismatch when there was no movement.

We mentioned that anosognosia is much more commonly observed with right than left hemisphere dysfunction. This feed-forward or motor intention hypothesis of anosognosia can also help us account for the observation that anosognosia for hemiplegia is more frequently associated with right than left hemisphere lesions. Normally warning stimuli can reduce reaction times because they allow the motor system to activate and prepare for the motor system for implementing a movement when the imperative stimulus is observed. To learn whether ther are right versus left hemisphere asymmetries in this motor preparation Heilman and Van Den Abell (1979) presented warning stimuli in either the right (directed to the left hemisphere) or left (directed to the left hemisphere) visual field and had normal subjects perform reaction times with either their right or left hands. We found that warning stimuli directed to the right hemisphere reduced reaction times for both hands, but warning stimuli directed to the left hemisphere primarily reduced the reaction times of the right hand. These results in normal subjects suggest that the right hemisphere's action preparation or intentional systems can help activate motor systems for both the right and left hands, but in contrast the left hemisphere can primarily only prepare the right hand for action. Akinesia, the inability to initiate an action, is a result of the failure to activate the motor system. Based on the results of this Heilman and Van Den Abell's study we would predict that left hemisphere injury may induce a less severe intentional deficit than right hemisphere injury because the right hemisphere can compensate for the left, but not vice versa and this asymmetry might result in a higher frequency of motor intentional deficits with right than left hemisphere damage. To test this postulate, Coslett and co-workers (1989) examined patients who had suffered either right or left hemisphere strokes for the presence of limb akinesia and found that limb akinesia was more often associated with right than left hemisphere lesions. Based on these hemispheric action-intentional asymmetries, a failure of the feed-forward system, described above, should be more commonly associated with right than left hemisphere injury.

Conclusions

Based on the research reviewed here, there does not appear to be a single mechanism that can entirely account for anosognosia for hemiplegia, a condition where patients confabulate that they have no weakness or disability. There is little doubt that for psychological reasons, people do deny disabilities, but this explanation of anosognosia for hemiplegia cannot explain why this disorder is

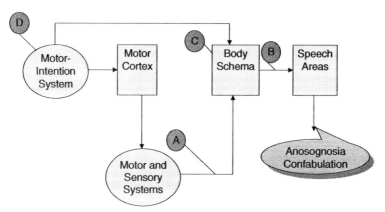

Figure 9.1 Model of system that allows explicit (verbal) awareness of hemiplegia and the possible causes for anosognosia of hemiplegia.

A = feedback anosognosia; B = verbal disconnection anosognosia; C = asomatognosia agnosia; D = action-intentional (feed-forward) anosognosia.

more frequently associated with right than left hemisphere dysfunction and why patients who had selective right hemispheric anesthesia were even unaware of their hemiparesis after it abated. It also cannot explain why patients may be aware of one deficit such as aphasia and unaware of an other deficit such as a hemiparesis. Anosognosia might improve in some, but not all patients when feedback is improved by moving their paretic left hand into right body hemispace and the right visual field. Therefore, those patients who recognized their weakness with this maneuver probably had a failure of feedback from either a sensory defect or hemispatial inattention (sensory neglect) or both. A directional or hemispatial akinesia-induced exploratory defect may also play a role in this feedback anosognosia.

If patients do not recognize that their left arm and hand belongs to them, they certainly will not recognize that they have a deficit in this limb. Therefore, the presence of asomatognosia might be another important factor in the development of anosognosia ('asomatognostic anosognosia'). However, this form of anosognosia appears to be relatively uncommon. When deprived of feedback some patients with a left hemiparesis feel that they are moving their paralyzed arm. However, this phantom movement is only rarely associated with anosognosia. Although right hemisphere dysfunction may induce a confusional state, many patients with anosognosia are without confusion. When the left hemisphere is disconnected from the right, the isolated left hemisphere may confabulate. However, this 'verbal disconnection anosognosia' also appears not to also be a major cause of anosognosia.

Finally, a person must have the intention to move and based on this intention they develop an expectation of movement. When there is a mismatch between the expectation of movement and the feedback that indicates a failure of movement a person is able to discover that they are weak. Thus, some patients may be unaware of their failure to move because they do not try to move ('feedforward or intentional anosognosia').

Based on the studies of anosognosia for hemiplegia reviewed here, it would appear that normal self-awareness depends on several parallel processes. We must have feedback systems that would allow us to monitor our body and we must be able to attend to different parts of space and to our own bodies. We must develop accurate representations of our body and this representation must be continuously modified by both expectations and knowledge of results.

References

Adair, J.C., Na, D.L., Schwartz, R.L., Fennell, E.M., Gilmore, R.L., and Heilman, K.M. (1995). Anosognosia for hemiplegia: Test of the personal neglect hypothesis. *Neurology*, **45**, 2195–2199.

Adair, J.C., Schwartz, R.L., Na, D.L., Fennell, E.M., Gilmore, R.L., and Heilman, K.M. (1997). Anosognosia: Examining the disconnection hypothesis. *Journal of Neurology, Neurosurgery and Psychiatry, 63*, 798–800.

Babinski, J. (1914). Contribution a l=etude des troubles mentaux dans hemiplegie organique cerebrale (anosognosie). *Reviews. Neurology, 27*, 845–847.

Breier, J.I., Adair, J.C., Gold, M., Fennell, E.B., Gilmore, R.L., and Heilman, K.M. (1995). Dissociation of anosognosia for hemiplegia and aphasia during left-hemisphere anesthesia. *Neurology, 45*, 65–67.

Carpenter, K., Berti, A., Oxbury, S., Molyneux, A.J., Bisiach, E., and Oxbury, J.M. (1995). Awareness of and memory for arm weakness during intracarotid sodium amytal testing. *Brain, 118*, 243–251.

Coslett, H.B. and Heilman, K.M. (1989). Hemihypokinesia after right hemisphere strokes. *Brain and Cognition, 9*, 267–278.

Durkin, M.W., Meador, K.J, Nichols, M.E., Lee, G.P., and Loring, D.W. (1994). Anosognosia and the intracarotid amobarbital procedure (Wada test). *Neurology, 44*, 978–979.

Dywan, C.A., McGlone, J., and Fox, A. (1995). Do intracarotid barbiturate injections offer a way to investigate hemispheric models of anosognosia? *Journal of Clinical Experimental Neuropsychology, 17*, 431–438.

Feinberg, T.E., Roane, D.M., Kwan, P.C., Schindler, R.J., and Haber, L.D. (1994). Anosognosia and visuoverbal confabulation. *Archiveof Neurology, 51*, 468–473.

Geschwind, N. (1965). Disconnexion syndromes in animals and man. *Brain, 88*, 237–294, 585–644.

Gilmore, R.L., Heilman, K.M., Schmidt ,R.P., Fennell, E.M., and Quisling, R. (1992). Anosognosia during Wada testing. *Neurology, 42*, 925–927.

Gold, M., Adair, J.C., Jacobs, D.H., and Heilman, K.M. (1994). Anosognosia for hemiplegia: An electrophysiologic investigation of the feed-forward hypothesis. *Neurology, 44*, 1804–1808.

Hecaen, H., and Albert, M. (1978). *Human Neuropsychology*. New York, Wiley.

Heilman, K.M. (1991). Anosognosia: Possible neuropsychological mechanisms. In *Awareness of deficit after brain injury* (ed G.P. Prigatano and D.L. Schacter), pp. 53–62. New York, Oxford University Press.

Heilman, K.M., and Van Den Abell, T. (1979). Right hemispheric dominance for mediating cerebral activation. *Neuropsychologia, 17*, 315–321.

Heilman, K.M., Watson, R.T., and Valenstein, E. (2003). Neglect and related disorders. In *Clinical neuropsychology,* (ed. K.M. Heilman and E. Valenstein), pp. 279–336. New York, Oxford University Press.

Heilman, K.M., Barrett, A.M., and Adair, J.C. (1998). Possible mechanisms of anosognosia: A defect in self-awareness. *Philosophical Transaction of the Royal Society of London Series B, 353*, 1903–1909.

Levine, D.N., Calvanio, R., and Rinn, W.E. (1991). The pathogenesis of anosognosia for hemiplegia. *Neurology, 41*, 1770–1781.

Lu, L., Barrett, A.M., Cibula, J., Gilmore, R.L., and Heilman, K.M. (1997a). Phantom movement during the Wada test. [abstract] *Epilepsia* 38, Suppl. **8**, 156.

Lu, L., Barrett, A.M., Schwartz, R.L., Cibula, J., Gilmore, R.L., and Heilman, K.M. (1997b). Anosognosia and confabulation during the Wada test. *Neurology, 49*, 1316–1322.

Mesulam, M.M., Waxman, S.G., Geschwind, N., and Sabin, T.D. (1976). Acute confusional states with right middle cerebral artery infarctions. *Journal of Neurology, Neurosurgery, Psychiatry,* **39,** 84–89.

Weinstein, E.A., and Kahn, R.L. (1955). *Denial of illness. Symbolic and physiological aspects.* Springfield, IL, Charles C. Thomas.

Chapter 10

Everyday confabulation

Thalia Wheatley

Truth must necessarily be stranger than fiction, for fiction is the creation of the human mind and therefore congenial to it.

G. K. Chesterton

The confabulations of patients read like fiction. Capgras patients claim that loved ones have been replaced by imposters, Anton's syndrome patients are blind but claim to see, and asomatognosic patients claim their paralyzed limbs belong to other people (Hirstein, 2005). The working of healthy brains seems boringly veridical in comparison: what you see is what you get. However, a wealth of evidence suggests that the healthy brain is far from veridical. In its attempt to create a coherent and predictable world, even basic cognitive processes such as perception and memory are actively constructed, manipulated and embellished, often without our awareness. This chapter highlights empirical demonstrations of how the healthy brain fills in gaps, alters perceptions of time and space, and subsequently generates false beliefs for the purpose of creating meaning from confusing and often contradictory inputs. As Chesterton suggests, fiction may be the creation of every *human* mind, not only diseased ones.

Everyday perception

Illusions of distance

The human visual system has the task of representing a three-dimensional world from two-dimensional retinotopic input. To do so, the system must make assumptions: converging lines indicate distance, a dark line is seen as an edge, and so on. Visual illusions are possible because they trick the brain into making these assumptions inappropriately. For example, in the Ponzo illusion, the perceived length of a line will differ by its placement between two converging lines. As converging lines are taken as cues to distance, a line placed closer to the point of convergence will appear longer than a line of equal length placed further from that point (see Figure 10.1).

Presumably, the brain is making the following calculation: if two objects are of the same size on the retina but one is assumed to be further away, the object further away must be bigger in real life. This is the reason why people in the distance are not assumed to be abnormally small and it is codified in Emmert's equation:

$$\textit{Perceived size} = (\textit{size of retinal image}) \times (\textit{perceived distance})$$

Visual illusions such as this demonstrate that basic visual perception relies on assumptions to turn impoverished two-dimensional cues into a three-dimensional model of the world. While such assumptions pale in comparison with confabulations of the diseased mind they demonstrate that, at the lowest levels of cognitive processing, the human brain prioritizes creating a sensible story over a faithful rendition of reality.

Illusions of motion

Cutaneous rabbit. Illusions of apparent motion reveal the extreme lengths to which the brain will take artistic license with sensory input. One such illusion, called the 'cutaneous rabbit', occurs when a person receives a series of five mechanical taps at the wrist then another five at the elbow and then five at the shoulder (Geldard and Sherrick, 1972). Rather than feeling the taps as they occurred, the person has the illusion that the taps were evenly spaced, as if a rabbit was hopping up the arm. The illusory perception of 15 equidistant locations (rather than three discrete ones) is interesting, but what is most

Figure 10.1 Ponzo illusion.

remarkable is that the rabbit appears to start hopping *right away*. This is not possible, of course, because there are five taps at the wrist before the elbow is tapped. As one might guess, when the taps are only given at the wrist, there is no rabbit illusion at all – only the experience of being tapped five times. Thus, the tap at the elbow is necessary for the rabbit to start moving (and know in which direction to move). But this tap doesn't happen until the sixth tap and the rabbit appears to start hopping up the arm four taps earlier. How is this possible? The only solution, barring extrasensory perception, is that conscious experience is delayed relative to unconscious sensation. This temporal buffer allows the brain a window of time to construct the best story and present that story to consciousness. In the case of the cutaneous rabbit, the buffer catches one or more taps at the next location and revises the perceptual story to be one of feeling regularly spaced taps across space and time.

Phi phenomenon. A visual demonstration of this temporal buffer exists in the phi phenomenon. First described by Max Wertheimer in 1912, the phi phenomenon is the experience of seeing illusory motion when still images or lights are presented in succession. That is, if a light is flashed briefly followed by a second light a short distance away, the perception will be of a single light that moved from the first location to the second. When the lights are of different colors, this illusory moving light will appear to change color mid-way between the two lights (Kohlers and vonGrunau, 1976).

Importantly, the viewer's experience is of seeing the motion in real-time. But, as with the cutaneous rabbit, the illusory motion could not be imputed until the second stimulus occurred. That is, the 'moving' light could not know the direction in which to move until the second light flashed. Of course, our conscious experience does not appear to be delayed at all. So, how does the brain accomplish this temporal slight-of-hand? Van der Waals and Roelofs (1931) proposed that the intervening motion is produced retrospectively, only after the second stimulus occurs, and then projected or 'referred' backwards in time. Just as observed in the cutaneous rabbit illusion, visual perception is largely constructive in nature.

Far more than the sum of retinal inputs, human perception uses the temporal buffer to incorporate one's knowledge about the world. For example, even though apparent motion is illusory, the brain requires that the illusion obey the laws of physics. The further the lights are apart, the longer the intervening interval must be for the illusion to occur; giving the 'moving light' an appropriate amount of time to get from point A to point B. Similarly, if a rectangle appears in the middle of the illusory path, the imputed motion will bend around it.

Apparent human motion. Perhaps the most compelling demonstration of the unconscious integration of perceptual knowledge was demonstrated by

Maggie Shiffrar and Jennifer Freyd in their paper 'Apparent Motion of the Human Body' (1990). In this seminal paper, Shiffrar and Freyd presented participants with slide pairs of human poses. In one such pair, the first slide showed a person standing with her legs together while the second slide showed the same person standing with her legs crossed. Showing these pairs in rapid succession produced the standard illusion of movement from the first to the second slide. Interestingly, the kind of movement that was perceived differed depending on how rapidly the slides were presented. With a very short interval between slides (<175 ms), subjects reported that they saw the shortest path of motion. In the leg example, they reported seeing one leg move through the other to get from the standing position (first slide) to the crossed position (second slide). However, when the interval was longer (<175 ms), subjects reported seeing the longer, anatomically correct path of motion: one leg moving around the other to get to the other side. In either time condition, the subjects reported seeing motion that was illusory. In the extra time condition, that illusory motion made anatomical sense. The brain used the additional time to create a better story; producing a more sensible conscious perception.

While it may seem strange that perception takes such artistic license with reality, one must remember that this system was selected under intense evolutionary pressures. Our hominid ancestors needed to make sense of impoverished information and do so quickly and efficiently. This pressure to 'make sense' prioritized the attribution of meaning over accuracy. It is far less costly to mistakenly impute a lion to a flash of yellow and a rustle of grass than process the color and sound veridically and miss the greater implications. Similarly, it is more advantageous to over-attribute connections between temporally close events rather than miss real cause-effect relationships. The priority of making sense over veridical accuracy selected for a perceptual system that takes an active role in imputing meaning to sensory input. As a result, we see things that are not there and rearrange time and space so that what we see conforms to our beliefs and expectations. Of course, our conscious selves are not privy to this manipulation and our perceptions appear as pristine as they are effortless. This assumption that perception is an inviolable given can lead to ill-grounded conclusions.

From false perceptions to false beliefs

Most illusions of distance and motion are such successful resolutions of incomplete information that we do not notice any disconnection with reality. Some sensations, however, are so unusual that our brains cannot resolve them with ease (e.g. out of body experiences (OBE), near death experiences (NDE), and sleep paralysis). In the last 20 years, science has discovered the sensory underpinnings of many of these psychological phenomena. Out of body experiences (OBE) have been associated with paroxysmal activity in the temporal lobe and have been produced empirically via electrical stimulation of the right angular gyrus within this region (Blanke et al., 2002). Sensations associated with a near death experience (NDE) such as floating, tunnel vision, a bright light, and a sense of calm are caused by a reduction of blood flow to the brain (cephalic nervous system ischemia) and have been reported by pilots subjected to extreme gravitational stress (Whinnery, 1997). Sleep paralysis is the lingering of the normal inhibition of the skeletal muscles during REM; the body's safeguard against the acting out of dreams.

These biological explanations have been around for a fraction of the time that people have experienced these phenomena, yet this does not mean that the preceding millenia left people scratching their heads. OBEs and sleep paralysis have been taken as evidence of witchcraft and alien abduction. The tunnel and bright light of NDEs have been assumed to support the existence of an afterlife. Strange percepts experienced by a normal mind are explained away by all manner of unsubstantiated beliefs.

The assumed wisdom of disgust. A recent empirical demonstration of the human need to explain used post-hypnotic suggestion to evoke disgust (Wheatley and Haidt, 2005). To determine hypnotizability, subjects were given abbreviated versions of the Harvard Group Scale of Hypnotic Susceptibility, Form A (Shor and Orne, 1962). This abbreviated version included an eye-closure induction, two hypnotic tests ('your hands are tightly interlocked, locked in place'; 'your hands are moving together'), a post-hypnotic suggestion to touch one's left ankle to a cue given after hypnosis, and an amnesia suggestion that they would not remember anything from the hypnosis session until cued to do so. Subjects were deemed highly hypnotizable if they were susceptible to the hypnotic tests (i.e. could not take their hands apart; moved their hands close together) and performed the post-hypnotic suggestion with amnesia for the true cause. In a subsequent session, these highly hypnotizable subjects were hypnotized to feel a 'pang of disgust' when presented with a neutral word (e.g. 'take'), but told that they would not remember this instruction. After being awakened from the hypnotic state, subjects were asked to rate a series of scenarios as to how disgusting and morally wrong the main action was. For example:

> Congressman Arnold Paxton frequently gives speeches condemning corruption and arguing for campaign finance reform. But he is just trying to cover up the fact that he himself will *take* bribes from the tobacco lobby and other special interests to promote their legislation.

When the hypnotic disgust word was present in the transgression, subjects rated the act as more disgusting and more morally wrong compared to other participants who read the same transgression without their hypnotic word. This was true even when the scenario was entirely neutral as in the case of a student council representative in charge of scheduling faculty–student discussions in which he tries to 'take up' topics that appeal to both professors and students. Subjects who read the neutral scenario with the hypnotic word rated the act as significantly more disgusting and morally repugnant than subjects who read the scenario without their hypnotic word. Some even confabulated reasons to explain why this reaction was legitimate (e.g. 'it just seems like he's up to something' and 'what a popularity-seeking snob').

We assume that what we see and feel is an objective read-out of the world, unvarnished by personal biases, contexts, and assumptions. Our perceptual experience is taken as read and our explanations tailored to fit. As such our explanations are only as good as our perceptions. Psychological evidence suggests that perception is a constructive process that relies upon assumptions. When those assumptions are inappropriate, errors occur. Thus, errors in perception lead to errors of explanation. The constructive nature of memory allows these errors to proliferate and can create additional distortions.

Everyday memory

Though life occurs in the present tense, the present is little more than a fleeting moment. We know ourselves from our memories: from childhood recollections to what we did 5 minutes ago. As the origin of our self-knowledge, we trust our memories and rely on their veracity. As described earlier, however, any reliance on information can lead to confabulation when that information is compromised. Memories are no exception. Though memory distortions differ based on whether and what kind of brain damage exists, all memory confabulations stem from the assumed veracity of the memory to be explained.

Memory distortions of patients can involve a disordered sense of time. Patients with orbitofrontal damage are sometimes unable to recognize the temporal order of stored information such that events that happened hours earlier feel as though they had *just* occurred (Schnider, 2003). Rather than recognize this temporal disorientation, patients confabulate around their deficit, assuming that their memory is the veridical piece to be explained. Patients with déjà vecu have a different temporal distortion: the illusion of having already experienced what is actually a novel event (Moulin et al., 2005). Like orbitofrontal patients, déjà vecu patients assume that their memories are true and fashion confabulations to fit. While the healthy brain does not have marked difficulties of temporal ordering, it is similarly susceptible to the assumption that memories are veridical. This assumption leads to confabulation when healthy individuals are pressed to explain memories of things that never occurred.

The classic false memory paradigm asks participants to memorize a list of words which is then tested by giving participants another set of words containing some of the words from the previous list, along with new words (Deese, 1959; Roediger and McDermott, 1995). The participant's task is to report which words had been previously seen. The typical finding is that participants erroneously recall having seen new words that are high associates of others on the list. For example, the word 'sleep' is likely to be erroneously recalled if semantically related words were memorized (e.g. 'dream', 'pillow'). Importantly, participants not only misremember having seen the semantic associate but also claim high confidence in that memory.

High confidence in false memories may be attributed, in part, to 'imagination inflation' (Garry et al., 1996). In essence, imagining an event leaves its own memory trace. As such, things that were previously imagined (or dreamt) have the potential to be misremembered as having actually occurred. In one empirical demonstration of this effect, participants heard simple action statements (e.g. 'break the toothpick') and sometimes also performed or imagined performing the action (Goff and Roediger, 1998). The more an action was imagined, the more likely it was to be misremembered as having been actually performed.

From false memories to false beliefs

Reporting the word 'sleep' erroneously and misremembering having broken a toothpick may seem innocuous but these findings have alarming real-world implications. Eyewitness testimony exerts a powerful influence in criminal trials yet appears to be just as easily manipulated and revised. Zaragoza and Mitchell (2005) demonstrated that participants' memories of a burglary video were influenced by the manner in which participants were interviewed afterward. For example, participants were asked, 'In the beginning of the scene, a young man dressed in jeans, a t-shirt and gloves entered the house. Did he enter through the door?' Although the burglar did not wear gloves in the video, the suggestion lead to later assertions by participants that they *had* seen the gloves. As in the word list paradigm, participants had the experience of 'remembering' rather than simply guessing or inferring. The illusory recollective experience is taken as evidence of the memory's veracity, not only by the author but also by the justice system writ large.

False memories themselves may not have the story-like quality of confabulation, yet such confabulations occur when people attempt to explain or defend those memories. Elizabeth Loftus has spent a career amassing evidence of how false memories can be embedded by an external source (e.g. experimenter, therapist) and subsequently embellished by the participant until they are strongly believed to be true (Loftus and Ketcham, 1994). This has been achieved in a number of experimental paradigms. In one experiment, parents were asked to remember events from the participant's childhood. Participants were subsequently told three stories ostensibly from their parents' recollections. What participants did not know is that one of the three stories was false. After the first telling of the stories, none of the participants claimed to have remembered the false story. However, when interviewed a couple of weeks later, 20 percent said that they remembered something about the false event (e.g. that a church friend had visited during a (false) emergency hospitalization; Hyman et al., 1995).

The finding that false memories can be implanted externally and then internally embellished has troubling implications for putative repressed memories. Indeed, several million dollar settlements have been awarded to patients who came to believe falsely, through psychotherapy, that they had been abused by family members (Loftus, 1997). One patient developed detailed memories of her father forcing her to use a coat hanger to abort fetuses conceived from repeated incest. Later, medical examinations revealed that she was still a virgin. These 'first-hand' accounts are compelling to the patients themselves as well as to the juries who unwittingly incarcerate innocent people based on this evidence.

Healthy people may not spontaneously confabulate or confuse the distant and recent past like confabulating patients, but their memories are hardly impenetrable. Real memories are revised by current contexts and confused with imagined events. False memories become strengthened by confabulated embellishments such that they are difficult to unseat. As Roediger and McDermott put it, 'all remembering is constructive' (Roediger and McDermott, 1995, p. 812).

Everyday action

Our experience tells us that we feel will when we do willful acts, not for mindless gestures or for things we didn't do, and certainly not for things other people did. Psychological research, however, suggests that this feeling of will may not always line up neatly with action. William James suggested such a notion over a hundred years ago:

> The willing terminates with the prevalence of the idea; and whether the act then follows or not is a matter quite immaterial, so far as the willing itself goes. I will to write and the act follows. I will to sneeze, and it does not. I will that the distant table slide over the floor towards me; it also does not. My willing representation can no more instigate my sneezing center than it can instigate the table to activity. But in both cases it is as true and good willing as it was when I willed to write. In a word, volition

is a psychic or moral fact pure and simple, and is absolutely completed when the stable state of the ideas is there.

(William James, 1910, p. 560)

The feeling that our actions are in lock-step with our conscious will is compelling. And yet, a growing body of evidence suggests that William James was correct, at least in part: the *feeling* of doing can be dissociated from the *actual* doing.

Libet's paradigm. In the 1960s, Kornhuber and Deecke discovered that if they asked participants to repeatedly perform a simple action (flexing a finger) while wearing electroencephalography (EEG) electrodes, they could average the electrical responses created by the motor cortex. They did so and found a change in the electrical activity in this region between 0.8 and 1.5 seconds before an action was performed. They called this shift in electrical activity a BEREITSHAFTSPOTENTIAL or 'readiness potential' since it indicated that participants' brains were getting ready for the act (Kornhuber and Deecke, 1965). The idea that the brain 'knew' about an upcoming action a whole second in advance fascinated a researcher, Benjamin Libet, in the physiology department at the University of California, San Francisco. Libet wondered whether people's conscious awareness of the urge to act ('will') would also appear so far in advance. In order to test this question, Libet devised a clever paradigm that would change how many people think about the conscious experience of will.

In order to study brain activity associated with initiating action, electrodes were placed on the participant's head. The more difficult measurement was marking exactly when the participant had the conscious intention to move. Requiring participants to say 'now' would be imprecise because formulating the 'now' would require several hundred milliseconds. To avoid this, Libet had subjects sit in front of a television screen that showed a spot moving clockwise in a circular path, akin to a dot version of the second hand of a clock. This spot took 2.56 seconds to make a complete rotation, and subjects noted the location of the spot when they first had the conscious intention to act. The accuracy of this time marking device was demonstrated by having a measurable stimulus (shock to the skin) and asking subjects to mark when they felt the shock, which they could do so accurately.

Once it was established that participants could use the clock to mark the occurrence of a stimulus, they were asked to flex a finger whenever they felt the urge to move and note the position of the spot at the moment of the urge. This paradigm gave Libet three pieces of information: (1) when participants felt the urge to move (intention), (2) when participants actually moved (recorded by an electrode on the finger), and (3) the onset of brain activity associated with the movement. Libet found that conscious knowledge of one's desire to act (intention) occurs approximately 400 ms *after* the advent of physiological changes in the brain associated with an impending action. In other words, the initiation of action occurs unconsciously and the feeling of will, the conscious urge to move, occurs quite a bit later. Despite the compelling nature of the illusion, the conscious experience of will cannot be the initiator of action.

Libet redux. Recently, John Dylan Haynes and colleagues published a study that would have undoubtedly pleased Libet, had he lived long enough to see it (he died 9 months earlier). In this study, Haynes updated the Libet paradigm by having subjects decide whether to press a button with their left or right hand while lying in a functional magnetic resonance imaging (fMRI) machine. Haynes found patterns of brain activity in the frontopolar cortex that predicted whether subjects would press a button with their left or right hand as much as 7 seconds in advance of that decision. This stood in stark contrast to the perception of subjects that their decisions were the outcome of conscious deliberation undertaken much later: on average about a second before they pressed the button (Soon et al., 2008).

Apparent mental causation

Akin to the perceptual illusions described earlier, the feeling of will may simply be an inference based on assumptions. And just as illusions can unmask the assumptions of the visual system, evoking sensations of will can unmask the inferential nature of volition. Wegner and Wheatley (1999) proposed that the 'feeling of will' rests on three assumptions and that mimicking these assumptions would produce an erroneous sensation of will. Specifically, the three assumptions are: priority (a thought occurs just prior to the act), consistency (the thought is consistent with the act), and exclusivity (the person is perceived to be the exclusive cause of the act). The assumption of priority was investigated first.

The 'I Spy' experiment. In this experiment, a participant and a confederate sat across a table from one another with their hands on a board mounted on a computer mouse. On the table, visible to both, was a computer monitor with a screen depicting a variety of objects (taken from the children's book 'I Spy'). The participant and confederate were instructed to move the mouse together in slow, sweeping circles and by doing so, move a cursor around the screen. They were also instructed to stop moving the mouse approximately every 30 seconds. After each stop they were to rate the stop for how much they had intended to make that stop at that time in comparison with their partner (the confederate). For four of the stops, the confederate actually made the participant stop on a particular object at a particular time. Both the confederate and the participant listened to headphones during the experiment and were told that they would be each listening to a different tape of words, ostensibly as a mild distraction for the task. Via headphones, the experiment manipulated when the participant heard a preview consistent with this forced stop. For example, if the confederate forced the stop on the swan, the participant heard 'swan' as a preview.

As the assumption of priority would predict, the amount of time between the preview and the forced act was important to the perception of will. If the preview occurred a few moments before the act, participants mistakenly perceived that they were responsible for (and had intended to do) the act. If the preview occurred too far in advance (e.g. subjects heard 'swan' 30 seconds before the confederate engineered a stop on the plastic swan in the picture) or immediately after the stop, subjects did not attribute the act to themselves (see Figure 10.2). Thus, the feeling of having intended an act can be erroneously imputed when conditions mimic the typical scenario in which will occurs.

Will by context. Recently, we completed a study in which subjects were asked to perform a series of action sequences in order to determine whether the attribution of will can also be manipulated by contextual cues. Each action in a sequence was performed without knowing which action would follow. All subjects were given the same 24 initial actions (e.g. make a fist) but subsequent actions in each sequence differed across subjects. In any given sequence, the set of actions made the entire sequence appear either *related* (make fist, knock on the desk with the fist), *unrelated* (make fist, knock on the desk with the other hand), *disrupted* by an intervening action (make fist, tap left foot, knock on the

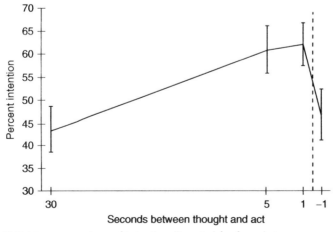

Figure 10.2 Mean percentage of intentionality rated for forced stops.

desk with the fist), or *delayed* (make fist, wait 5 seconds, knock on the desk with the fist). Each subject performed each of the action sequences once only; counterbalancing ensured that the endings for each action were balanced across subjects. Immediately after each sequence was performed, subjects were asked to rate the first action, last action, or entire action sequence for how much they felt that they had performed it willfully (described as feeling as though one is an active participant and conscious author of one's action) versus mechanically (described as operating on autopilot, similar to mindless participation in a game of 'Simon Says'). The key question was whether the first actions would be misremembered as more or less willful depending on the subsequent context. As this context was unknown at the time of the action, any influence of the context on those ratings would be an immediate revision of reality.

As predicted, we found that the ratings of the first action differed significantly depending on the subsequent context. Specifically, actions followed by a related sequence were deemed to have felt more willfully authored at the time of action compared to action sequences that were disrupted or unrelated (see Figure 10.3). Thus, the experience of will was almost immediately negated and revised by what followed. Uncharacteristically, William James was incorrect when he stated that, 'The willing terminates with the prevalence of the idea; and whether the act then follows or not is a matter quite immaterial'. The context colors will, even retrospectively.

These studies demonstrate that conscious will is perceived and remembered whenever contexts imply that perception. Here again, the brain makes the

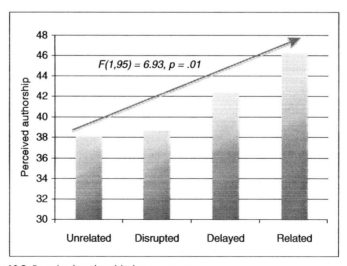

Figure 10.3 Perceived authorship by sequence.

most sensible story given a temporal slice of information. Actions preceded by related thoughts/actions are assumed to have been willed compared to actions preceded by unrelated thoughts/actions. While this calculation is rational, it is not veridical. The system relies on assumptions and is duped whenever stimuli mimic the rules.

Clinical dissociations of will and action. Demonstrations that reveal the dissociation between action and the feeling of will may be less surprising when one considers the number of clinical disorders in which this occurs. Patients with motor disorders (e.g. Parkinson's, Huntington's) experience the frustration of commanding unresponsive limbs. Patients with phantom limbs ineffectively will limbs that do not exist at all in hopes of alleviating painful sensations of contortion (Ramachandran and Blakeslee, 1998). Other patients perform actions with an erroneous *lack* of authorship: patients with alien hand syndrome believe that one of their hands is a free and often malicious agent that may undress or strangle its owner at any moment (Biran and Chatterjee, 2004). Patients with Schizophrenia are unaware that their own subvocal speech is the source of their auditory hallucinations (Bick and Kinsbourne, 1987).

Certainly, the particular ways that will and action are uncoupled in these patients reflect their particular disorders. However, the fact that this uncoupling occurs at all suggests that will and action are not as inextricably linked as they appear in normal consciousness. Akin to the brain's vulnerability to conflate internally generated imagery with stimulus-driven perception (Johnson, 1991), the sensation of will and the perception of action may be easily conflated in normal consciousness, leading to misperceptions of willed acts.

When false will leads to false beliefs

Converging evidence has demonstrated that the feeling of will is largely impotent, occurring several hundred milliseconds after the initiation of a specific act (Libet, 1985) and several *seconds* after the brain biases action outcomes (Soon et al., 2008). Yet the phenomenology that we, our *conscious* selves, are the deciders of our own behavior is tremendously compelling. It feels like it must be true. However, taking this *feeling* as prima facie evidence of an actual, conscious decision can lead quickly down the path of confabulation.

Telling more than we can know. Possibly the single richest source of experiments showing how our phenomenological experience of action can be erroneous and lead to confabulated explanations is Nisbett and Wilson's (1977) review paper entitled 'Telling More Than We Can Know'. In one study, participants were asked to choose their favorite pair of panty hose from four choices (all of which were the same). People overwhelmingly chose the right-most pair, presumably because they examined the hose from left to right. However, the participants never recognized the position effect, claiming instead to have chosen based on weave, silkiness, and a host of other plausible factors. Their conscious experience was one of being rational decision makers, acting according to 'sensible' causes. In fact, when asked after the experiment whether they thought position had an effect on their choice, all participants denied it '…usually with a worried glance at the interviewer suggesting that they felt either that they had misunderstood the question or were dealing with a madman' (Ibid).

In another experiment, participants were asked to tie together two ropes hanging from the ceiling that were far enough apart that they could not be reached simultaneously (Maier, 1930). One solution was to weight one of the ropes with a heavy object (pliers were intentionally left lying on the floor for this purpose) and to set that weighted rope in motion so as to be caught while holding onto the other rope. Importantly, participants never arrived at this solution independently. To get there, Maier had to give them a hint. He would walk around the ropes and surreptitiously set one in motion by brushing it with his shoulder. A few seconds later, participants would attach the pliers to a rope and swing it over to the other rope to complete the task. When asked how they arrived at this solution, no one mentioned Maier's shoulder brushing act. Instead, each claimed to have had a personal epiphany at that very moment (e.g. 'I thought of monkeys brachiating through trees'). When people are asked why they did something, they will offer an explanation. Nisbett and Wilson famously demonstrated that these explanations can be confabulatory. The key difference between normal and patient confabulations may be that the former *sound* better because they are based on apriori, causal theories shared by healthy minds. Confabulations that do not adhere to such plausible, common theories fail to meet a psychological threshold of verisimilitude or 'truthiness'.

Truthiness

'Truthiness' was first used in a satirical sense by comedian Stephen Colbert to describe the quality of seeming true on a gut or intuitive level without regard to factual evidence. Since, by definition, neither normal nor abnormal confabulations can be factually true, truthiness may best characterize the dividing line. Differences in truthiness may be the reason why abnormal confabulations are salient (truthiness failed) and why normal confabulations go undetected (truthiness passed).

The truthiness of 'normal' belief has a wide birth. Hundreds, if not thousands, of supernatural beliefs flourish across continents including beliefs in aliens, witches, ghosts, and deities of all shapes and sizes. Under the assumption that at least some of the world's religions are mutually exclusive; millions of people are praying to illusory supernatural agents. Yet, the general public and the DSM-IV-R sanction this behavior as normal rather than deluded. To quote from George Orwell's '1984': sanity is statistical.

> [Winston] could not fight the Party any longer. Besides, the Party was in the right. It must be so: how could the immortal collective brain be a mistake? By what external standard could you check its judgments? Sanity was statistical. It was merely a question of learning to think as they thought.

(Orwell, 1949, p. 228)

The beliefs of the masses dictate the acceptable norms. Presumably, the belief that the earth is 'carried in the pincers of two giant green lobsters named Esmerelda and Keith' (Dawkins, 2006, p. 53) would be deemed 'normal' if enough people believed it. There appears to be little objectivity in what counts as a normal versus an abnormal confabulation. While patient confabulations appear outrageous, a quick catalog of 'normal' religious beliefs should provide a sobering perspective.

An illustrative example. In the year between college and graduate school, I worked as an intake specialist at a psychiatric clinic in a poor area of south Austin. I was the first person that incoming psychiatric patients saw, and my primary responsibility was to assign each of them a psychiatric diagnosis. I was woefully unqualified and resorted to matching their self-reports to DSM-IV checklists as best I could.

One day, an older woman came in with her daughter who served as her guardian and translator. Toward the end of the session, I asked whether the older woman saw or heard things that other people did not. Through her daughter, she recounted that a bird recently flew into her car windshield as she was driving. She believed the bird was her deceased husband who had taken avian form in order to tell her something important. As animistic beliefs are common in certain cultures and the DSM-IV exempted such beliefs, I was unfazed. Her daughter, clearly annoyed that I was not taking this as evidence of psychosis, asked her mother to tell me what the bird had said. The mother replied earnestly, 'he said that I should have taken a left'.

Believing that a dead relative takes avian form is considered to be within the realm of normal belief. When the President claims he talks with God everyday, this is taken as a sign of wisdom. However, if the bird says something inane or the President claims to talk with a hairdryer, the mental health conclusions would be markedly different. The difference lies not in the presence of confabulation per se, but in whether the contents of those confabulations meet standards of acceptability within the cultural zeitgeist.

Truthiness in the brain. Recent work from Elliott, Moscovitch and others points to the ventromedial prefrontal cortex as a region that may subserve 'felt rightness': the ability to quickly appreciate the apparent appropriateness of a response given current goals (Moscovitch and Winocur, 2002). The evaluation of 'rightness' appears to precede more rational analyses and may be akin to the hypothesized mechanism of somatic marking which binds a positive or negative valence to a behavioral action in order to speed judgment (Damasio, 1996). Elliott and colleagues (Elliott et al., 2000) reviewed converging evidence that vmPFC subserves this feeling of 'rightness' or 'closure' and that this sensation is distinct from subsequent, cognitive assessments of appropriateness and veridicality (e.g. verifying that 'felt right' memories are compatible with other sources of knowledge). Consistent with the vmPFC as 'rightness' or 'truthiness' detector, patients with damage to this region may spontaneously confabulate (Schnider, 2001) and have difficulty automatically accessing the kind of overlearned associations that become knee-jerk intuitions in normal volunteers (e.g. gender stereotypes – Milne and Grafman, 2001). One vmPFC patient described by Moscovitch had no 'feeling of rightness' even when he gave correct responses: insisting that he was guessing each time (Moscovitch, 1989). While our perceptual, memory, and action systems can be lead astray by faulty assumptions, the output has to feel 'right'. Even when perceived veridicality is ill-grounded, this truthiness check constrains our perceptions such that they remain within the bounds of rationality. This latter benefit has important implications for health and social functioning.

Healthy vs unhealthy confabulation

The human need to make sense of the world is a helpful one. Without it we would bump into walls, fail to notice cause and effect of relationships, and believe the world to be an unpredictable world governed by chance events. The assumptions of our perception, action, and memory systems subserve an efficient, coherent model of the world that is correct enough of the time to be worth the inaccurate artistic flourishes. Beyond cognitive efficiency, the proclivity to impute meaning – even illusory meaning – protects against disease, depression, and death (George et al., 2002; Taylor et al., 2000). These benefits are not trivial and are protected by cognitive processes that insulate our beliefs from contradictory arguments and disconfirming evidence (Gilovich, 1991). It is not the case, however, that *any* meaning will do. Healthy confabulations are cognitively efficient models of the world. Patient confabulations are cognitively inefficient models hampered by confusions of time and space. Healthy confabulations incorporate cultural norms and shared beliefs thereby providing a meaningful, communal dialogue. Patient confabulations are often idiosyncratic and peculiar, leading to estrangement from family and friends.

Summary

The healthy, human brain is not a veridical recorder of events but rather a meaning machine that fills in gaps, rearranges time and space, delays conscious experience, and generates false explanations via available cultural theories. To confabulate is human. A key difference between normal and abnormal confabulations lies in their apparent truthiness and whether the contents therein are adaptive and shared, or maladaptive and peculiar. Patient confabulations are the output of disrupted human minds *not* altogether alien ones. While we marvel at eccentric notions of impersonated loved ones and disowned limbs, we should remember that storytelling is not solely the purview of diseased minds. Rather, storytelling is an ancient and fundamentally *human* art.

References

Bick, P.A. and Kinsbourne, M. (1987). Auditory hallucinations and subvocal speech in schizophrenic patients. *American Journal of Psychiatry,* **144**, 222–225.

Biran, I. and Chatterjee, A. (2004). Alien hand syndrome. *Archives of Neurology,* **64**, 292–294.

Blanke, O., Ortigue, S., Landis, T., and Seeck, M. (2002). Stimulating illusory own-body perceptions. *Nature,* **419**, 269–270.

Damasio, A.R. (1996). The somatic marker hypothesis and the possible functions of the prefrontal cortex. *Philosophical Transactions of the Royal Society of London. B Biological Sciences,* 1413–1420.

Dawkins, R. (2006). *The God Delusion.* Boston, Houghton Mifflin.

Deese, J. (1959). On the prediction of occurrence of particular verbal instructions in immediate recall. *Journal of Experimental Psychology,* **58**, 17–22.

Elliott, R., Dolan, R.J. and Frith, C.D. (2000). Dissociable functions in the medial and lateral orbitofrontal cortex: Evidence from human neuroimaging studies.*Cerebral Cortex,***10**, 308–317.

Garry, M., Manning, C.G., Loftus, E.F., and Sherman, S.J. (1996). Imagination inflation: Imagining a childhood event inflates confidence that it occurred. *Psychonomic Bulletin and Review,* **6**, 313–318.

Geldard, F. A. and Sherrick, C. E. (1972). The cutaneous "rabbit": A perceptual illusion. *Science,* **178**, 178–179.

George, L. K., Ellison, C. G., and Larson, D. B. (2002). Explaining the relationships between religious involvement and health. *Psychological Inquiry,* **13**, 190–200.

Gilovich, T. (1991). Seeing what we expect to see: The biased evaluation of ambiguous and inconsistent data. *How We Know What Isn't So.* New York, The Free Press. 49–72.

Goff, L.M. and Roediger, H.L. (1998). Imagination inflation for action events: Repeated imaginings lead to illusory recollections. *Memory & Cognition,* **26**, 20–33.

Hirstein, W. (2005). *What is Confabulation?* In *Brain Fiction.* Cambridge, MA, MIT Press.

Hyman, I.E., Husband, T.H. and Billings, F.J. (1995). False memories of childhood experiences. *Applied Cognitive Psychology,* **9**, 181–197.

James, W. (1892). *Psychology-Briefer course*. New York, Henry Holt. New edition, New York, Harper and Row, 1961

Johnson, M.K. (1991). Reflection, reality monitoring, and the self. In *Mental Imagery* (ed. R. Kunzendorf), pp. 3–16. New York, Plenum.

Kohlers, P. A. and von Grunau, M. (1976). Shape and color in apparent motion. *Vision Research,* **16**, 329–335.

Kornhuber, H.H. and Deecke, L. (1965). Hirnpotentialänderungen bei Willkürbewegungen und passiven Bewegungen des Menschen: Bereitschaftspotential und reafferente Potentiale. *Pflügers Archives,* **284**, 1–17.

Libet, B. (1985). Unconscious cerebral initiative and the role of conscious will in voluntary action. *Behavioral and Brain Sciences,* **8**, 529–566.

Loftus, E.F. (1997). Creating false memories. *Scientific American,* **277**, 70–75.

Loftus, E. and Ketcham, K. (1994). *The Myth of Repressed Memory: False Memories and Allegations of Sexual Abuse.* New York, St. Martin's Press.

Maier, N.R.F. (1930). Reasoning in humans: I. On direction. *Journal of Comparative Psychology,* **10**, 115–143.

Milne, E. and Grafman, J. (2001). Ventromedial prefrontal cortex lesions in humans eliminate implicit gender stereotyping. *Journal of Neuroscience,* **21** (RC150), 1–6.

Moscovitch, M. (1989). Confabulation and the frontal systems: Strategic versus associative retrieval in neuropsychological theories of memory. In *Varieties of Memory and Consciousness: Essays in Honor of Endel Tulving* (eds. H.L. Roediger and F.I. Craik). Hillsdale, NJ, Lawrence Erlbaum.

Moscovitch, M. and Winocur, G. (2002). The frontal cortex and working with memory. In *Principles of Frontal Lobe Function* (eds. D. T. Stuss and R. Knight). New York, Oxford University Press.

Moulin, C.J.A., Conway, M.A., Thompson, R.G., James, N., and Jones, R.W. (2005). Disordered Memory Awareness: Recollective Confabulation in two cases of Persistent Déjà vecu. *Neuropsychologia,* **43**, 1362–1378.

Nisbett, R. and Wilson, T. D. (1977). Telling more than we can know: Verbal reports on mental processes. *Psychological Review,* **84**, 231–259.

Orwell, G. (1949). *Nineteen Eighty-Four. A novel.* London, Secker and Warburg.

Ramachandran, V.S. and Blakeslee, S. (1998). *Phantoms in the Brain: Probing the Mysteries of the Human Mind.* New York, William Morrow.

Roediger, H.L. III. and McDermott, K.B. (1995). Creating false memories: Remembering words not presented in lists. *Journal of Experimental Psychology: Learning. Memory and Cognition,* **21**, 803–814.

Schnider, A. (2001). Spontaneous confabulation, reality monitoring, and the limbic system—A review. *Brain Research Reviews,* **36**, 150–160.

Schnider, A. (2003). Spontaneous confabulation and the adaptation of thought to ongoing reality. *Nature Reviews Neuroscience,* **4**, 662–671.

Shiffrar, M. and Freyd, J.J. (1990). Apparent motion of the human body. *Psychological Science,* **1**, 257–267.

Shor, R.E. and Orne, E.C. (1962). *Harvard Group Scale of Hypnotic Susceptibility: Form A.* Palo Alto, CA, USA, Consulting Psychologists Press.

Soon, C.S., Brass, M., Heinze, H.J., and Haynes, J.D. (2008). Unconscious determinants of free decisions in the human brain. *Nature Neuroscience,* **11**, 543–545.

Taylor, S.E., Kemeny, M.E., Reed, G.M., Bower, J.E., and Gruenewald, T.L. (2000). Psychological resources, positive illusions, and health. *American Psychologist,* **55**, 99–109.

Van der Waals, H.G. and Roelofs, C.O. (1931). Optische Scheinbewegung, *Zeitschrift fr Psychologie und Physiologie des Sinnesorgane,* **115**, 91–190.

Wegner, D.M. and Wheatley, T. (1999). Apparent mental causation: Sources of the experience of will. *American Psychologist,* **54**, 480–492.

Wertheimer, M. (1912). Experimentelle Studien uber das Sehen von Bewegung. (Experimental Studies of the Perception of Motion). *Zeitschrift fur Psychologie,* **61**, 161–265.

Wheatley, T. and Haidt, J. (2005). Hypnotic disgust makes moral judgments more severe. *Psychological Science,* **16**, 780–784.

Whinnery, J.E. (1997). Psychophysiologic correlates of unconsciousness and near-death experiences. *Journal of Near-Death Studies,* **15**, 231–258.

Zaragoza, M.S. and Mitchell, K.J. (1996). Repeated exposure to suggestion and the creation of false memories. *Psychological Science,* **7**, 294–300.

Chapter 11

Temporal consciousness and confabulation: Escape from unconscious explanatory idols

Gianfranco Dalla Barba

'How did your disease begin?' the doctor asks patient CA

'It started with a strong sore throat… I couldn't swallow anything… so I couldn't go to school… my mother called the doctor', answers the patient.

'How did your disease begin?' the same doctor asks another patient, CD

'It started with a strong headache… one morning I woke up with a strong headache and then I started throwing up and I remember I couldn't keep my eyes open', answers the patient.

One of these two patients is confabulating, whereas the other one is reporting the memory of an event she has really experienced. But who is confabulating, CA or CD? As you can see, there is nothing in the patients' reports that can help you to tell which patient is confabulating. However, if I tell you that CA is a 67-year-old woman with Korsakoff's syndrome (Dalla Barba et al., 1990) and that CD is a 33-year-old woman reporting the onset of her Herpes meningitis, things become much more clear and these additional pieces of information allow you to identify CA as the confabulating patient. This is not so much because you know that patients with Korsakoff's syndrome confabulate, but rather because you know that it is quite unlikely that somebody who is 67-year-old goes to school and has a mother who calls the doctor for her sore throat. In addition you know that headache, vomiting, and photophobia are common in the onset of Herpes meningitis, which suggests to you that CD is not confabulating. Nevertheless, CA's and CD's reports have something in common. They are *semantically appropriate* (Dalla Barba, 1993), in the sense that a hypothetical observer not familiar with the patients' history could hardly tell whether their reports are confabulatory or not. In other words, the semantic structure of CA's and CD's memories is *internally* consistent, but the content of CA's memory is *externally* inconsistent with the patient's past and present situation. CA remembers 'another' past (Dalla Barba et al., 1997b), in the sense that she is aware of a personal past that is different from the past she would have remembered if she wouldn't have had a severe amnestic-confabulatory syndrome. The case of patient MG (Dalla Barba et al., 1997a) well illustrates how semantically appropriate confabulations can go undetected when the real present and past situation of a patient is unknown. While he was waiting to undergo a CT scan, MG told the radiologist that he had accompanied a friend to be admitted to the neurology department that day. The neurologist who was taking care of MG's (non-existent) friend realized that MG also had neurological problems and so decided to refer him to the radiology department for a CT scan. On that occasion the radiologist did not even suspect that MG was confabulating.

However, patients who confabulate like CA, not only remember 'another' past, but are also disoriented in time and place. They are living 'another' present, in the sense that they *are present* to a world which differs from the world to which an observer is present. Consider the following example.

'How old are you?' the doctor asks patient PL, a 57-year-old woman, hospitalized following cardiac arrest (Dalla Barba et al., 1998).

'I'm 20'

Then the doctor asks her to look at herself in the mirror.

'Well, I look 50 years old, but it's because I was sick. I fell in a ditch while I was playing with my brothers. That's why I damaged my face.'

'Where are you now?'

'I'm in a school to learn.'

'Why then do you wear a night gown?'

'Well I was hospitalized… I was hospitalized somewhere… I don't even know what the problem was. You should ask my teacher'

'How many children do you have?'

'Two' (actually 3).

'What are their names?'

'Roberto and Susy' (actually Lucia, Luisella and Georgia).

'How old are they?'

Roberto is three and a half, Susy… I don't know (her children were actually 36, 33, and 10).

So, what is PL's present? It is the present of a 20-year-old woman, with two little children, who is at school to learn. She is present to a world which is in sharp contrast with the *real* world, that of a middle-age woman, with a young daughter and two other adult children, who is hospitalized for a severe medical condition. However, the distorted world to which PL is present is a *real* world *for her*, as *real* as the remembered distorted past and the distorted present world for patients who confabulate. In fact, confabulators deeply adhere to their confabulatory world and tend to act upon their confabulations. Metcalf's and co-workers' patient (Metcalf et al., in press), for example, upon his return home from the hospital, would awaken each morning with the conviction that he was required to attend a swimming carnival at school that day and would attempt to search for his swimming costume, despite being 36 years old and unable to walk due to injuries sustained in the accident that provoked his confabulatory amnesia.

So far we have seen that confabulation involves the patient's past, as revealed by confabulatory memories, and present, as shown by confabulatory reports and acts about the present. Is that it? Is confabulation limited to past and present? Certainly, it would be quite surprising that a patient who lives with distorted personal past and present would live without a personal future. In fact this is not the case since these patients also confabulate about their personal futures. Patient MB (Dalla Barba, 1993), for example, while he was hospitalized, said on one occasion that he was looking forward to the end of the testing session because he had to go to the general store to buy some new clothes, since he hadn't been able to the day before, because he had gotten lost in the center of Paris, where he had fortunately met a nurse who kindly took him back to the hospital. On that occasion the patient actually attempted to leave his hospital room, claiming that there was a taxi waiting for him downstairs. This is obviously not the only example of confabulation about personal future. When asked to report their plans or projects about their future, confabulators typically report as personal plans their habits and routines. Patient GA (Dalla Barba et al., 1997b), for example, to the question 'What are you going to do in a few minutes?' answered 'I'll go home to cook supper', whereas since her disease she never cooked and she was living one and a half hours from the hospital she was admitted to. To the question 'What are you going to do tomorrow?', she replied 'I'll go out shopping alone by car', whereas she never did that since her disease and she would certainly not do it in the following day.

Plausible verbal reports and acts involving the patient's past, present, and future are not the only example of how confabulating patients can interact with their worlds. Actually, confabulation is sometimes described as a heterogeneous phenomenon. In fact, some patients tend to confabulate spontaneously, while others confabulate more when in response to direct questioning. The content of confabulation can also vary considerably, being in some cases frankly implausible. The main difference between these cases and cases in which confabulation is plausible is that confabulation can be detected without knowing anything further about the patient. Consider the following example.

'What did you do yesterday?' the doctor asks patient SD

'Yesterday I won a running race and I have been awarded with a piece of meat which was put on my right knee'.

In order to tell that SD's report is confabulatory, you don't need to know that he is a 37-year-old patient who reported a severe head trauma. In fact, SD's confabulation describes an event that not only is he unlikely to have experienced at that particular time, but it is also unlikely that anyone would have, or ever will, experience. The content of SD's confabulation is *semantically anomalous*, in the sense that it carries meanings, which are inconsistent with knowledge and information shared by members of the society. Confabulations often described as *fantastic* or *implausible* actually contain semantic anomalies (Weinstein and Lyerly, 1968; Stuss et al., 1978; Baddeley and Wilson, 1986; Joseph, 1986; Sandson, Albert et al., 1986). However, although semantically anomalous, these confabulations are often made of autobiographical elements put together in an inappropriate semantic structure. Consider again SD's example. SD was actually involved in running races and had spent most of his time off work in this kind of activity. It was actually during a running race in the mountains that he fell, sustaining a severe head trauma and an open wound to his right knee. So, his confabulation about having won a running race and having been awarded with a piece of meat on his knee actually contains autobiographical elements inserted in an inappropriate semantic context.

From the description of confabulating patients reported so far emerge three characteristics of confabulation: (1) confabulation affects memory, in particular, but not exclusively, episodic memory (Tulving, 1972, 1983), and manifests itself when patients retrieve personal episodes from their pasts. (2) The content of confabulation can vary considerably, ranging from semantically appropriate to semantically anomalous. (3) Confabulation is not only limited to the patients' past, but also involves their presents and their personal futures.

Why confabulating patients make such errors when retrieving their pasts? Why is confabulation on some occasions indistinguishable from a true memory, whereas on other occasions it has such bizarre or semantically anomalous content? Is confabulation a pure memory disorder, or does the fact that it involves the patient's past, present, and future reflect a disruption of how personal temporality is experienced? In the following sections we will address these questions.

Memory and past

Confabulation affects memory and memory, by definition, is memory *of* the past. So, at first glance it seems that in confabulating patients there is something wrong in the way they retrieve their past. Are these patients retrieving the 'wrong' past or remembering 'another' past, as we said earlier? Or, putting it in a different terminology, are they activating the wrong memory trace, as proposed by some theorists (e.g. Schnider and Ptak, 1999)? In order to answer these questions, we need first of all to know what the past is. Although a presupposition about the nature of the past is necessarily implicit in any theory of memory, this presupposition has never been clarified. The being of the past is somehow negated in these theories, in the sense that the past is considered as what *is no longer*. This assumption has produced the theory of memory traces: if something is no longer present but continues to exist in the form of memory, it must be preserved in the form of a more or less stable modification in the organism which remembers. Accordingly, if I now perceive the image of this cup of coffee on the table, tomorrow I will be able to remember it because this image has, so to speak, been deposited in some part of my brain in the form of a *memory trace*. In other words, the event of 'cup-on-the-table-on-such-and-such-an-afternoon' has caused a modification in the equilibrium of my brain which I call memory trace of the event, or, to use more elegant terminology, an engram, in which the event is deposited in the form of a representation. The activation of the trace, that is, its subsequent passage from a passive to an active state (as in copy theories of remembering) or its interaction with a present cue (as in reconstructive models of memory), will result in recollection of the event. Figure 11.1 depicts this point of view: event E is stored in memory as memory trace E′; the activation of E′, with or without the involvement of a retrieval cue, results in E″, i.e., the conscious remembering of E.

Present-day versions of this now classical way of thinking have been reformulated more or less explicitly in current functionalist theories. Functionalism maintains that mental operations are expressible in an abstract and physically neutral language that designates functions and functional relations (Marcel, 1988). As far as memory is concerned, functionalist theories substitute the physical trace with a functional trace which is preserved in the architecture of a system which is no longer physical (the brain), but virtual (the cognitive system). It is easy to see that, however reformulated, any theory which bases the ability to recollect on the preservation of an event inside a trace contains a paradox, fruit of a misleading assumption, that is the belief that time can exist in things. The past event which I now remember, for example my dinner yesterday with Paul, is present to my consciousness as a past event, in that as

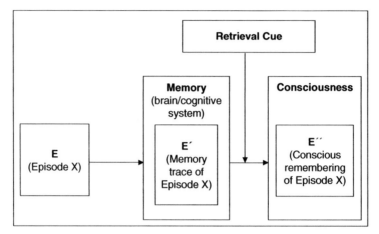

Figure 11.1 The relation between memory and consciousness in some current theories of memory (see the text).

such, that is in being past, that event was contained in the memory trace whose activation produced the recollection. In other words, the past of that event, or its 'pastness' as in Bergson (1896), is already there, enclosed in that 'thing', physical or abstract as it may be, which I call memory trace of the event. But it should be clear that 'things' as such are not temporal. Objects of the world are neither present, nor past, nor future, but they acquire a temporal dimension only in the presence of a person who goes to the trouble of making them temporal. Time cannot even be found in a 'thing' like the brain, however much one would like to give it a particular status in the universe. This erroneous assumption, on which theories of memory are founded, is directly reflected in the paradox to which these theories fall victim. The paradox of the memory trace, as we shall call it, consists in seeing memory, that is, what is given to consciousness as past, as originating in elements borrowed from the present. Let's see why.

The memory trace paradox

The event which I now perceive, for example, the glass which is on the table in front of me, is without doubt a present event. This event of glass-on-the-table determines a modification in the equilibrium of a system, be it physical (the nervous system) or virtual (the computational level), which I call a memory trace. What is the temporal nature of this modification, namely of the memory trace? Without doubt present. The glass-on-the-table which I now perceive is present and if one accepts that this event produces a modification somewhere in my brain or in my mind, one will have to accept that said modification will be present and that the event represented by that modification will also be present. In short, depending on the level of description that one wants to adopt, be it a case of the synthesis of new proteins, of the growth of new dendritic spines, of the activation or the reinforcement of synaptic circuits, or of the particular codification of information, it will always be a matter of present modification of something. What happens when that event contained in the trace is recollected in memory? When the event of 'glass-on-the-table' is recollected, it happens in the present, that is, as the result of the reactivation of the modification that the event caused on a physiological, biochemical, neurocibernetical, neurocomputational or functional level. And so it is not at all clear how memory, whose basic characteristic is being memory of the past, can stem from a combination of present phenomena, perception, the preservation of the trace, and recollection, which do not reflect any notion of past. Figure 11.2 depicts this situation: event 'E' is *present* and stored as *present* 'E' in the memory trace. When E' is retrieved this happens as a consequence of a *present* process. Depending on whether a *present* cue is involved or not, the result of this processing is E", i.e. the conscious remembering of E as 'past'.

Activation of the memory trace should, if anything, coincide with a new perception of the event contained within the trace, not with its memory since the event contained in the trace was present as it ended up in the trace and continued to be so for as long as it remained enclosed in the trace. The paradox of the memory trace, which current theories on memory overlook had already been clearly reported over 60 years ago. Merleau-Ponty (1945) wrote,

'...our very best reason for rejecting physiological preservation of the past is also a reason for rejecting 'psychological preservation', and this reason is that no preservation,

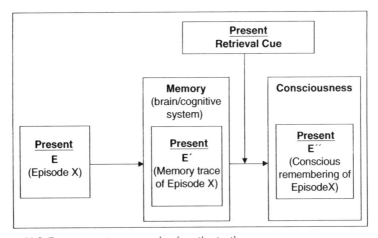

Figure 11.2 Tre memory trace paradox (see the text).

> no physiological or psychic 'trace' of the past can enable comprehension of consciousness of the past. This table carries traces of my past life, I have carved my initials, I have left ink stains. But, alone, these traces do not refer back to the past: they are present and, if I find there signs of some 'previous' event, I find them because, by other means, I have a sense of the past, because I carry in me this meaning. – a preserved perception (in a 'physical' or 'psychic' trace) is a perception, it continues to exist, it is always in the present, it does not open behind us that dimension of escape and of absence that is the past.'

If, on the other hand, I recognize that particular event as past, this happens because I attribute a precise meaning to it, that of being past, a meaning which by definition cannot be contained in the trace since, in every moment of its existence, it has never ceased to be present.

This does not mean that events do not cause modifications in our brains or in our cognitive systems, but these modifications cannot be used to explain recollection. Besides, any object in the universe undergoes modification on account of events. Any object carries with it the marks of the past, and yet no one would think of attributing the possibility of recollection to objects, if not metaphorically. The signs that events have left on objects acquire the meaning of *past* only by virtue of a consciousness which attributes it to them. Even the impression on the cushion on the sofa in front of me bears witness to past events, but in itself it is present and has never ceased to be so in any single instant of its existence. If I find in it signs of some past event, if I remember the thousands of times that my guests and I myself have sat on that sofa, it is because I attribute a meaning to those marks, that of being past. The 'me-ness' of memory of which Claparède (1911) speaks, the 'warmth and intimacy' with which James (1890) describes memory, or the 'pastness' of Bergson (1896) describe certain characteristics of memory well, but tell us nothing about its nature. Indeed, they either describe only one present characteristic of memory, and so they remain in the present, or else if they are already dealing with the past, they presuppose that which they want to explain. Certainly, there are events that seem to be 'themselves' past without belonging to the personal experience of any particular individual. For example, the big bang itself *exists in the past*, but no human experienced it. Would that allow us to make a distinction between the past itself and a *human past*, or our concept of past? Certainly no. The very necessary condition to be satisfied for the big bang to be past is the existence of a present consciousness that considers it *as* past. Without such a consciousness, the big bang is neither past, nor present nor future: it just doesn't exist. At the most, a distinction must be made between a generic impersonal past and *my* past. When I say that I remember the big bang, I'm not remembering my personal past, I'm just conscious of a piece of information, a notion, that contributes to my knowledge of the world: the big bang is an hypothesis concerning the origin of the universe. We will analyze this in more detail when we will discuss the distinction between Knowing Consciousness and Temporal Consciousness.

Tags, labels and the past

In support of the hypothesis of the memory trace as a condition for recollection it could be stated that it is not at all necessary for episodes to be contained in the memory trace as past. Indeed, for recollection to be possible, it is enough for 'something' in the trace to indicate that its content concerns some past event. In short, it would be enough for the episodes registered in the trace to be in some way marked, for example, with a type of tag stating the date they took place or simply indicating that what is contained in that trace is past, e.g. Anderson and Bower (1972), (1974); Hintzman (1978); Morton et al. (1985). It is easy to see how yet again a hypothesis of this type presupposes the past instead of explaining it. Any tag or indicator added to the episode contained in the trace would indeed be an indicator in itself present just as the episode which it accompanies. The date or the 'past' information of the indicator, in themselves, tells us nothing, they are not past but they become so only if the past is already given for the consciousness which picks up that indicator. In other words, the label or indicator of pastness of an episode does not precede nor, even less so, does it create the past. In contrast, it is in some way the consequence of it, it assumes its function as indicator of pastness because I already carry in me this meaning and am capable of attributing it to it. The knot I tie in my handkerchief to remind me that yesterday I made an appointment with Paul is not past and if I ignore it, it isn't even present. When I put my hand in my pocket to take out my handkerchief and realize it has a knot, I attribute a meaning to that knot, that of being an indicator of a past event which I have to remember so as not to cut a poor figure with Paul. If I didn't already possess the past as meaning, that knot would simply remain what it is and not an indicator of something past. The date, the indicator of pastness or what have you, say absolutely nothing about the past, nor do they bear witness to it. If I am able to recollect the appointment with Paul, this episode will appear to me in the past not because of the date but because of the meaning I attribute to that date, namely the meaning of the past that I attribute to that episode. In short, for however many tags, indicators, or whatever else you may choose to attach to the memory trace, it will never contain the past.

The order of succession

On the other hand, it would be pointless to attribute the order of succession to the contents of the trace, that is something that specifies that episode B took place before episode C and after episode A. The order of succession, the very idea of a before and of an after precedes the episode, it is not part of it. If I say that B comes after A and before C, I am temporalizing A, B, and C according to an order of succession that does not depend on the elements themselves, but on the temporalizing act which I perform in accordance with an idea of succession which I already possess and which precedes the elements themselves. The relationship of succession between A, B, and consciousness is not an external relationship between atemporal elements, but rather an internal relationship between elements that are temporalized thanks to their relationship. If I say 'I like A and I dislike B', the relationship between A and B is external because there is nothing in A that tells me that I dislike B and nothing in B that tells me that I like A. By contrast, when I say that A comes before B, the relationship between A and B is internal because the anteriority of A presupposes in the nature of A an 'incompleteness' of A (instant or state) that points toward B. If A is anterior to B, it is in B that A can receive this determination. Otherwise B isolated in its instant could never confer to A, isolated in its instant, any particular quality. In the same way, in order to be posterior to A, B needs to be in some way referred to A to have the characteristic of posteriority.

Now, the question is, who is the author of this temporalization of A, B, and C? When I say 'my last dinner with Julie was before I had a cold and after I gave a lecture in Lyon', where does this succession come from? Certainly not from the elements themselves. My dinner with Julie, my cold, and the lecture in Lyon are just episodes without any intrinsic notion of succession. If in the memory trace of the episode 'having had dinner with Julie' there were 'something' specifying that it was before my cold and after my lecture, then every time I thought of that dinner, an order of succession would rise in my mind, which is clearly not the case. In fact I can think of that dinner with Julie without having the phenomenal experience that the dinner was before my cold and after my lecture in Lyon. If I can see an order of succession in these three episodes it is because I am the author of the temporalizing act that puts these three episodes in an order of succession. And when I say 'I', I mean consciousness. It is consciousness that places these episodes in an order of succession, such order is not intrinsic to the memory trace.

What conclusion can be drawn from this discussion? First of all that current theories about memory imply an insoluble contradiction which we described under the name of the paradox of the memory trace. However many experimental data may be collected, these theories will never be able to explain recollection as consciousness of the past because from the start they break off any connection between consciousness *and* past. Once consciousness of the past has been separated from the past itself, the various theoretical attempts to reunite the past and consciousness are absolutely pointless. However, the memory-trace paradox does not represent the only problem with current theories of remembering. Another problem which deeply undermines the heuristic value of these theories is what we will refer to as the fallacy of the *homunculus*.

Memory, consciousness, and monitoring processes

The assumption that the past is preserved in a memory trace contains, as we have seen, a paradox in that the past is seen to derive from present elements, but how this happens is not explained. The past is thus assumed but not explained, and any possibility of understanding the nature of recollection, true or distorted, is therefore lost. But the paradox of the memory trace is not the only problem with current theories of memory. According to some theories of memory (Baddeley and Wilson, 1986; Moscovitch, 1989; Johnson, 1991; Burgess and Shallice, 1996; Conway and Tacchi, 1996; Moscovitch and Melo, 1997), in order for the recollection of a memory or of knowledge to be correct, that is for it to be the recollection of a memory or of information that we wanted to evoke, certain selection and verification mechanisms of the memory trace must be called into play. Depending on what the subject wants to remember, these mechanisms first make a selection from the various traces stored in the memory systems, and then check whether the result of the selection meets the conditions set by the recollection task. If these conditions are not met, due to contradictions between the selection result and verification criteria, the mechanisms in question continue to make new selections until a satisfactory choice is made, a choice which does not contradict the verification criteria and which also meets the demands of the recollection task. If, for example, I remember eating in a restaurant yesterday evening, according to these theories this is due to the fact that the trace 'dinner in restaurant' has been selected from a host of other traces for example, 'dinner at home', 'dinner at a friend's', in accordance with the criteria and mechanisms which guarantee the selection of the correct memory. The most widespread explanation of confabulatory symptoms provides a good example of an interpretative application of this hypothesis.

According to this hypothesis, confabulation is the result of the dysfunction of memory-monitoring mechanisms, that is, of the selection and verification mechanisms of the memory trace. The breakdown of these mechanisms is thought to prevent the inhibition of inappropriate answers, which are produced as confabulatory answers. If, for example, I want to remember what I did last night, according to the hypothesis in question, memory-monitoring mechanisms start searching among my memory traces and make a selection, the result of which is, let's suppose, 'I had dinner at home'. This is then checked in accordance with criteria of plausibility and coherence with other associated memories, for instance 'last night I went out', and is then rejected since it does not correspond to these criteria. At this point the same mechanisms begin a new selection and check other possible memories until they find the appropriate memory, 'last night I had dinner in a restaurant'. If, however, the memory-monitoring mechanisms are dysfunctional, 'I had dinner at home' is accepted as appropriate and is produced as a confabulatory memory. So according to this reasoning, the possibility of recalling an appropriate episode or meaning requires the preliminary examination of various possible answers, followed by the inhibition of inappropriate answers. Now, it is crucial to know whether monitoring processes act on a conscious, voluntary basis or, alternatively, if it is possible to assume that they operate outside consciousness and are inaccessible to it.

Are monitoring processes conscious?

If monitoring processes were conscious and voluntary, then their action would be transparent to reflexive analysis since they would be operations of consciousness. The subjective experience of reflection would, then, show me that when I am engaged in a recollection task, I consciously carry out the operations of selection and verification attributed to monitoring mechanisms. In practice this would mean that while recalling I consciously select a memory, judge whether its contents meet the conditions of the recollection task that I have set myself, reject it if they don't and begin a new selection or accept it as a memory if it meets the conditions of the task. Reflexive analysis, however, demonstrates that this is not at all the case. If, for example, I try to recall what I did last night, I don't need to subsequently recall a number of different memories and monitor each of them until I find the good memory, the memory that reflects what I actually did last night. Last night I watched a Woody Allen movie on television. I remember this without any searching and monitoring. Sometimes, however, the act of remembering needs searching. If, for example, I try to recall what I did last Wednesday at five o'clock in the afternoon, I need to search by successive approximation. I will remember, for instance, that on Friday morning I gave a talk in such and such place, that on Thursday afternoon I took the train to get to the city where I was going to give the talk, and that on Wednesday afternoon at five o'clock I was working on the talk for Friday. In other words, I operate a reconnaissance in my past, I move from memory to memory until I select one, the one which seems to best answer the question 'what was I doing last Wednesday at five o'clock in the afternoon?' But each of these recollections immediately appears to my consciousness as real, that is as a past image of a certain subject in which I recognize myself and to which I am intimately tied by an ontological relationship which does not allow for doubt: I was that person who was preparing the talk, taking the train, giving the talk, etc. Where I may hesitate is not on the content of my recollections, but on the date: I may not be sure that it really was Wednesday or that it was five o'clock not six. The process of selection and verification of the memory that best answers the question I ask myself does not concern the veracity of the memory, which is already given and, one could say, emanates from the memory itself; it concerns the possibility of placing it correctly in the sequence of recollections which constitutes my past. Sometimes, very rarely, I may hesitate about the source of a memory. I remember an episode, but I don't know whether that episode was actually experienced, imagined, or dreamed. But the point is that I don't hesitate about the fact that I am remembering an episode, but about its origin – direct experience, imagination, dreams, and so on.

But what reflexive analysis shows me above all is that during recollection I never come up with memories like those produced by patients who confabulate. For example, I never come up with memories like confabulations produced by patient SD. When asked what he had done the previous day would claim to have won a running race for which he was awarded a piece of meat which was placed on his right knee. When asked to give a definition of the word 'synagogue' he would reply that it was something to do with physiotherapy. Now according to the hypothesis, which sees memory and knowledge as the result of the verification and inhibition of inappropriate answers by special monitoring mechanisms, in order to be able to attribute the correct meaning to the word 'synagogue' one would have to choose from different possible alternatives such as, let's say 'a church', 'a Jewish place of worship', 'a type of fruit' or 'something to do with physiotherapy'. Only if one manages to inhibit all the inappropriate responses will 'Jewish place of worship' be selected otherwise, as in the case of our patient, 'something to do with physiotherapy' or any other answer could be given. This reasoning also implies that if, before his amnesia, the patient was asked what he had done the previous day, he would have consciously examined and rejected the possibility of having won a running race and being awarded a piece of meat which had been placed on his right knee and would instead have produced the correct answer. There is no evidence that, in order to recall an episode or a piece of information, subjects are engaged in consciously evaluating and rejecting candidate memories and information of the type described above.

Certainly confabulation is more often far more plausible than the examples given of the running race and the definition of 'synagogue'. In fact, most patients who confabulate produce confabulatory memories which cannot be distinguished from 'real' memories by an interlocutor who does not know the patient's history and current situation. But even in the case of the most plausible confabulation, like the one produced by patient MG (see above), it is difficult to imagine that on asking someone in hospital why he is there, this person, when answering, should consciously consider, among others, the possibility of being in hospital to accompany a friend. But even if that were the case, that is if recalling an episode or a meaning were possible due to conscious and voluntary inhibition of inappropriate answers, something which reflexive analysis leads us to exclude, it remains to be decided on what basis the correct answer is selected. One criterion could be that of plausibility. Less plausible answers are inhibited while the more plausible are accepted. But isn't plausibility itself a meaning which is attributed to a possible answer, in which case shouldn't plausibility also be subject to a process of verification like any other meaning? And shouldn't the criterion which I use to determine plausibility also be verified, and so on endlessly, like in a game of Chinese boxes? It is not worth arguing (Johnson and Raye, 1981; Johnson, 1988; Johnson, 1991) that in recollection the correct choice from various alternatives is based on the evaluation of the qualitative characteristics of information, for example the amount of perceptual detail and the quantity and type of memories associated with the episode we want to recall. Indeed, is it once again a question of *quis custodet custodes?* Who can assure me that when I remember meeting Paul the other evening, the bright red of his pullover is a perceptual detail which comes from my memory and not my imagination? Why should I grant these so-called perceptual details the status of veracity which I deny the memory itself? Similarly, who can assure me, for example, that the fact that in my memory Mary is with Paul is an 'associated memory' which guarantees the veracity of the main one, that is the meeting with Paul, and not a confabulation? As you can see, there is no way of escaping this circularity.

Are monitoring processes unconscious?

The subjective experience of reflection thus leads us to exclude the notion that, *with some rare exceptions,* the processes of information selection and verification are voluntary and conscious. Are they then processes which work outside consciousness and which are inaccessible to it? But to accept the hypothesis of unconscious monitoring mechanisms means falling into what we call *the homunculus fallacy,* that is the contradiction of postulating the existence of a sort of *unconscious consciousness,* that is of unconscious monitoring mechanisms endowed with intentionality which select, evaluate, and reject false memories and provide *conscious consciousness* with only real memories. It is unclear on the basis of what theoretic assumption one can attribute intentionality to this kind of process. Since Brentano (1874 (1973)), intentionality has been a characteristic of consciousness and, as Husserl (1950) says, represents the need of consciousness to exist as consciousness *of* something. Attributing intentionality to an unconscious process, then, is equivalent to giving unconsciousness the attribute of being *subject*, that is attributing consciousness to the unconscious. Moreover, this unconscious consciousness is inaccessible to the real sense of consciousness. As in a game of Chinese boxes, one personality would contain another personality, a *homunculus* to be precise, endowed with a shady, inaccessible consciousness which is busy resolving problems like rejecting false memories and is ready to provide conscious consciousness with the result of this detailed selection. But let's examine this problem more closely and see why it is illusory to attribute intentionality to the unconscious.

The fallacy of the homunculus

Let us first of all clarify what is meant by intentionality. I am conscious of this glass on the table. In other words, I have perceptual consciousness of glass-on-the-table. I also perceive the glass from a certain angle, not only visual but, let's say, existential: it exists before me, it presents itself to me in a certain perspective and, as an object among other objects, it has a certain relationship with these. Here again, this relationship is not only spatial (proximity, distance, adherence, etc.) but also functional, aesthetic, etc. In short, the being of the glass-on-the-table is a certain, specific, and original being which my consciousness is at this moment selecting.

What can be deduced from this? If we were idealists, we would say that the glass-on-the-table exists as 'content' of my consciousness, which in some way absorbs it. If we were realists, we would instead tend to consider the glass-on-the-table as an element of a reality which precedes and transcends consciousness, and to which consciousness can only adhere. And, in his cognitivist diversity, the realist would say that this information, 'glass-on-the-table', entered my cognitive system where it underwent a series of computational transformations before becoming perceptual consciousness of the glass-on-the-table. Nevertheless, if we free ourselves from what Sartre (1939) called alimentary philosophies, that is, from realism's tendency to make the object 'eat' the subject and idealism's tendency to make the subject 'eat' the object, we discover the true relationship between consciousness and world, between subject and object. These are born *together*. They are involved in a relationship where, although they retain their autonomy, neither term can exist without the other. The result of this relationship between subject and object, between consciousness and world, is intentionality, that is, the need of consciousness to always be consciousness *of* something.

Intentionality then, as relationship between consciousness and world, is a basic characteristic of consciousness which has no 'inside' but which defines itself by being 'outside', intentionally oriented toward things. At this point we must ask whether intentionality can also be attributed by right to the unconscious. Searle (1983), while rejecting functionalist positions, draws a distinction between consciousness and intentionality, maintaining that there can be non-intentional conscious states, for instance a sudden feeling of excitement, and unconscious intentional states, for example those beliefs which I am not thinking of at this moment but which determine my behavior. But why should a sudden feeling of excitement be a state of non-intentional consciousness? Excitement, or its opposite, depression, *are* states of consciousness, as Searle calls them, on the same level as any other consciousness. Like any other state of consciousness, that of excitement or depression does not escape its own law, that is of being destined to come out of itself in order to come to terms with the thing, that world which it is trying to reach and which continues to escape it. Accepting the existence of non-intentional states of consciousness is the same as making consciousness coincide with the thing. Non-intentional consciousness is quite unthinkable because it would be consciousness deprived of its original essence, that is, the negation of itself as 'thing'. One must not fall into the trap of thinking that *first* I am excited and *then* I am conscious of the glass-on-the-table, or that a sudden state of excitement *joins* my perception of the glass-on-the-table *from outside*. What one should say is that *in* a state of excitement I am aware of the glass-on-the-table. Mine is excited consciousness of the glass-on-the-table. Therefore, once again there are no exceptions to the law of consciousness: all consciousness is intentional in that it must, by nature, be consciousness *of* something.

Searle maintains that the idea that consciousness must exist as consciousness *of something* neglects a fundamental distinction,

> 'when I have a conscious experience of anxiety, there is indeed something my experience is an experience of, namely anxiety, but this sense of "of" is quite different from the "of" of Intentionality, which occurs, for example, in the statement that I have a conscious fear of snakes; for in the case of anxiety, the experience of anxiety and the anxiety are identical; but the fear of snakes is not identical with snakes.'

(Searle, 1983, p. 2)

But in proposing this example Searle confuses the essential structure of a reflexive act with that of a non-reflexive act. He seems to ignore the fact that there are always two possible forms of existence for consciousness: non-reflexive consciousness, that is which appears when 'I am afraid of snakes' and reflexive consciousness, that is consciousness 'of me-as-anxious'. These are two different types of consciousness, but both are intentional. The trick Searle uses involves comparing two different degrees of consciousness. In the case of anxiety, he makes the example of reflexive or second-degree consciousness; I am aware of being anxious. But first degree or non-reflexive consciousness is only anxiety, anxiety which opens onto the world like any consciousness and like any consciousness it is intentional in that it is outside itself, as anxiety, toward the world. It is by no means true that 'in the case of anxiety, the experience of anxiety and anxiety itself are identical'. The anxiety which pervades me in this case is the object of my consciousness, which makes itself conscious *of* anxious consciousness. Without this second-degree reflexive act, which gives me a point of view on my consciousness, my anxiety *is* my consciousness without my being aware of it: I will anxiously drink from the glass-on-the-table without being able to avoid the intentionality of my consciousness which will be *anxious consciousness of the glass-on-the-table*. There is, then, no difference regarding the degree of intentionality between my consciousness of *fear of snakes* and my *consciousness of anxiety*. They are both intentional. The difference is that the former is non-reflexive consciousness while the second is reflexive consciousness, that is consciousness which makes anxious consciousness its intentional object.

   If we then analyze the possibility maintained by Searle of unconscious intentional states, that is the so-called beliefs to which we fall victim without being conscious of it, it is clear that these supposed beliefs are not at all that unconscious background which Searle talks about, but they constitute consciousness itself. Searle says 'I believe that my paternal grandfather never once left the American continent, but until now, I had never formulated or clearly examined this belief'. What was this belief of Searle's before it became conscious? Searle maintains that it already existed in his unconscious in its intentional form of 'my grandfather never left the American continent'. This seems to be a rather rushed interpretation of the facts. Essentially Searle is saying that, in some way, the fact that his grandfather never left the American continent is something that he had always known, even if this thought has only now become conscious. If, then, it has always existed it must have been stored somewhere, and where or what is this place where thoughts are stored before becoming conscious, if not the unconscious? There is almost no need to emphasize the absurdity of such a hypothesis. Even if the unconscious does exist, who will believe that it contains pre-established thoughts and beliefs? This type of explanation, which has a long tradition in psychology, stems from the fact that spontaneity of consciousness is not accepted and thus is traced back to an 'elsewhere', the unconscious, the cognitive system, etc., where already formulated thoughts are believed to exist in a passive mode, in propositional form, which will then become conscious. What has not been seen is that such a hypothesis, in trying to trace the spontaneity of consciousness to another, unconscious location, only puts off the problem of the existence of beliefs and thought in general, a problem which sooner or later will have to be formulated. An unconscious and intentional thought or belief does not only present the paradox of passivity, that is of the existence of inactive intentional states, but it also implies another question: who, in this unconscious, believes, has believed, and will continue to believe that Searle's grandfather never left the American continent? The problem of the existence of an unconscious subject who believes thus arises. We shall come back to this problem shortly. For the moment it is enough to emphasize how even if an unconscious subject were admissible, he or she would in turn have to draw his or her thoughts and beliefs from another 'elsewhere', because if the spontaneity of consciousness is not accepted, there is no reason to accept spontaneity of the unconscious. The attempt to trace the origins of spontaneity to an unconscious elsewhere is nothing but an absurd, naive attempt to free oneself from the anguish we feel assisting the unceasing ex nihilo creation of consciousness which we do not create ourselves. You could object that consciousness of 'grandfather-never-left-the-American-continent', however spontaneous we may consider it, is still coherent with a given fact, that is, that Searle's grandfather never actually left the American continent. However, we will have to ask ourselves where this consistency between consciousness and reality comes from. There is no need to resort to explanatory idols such as the existence of unconscious beliefs. Consciousness, as intentional consciousness of the world, can only be a perpetual synthesis of past and present consciousness. In short, it is not by resorting to mechanistic determinism, which claims that consciousness comes from unconscious intentional states, that we will be able to understand spontaneous, intentional existence. Saying that consciousness is the synthesis of states of past consciousness with present consciousness does not mean tracing its origins to somewhere else, it simply means acknowledging to consciousness an existence *ex novo* in accordance with a certain synthetic form.

As an example of unconscious intentional states, that is of background, Searle gives that of Carter who formulates the intention of presenting himself as a candidate in the presidential elections of the United States. To be more precise, Searle maintains that

'an intentional state only determines its conditions of satisfaction – and thus only is the state that it is – given its position in a *Network* of other Intentional states and against a *Background* of practices and preintentional assumptions that are neither themselves intentional states nor are they parts of the conditions of satisfaction of Intentional states'.

(Searle, 1983, p. 19)

In order to express his intention of presenting himself at the presidential elections, Carter has to know that the United States is a Republic, that there are regular presidential elections where two large parties are rivals in the race for presidency, etc. Whoever presents himself as a candidate has to have the backing of his/her party, be actively supported by a large number of people, and finally, in order to become president must be voted for by the majority of voters. Well, concludes Searle, even if none of these *states* has a direct link with Carter's intention to candidate himself, he could not form such a plan, that is 'the intention of presenting himself for the American presidential elections', without such a *network* of intentional unconscious states.

> 'We might say that his intention "refers" to these other Intentional states in the sense that it can only have the conditions of satisfaction that it does, and thus can only be the intention that it is, because it is located in a Network of other beliefs and desires. Furthermore, in any real life situation, the beliefs and desires are only part of a larger complex of still other psychological states; there will be subsidiary intentions as well as hopes and fears, anxieties and anticipations, feelings of frustration and satisfaction. For short, I have been calling this entire holistic network, simply, the "Network"'.

(Searle, 1983, p. 141)

What Searle wants to explain is that our acts are not fortuitous but presuppose a 'Network' of meanings which condition their realization.

> 'We understand completely what it is for a man to intend to become President, but we have no clear idea at all what it would be for a man to intend to become a coffee cup or a mountain, because - among other reasons – we don't know how to fit such an intention into the Network'.

(Searle, 1983, p. 142)

What is difficult to understand is how this network can exist and how it can be made up of unconscious intentional states. In fact, if we accept its existence we also have to face the problem of its origins. What is the nature of this unconscious and intentional Network? Even though he vigorously rejects every functionalist hypothesis, Searle seems to make a similar mistake to that which he accuses the functionalists of making. Like them, he resorts to the unconscious in order to explain consciousness. Searle's is not an unconscious made of information processing, but one of beliefs or meanings which condition conscious life as much as the functionalist unconscious does. But Searle's hypothesis is presented with exactly the same problem as is functionalism: that of explaining, once and for all, how man's conscious life can be the result of something which happens in the unconscious in accordance with rules fixed by consciousness, Searle's in this case. We shall come back to the illusiveness of considering consciousness as an 'effect'. For now, it is enough to understand that unless its ontological origin is clarified, Searle's Network is nothing but a figure of speech. Actually, there is no apparent reason to make reference to an unconscious intentional Network of meanings to explain the fact that formulating the intention of presenting oneself for presidential elections is plausible and comprehensible, while formulating the intention of becoming a piece of amethyst is not. As we have already said, consciousness cannot but be a perpetual synthesis of earlier states of consciousness.

My present consciousness is new consciousness which is born ex nihilo and does not resemble anything before it. But this does not mean that my earlier states of consciousness are not synthetically represented in it. Soon I will leave the house to go to the cinema. This will happen, not because I have a sort of redeeming Network which allows me to do this but forbids me to leave the house to hunt a jaguar, but simply because my present consciousness is mundane consciousness of a being which is me, a being which carries around its past without any possibility of getting rid of it. There is, then, no Network of beliefs and meanings on one side *and* a consciousness which is determined by it on the other side. My consciousness *is* the network of the beliefs and meanings of which it is made up. Beliefs and meanings which are not in an unconscious *elsewhere* in a strange state of *active passivity*, that is in an oxymoron – meanings and beliefs whose origin as well as the present state need explaining. In fact either they are passive in the unconscious and so have no way of influencing conscious life or they are active, in which case, where their activity is supposed to stem from needs explaining. Carter's consciousness in formulating his intention of presenting himself at the presidential elections is such as it is, also because at a certain point in his life Carter became conscious of living in a country where there are presidents, presidential elections, etc. His present intention is not the result of unconscious intentionality made up of unconscious beliefs, but is the present form of his present consciousness which implies, and is, the synthesis of all his earlier states of consciousness.

If I now take a cigarette to my lips and inhale the smoke, this does not happen as the result of a series of unconscious presuppositions. It is not because I have the unconscious and intentional belief that, for instance, 'there are objects called cigarettes of a certain shape which serve a certain purpose, which are bad for your health but also give pleasure, which in order to smoke you must go through a series of movements which involve the contraction of certain arm muscles but not of others, and that each movement consumes a certain amount of energy which is reflected in the consumption of oxygen and carbon compounds, etc.' This is only one of the countless explanations which I can give for my act of smoking, or to put it another way, one of the possible ways my consciousness thematizes my act of smoking in order to assign it a meaning. Meanings and beliefs do not *precede* consciousness, if anything they *follow* it, that is they are possible thematizations of the world on behalf of consciousness. Consciousness itself has no need for meanings and beliefs which precede it and guide it out of the darkness of the unconscious. Consciousness *is* the synthetic combination of these meanings which, with a secondary operation, can become theses for consciousness which, in this case, ceases to *be them* in order to detach itself from them and make them the object of its own thematization. In short, there may be a metaphysical problem in consciousness but there is definitely not an ontological problem: my present consciousness is *made up* of my earlier states of consciousness. We will see later, when our discussion leads us to the problem of temporality, what exactly is meant by this. For now, it is enough to have clarified the impossibility of supposing the existence of an unconscious intentional world.

We have just seen that hypothesizing the existence of intentional, unconscious beliefs involves the problem of supposing the existence of an unconscious subject who 'believes' something (for example that Searle's grandfather never left the American continent). This unconscious subject, then, is supposed to reveal itself just when the conscious subject is ready to thematize this type of pre-packaged thought, stored in the frozen unconscious, together with the unconscious subject, passively waiting for consciousness to defrost it, as if by magic. This type of interpretation, which does not seem to deserve comment, is however worth analyzing once and for all.

The first question to be asked clearly concerns the nature of the subject, this unconscious *who* that *believes*. A first objection could be raised at this point, and that is that in reality questioning the nature of an unconscious subject is the same as posing a false problem. In fact, there is no need to presuppose an unconscious subjectivity as author of acts like believing or thinking. Beliefs and thoughts could be unconscious without needing to be the beliefs and thoughts *of* someone, that is of an unconscious subject. They would be kinds of pure representations which in themselves were complete and self-sufficient. In other words, that network of meanings which, according to Searle, 'are in one's head'.

Let us suppose that shortly I leave the office to go and buy cigarettes at the bar on the corner. According to the hypothesis in question, this project of mine is plausible inasmuch as a series of unconscious beliefs make it so. The belief, for instance, that there are shops that sell cigarettes, that these shops have certain opening hours compatible with the time I go to one of these to fulfill my objective, that I am a great consumer of cigarettes, and so on. Good. These beliefs, which make my objective possible, supposedly lie passively in the unconscious, waiting to intervene, and guide my behavior when necessary. Question: who informs them when it is their turn? How do they come out of their passive state to become active? You might say they are *activated*, as functionalist literature does. A group of representations or of neurons are activated in order to attain said goal. But, once again, *who* activates these representations? Certainly not my consciousness. The moment I go to buy my cigarettes my consciousness is pure, non-reflexive consciousness, consciousness without a subject, consciousness of-cigarettes-to-be-bought. They could be said to activate themselves, that is, to pass from their passive state to an active one without the intervention of any external factor. But why them in particular? Why should only those beliefs which are useful to one's purpose be activated, and not others? You could object further that it is precisely the need to reach one's goal which activates them. But even if we accept this kind of reverse teleology, which in any case needs clarifying, who is it that goes and tells the beliefs necessary for the purpose that it is they, and not others, that are necessary? There could be said to be a system of beliefs which is in some way always active in the unconscious and ready to face the needs of the moment. But how could a system of beliefs which is in a state of continuous activation, in a sort of erethism, work? In a similar condition, there would be beliefs in contradiction with each other and in an equivalent state of activation. For example, the beliefs 'there are shops that sell cigarettes' and 'man has been on the moon' would be activated contemporarily. If both these beliefs are activated at the same time, who can assure me that halfway from the office to the bar I will not decide to go to the moon? This demonstrates, then, that a problem of priority among beliefs arises, dictated by the necessity of the moment. And this priority takes us back to the problem of selecting the appropriate beliefs; since this is not carried out by a conscious 'who', the existence of an unconscious 'who', author of this choice, must be presupposed.

So here we are, once again, struggling with the nature of a *who*, an unconscious subject who intentionally turns to an unconscious world made up of beliefs, meanings, thoughts, memories, and so on. Who is this unconscious subject, this *homunculus* who lives in the shadow of the unconscious, master and origin of conscious life?

The problem of an unconscious 'who'

First of all it is plain to see that the unconscious *homunculus* is distinct from the object it intentionally addresses, beliefs, memories, etc. In a certain sense then, we find the same relationship between the *homunculus* and the object it addresses as that which exists between consciousness and its object. In short, one could say that the *homunculus* is *conscious* of beliefs, of the meanings of the thoughts and memories it has to select, activate, etc. But *what is the unconscious homunculus conscious* of? What is the nature of unconscious meanings, memories, beliefs? Let us go back to the case of memory, which is that which interests us most. In its work of selecting and checking memories, the *homunculus* deals with both true and false memories. Its task is that of selecting memories, *sending* the real ones to consciousness and rejecting the false ones. Now, it is obvious that if we accept such a hypothesis, we must also accept that the memories that the *homunculus* examines or, in functionalist terms, the information that the monitoring systems elaborate, must be already specified in syntactic-grammatical terms. Since no active role is attributed to consciousness, all that arrives there must already exist *first*, in the unconscious, in the form that it will have *afterwards* in consciousness. For example, our patient's confabulatory memory of 'having won a running race' will be exactly the same in the unconscious, in a sort of state of inactivity, waiting to be evaluated by the *homunculus* as a possible memory. In this way the *homunculus* fallacy not only postulates the existence of an unconscious consciousness, that is, it is based on an oxymoron, but since this unconscious consciousness must have an object to turn to, it also postulates unconscious mnemonic activity already specified in syntactic-grammatical terms. In other words, as in a photocopy of conscious life, memories are found in exactly the same form in the unconscious, ready to be selected by our *homunculus*, and *sent* to that kind of passive container which is thought to be consciousness.

At this point one may object that memories do not need to exist in the unconscious in the form that they have in consciousness, because consciousness can be considered as having emergent properties. Searle (1983), for example, maintains that the liquidity of water, just like consciousness, digestion, photosynthesis or cell reproduction, is caused by elements which precede it in the causal chain and takes form in the structure which regulates the relationship among these elements. But the molecular structure of water does not, by any means, reveal its *liquidity*. If I look for its chemical structure, what I find is a certain relationship between pieces of matter which are called atoms, and I express this relationship with a conventional symbol: H_2O. In H_2O there is no *liquidity*, just as there is no solidity or gaseous state. In order for H_2O to be liquid, something which has nothing whatsoever to do with its molecular structure is required. That is, H_2O needs to be found at a certain temperature and under certain pressure conditions. But even if the conditions of temperature and pressure are met, we still have not discovered the liquidity of water. In order for water to be liquid, consciousness must notice it. Without consciousness bothering to discover water *as liquid*, water, assuming its chemical structure is known, is nothing but H_2O. If its chemical structure is unknown, water is simply *water*, that *thing* we are all familiar with and which we know has certain characteristics, among these liquidity, a term we use to distinguish one state of matter from another. As for temperature and pressure, they only become significant when a consciousness which knows a bit of physics recognizes that these two variables are essential in order for water to be liquid. In other words, the molecular structure of water is neither necessary nor sufficient for its liquidity. It is not necessary as water can be considered to be liquid *before*, and quite apart from, any knowledge of its molecular structure. It is not sufficient since even if by some absurdity there were someone in the universe who knew the molecular structure of water *before* knowing that it was liquid, from the former he could never derive the latter. Searle's causality could, in reality, be easily turned upside down. It could be maintained that it is the molecular structure of water that is caused by, and realized in its liquidity. It is because water is liquid that it has a certain molecular structure. But if we decide, once and for all, to leave aside the circularity of causal thought, it is clear that neither the liquidity of water nor its structure can lay claim to priority over the other. They both come into being as meanings, that is, as objects which present themselves to consciousness in accordance with different points of view. Water is both liquid and H_2O without one of these being cause of the other.

In short, in order to maintain that liquidity is an emergent property of H_2O and that conscious remembering is an emergent property of memories that exist in the unconscious in a form that is different from the form they have in consciousness, one should show how these properties, liquidity and conscious remembering, *emerge* from different states. In the absence of a clear specification about the passage from one state to another, the liquidity of water and conscious remembering are nothing but a figure of speech.

Turning back to the problem of the *homunculus,* we see that we have gained nothing in supposing its existence. In fact, we find ourselves with an unconscious made up of the same elements we left in conscious life: on the one hand a subject with its baggage of intentionality, the *homunculus,* on the other a pre-fabricated unconscious world that the homunculus intentionally addresses. At this point it is clear that what we had invoked to *explain* conscious memory requires an explanation itself. In fact, if the existence of unconscious monitoring mechanisms, the *homunculus,* has been set as a condition to explain the conscious emergence of memory, the criteria in accordance with which these unconscious monitoring mechanisms are supposed to operate also need explaining. In other words, on the basis of what criteria does the *homunculus* distinguish a true memory from a false one? In order to reject false memories, the *homunculus* needs to know what it is rejecting. The *homunculus* in fact has to *choose* among memories and in order to do so it must be able to represent these memories to itself. Otherwise how could it accept true memories and reject false ones? But it is not sufficient for the *homunculus* to be able to distinguish between memories. It must also recognize false memories *as 'to be rejected'* and that implies that the *homunculus* must be able to represent its own activity to itself. Indeed, how could the *homunculus* recognize memories 'to be rejected' without being conscious of recognizing them as *to be rejected?* In short, the *homunculus* implies not only a conscious representation of memories 'to be rejected', but also a consciousness of what the *homunculus* must do in order to carry out its action correctly. But what kind of self-consciousness is the self-consciousness of the *homunculus?* It must be consciousness of the tendency to reject false memories, but precisely for the aim *of not being conscious of that tendency.* An unconscious consciousness that is conscious of itself in order not to be so. At this point wouldn't this *homunculus* in bad faith (Sartre, 1943) also need its own unconscious *homunculus* to help it distinguish real memories from false ones? The game of Chinese boxes continues and what we are left with is only a *reductio ad infinitum* which is clearly of no explanatory value.

Is a scientific theory of consciousness possible?

Up until now our discussion dealt with present theories of memory and their possible application to the interpretation of confabulation. We have shown that these theories are based on a paradox, that is, on the idea that the past is passively preserved in memory traces, and on a fallacy, the fallacy of the *homunculus*, that is, the assumption of the existence of a sort of unconscious consciousness in bad faith. So, memory traces and monitoring processes are just explanatory idols which theories of memory should get rid of. The problem is that there is a tendency to think of memories as unconscious items that one brings to consciousness. But we have to understand consciousness before we can assume that memories simply 'rise' to it or are tacked onto it. In particular, it must be ascertained whether memory and consciousness are part of the same structure or not. The question we have to ask at this point is whether a scientific theory on the relationship between memory and consciousness is possible.

Given that the aim of science is to achieve objective knowledge and that its method is the establishment of quantitative relationships, the consequence is that a scientific theory of consciousness will have as aim its the objectivation of consciousness and the determination of the quantitative relationships that describe it. In other words, in order for a science of consciousness to be possible, consciousness must be a measurable object which is independent of the observer and of the point of observation. Yet, to objectivise consciousness, i.e. to consider it as an object, means to transform consciousness into something it is not. Consciousness by definition is subjectivity that describes itself according to rules of quality and not of quantity. This flowerpot standing in front of me, the memory of meeting Paul last night, the blue I am now imagining are present to my consciousness, establishing that subjectivity that is me. And I am the only being responsible for this subjectivity. Of course, at the same time that being that I am subjectively is not only *for itself* but also *for the others*. I am continuously observed, an object for other consciousnesses like other consciousnesses are objects *for myself*. However, this objective consciousness has not the characteristics of consciousness because it is an object and my consciousness is not object but subject. The only being that for me has the characteristics of consciousness is *my* consciousness. And even when my consciousness becomes object not for others but for me, i.e. when with a reflective act I become conscious of my consciousness, the consciousness I am conscious of is a me which is *not me*, that does not have the characteristics of consciousness. The objectivation of consciousness, therefore, reflects a radical metamorphosis. Even if I could *see myself* distinctively as an object, what I would see would not be an adequate representation of what I am, but only the perception of the distance that separates me from myself, that is the objective perception of my being *other*, which is radically different from my being for myself, that is from that being that I am in the irreflective mode. My considering myself *honest*, for example, does not describe at all what I am for myself, because I cannot be honest for myself, that is, in the irreflective mode of consciousness. The qualification of 'honest' characterizes me as object: it is that being of which my consciousness is conscious that is honest, not what I am in the irreflective mode, that is my consciousness.

Even considering my consciousness as object for the consciousness of others, we can see that this does not establish how I am for myself but how I am *for others*. When somebody describes my character saying that I am 'jealous', 'nice', or 'irascible', I don't *recognize* myself at all in this description, nevertheless I know that *it is me*, an objectual 'I' that I cannot deny being but that does not describe at all what I am for myself. In this way the 'I-object', or objective consciousness, establishes a knowledge that does not refer to the reality of consciousness, that is, to what I concretely am as subject, but to a metamorphosed consciousness, a consciousness transformed into object. And this is the metamorphosis of consciousness that science requires in order to establish consciousness as the object of its investigation. Therefore, any scientific theory of consciousness can only be a theory that concerns objective consciousness, that is a degraded form of consciousness, and will have to renounce, by definition, the possibility of having 'fresh' information concerning consciousness because consciousness in its entirety defines itself precisely as what is not object.

Earlier in this chapter we argued that intentionality is a characteristic of consciousness since it describes the necessity of consciousness to always be consciousness *of* something. We would now like to add that consciousness is always consciousness of something *in a certain way*. This means that consciousness takes a certain point of view of its object and of the same object consciousness can take various points of view. The first consequence of this statement is that different *modes* of consciousness exist and each of these represents an original and irreducible mode of addressing the world. By 'original' we mean that each mode of consciousness is different from any other. By 'irreducible' we mean that the existence of each original mode of consciousness cannot be traced back to something else that precedes it in causal or ontological terms. A taxonomy of the different modes of consciousness is far beyond the aims of this work. Our aim is rather to operate certain distinctions that will allow us to see, though at a rather general level of description, the differences between two modes of consciousness, namely what we will indicate as *knowing consciousness* (KC) and *temporal consciousness* (TC).

Knowing consciousness and temporal consciousness

KC describes what is usually referred to as semantic memory. A substantial difference, however, distinguishes KC from what is presupposed in the idea of semantic memory. Unlike semantic memory, KC is not based on the idea of unconscious mental representation. KC is consciousness of the object, it is already *outside itself* and directed toward the object to be known. And it is consciousness of the object *in a certain mode*, an original mode that makes it impossible that what I know, for example, can be mistaken for what I remember or imagine. It can be argued that I could never, for example, recognize this packet of cigarettes as *red* if I had not *already* somewhere in my mind and my brain an *idea of red*. But this kind of argument is unintelligible because it presupposes the existence and the activation of unconscious representation and in so doing falls into the fallacy of the *homunculus*. If I recognize the packet of cigarettes as red it is not because I operate, unconsciously, a sort of correspondence between the packet I perceive and a mental representation that I carry in me. What one should say is that I am conscious of this packet of cigarettes as red because my present consciousness, since it is a synthesis of all my past consciousnesses, is also consciousness of red. But I can also see this packet of cigarettes as ugly, dangerous, attractive, almost finished. In short, the meanings I attribute to the packet of cigarettes are concretely infinite and depend on my being conscious here and now as synthesis of what I have been before and elsewhere. In this sense KC is temporal since it is a synthesis of what I have been and *we are our past* or *wesen ist was gewesen ist*, as in Hegel. But at the same time KC, which is temporal, is also atemporal in the sense that the time of which it is made is not recognizable. KC *is* the past but it is not consciousness *of* the past, nor of the present or of the future. There is no time in the packet of cigarettes in front of me although it is thanks to time, that is, of the past I am made of, that I can see the packet as red, dangerous, as so an.

Consciousness *of* time, i.e. the thematization of the object in the mode of temporality, is what we have called TC. TC, as far as it poses its object according to the structures of time, i.e. the past, the present, and the future, is an organized, original, and irreducible form of consciousness, for addressing the world. Unlike KC, TC transcends the mere presence of the object in order to set it in time. When I say that I remember yesterday's dinner, that now I am in my office, and that later I will go out to buy some cigarettes, knowledge is presupposed, as we will see later, but it is not the aim of the temporalizing act that I am making. In order to remember yesterday's dinner, to affirm that I am *now* in my office, and to plan the act of buying cigarettes, I have to *know* what a dinner, an office, and cigarettes are. However, this knowledge is only the structure on which my act is founded. It is *through* knowledge that the temporalizing act is realized but it is not *for* knowledge that it is realized. Although TC is an organized structure of consciousness because past, present, and future are not isolated dimensions but continuously refer to one another, consciousness of the past, of the present, and of the future are nevertheless subordinate structures of TC, and for the sake of clarity, we will describe them separately.

Consciousness of the past is an act through which the object of consciousness is seen as absent, or as non-present. But, in contrast with imagining consciousness, which sees the absent object as non-existent, for consciousness of the past the object is absent *in* the past. It is this consciousness of the past that we call remembering. But consciousness of the past is not consciousness of a generic and impersonal past. When I say that I remember that Kennedy was killed in 1963 in Dallas or that Dante wrote the *Divine Comedy*, I am not conscious of the past but of a piece of information, a notion, that joins other notions to form a certain type of knowledge. Kennedy is president of the United States *and* past, Dante is a poet, Italian and past. In other words, it is about a generic and impersonal past, not *my* past. In order for consciousness of the past to exist, i.e. remembering in the mode of TC, there must be a deep link between the being I am now and a being I was before. It is to that past being of mine that consciousness of the past refers, and it is that past being that remembering represents.

In order for consciousness of the past, i.e. remembering, to exist, there needs to be a present of which the past is past. It is present consciousness that is consciousness of the past. It must be emphasized here that by 'present' we mean subjective or phenomenological present, which distinguishes itself from «objective», or clock-measured present. Objective present, as measured in neurophysiological experiments for example, lasts a few milliseconds and is practically an instantaneous present. Accordingly, present consciousness would also last a few milliseconds and as a consequence it would be either instantaneous or always 'behind' already in the past. However, the subjective phenomenological present cannot be measured in objective time. The phenomenological present is not an instant, but a dimension that distinguishes itself from the clock-measured present with its characteristic of *presence*. So present consciousness is not an instant, or something that is always already past, but is the relationship between the subject and its object in the mode of presence. But present consciousness can also be consciousness *of* the present. Consciousness of the present is an act that temporalizes the world in the present form and that does not confuse itself with perception which is the mere presence of consciousness to the object. There is no temporal dimension in my perception of this chair. It is only when I feel myself contemporary to this chair, to this table, to the city, to the world that the present comes to the world as consciousness of something in the present mode. So consciousness of the present, far from coinciding with perception, represents thematization of perception in the present mode.

The third subordinate structure of temporality is consciousness of the future. Consciousness of the future puts its object in the future mode. It is thematization of my possibility in the future mode. By 'possibility' we mean what is founded on knowledge of my past and present, and this radically distinguishes consciousness of the future from wishes. Tomorrow I will be in Paris and I will continue working on this paper. This is one of my possibilities, a thematization in the future mode of my being that founds itself and is a synthesis of knowledge of my being in the world: I know that I live in Paris, that I am writing this paper and that tomorrow is not Sunday. When instead I say 'I would like to be an astronaut' I don't express a possibility, but something that transcends the knowledge of the mundane being that I am.

So TC opens the possibility of a temporal existence for the subject. A subject who is conscious of a personal past when remembering a personal present, in which he/she is oriented, and a personal future, in which he/she is projected. But before proceeding further to see what is the relationship between TC and confabulation, which is what interests us more, we need to know what the normal operations of TC are.

Uniqueness and multiplicity

Consciousness, we have seen, must always be consciousness *of* an object. One of the characteristics of the object of consciousness is that it represents and reveals to consciousness a *uniqueness* (U) and a *multiplicity* (M). Let's consider this point more closely. This pen on the desk is both *a pen* and *the pen*. In the first case, it is an undetermined pen, something that belongs to the category of 'pens', an object that I recognize and use appropriately because I recognize it. In contrast, in the second case 'the pen' is a determined object, it is exactly this pen in front of me, the pen I bought yesterday and that I will be using tomorrow. So the pen reveals a U and a M. M is reflected in its being a pen and not a different object. U manifests itself in its being this precise pen and not another. However, the U and M of the pen are not adjacent qualities, external to one another. There is a sort of hierarchy that establishes the relationship between the object as representative of an M of objects and the object as representative of itself, in being *this* object that distinguishes itself from all the other objects of the world. The U of the object, of this pen, of the room, of my feeling happy is *this*, i.e. they manifest a U that distinguishes them from the *other* pen, room, or feeling of happiness. But their U is founded on an M, the M that acts in such a way that these objects manifest themselves to consciousness as unique but under a certain, already distinguished form, i.e. pen, room, happiness. If we consider the opposite condition, we see that for the undetermined object there is no need to represent the U. I can think of a flower, a love, a city, a world without these objects needing to be *this* flower, *this love*, etc.

But what happens when in front of me there is an object I have no experience of, that I don't know? At first sight one would say that any object that I see for the first time is unique and doesn't carry in itself that M that we attributed to known objects. But in actual fact, as soon as an unknown object shows up, all the M of which it is made manifests itself instantaneously. This geometric form that I have never seen before is *already* 'geometric form that I have never seen', that is it summarizes and represents in the negative form what my consciousness has been before. And this can happen without my needing to notice the U of the object. So the object, be it known or unknown, is first the expression of an M and then becomes *this* object, i.e. declares its U.

However, in order for the U of the object to be revealed, it must be addressed by consciousness in the mode of TC. In other words, in order to achieve the passage from the M to the U of an object, there must be an act of consciousness that selects its object as a *this*, and this can happen only if consciousness transcends the knowing mode to put itself at the level of the temporalization of the object. One would certainly want to argue that in what we have called KC the object also appears to me as unique. The cup in front of me is in any case *this* cup, it is with this cup that I interact and not with a generic cup when I pick it up and bring it to my lips. Of course, but its U is revealed only if I consider it as a *this*, that is when I notice its presence as an object that is not my consciousness, and to which my consciousness is contemporary. When I simply use it, when I execute the appropriate sequence of gestures in order to pick it up and bring it to my lips, or when I look at it wondering whether it is full or empty, there is no U in my consciousness. I do not even need to be conscious of the cup in order to use it and when I wonder whether it is empty or full I am aware of a problem to be solved, not of the presence of *this* cup. In short, there is the continuous possibility of varying the relationship between U and M and this possibility depends on the mode in which consciousness addresses the object.

However, one could ask, where is the evidence that in TC the object manifests itself to consciousness as unique and not according to its M. I can easily, for example, remember a generic walk along the shore without being able to locate it in any specific time but only in the past in general. But this does not mean that the walk I remember is not a particular walk but instead the general idea of walking along the shore. The fact that in this memory certain details are missing, where and when, for example, does not mean that I am not remembering a specific walk. Remembering cannot be anything other than remembering an object in its U, because the U of an object is precisely one of the elements that describe the relationship between remembering consciousness and its object.

Memory, consciousness, and temporality

The ideas we have expressed so far are part of a theory, the memory, consciousness and temporality theory (MCTT), that we have detailed elsewhere (Dalla Barba, 2002). Aspects of the MCTT relevant to the interpretation of confabulation are summarized below and schematically represented in Figure 11.3.

(1) Events produce atemporal and aspecific modifications in the organism and, within the organism, in the brain. These modifications, represented in Figure 11.3 as X, Y, and Z, are atemporal in the sense that they do not contain any information concerning time. They do not represent the past, the present, or the future, nor are they organized according to the order of succession, i.e. there is nothing in Y, for example, that encodes that Y comes before Z and after X. They are aspecific in the sense that they do not contain any information specifying that they are representing episodes, meanings, rules, procedures, algorithms, etc.

(2) The modifications in the brain can be more or less stable and more or less vulnerable depending on a number of variables. These variables include, among others, attention at encoding, emotional value of the event, depth of encoding, rehearsal and repeated experience of the same event, and so on.

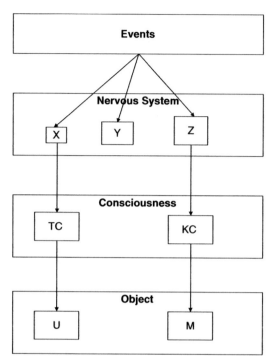

Figure 11.3 A hypothesis concerning the relation between memory, consciousness, and temporality. NS = nervous system; X, Y, Z = less stable (X), more stable (Z) patterns of modification of the nervous system; TC = temporal consciousness; KC = knowing consciousness; U = uniqueness; M = multiplicity.

(3) Consciousness means to be conscious *of something in a specific way.* That means that consciousness is not an aspecific dimension that passively receives and becomes aware of different types of already specified information, but rather that different types of consciousness exist, each representing an original and irreducible way of addressing the world. Different types of consciousness include, among others, TC and KC. TC means to become aware of something as part of a personal past, present, or future. KC means to become aware of something as a meaning or as an element of impersonal knowledge or information.

(4) The object of consciousness represents a determination and an indetermination, what we have called U (uniqueness) and M (multiplicity). TC addresses the object's U, whereas KC addresses its M.

(5) Less stable and more vulnerable patterns of modifications of the brain are necessary, but not sufficient, for the interaction between TC and the object's U, whereas more stable and less vulnerable modifications of the

brain are necessary, but not sufficient, for the interaction between KC and the object's M.

Temporal consciousness and confabulation

How do the ideas that we have described apply to the interpretation of confabulation? Confabulation, as we have seen in the first part of this chapter, is not limited to remembering personal past episodes, but also involves the patient's present and future. According to the MCTT, in confabulating patients TC is still there, as in normal subjects, and addresses the object's U, just as in normal subjects. These patients can still remember their pasts, they are present to a world, and can project themselves into a personal future. But in doing this they make errors, sometimes frankly bizarre errors. Actually, what is happening in these patients is that TC is still there but is not interacting with less stable patterns of modification of the brain. Most frequently the result of this condition is that personal habits and routines are considered in a personal temporal framework. When asked what they have done the previous day or what they are going to do the following day, confabulating patients typically answer with memories and plans that they usually had in their daily lives. Although admitted

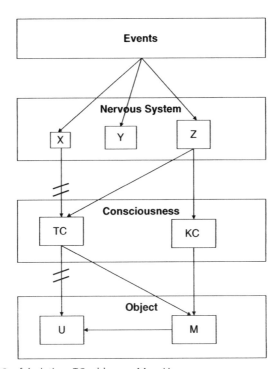

Figure 11.4 Confabulation: TC addresses M as U.

to the hospital, they will say, for example, that the previous day they went out shopping and that the following day they will be visiting some friends, acts that presumably were part of their routine lives. According to the MCTT, in this condition TC interacts with more stable patterns of modification of the brain and addresses the object's M, habits, routines, repeated events, *as* U, a specific, unique past event.

It could be argued that patients who confabulate in episodic memory, orientation, and planning tasks are not necessarily conscious of a confabulatory past, present, and future but rather they simply produce the more plausible answer without having a subjective experience of remembering of being in that place at that time or of planning their future. If this were the case, our account of confabulation in the past, present, and future would be dismissed because TC wouldn't play any role at all in confabulation. Confabulation would be just a sort of 'best guess' produced as a consequence of a faulty memory. Yet, there is evidence that patients who confabulate actually do become aware of their confabulatory past, present, and future. For example, patient MB (Dalla Barba, 1993) when asked to attribute a ' remember' or a ' know' judgement to his confabulations, systematically gave 'remember' judgements. Also, the same patient showed he was ready to carry out his confabulatory plans (see also Baddeley and Wilson, 1986; Moscovitch, 1989; Burgess and McNeil, 1999; Metcalf et al., in press). In addition, from a clinical point of view, confabulating patients do not look like subjects who produce their 'best guess' in answering questions, but rather they seem to adhere completely to their confabulatory reports.

However, although habits, routines, and repeated events are the most frequent content of confabulation (Dalla Barba and Boissé, in preparation), confabulations are sometimes made of elements that cannot be traced back to any aspect of the patient's history, present, or future situation. This is the case, for example, of patient MG who told the radiologist that he had accompanied a friend to be admitted to the neurology department and that the neurologist who was taking care of his friend realized that he also had neurological problems and so decided to refer him to the radiology department for a CT scan. Does the MCTT account for this case?

Well, it is clear that MG is immersed in a temporal existence: he *remembers* accompanying a friend to the hospital and he is *there*, undergoing a CT scan *because* the neurologist noticed by chance that he had neurological problems. So TC is working in this case and, as it usually does, is addressing the object's U, the specific past episode he remembers and the specific present situation he is involved in. Can we say in this case that TC interacts with more stable patterns of modification of the brain, as we said it did for habits, routines, and repeated events? Clearly there is no evidence in this sense. In this case, confabulation appears to be created ex nihilo. This is difficult to understand only if we are prisoners of the memory trace paradox and of the *homunculus* fallacy. MG's confabulation is not a matter of *failing to inhibit currently irrelevant memory traces*, as Schnider believes (Schnider and Ptak, 1999). MG's past and present world is not made of currently irrelevant memory traces. And it is not the result of the confusion between reality and imagination, as Johnson would say, unless one wants to think that MG had once imagined the situation he is remembering and involved in, which is quite hard to believe. But if we consider that in MG TC is still there, the appearance of ex nihilo confabulations is not a problem, since we don't need to trace confabulation back to an unconscious elsewhere, memory traces or imagination. In fact, TC cannot escape the general rule that consciousness is always consciousness *of* something. So, if TC is there, it must be consciousness of something, i.e. it must temporalize its object according to the subordinate structures of temporality, past, present, and future. There is no need to ask where the object of this temporalization comes from because it doesn't come from any sort of unconscious world. It is not *behind* consciousness, it is down there, right in front of consciousness. If we are not in a psychoanalytic perspective, do we ask where thoughts or imagined objects come from? We don't. So why should we ask this question for TC? All we can say is that when TC temporalizes its objects, under normal conditions we can recognize a *true* temporal world, a real past, present, and future, *probably* because TC interacts with less stable patterns of modification of the brain. When TC temporalizes its object in confabulatory conditions, sometimes we can recognize habits, routines, and repeated events, *probably* because TC interacts with more stable patterns of modification of the brain, other times we don't recognize any meaningful element of the patient's history, present, and future situation.

So, the difference between normal memory and confabulation is that in the case of patients who confabulate we are faced with a confabulatory consciousness in which past, present, and future are somehow distorted. Distorted with respect to what? The truth, you will say; with what *actually* took place, is taking place, or will take place. But who establishes the truth? If temporality, and therefore its subordinate dimensions, is inherent to consciousness, what relationship of truth can there be between what you suppose to *actually* have taken place, to be taking place, or to be going to take place and the reality of TC? And yet for a witness, the doctor or the psychologist observing the patient who confabulates, his stories about the past, his perception of the present, and his future plans are confabulatory, in that they are totally at variance with what the listener expects as an answer, so much so that they push him to consider the patient's answers as not normal, namely as confabulatory.

Where does this discrepancy between what the observer expects and the answers he receives come from? In other words, what is the origin of this confabulatory temporality?

The answer to this question can only be a biological one. There is a biological difference between normal subjects and confabulators. This biological difference is represented by the brain lesion, which prevents the interaction between TC and less stable modifications of the brain.

It could be argued that we made us of an easy shortcut since we have established an interaction between the biological level (patterns of modification of the brain) and the psychological level (TC). However, this is not a shortcut because TC depends on brain function and can be altered or abolished by a brain lesion. TC works normally in subjects without brain lesions, is altered in patients with brain lesions that cause confabulations, and is abolished, as we will see, in patients with brain lesions that cause amnesia. Now, the question is what are the brain structures which need to be intact for the normal functioning of TC, altered in confabulation, and damaged in amnesia? This is an experimental problem which needs more experimental work to be answered appropriately. However, the literatures on amnesia and on confabulation indicate that the hippocampus and the medial temporal lobe are good candidates as brain structures involved in the functioning and dysfunction of TC.

Temporal consciousness and brain: Is the medial temporal lobe 'temporal'?

Patients with medial temporal lobe (MTL) lesions are known to be deeply amnesic for personal past episodes and to have relatively preserved general knowledge or semantic memory (see Kopelman, 2002 for a review). Patient HM was the first well-documented example of this condition (Milner, 1958). However, amnesic patients do not consciously remember their pasts, nor can they imagine their personal future. These patients are lost in a *non-time*, or in a sort of instantaneous present. The patient, N.N., described by Tulving (1985) is a good example of this condition. Tulving's patient had preserved semantic abilities, but was unable to retrieve any episode from his personal past or to say anything about his future.

> N.N. has no difficulties with the concept of chronological time. He knows the units of time and their relationships perfectly well, and he can accurately represent chronological time graphically. But in stark contrast to his abstract knowledge of time, his awareness of subjective time seems to be severely impaired. When asked what he did before coming to where he is now, or what he did on the previous day, he says that he does not know. When asked what he will be doing when he leaves 'here', or what he will be doing 'tomorrow', he says he does not know.

Here is part of the transcript of the interview with me as the interviewer:

E.T: 'Let's try the question again about the future. What will you be doing tomorrow?' (there is a 15-second pause.)

N.N. smiles faintly, then says: 'I don't know'.

E.T: 'Do you remember the question?'

N.N: 'About what I'll be doing tomorrow?'

E.T: 'Yes. How would you describe your state of mind when you try to think about it?' (A 5-second pause.)

N.N: 'Blank. I guess'.

... When asked to compare his state of mind when he is trying to think about what he will be doing tomorrow with his state of mind when he thinks about what he did yesterday, he says it is the '*same kind of blankness*'.

(Tulving, 1985, p. 4)

As emerges from the description of this patient, what characterizes the core deficit of N.N. is a loss of TC. Past and future have disappeared as possible objects of his consciousness and the result is that N.N. is shut in an atemporal instantaneous present.

Further evidence of selective loss of TC in amnesia comes from patient DB described by Klein et al. (2002). DB suffered severe amnesia for the personally experienced past. By contrast, his knowledge of the non-personal past was relatively preserved. A similar pattern was evidenced in his ability to anticipate future events. Although DB had great difficulty what his experience might be like in the future, his capacity to anticipate issues and events in the public domain was comparable to that of neurologically healthy, age-matched controls. These findings show a dissociation between TC, which is impaired, and KC, which is preserved. Impairment of TC has also been documented in Alzheimer's disease (Dalla Barba et al., 1999).

So, there is increasing converging evidence that lesions which produce amnesia also produce deficits of TC. This suggests that the integrity of the MTL and related structures is crucial for the normal functioning of TC. Further evidence on the involvement of the MTL in TC comes from a recent neuroimaging study which showed that in normal subjects the hippocampus was activated both when individuals remembered their past and when they imagined their future (Addis et al., 2007).

Now, if the integrity of the MTL is crucial for the functioning of TC, what happens in confabulation, where TC is present but functioning in an abnormal way? The most plausible answer to this question is that in confabulation the MTL is intact, but lesions to other brain structures prevent its normal functioning, which is the biological counterpart of the claim that in confabulation TC is preserved but no longer interacts with less stable modifications of the brain. This seems actually to be the case. Gilboa and Moscovitch (2002) found that only 2 out of 79 patients with confabulation had lesions involving the MTL. These patients had lesions in more than 20 brain regions, although the frontal lobe was preferentially affected, but almost all these patients had preserved MTL. Twenty-eight additional confabulating patients not included in Gilboa's and Moscovitch's review also had preserved MTL (Dalla Barba, Cipolotti et al., 1990; Dalla Barba, 1993; Dalla Barba et al., 1998; Fotopoulou et al., 2004; Ciaramelli et al., 2006; Ciaramelli and Ghetti, 2007; Fotopoulou et al., 2007). So, what these data show is that what confabulators have in common is not a specific lesion site but rather the integrity of the MTL, which is consistent with the idea that the MTL is essential for the function of normal and confabulatory TC. In this sense the MTL is 'temporal' because its integrity allows individuals to be consciously aware of a personal past, present, and future.

There are a number of important questions that we have not addressed because they were far beyond the aims of this work. Why is confabulation often a transitory symptom? Does confabulation reflect a disconnection of the MTL? Why does amnesia, i.e. loss of TC, occur for lesions outside the MTL? Is it also a matter of disconnection of the MTL? And if this is the case, what is the difference between confabulators and non-confabulating amnesics with preserved MTL? What is the exact role of frontal lesions in confabulation, if we reject, as we do, the possibility of unconscious monitoring? What is the exact nature of what we indicated as patterns of modification of the brain, if we reject, as we do, the notion of memory traces which would contain the past? Some of these are experimental questions that will be answered by experimental work. Others are theoretical and their discussion couldn't have been included in these pages. What we have shown in these pages is that understanding confabulation is a difficult and ambitious enterprise. An enterprise is doomed to failure if based on theoretically untenable and experimentally undemonstrated explanatory idols like memory traces and unconscious monitoring. Confabulation is a conscious phenomenon, indeed a phenomenon that involves TC. A better understanding of TC, including its neurobiological correlates, is therefore demanded, legitimate and necessary.

References

Addis, D.R., Wong, A.T., and Schacter, D.L. (2007). Remembering the past and imaging the future: Common and distinct neural substrates during event construction and elaboration. *Neuropsychologia*, **45**, 1363–1377.

Anderson, J.R. and G.H. Bower. (1974). A propositional theory of recognition memory. *Memory and Cognition*, **2**, 406–412.

Anderson, J.R. and J.H. Bower. (1972). Recognition and retrieval processes in free recall. *Psychological Review*, **79**, 97–123.

Baddeley, A. and B. Wilson. (1986). Amnesia, autobiographical memory and confabulation. *Autobiographical Memory* (ed D.C. Rubin). Cambridge, UK, Cambridge University Press. pp. 225–252.

Bergson, H. (1896). *Matière et mémoire*. Paris, Alcan.

Brentano, F. (1874 (1973)). *Psychology From an Empirical Standpoint*. London, Routledge and Kegan Paul.

Burgess, P.W. and J.E. McNeil (1999). Content-specific confabulation. *Cortex*, **35**, 163–182.

Burgess, P.W. and T. Shallice (1996). Confabulation and the control of recollection. *Memory, 4*, 359–411.

Ciaramelli, E. and S. Ghetti (2007). What are confabulators' memories made of? A study of subjective and objective measures of recollection in confabulation. *Neuropsychologia*, **45**(7), 1489–500.

Ciaramelli, E., Ghetti, S., Fraltarelli, M., and Ladavas, E. (2006). When true memory availability promotes false memory: Evidence from confabulating patients. *Neuropsychologia*, **44**(10), 1866–1877.

Claparède, E. (1911). Recognition et moïté. *Archives de Psychologie*, **11**, 79–90.

Conway, M.A. and P.C. Tacchi (1996). Motivated confabulation. *Neurocase*, **2**, 325–339.

Dalla Barba, G. (1993). Confabulation: Knowledge and recollective experience. *Cognitive Neuropsychology*, **10**(1), 1–20.

Dalla Barba, G. (1993). Different patterns of confabulation. *Cortex*, **29**, 567–581.

Dalla Barba, G. (2002). *Memory, Consciousness and Temporality*. Boston, Kluver Academic Publishers.

Dalla Barba, G., Boissé, M.-F., Bartolomeo, P., and Bachoud-Levi, A.C. (1997a). Confabulation following rupture of posterior communicating artery. *Cortex*, **33**, 563–570.

Dalla Barba, G., Cappelletti, Y.J., Signorini, M., and Denes, G. (1997b). Confabulation: Remembering "another" past, planning "another" future. *Neurocase*, **3**, 425–436.

Dalla Barba, G., Cipolotti, L., and Denes, G. (1990). Autobiographical memory loss and confabulation in Korsakoff's syndrome: A case report. *Cortex*, **26**, 525–534.

Dalla Barba, G., Mantovan, M.C., Cappelletti, Y.J., and Denes, G. (1998). Temporal gradient in confabulation. *Cortex*, **34**, 417–426.

Dalla Barba, G., Nedjam, Z., and Dubois, B. (1999). Confabulation, executive functions and source memory in Alzheimer's disease. *Cognitive Neuropsychology*, **16**(3/4/5), 385–398.

Fotopoulou, A., Conway, M., and Solms, M. (2007). Confabulation: Motivated reality monitoring. *Neuropsychologia*, **45**, 2180–2190.

Fotopoulou, A., Solms, M., and Turnbull, O. (2004). Wishful reality distortions in confabulation: A case report. *Neuropsychologia*, **42**(6), 727–744.

Gilboa, A. and Moscovitch, M. (2002). *The CognitiveNeuroscience of Confabulation: A Review and a Model. The Handbook of Memory Disorders* (eds. A. Baddeley, M. Kopelman, and B. Wilson). Chichester, John Wiley & Sons Ltd.

Hintzman, D.L. (1978). *The Psychology of Learning and Memory*. San Francisco, W.H. Freeman.

Husserl, E. (1950). *Ideen Zur Einen Reinen Phänomenologie*. Hen Haag, Martinus Nijhoff.

James, W. (1890). *Principles of Psychology*. New York, Holt.

Johnson, M. (1988). *Discriminating the Origin of Information. Delusional Beliefs* (eds. F. Oltmanns and B. Mahers). New York, Wiley. pp. 34–65.

Johnson, M.K. (1991). *Reality Monitoring: Evidence from Confabulation in Organic Brain Disease Patients. Awareness of Deficit After Brain Injury* (eds. G.P. Prigatano and D.L. Schacter). New York-Oxford, Oxford University Press. pp. 176–197.

Johnson, M.K. and Raye, C.L. (1981). Reality monitoring. *Psychological Review*, **88**, 67–85.

Joseph, R. (1986). Confabulation and delusional denial: Frontal lobe and lateralized influences. *Journal of Clinical Psychology*, **42**, 507–520.

Klein, S.B., Loftus, J., et al. (2002). Memory and temporal experience. The effects of episodic memory loss on an amnesic patient's ability to remember the past and imagine the future. *Social Cognition*, **20**, 353–379.

Kopelman, M.D. (2002). Disorders of memory. *Brain*, **125**, 2152–2190.

Marcel, A.J. (1988). Phenomenal experience and functionalism. *Consciousness in Contemporary Science* (eds. A.J. Marcel and E. Bisiach). Oxford, Oxford University Press. pp. 121–158.

Merleau-Ponty, M. (1945). *Phénoménologie de la Perception.* Paris, Librairie Gallimard.

Metcalf, K., Langdon, R., et al. (in press). Models of confabulation: A critical review and a new framework. *Cognitive Neuropsychology*.

Milner, B. (1958). *Psychological Defects Produced by Temporal lobe Excision. Association for Research in Nervous and Mental Disease. The Brain and Human Behavior.* Baltimore, Williams and Wilkins.

Morton, J., Hammersley, R.H., and Bekerian, D. (1985). Headed records: A model for memory and its failures. *Cognition*, **20**, 1–23.

Moscovitch, M. (1989). Confabulation and the frontal systems: Strategic versus associative retrieval in neuropsychological theories of memory. *Varieties of Memory and Consciousness: Essay in Honor of Endel Tulving* (eds. H.L. Roedinger and F.I. Craik). Hillsdale NJ, Lawrence Erlbaum. pp. 133–160.

Moscovitch, M. and Melo, B. (1997). Strategic retrieval and the frontal lobes: Evidence from confabulation and amnesia. *Neuropsychologia*, **35**(7), 1017–1034.

Sandson, J., Albert, M.L., et al. (1986). Confabulation in Aphasia. *Cortex*, **22**: 621–626.

Sartre, J.-P. (1939). Une idée fondamentale de la phénoménologie de Husserl: l'intentionnalité. Situations I. Paris, Gallimard.

Sartre, J.-P. (1943). *L'être et le néant.* Paris, Gallimard.

Schnider, A. and Ptak, R (1999). Spontaneous confabulators fail to suppress currently irrelevant memory traces. *Nature Neuroscience*, **2**(7), 677–681.

Searle, J.R. (1983). *Intentionality.* Cambridge, Cambridge University Press.

Stuss, D.T., Alexander, M.P., Leiberman, A., and Levine, H. (1978). An extraordinary form of confabulation. *Neurology*, **28**, 1166–1172.

Tulving, E. (1972). Episodic and semantic memory. *Organization of Memory* (eds. E. Tulving and W. Donaldson). New York, Academic Press.

Tulving, E. (1983). *Elements of Episodic Memory.* Oxford, University Press.

Tulving, E. (1985). Memory and consciousness. *Canadian Psychology*, **26**, 1–12.

Weinstein, E. and Lyerly, O. (1968). Confabulation following brain injury. *Archives of General Psychiatry*, **18**, 348–354.

Chapter 12

Disentangling the motivational theories of confabulation

Aikaterini Fotopoulou

Introduction

Confabulation has long been described as motivated by personal goals and emotions (see Talland, 1961 for review; Berlyne, 1972; Weinstein, 1996). Historically, motivational factors in confabulation were thought to arise as a secondary consequence of the brain injury as a whole and not as the specific consequence of a particular neurocognitive deficit (e.g. Weinstein and Kahn, 1955). These kind of models were criticised for considering the motivated content of confabulation as independent of the neuropathology that causes confabulation in the first place. As a consequence, these theories were seen as inadequate to explain the occurrence of confabulation. Moreover, they were not empirically supported. In this chapter, we will review the tension between cognitive and motivational theories of confabulation and we will argue that it lies in residual notions of an outdated and rigid distinction between functional and organic explanations. By contrast, the more recent motivational accounts of confabulation presented here attempt to escape this implicit dualism (Fotopoulou et al., 2008). A number of recent systematic studies on the emotional content of confabulation have shown that, given the trade-off between the influence of cognitive control and motivational influences on memory, impairment in one aspect may generate exaggeration in the other; when irrelevant memory representations are not inhibited and memories are not retrieved in appropriate manner, motivational factors may acquire a greater role in determining which memories are selected for retrieval and accepted as true (see also Fotopoulou et al., 2004, 2007b).

What is confabulation?

Confabulations are false memories produced without conscious knowledge of their falsehood. Amnesic confabulatory behaviour is considered pathognomonic of Wernicke-Korsakoff's syndrome, but confabulation has been observed in many other neuropathologies including anterior communicating artery (ACoA) aneurysms, Alzheimer's disease, and traumatic brain injury (TBI) (see Johnson et al., 2000; Gilboa and Moscovitch, 2002 for extensive meta-analyses). Confabulation is frequently associated with lesions to the ventromedial prefrontal cortex, as well as other surrounding areas, including the orbitofrontal cortex, the basal forebrain, the anterior cingulate cortex, and other 'anterior limbic' areas (Johnson et al., 2000; Schnider, 2003).

Confabulation can take various forms, e.g. it can occur spontaneously or it can be provoked by questions; it may include the fabrication of new events or the misplacement of true experiences in time or space; it can include plausible recollections or completely implausible and non-realistic descriptions (e.g. Berlyne, 1972; Kopelman, 1987). Beginning with Korsakoff (1889/1995), some authors describe confabulatory manifestations on a continuum of severity (e.g. DeLuca and Cicerone, 1991). There is however some evidence suggesting that spontaneous confabulation is etiologically different from other, less severe forms of provoked memory distortion or intrusion (Kopelman 1987; Schnider, 2003). Nevertheless, to date, the exact taxonomy of these characteristics and possible subtypes of confabulation remains unclear (for discussions see DeLuca, 2000; Metcalf et al., 2007).

The several proposed etiological accounts of memory-related confabulation can be summarised under three main types: (a) those explanations which consider confabulation as a dysfunction of *the normal memory retrieval mechanisms* and try to identify the *cognitive impairment(s)* responsible for confabulation; (b) those accounts which consider confabulation as a *compensating mechanism* resulting from memory loss or distress and try to explain *the motivational aspects* of the symptom; and finally (c) those models which aim to explain both *the negative and positive features of confabulation* (in the Jacksonian sense, 1932). In other words, they try to assess the etiological role of *both cognitive and emotional mechanisms*.

Damage to 'normal' cognitive mechanisms: Deficit theories

Memory deficit

Confabulation is traditionally linked with severe amnesia, yet the exact etiological role of amnesia in confabulation is debated among researchers. Certain authors have considered amnesia as the necessary prerequisite for some forms of memory-related confabulation (e.g. Talland, 1965; Berlyne, 1972; DeLuca, 2000). However, it has also being argued that amnesia is not sufficient to explain confabulation, particularly in its more severe forms (e.g. Moscovitch and Melo, 1997; Benson et al., 1996; Johnson et al., 1997; Kapur and Coughlan, 1980; Kopelman et al., 1997; Talland, 1965; Wyke and Warrington, 1960); and perhaps not even necessary (Dalla Barba et al., 1990; Dalla Barba, 1993a; Papagno and Baddeley, 1997; Villiers et al., 1996). The simplest evidence against the impaired memory explanation of confabulation is the fact that not all amnesic patients confabulate. This is particularly true for patients with discrete lesions of limbic and medial temporal lobe regions (e.g. Parkin, 1984; Moscovitch and Melo, 1997). In addition, patients have been reported whose confabulation cleared after a few weeks, while their memory impairment remained unaffected (Benson et al., 1996; Kapur and Coughlan, 1980). Furthermore, patients have been reported who confabulate without being clinically or globally amnesic (Nedjam et al., 2000; Papagno and Baddeley, 1997; Villiers et al., 1996) or who do not confabulate in tasks in which their memory is defective (Dalla Barba et al., 1990; Dalla Barba, 1993a).

Thus, it appears that although the clinical association of amnesia and memory-related confabulation is well-established, general memory impairment is not sufficient to explain the presence of confabulation in certain patients and clinical amnesia may not be necessary for confabulation to occur. The possibility remains that certain memory processes, e.g. control of retrieval or temporal confusion, have an etiological role in the production of confabulation. These will be addressed below.

Executive Functions Deficit

Spontaneous confabulation has by some authors been attributed to general executive dysfunction, resulting from frontal lobe lesions and leading to disinhibition, perserveration, defective self-monitoring, lack of awareness, and other related deficits (Baddeley and Wilson, 1986; Benson et al., 1996; Joseph, 1999; Kapur and Coughlan, 1980; Luria, 1976; Papagno and Baddeley, 1997; Stuss et al., 1978). Commonly this view explains the degree of incidence and bizarreness of confabulation, or the spontaneity of its production (Kopelman, 1987) as determined by the degree of executive ('frontal lobe') dysfunction, superimposed on amnesia (Stuss et al., 1978; DeLuca, 1993; Fischer et al., 1995). This explanation has not gone unchallenged. For example, Dalla Barba (1993a) described a patient showing profound confabulation in the absence of any direct evidence of frontal lobe pathology, although further testing might have indicated otherwise (see also Dalla Barba et al., 1990, 1997a, 1999 Delbecq-Derouesne et al., 1990). Moreover, the lesions of confabulating patients frequently involve ventromedial prefrontal cortex and associated regions. Such lesions have been most frequently associated with disinhibited or socially inappropriate behavior, impairments in decision-making and emotional regulation (e.g. Bechara et al., 2000; Berlin et al., 2004; Stuss and Benson, 1986). However, standardized frontal tests are not sensitive to such impairments. Crucially, a general executive dysfunction is not sufficient to explain content-specific confabulation (Burgess and McNeil, 1999). Indeed, more recent studies have argued that frontal lobe damage, i.e. a constellation of various and potentially dissociable functional circuits, is not sufficient to explain confabulation (Burgess and McNeil, 1999; Benson et al., 1996; Cunningham et al., 1997; DeLuca, 1993; Kopelman et al., 1997; Johnson et al., 1997; 2000; Moscovitch and Melo, 1997). Thus, some have argued in favor of assuming specific rather than general executive dysfunction as causative of confabulation. These approaches will be examined next.

Deficit in the control of recollection ('retrieval theories')

According to the memory control explanations, confabulation arises when the executive components of memory recollection are specifically impaired (Burgess and Shallice, 1996; Gilboa et al., 2006; Moscovitch and Melo, 1997; Schacter et al., 1998). These models emphasize that confabulation is associated with the retrieval rather than the encoding or the storage stages of memory (Moscovitch, 1995; although see below, Schacter et al., 1998). This is mainly based on the observation that patients tend to give erroneous accounts of events that occurred prior to their lesion, i.e. events that were normally encoded and stored. Thus, for example, Moscovitch (1989) postulated a deficit in the strategic component of retrieval processes. This results in memory retrieval being guided solely by associative cue-dependent rules, instead of by the appropriate effortful and goal-directed processes of editing and monitoring stored information. Somewhat similarly, Kopelman (1987) attributed spontaneous confabulation to the 'completely incoherent and context-free retrieval of memories and associations'. These views also approximate Luria's descriptions of the phenomenon of 'equalization of excitability' of traces, i.e. the lack of selectivity of traces, leading to confusion and confabulation (Luria, 1973).

In Burgess and Shallice's (1996) variant of this hypothesis, confabulation may occur in various forms, depending on the damage to the three principal memory control systems. Specifically, these include 'description' mechanisms (specifications of what it is that is being asked of the memory store); 'editing' operations (i.e. verification, checking, and comparison operations); and 'mediator' processes (i.e. pure problem-solving routines involved in reasoning). Hence, according to this model, bizarre or fantastic confabulations are evidence of damaged 'mediator' processes and more generally reasoning errors, while the possible lack of self-correction can be linked to impaired 'editor' processes. Finally, impaired cue retrieval (ambiguous and misleading cues) is evidence of damaged 'descriptor' processes (see also Burgess and McNeil, 1999; Dab et al., 1999).

Similarly, Schacter et al. (1998) have recently put forward a general 'constructive memory framework' (CMF), emphasizing both encoding operations (binding the different features of events to form a coherent representation and also representing similar features in distinguishable ways) and retrieval processes (focusing retrieval descriptions of the sought-after event and also monitoring retrieval information according to source and contextual information). Confabulation in this framework would result from a deficit in either focusing processes (failure to discriminate between the sought-after trace and competing episodes) or monitoring processes (verifying or rejecting information according to the individual's present internal and external environment).

These explanations are particularly informative with regard to the specification of the memory processes affected and unaffected by confabulation. For example, they have been employed to explain why recall tests and episodic tasks pose a greater challenge for confabulating patients than recognition or semantic tasks. According to Moscovitch and Melo (1997) the latter pose fewer challenges to memory search mechanisms and are thus less likely to be affected in confabulating patients (Moscovitch and Melo, 1997; Dab et al., 1999). More generally, theses accounts are able to explain why specific memories cannot be appropriately identified, selected, monitored and even 'deactivated'. However, they cannot explain which memory traces are actually selected and activated. These are eventually turned into simple or more elaborate confabulations which patients believe are real and even part of their own personal histories. In other words, such models have difficulty addressing some of the positive features of confabulation and lead to the assumption that the confabulatory content is random.

More recently, some of these theorists acknowledged that certain features of confabulation, e.g. the potential selectivity and stability of confabulations (Burgess and McNeil, 1999; Conway and Tacchi, 1996), require a change of emphasis within these models. Specifically, both preserved and impaired recollective processes need to be considered and assumed to be responsible for confabulation (see Burgess and McNeil, 1999; Dab et al., 1999; Gilboa et al., 2006 for discussions). Thus, for example, Burgess and McNeil (1999) proposed that 'the marked personal significance for the individual' (Burgess and McNeil, 1999, p. 179) of some generic memories render them capable of 'motivating the emergence of this particular generic memory over others' and thus lead to the 'intrusion' and 'schematization' of certain specific confabulations (e.g. Burgess and McNeil, 1999). More generally, although some of these models allow for preserved memory processes to be implicated in the construction of confabulations, their conceptualizations tend to emphasize the observed cognitive impairments. In parallel, they tend to de-emphasize some of the emotional features of confabulation and their potential explanation.

Temporal context deficit

In this type of model, 'context' or 'source' information forms the core element in explaining confabulation. This is a persistent view in the literature on confabulation. Korsakoff (1889/1996) had first placed emphasis on the temporal confusions observed in confabulating Korsakoff patients and this explanation was taken up by many other authors (e.g. Moll, 1915; Talland, 1961, 1965; Talland et al., 1967; Van der Horst, 1932). More recently, Dalla Barba and his colleagues (1993a; 2000; Dalla Barba et al., 1997b) described dysfunctions in the subjective experience of temporality. These led patients to make temporal judgments based only on information about temporality, well established in their long-term memory stores, but irrelevant to their present situation or to specific points in episodic memory.

Somewhat similarly, Schnider and his colleagues (1996) emphasized temporal context memory impairments, resulting in confusion about the temporal relevance of memory information. Indeed, in a series of more recent studies, Schnider and his colleagues (see Schnider, 2003 for review) demonstrated that confabulating patients with orbitofrontal and basal forebrain lesions showed increased temporal memory confusion in comparison with amnesic patients of other etiologies. This emanated from the inability of the confabulating patients to suppress previously activated, but currently irrelevant memory traces. Furthermore, in a recent high-resolution event-related potential study, Schnider and colleagues (2002) have provided evidence for the assumption that normal subjects filter, or deactivate, currently irrelevant memory traces (e.g. memories of a different temporal source), before the conscious stages of learning and recognition. On this basis they have argued that the deactivation of currently irrelevant memories is a pre-conscious mechanism, intervening before the content of a memory is consciously recognized and consolidated. These findings were confirmed by PET investigations that demonstrated circumscribed posterior medial orbitofrontal activation in healthy adult volunteers, during a specific experimental task which required the selective recognition of mental associations that pertain to ongoing reality (Schnider et al., 2000).

However, not all patients with temporal context memory impairment show confabulation (Shimamura et al., 1990; Kopelman, 1989) and some confabulating patients do not show temporal confusion (e.g. Dab et al., 1999;

Johnson et al., 2000). Thus, as Kopelman has supported (Kopelman et al., 1997) context memory impairment may be a necessary, but not a sufficient condition for spontaneous confabulation to occur. Moscovitch (1995) has even more controversially argued that deficits in chronology are prominent yet secondary features of confabulation. These difficulties merely represent the consequences of other primary retrieval impairments. Crucially, deficits in temporality alone would not easily account for the bizarre, unrealistic stories told by some confabulating patients (e.g. Damasio et al., 1985). Dalla Barba, 1993a; 1993b) has explained these on the basis of an additional impairment in semantic abilities. This proposal however would only explain confabulations which are internally inconsistent and incoherent, but it does not explain con-fabulations which are bizarre in their content and irrelevant with one patient's life, without being incoherent, e.g. alleged trips to space (Damasio et al., 1985), or even previously desired, but never actualized trips to other counties (Villiers et al., 1996; see also Kopelman et al., 1997). Thus, this type of explanation, as the previous one, is capable of explaining some of the 'negative' characteristics of confabulation (e.g. temporal displacement), but it cannot address some of the 'positive' features of the symptom (e.g. bizarre content and motivation).

Source deficit

More generally, Johnson and her colleagues (for reviews see Johnson, 1991; Johnson et al., 2000) proposed an explanation of confabulation based on a 'source monitoring framework' (SMF). This model emphasizes the role of a set of 'source or reality monitoring' processes, involved in making attributions about the origins of memories, knowledge, and beliefs. More generally, source monitoring is defined as the ability to attribute a mental representation to its appropriate source (e.g. a past true experience, a dream, etc). Its related dys-function in memory has been termed 'source amnesia' (Schacter et al., 1984). Johnson proposed that confabulation is not caused by the inability to monitor the correct chronology of events, as the previous explanations have. Confabulation is caused by a more general inability to monitor the source of mental representations that reach consciousness (e.g. internal mental associa-tion versus external perception, past versus current representation). In Moscovitch's terms (1989) 'confabulation is source amnesia magnified and extended to include an entire life-time of experience' (Moscovitch, 1989, p. 138). In this framework, confabulation may result from a wide range of source monitoring deficits such as (1) inadequate feature binding, (2) disrupted reacti-vation and consolidation processes, (3) failure to engage in evaluation processes or to use situationally appropriate feature weights and criteria, (4) poor self-initiated cuing and retrieval of supporting information, (5) failure to access or to use general in knowledge generating appropriate retrieval cues, weighting features, and crucially distinguishing between 'the real' and 'the imagined' (Johnson and Raye, 1998). This hypothesis initially emphasized specific processes of reality and source monitoring, over and above other memory processes and influences. However more recently, Johnson and colleagues have acknowledged that the exact nature of confabulation depends on a constellation of different intact and preserved memory control processes as well as other emotional and social factors (Johnson et al., 1997, 2000). Thus, this view will be reconsidered below.

Compensatory psychological mechanisms

In the beginning of the 20th century, several clinicians observed the presence of motivational and emotional biases in confabulation. These fell under five different, yet at times overlapping, categories which are still discussed in recent studies on confabulation. (a) The motive of embarrassment; (b) the motive of suggestibility; (c) motives based on patients' premorbid personality; (d) the motive of denial; (e) other psychodynamic models.

The motive of embarrassment

The 'gap-filling' hypothesis is perhaps the oldest motivational theory of confabulation. According to it, confabulation occurs as a purposive act contrived by the patient to spare him from the embarrassment of not being able to remember the events of his life (Bonhoeffer, 1901, cited in Talland, 1961). This perspective explains confabulation as the result of *some compensatory motivational mechanism*, which is essentially unrelated to normal memory processes. However, this hypothesis is untenable even at a conceptual level, as confabulation is by definition exclusive of conscious intention to deceive one's listener. Furthermore, given the associated unawareness of deficit, it is clinically invalid to describe confabulating patients as consciously attempting to conceal what they seem to ignore, i.e. their memory deficit. Finally, this hypothesis has been countered by experimental evidence. A number of confabulating patients did not show a tendency to increase their confabulation rate when they were confronted with questions to which they did not know the answer (e.g. Dalla Barba et al., 1997b; Kopelman et al., 1997; Mercer et al., 1977; Schnider et al., 1996). Despite all these counter indications, the gap-filling hypothesis has had a lasting impact in the literature on confabulation. It has persisted and has dominated definitions of confabulation for decades (see Whitlock, 1981) and it is still mentioned in most recent papers, even if only to be rejected. This rather unusual persistence of a highly controversial hypothesis relies on the multiple and often conflicting uses of the gap-filling notion (see Berrios, 1998). A brief clarification will be undertaken below.

At least four interrelated, yet distinct, uses of gap-filling have been described in the literature. (a) On a first descriptive level, 'gap-filling' has been used to highlight the occurrence of confabulation against the background of amnesia, i.e. confabulation appears when accurate memory is absent. More recently, these gaps have been conceptually extended to include not only memories, but also other types of unavailable or inaccessible knowledge (e.g. Hirstein, 2005); (b) on a related etiological level, the tendency to fill memory or knowledge gaps with false answers has been considered as evidence for the etiological role of amnesia in confabulation (see Berrios, 1998; DeLuca, 2000 for discussions); (c) on a second descriptive level, the notion of 'gap-filling' is used to provide a classification of confabulation severity. Gap-filling confabulations represented simple, momentary, passive or reactive, i.e. provoked only by questioning, confabulations (e.g. see Berlyne, 1972; Whitlock, 1981). These are contrasted with fabrications or fantastic confabulations produced spontaneously (e.g. Bonhoeffer, 1901 in Talland, 1961; Berlyne, 1972; see also above). More recently, Moscovitch (1989; see also Gilboa and Moscovitch, 2002) has noted that such gap-filling confabulations do in fact make their appearance in confabulating patients. They represent efforts to correct or further support their previous claims. However, they should not be identified with provoked or less severe forms of confabulation. Instead, they should be considered as secondary forms of the symptom and explained as such. Interestingly, almost 100 years ago in a systematic exploration of types of confabulation, Moll (1915) had ascribed a similar and peripheral role to ad hoc concoctions, i.e. gap-filling confabulations; (d) on a second etiological level, the tendency to confabulate by filling memory gaps has been linked to the potential etiological role of suggestibility in confabulation (Pick, 1905 in Talland, 1961). This view will be addressed below.

In light of the above, any theoretical or empirical consideration of the gap-filling hypothesis that does not carefully clarify whether it addresses the motivational claims of embarrassment, the descriptive or etiological association to amnesia, the clinical description of a secondary form of confabulation or the causative role of suggestibility, is likely to cause conceptual confusion. This is exactly what has taken place in the literature (for critical reviews see DeLuca, 2000; Berrios, 1998; Gilboa and Moscovitch, 2002). This conceptual confusion has also, at least in part, contributed to certain superficial rejections of *any* type of motivational etiology in confabulation (e.g. Schnider, 2003; Whitlock, 1981).

Suggestibility motives

Pick (1905, 1915 in Talland, 1961) and Korner (1935 in Talland, 1961) noticed that the statements of confabulating patients can be easily steered by leading questions. Thus, they argued that 'suggestibility' has a causal role in the gap-filling forms of confabulation. This explanation relates to the above discussions about the complex connotations of the gap-filling notion. Specifically, the motive of suggestibility has been treated as synonymous with the embarrassment gap-filling motive. Furthermore, it has been rejected as such, i.e. by asking confabulating patients to answer questions with generally 'unknown' or 'hard to access' answers (e.g. Berlyne, 1972; Dalla Barba, 1993a, 1993b; Mercer et al., 1977; Schnider et al., 1996), or by measuring the amount of prompting patients require, before confabulating (e.g. Moscovitch and Melo, 1997). However, this hypothesis also includes a different component. Berlyne, (1972) notes how suggestibility in Pick's descriptions is dependent on clouded consciousness, weakened judgement, and lively fantasy. The latter has been supported by Johnson and colleagues (1997) who recently have reported a patient who among other deficits showed 'a propensity towards detailed imaginations' (Johnson et al., 1997, p. 203; see also Johnson et al., 2000). In this sense, suggestibility may be seen as part of one's personality structure, or more generally an individual predisposition to external suggestion and compliance.

The only study known to the author that directly addressed suggestibility in this context is by Mercer and colleagues (1977). They deceived their patients into believing that they had responded earlier to questions, in which in reality they had responded 'I don't know' and asked them to re-answer the questions. The results indicated that severe confabulators changed their replies on 31% of the occasions, while mild confabulators did so on 28% of the occasions. Based on this similarity, the authors concluded that their results did not support the suggestibility hypothesis. However a re-examination of their results leads to a more complex interpretation. First of all, the study does not report the percentage of change of responses in non-confabulating patients. If the latter did not change their responses at all, then suggestibility might have a role in confabulation, albeit a secondary one. In addition, the authors report that mild confabulators never produced a confabulation when altering their responses, while severe confabulators did so at every question. The latter finding suggests that the production of confabulations is influenced by suggestion. However, the question of whether the influence of suggestibility is causative of confabulation across patients or whether it is a secondary phenomenon (e.g. Moscovitch, 1989) requires further investigation. Interestingly, similar phenomena have been observed and studied in a forensic context (e.g. Gudjonsson and Sigurdsson, 1995; see also Kopelman, 2002 for review). Although confabulation in these contexts may represent a different phenomenon, the conclusions of these studies about the partial role of suggestibility in 'forensic confabulation' warrants direct investigation of the phenomenon in the case of neurological confabulation (Fotopoulou et al., 2007a).

Motives based on premorbid personality

Williams and Rupp (1938) attributed the occurrence of confabulation, in part at least, to tendencies inherent in the patient's premorbid personality struc-ture. They emphasized that confabulating patients combine the extremes of introversion and extraversion, including uncommunicativeness and apathy at the one end and superficial sociability and realism at the other. Talland (1961) noted that confabulation is 'an interaction effect of the amnesic syndrome and basic personality structure' (p. 380). More specifically, he concluded that con-fabulation was secondary to amnesic derangement. The latter 'creates an occa-sion for each occurrence, and dispositions characteristic of the individual patient will determine its presence, rate and quality'. Berlyne (1972) confirmed the above views. He observed that five out of the seven Korsakoff patients he studied were premorbidly extraverts and 'no less than four showed features of Schneider's 'hyperthymic' personality type (Schneider, 1958)'. He also observed three cases of fantastic confabulation of paranoid content in patients with senile dementia. All three had a 'sensitive' premorbid personality. Berlyne concluded that premorbid personality traits may determine the content of confabulation.

In a study on confabulation in the context of senile dementia, Gainotti (1975) conducted what remains until today the most systematic study of this hypothesis. He asked relatives to describe the premorbid personality of eight confabulating patients and 22 non-confabulating control patients. Specifically, he investigated the following features: (i) attitudes toward work, health, and illness; (ii) interpersonal patterns, e.g. need for prestige and superiority, toler-ance or hypersensitivity to criticism; and (iii) reaction to stress, e.g. depression, overt anxiety. The results indicated opposite personality traits between the two groups. More specifically, 75% of the target patients were described as having a strong tendency to deny, ignore, or rationalize illness. In addition, the pre-dominant feature of their interpersonal relationships was the need for prestige and domination, over emotional and intimacy concerns. None of the confabu-lating patients were hypochondriacal or concerned with their somatic functions but five of them were described as having violent reactions to anxiety. The con-trol group showed a very different balance of personality characteristics along all three axes. Gainotti concluded, similarly to Talland (1961), that although the memory and intellectual deterioration observed in this neuropathology is necessary for confabulation to occur, the presence of confabulation in some, but not other patients, suggests a role of personality traits and coping mechanisms in the emergence of the symptom. Finally, given that most of the confabulating, but not the control, patients of the study came from particular social and national backgrounds, the study also highlighted the influence of cultural norms and expectations in the formation of confabulation (see also Kopelman, 1997).

Similar conclusions about the role of premorbid personality traits in confabulation have been drawn by Weinstein and his colleagues in a series of clinical studies (Weinstein and Kahn, 1955; Weinstein, Kahn and Malitz, 1956; Weinstein and Lyerly, 1968). They found that the patients most likely to show confabulation and denial of deficit were the ones characterized by their relatives as premorbidly stubborn, introverted with regard to their feelings, prestige- and power-seeking. In addition, these patients had premorbidly been using coping mechanisms such as denial and minimization, when confronted with other health issues. This view will be considered in detail below.

Finally, in two more recent case reports, Conway and Tacchi (1996) and Fotopoulou and colleagues (2007a) investigated mood and personality changes in two confabulating patients. In both cases, the patients' current goals and preoccupations had influenced the content of their confabulations in ways that were described as compatible with the patients' premorbid personalities as described by relatives. In conclusion, although this hypothesis has received some support, it remains unclear how, and at what etiological level, the individual's personality interacts with the neurocognitive dysfunction in order for confabulation to occur, or in order for the content of confabulation to be colored in a particular way. Thus, the issue awaits further investigation.

The motive of denial

Lidz (1942 in Talland, 1961) had discussed confabulation as a response to overwhelming anxiety and Zangwill (1953 in Berlyne, 1972) had conceptualized confabulation as a defense against 'a catastrophic reaction', i.e. a depressive reaction to one's illness. However, the hypothesis that confabulation is a form of 'psychological denial', i.e. a compensatory coping mechanism instigated by excessive anxiety, is mostly related with the work of Weinstein and his colleagues (for a review see Weinstein, 1996). It was their studies on anosognosia and a number of other related syndromes that led to the formulation of this psychodynamic hypothesis. This theory did not only focus on the premorbid predispositions of certain individuals to confabulate (see above), but also further emphasized two aspects of the syndrome; the symbolic nature of its content and the accompanying implicit awareness of deficit (see also Feinberg, 2001).

Thus, Weinstein and colleagues claimed that although confabulations frequently involve references to past events, they are to some degree, symbolic representations, dramatizations, or explanations of some current personal experience, preoccupation or disability (Weinstein et al., 1956). These symbolic functions are based on kernels of awareness of deficit, i.e. confabulations implicitly express illness preoccupations and anxieties, which the patient is not capable of fully appreciating and explicitly expressing. More generally confabulation itself represents an indication of a selective and partial awareness of deficit (Weinstein and Kahn, 1955). Finally, the symbolic function of confabulation, although is at *face value* aberrant with reality, it seems to have an ultimate adaptive role. Weinstein observed, following Bonhoeffer (1901 cited in Weinstein, 1996) that during the narration of confabulations, patients become engrossed in detail, lose their previous irritability, and then appear utterly relaxed.

Although these views have highlighted the positive aspects of confabulation, there has been little experimental evidence in their support. Moreover, these psychological coping mechanisms are considered independent of the specific neuropathological features of the syndromes they aim to explain. Thus, their explanatory power with regard to the syndromes themselves is limited. Indeed, Weinstein (1996) acknowledged that the above descriptions are less likely to be relevant to spontaneous confabulation with vivid imagery, as reported in patients with ACoA aneuryrms and anterior cingulectomy.

Other psychodynamic models

In the early explorations of the nature of confabulation, a series of clinicians observed motivational biases in the manifestations of confabulation. For example, Moll (1915) noted the influence of former habits and emotional complexes. Some psychoanalytically oriented clinicians recognized in the content of confabulation the mark of psychodynamic mechanisms (for reviews see Berlyne, 1972; Betlheim and Harman, 1924; Davidson, 1948). For example, Betlheim and Hartman (1924) noted 'If we start out from the general view that there is a close relationship between-organic-cerebral and psychic mechanisms, it seems justified to raise the question whether the psychologically well-described and well-known processes of repression, displacement and condensation have their counterpart in the realm of organic disorders' (Betlheim and Harman, 1924, p. 288). Most importantly, the disorganized, atemporal, free of counter-ideas, and at times, wishful and vivid quality of confabulations was reminiscent of the recollective quality of dreams (Berlyne, 1972; Betlheim and Hartman, 1924; Pick, 1905, 1915 in Talland, 1961; Scheid, 1934 in Berlyne, 1972; Van der Horst, 1932; Whitty and Levin, 1957; see also

Damasio et al., 1985; Stuss et al., 1978). This led some authors to suggest that the individual's wishes and interests guided confabulation in the same way as they controlled dream fantasy (Berlyne, 1972; Betlheim and Hartman, 1924; Van der Horst, 1932).

However, these explanations, unlike the ones examined above, did not consider these emotional mechanisms in isolation. Instead, they regarded the emotional manifestations as the direct consequence of the cognitive dysfunction. For instance, Bertlheim and Hartman (1924) argued that the characteristic amnesic derangement of the Korsakoff syndrome caused a lack of cognitive restraint. This in turn, allowed the normally implicit effect of primitive, emotion-based forms of cognition to become more explicit and color recollection even under controlled experimental conditions. These views echoed Korsakoff's (1889) initial suggestion that the frequency of death and funeral themes in these patients' false memories was based on unconscious associations (in Talland, 1961).

Although at first sight, these psychodynamic views appear similar to the denial hypothesis, in fact they are significantly different in at least one fundamental aspect. Confabulation in these psychodynamic theories is not conceived as caused, nor colored, by any compensatory defense, filling-in tendency, or personality-related mechanism. Instead confabulation, including its negative and positive features, is regarded as the direct result of an organically caused dysfunction of the normal mechanisms of remembering. Given this dysfunction, the necessary mixing and editing of memory material has now produced an almost grotesque outcome. Yet it still bears the influence of its basic ingredients, including basic emotional tendencies and cognitive elaborations. In Bertlheim and Hartman's (1924) terms,

> that the memory disorder of the Korsakow syndrome is organically founded is conceded by all investigators. But one can assume as Bonhoeffer did long ago, that there is also a functional factor and that only its interaction with the organic-cerebral factor yields the total psychological picture of the Korsakow syndrome. The functional factor of the memory disorder seems clearest in post-traumatic cases. Even if we consider the functional factor secondary, it is permissible to assume that in our cases too, psychologically demonstrable tendencies make use of organically pre-formed distortion mechanisms. The aim of our investigation was to demonstrate through the study of symbolic distortions how the deliberate application of psychological insight affords a partial glimpse into the operation of these organic mechanisms.

> (Bertlheim and Hartman, 1924, p. 307)

Yet in the following decades this perspective received little experimental attention. Perhaps given that the neurocognitive basis of confabulation remained obscure until a few decades ago (Schnider, 2003), this early and rather ambitious effort to explain the emotional features of the syndrome in organic terms fell into a theoretical vacuum. Instead, the more simple defense or filling-in explanations were established as *the* motivational hypotheses, only to be de-emphasized and largely dismissed as more sophisticated neurocognitive models of confabulation came to the foreground (for review see DeLuca, 2000). The subsequent revision of some of the above psychodynamic hypothesis will be addressed in the following section.

Combinations of damaged and spared mechanisms

The discussion of the aforementioned controversial theoretical explanations of confabulation has hinted at the fact that the endeavor to define a single cognitive deficit, or a single compensatory mechanism, underlying confabulation has proven far from straightforward. Indeed, more recently various investigators have noted that the variety of reported features of confabulation requires a theoretical account capable of incorporating multiple contributing factors (Burgess and McNeil, 1999; Fotopoulou et al., 2004; Johnson, et al., 1997, 2000; Kopelman et al., 1997; Shapiro et al., 1981; Gilboa et al., 2006; Metcalf et al., 2006). Crucially, any appropriate theory should be in the position to integrate both 'negative' and 'positive' features of confabulatory manifestations since positive or adaptive aspects of confabulation have been reported in confabulation case studies in parallel with negative ones (e.g. Burgess and McNeil, 1999; Conway and Tacchi, 1996; Downes and Mayes, 1995; Jorn and Rybarczyk, 1995; Sabhesan and Natarajan, 1988; Villiers et al., 1996).

For example, Villiers and his colleagues (1996) report a patient who was found confused in his hotel room and who, although presenting no amnesia or confabulation upon formal neuropsychological testing (see also Papagno and Muggia, 1996; Conway and Tacchi, 1996), repeatedly described an alleged one-day trip to Tokyo on the day before his admission. Relatives verified that, although the patient had always wished to work in Tokyo, he had never been there. Therefore, it appears that in such cases, although confabulation may involve 'some kernels of truth of genuine experience' misattributed in time and space (Talland, 1965), it may also be influenced by factors of great affective stamp (Mercer et al., 1977), marked personal significance (Burgess and McNeil, 1999), or, wish-fulfillments (Berlyne, 1972; Betlheim and Hartman, 1924; Downes and Mayes, 1995; Van der Horst, 1932; Flament, 1957 cited in Berlyne, 1972; Clarke et al., 1958 cited in Talland, 1961).

As described above, initial attempts to address these 'positive' features and adaptive functions within neurology and psychiatry have been rather unsuccessful. However, recent advances in neuroscience and the broadening of its interests to topics which were once considered not amenable to empirical research (e.g. affective regulation) have allowed emotional features of confabulation to be reconsidered. This happened within two different traditions, cognitive psychological research on 'normal' memory distortion, and a small branch of psychodynamically informed neuroscience.

Recent 'combination' models

Following the pioneering studies of Bartlett (1932), a tradition within cognitive psychology focused on the constructive nature of memory. Within this paradigm, memories are understood as dynamic, fluid, and situationally bound constructions, which are influenced by the context in which they are produced (Conway, 1992). A number of emotional and cognitive factors render memories prone to distortions and misattributions (Johnson and Raye, 1998). More generally errors of commission are considered as defining for the nature of memory as errors of omission (e.g. Conway and Pleydell-Pearce, 2000; Johnson et al., 2000; Loftus, 1993; Schacter et al., 1998).

Similarly, investigations of autobiographical memory within cognitive and social psychology (Conway and Pleydell-Pearce, 2000; Ross, 1989; Pillemer, 2001; Singer and Salovey, 1993; Woike et al., 1999) have put forward an equally dynamic conceptualization of remembering. For example, in a series of studies McAdams (for review see McAdams, 2001), argued that individuals reconstruct the past in terms of an internalized and evolving self-story, a coherent narrative of self that weaves together diverse experiences and creates a sense of unity over time and a defined purpose for future action. Crucially, 'these life stories are based on biographical facts, but they also go considerably beyond the facts as people selectively appropriate aspects of their experiences and imaginatively construe both past and future to construct stories that make sense to them and to their audiences, that vivify and integrate life and make it more or less meaningful' (McAdams, 2001, p. 101).

Stemming from these traditions, certain models have proposed equally dynamic conceptualization of memory distortion and falsification in neurological syndromes (for review Conway and Fthenaki, 2000). They suggest that memory following brain damage will remain constructive in nature and show similar patterns of source misattributions, distortions, and fabrications as observed in normal memory distortion, albeit in an exaggerated form. *Thus, confabulation may be best understood as the magnification of existing 'normal' misremembering experiences, rather than a dysfunction of the previously flawlessly functioning memory system* (Burgess and Shallice, 1996; Conway and Fthenaki, 2000; Fotopoulou et al., 2004; Johnson, 1991; Schacter et al., 1998). Moreover, the particular combination of preserved and impaired memory processes will determine the exact form and content of confabulatory memories, including both 'positive' and 'negative' features. Indeed, as also described above, some studies have already begun to recognize and address such complexities in the production of confabulation (Burgess and McNeil, 1999; Conway and Tacchi, 1996; Johnson et al., 1997; Kopelman et al., 1997). For example, Kopelman and his colleagues, 1997 concluded that frontal lobe pathology and context memory disorders are not sufficient to produce confabulation. Instead, factors such as a high rate of perserverations and a tendency to respond indiscriminately to the immediate social and environmental context may have some role in causing confabulation.

However, while some of the above models have focused on the cognitive mechanisms of memory distortion, others emphasized both cognitive and emotional critical factors (Conway and Fthenaki, 2000; Fotopoulou et al., 2004; Johnson et al., 2000). For instance within the proposed source monitoring framework (SMF), Johnson and colleagues (for reviews see Johnson et al., 2000) have recently broadened their conceptualization of confabulation. They (Johnson et al., 1997) emphasized that source-monitoring deficits alone could not account for all the instances of confabulation in their patient. Since the latter is based on a confluence of factors, such as source monitoring deficits, impoverished autobiographical memory retrieval, and a propensity toward vivid imagination. More generally, in their model, the retrieval of memories is not described as a process of search and identification of memory traces. Rather mental experiences and representations are attributed to memory by ongoing judgment processes (Johnson, 1991). In a recent review paper, Johnson (2001) outlined four key features of these complex attribution mechanisms. (a) They are depended upon the qualitative characteristics of mental experience, including perceptual, spatial, temporal, and emotional details; (b) They are influenced by the embeddedness of mental experiences, i.e. the availability of supporting memories, the consistency with previous knowledge, and their internal consistency; (c) They are based on flexible criteria, which may vary according to the context in which mental experiences are judged; (d) Goals, beliefs, motivational, and social factors influence what characteristics are looked for, how much embedding occurs and which criteria are applied. In other words, *motivational factors have a determining role on all four other key aspects.* More generally, all these components are imperfect and interact in a dynamic way to produce both accurate and faulty attributions. Based on this framework, Johnson and colleagues (e.g. Johnson and Raye, 1998) proposed that deficits in one or more of these components will lead to confabulation. The nature of the latter will depend on the exact amount and combination of processes impaired and preserved.

In a similar model, Conway and colleagues (for a review see Conway, 2001) stressed the interdependence of motivation and autobiographical memory.

They have conceptualized autobiographical memory as a database of information in the service of the 'working-self', which is conceived as a hierarchical template of currently active goals. The latter, in conjunction with input from the autobiographical memory base, sets goals, determines accessibility to autobiographical memory, and supervises its output. Within this model, confabulation is regarded as resulting from a combination of preserved and damaged memory processes in autobiographical memory 'construction' (Conway and Tacchi, 1996; Conway and Fthenaki, 2000; Fotopoulou et al., 2004). Dysfunctional executive control processes compromise both the search in autobiographical memory and the evaluation of long-term memory output. Thus, patients are unable to distinguish between memory constructions created by the 'current self' and the ones grounded in and constrained by autobiographical knowledge. As a consequence, the degree of involvement in memory construction of the wished-for-self (ungrounded goals and plans) is disproportionately larger than of the 'actual' self (Conway and Pleydell-Pearce, 2000). For example, the frontal patient OP, reported by Conway and Tacchi (1996) persistently maintained a set of plausible but confabulated memories. These rewrote the disappointments in familial interactions of her past into a history of successful and supportive intimacy with certain family members.

From a different perspective, Solms and his colleagues (for review see Solms, 2000) have proposed a neuroscientific revisiting of old psychodynamic hypotheses of confabulation. More generally this approach, summarized under the term 'neuro-psychoanalysis', aims to assess the validity and scope of fundamental psychoanalytic hypotheses using empirical neuropsychological and neuroscientific research. This endeavor has met with significant obstacles, mainly due to the scepticism of clinical and experimental neuroscience toward psychoanalysis, as well as the retreat of the latter into scientific isolation (see for discussion Solms and Turnbull, 2002). This mutual avoidance of the two fields is also rooted in the historical discrediting of psychoanalysis by biologically orientated psychiatry during the second half of the 20th century. However, as misleading concepts such as the rigorous distinction between 'functional' and 'organic' have recently become outdated, various scientific authorities have begun to recognize the benefits of reconciliation (e.g. Nobel-laurate Eric Kandel, 1999). Simultaneously, the softening of positivism within neuroscience has allowed the study of topics such as emotions and 'the self', on which psychoanalysis has traditionally focused, to gain scientific credibility.

Confabulation has served as a particularly useful arena for this interdisciplinary exchange (e.g. DeLuca, 2000; Fotopoulou and Conway, 2004; Johnson, 2000; Feinberg, 2004; Kinsbourne, 2000, 2004; Schnider, 2004; Turnbull, 2004b). Based on the description of a series of severely confabulating patients with bilateral ventromedial prefrontal cortex lesions, Solms and colleagues (Kaplan-Solms and Solms, 2000; see also Turnbull et al., 2004b) proposed that the characteristics of confabulation result from the combined effect of executive disinhibition, disorganization of memory recollection, and the release of primitive mental mechanisms. This view is grounded in traditional psychodynamic models (Freud, 1915). In such models, mental functioning is conceived as dominated by mature conscious and unconscious cognitive functions of self-representation and organization, termed 'ego functions', which include processes of inhibition, selectivity, binding, pacing, organization, and control. These are further conceived as built upon the phylogenetic and ontogenetic foundations of more primitive and largely unconscious mental functions. According to this perspective, the latter are persisting in implicit form and under the dominating supervision of 'ego functions'. Nevertheless, unconscious mental processes continue to exert an effect on more mature cognitive operations, particularly when the latter are defective or simply overwhelmed.

Solms (2000) focused on the similarity of these primitive unconscious processes and the clinical characteristics of confabulation. These include tolerance of mutual contradiction, timelessness, attribution of internal representations or emotions to external sources, associative thinking, i.e. frequent superficial displacements, and condensations of thoughts and memories. These very characteristics, observed directly by several neurologists and neuropsychologists in confabulating patients, have also been described in traditional psychodynamic models. However in the latter case, these characteristics had been inferred from psychoanalytic inquiry into psychopathological symptoms and certain everyday phenomena such as dreams (Freud, 1915). Based on this similarity, Solms (2000) proposed that in confabulating patients damage to the ventromedial prefrontal cortex and the resulting lack of executive control of memory recollection (a deficit hypothesis) leaves memory at the mercy of disproportionally powered inner needs and desires, with little regard for adaptive considerations (a complementary motivational hypothesis).

Despite this increased theoretical attention to the potential motivational nature of confabulation, there has been little experimental work investigating these issues (see below). Instead the motivational accounts outlined above are based mostly on anecdotal clinical descriptions of a few confabulating patients (e.g. Conway and Tacchi, 1996; Kaplan-Solms and Solms, 2000).

The motivated content of confabulation: Experiments at last

To investigate the validity of the above theoretical framework, a number of recent studies set out to systematically investigate the emotional content of confabulation (see Fotopoulou et al., 2008b for review). The main hypothesis put forward by these investigations was that the false recollections of confabulating patients should show a self-serving bias that is greater than that typically encountered in studies on healthy volunteers (Walker et al., 2000). Of course, the vicissitudes of human motivation extend far beyond self-serving biases, but this definition of motivated confabulation was considered a useful first approach to the challenge of systematically studying the complex role of motivation in confabulation. This exaggeration in self-serving biases was primarily expected due to the reported damage of the ventromedial frontal cortex in confabulation, which is more generally thought to be responsible for affective regulation.

Consistent with the above hypothesis, the content of spontaneous confabulation has been found to contain mostly positive and wishful descriptions in a number of single-case and group studies (Fotopoulou et al., 2004; Fotopoulou et al., 2008a; Turnbull et al., 2004a). For example, patients described themselves as healthy and as being in familiar surroundings, in professional or leisure activities instead of the hospital. Some of these errors could of course be attributed to their amnesia for recent life periods. However, patients often accurately remembered neighboring pleasant events of the same time period (Fotopoulou et al., 2007b). Patients also often minimized their current disabilities and attributed them to premorbid traits and attitudes. This can be seen as an extreme adherence to one's premorbid self-identity and a need to maintain a coherent self-narrative that is healthy, independent, and competent. Given the neurocognitive deficits of these patients these needs for self-coherence were met with poor executive control and reality monitoring. Thus, their memory could not adequately respond to the demand for reality correspondence and patients maintained a continuous, yet false, self-identity.

Moreover, some confabulating patients persistently denied the death of close relatives and other unpleasant events of the remote or recent past, and they were noted to inflate their abilities, exaggerate their previous professional skills, and overstate their social and financial position (Fotopoulou et al., 2007a). Often these descriptions were accompanied by dramatization of the circumstances or of the consequences of their injury and hospitalization. This can be seen as a form of idealization of one's self-identity (see Fotopoulou, 2008a for more examples).

The above observations on spontaneous confabulation were also supported by studies that experimentally manipulated the emotional content of memories. For example, a recent study showed that confabulating patients were more likely to misrecognize past self-referent events as currently true when these were of pleasant rather than unpleasant consequences (Fotopoulou et al., 2007b).

Similar emotional biases were observed in the amnesic non-confabulating group but their overall errors were far less, and thus the effect was of lesser importance in the construction of their self-representation. By contrast, the combination of poor memory monitoring and self-enhancement motivation led the confabulating patients to even accept as part of their autobiography a number of suggested pleasant events that had never taken place. These errors were only minimal in the case of unpleasant events. Thus, for example, a patient was significantly more likely to falsely claim that he actually remembered winning the lottery recently than to falsely claim that he remembered losing his job.

In a recent prose recall study, confabulating patients showed a selective bias in recalling negative self-referent stories, in that they recalled such information in a manner which portrayed a more positive image of themselves (Fotopoulou et al., 2008b). This positive bias was not present in stories that were not encoded in a self-referent manner. This study shows that confabulating patients do not have a difficulty in processing negative emotions in general. Instead, they show a specific self-related motivational bias in their memory. This has implications for the provision of information to confabulating patients using 'the third person'. More generally, this study shows that given the deficits of confabulating patients in the control and regulation of memory retrieval, their recall is highly susceptible to motivational distortions, and their confabulations may reveal the influence of their self-related wishes, concerns, and preoccupations.

Finally, in a recent study, we found that although all of the 10 tested patients showed a positive bias in their confabulations, the greater the patients' self-reported depression, the greater their tendency to produce self-enhancing and wishful confabulations (Fotopoulou et al., 2008a). No relation was observed between patients' self-reported anxiety and the emotional content of their confabulations. This association between depression and confabulation may suggest that the production of positive confabulations is most frequently associated with low mood, or with topics that diminish one's self-esteem (see also Bentall et al., 2003; McKay et al., 2005 for similar findings in delusions). This raises the possibility that confabulations have a direct adaptive function (as originally proposed by psychodynamically oriented authors, e.g. see Weinstein, 1996), but on the other hand it highlights that even if confabulations have a mood-regulatory (or, defensive) function, their effect must be temporary or incomplete for patients to remain depressed. It is thus hard to conclude reliably that correction or spontaneous recovery from confabulation may lead to increased sadness. Furthermore, given that patients are typically unaware of their symptoms it is unlikely that mood regulation occurs at a conscious level. The highly complicated and dynamic relation between motivated confabulation, mood, and awareness requires further investigation and conceptual clarification.

More generally, social psychology has provided considerable evidence that people are motivated to view their current self favorably and engage in considerable memory distortion in order to maintain such a view (Walker et al., 2000; Wilson and Ross, 2003). This is particularly evident in older adults who show a strong self-serving positivity bias in their autobiographical recollections, and this seems to have positive effects on their mood and well-being (for review see Mather and Carstensen, 2005). Older adults and confabulating patients show deterioration and dysfunction respectively in prefrontal brain regions, and we therefore have claimed that the exaggeration of self-enhancement and self-coherence through memory maybe linked to the resulting deterioration of executive memory processes (Fotopoulou et al., 2008b). This proposal is consistent with recently emerging models of confabulation that include personal goals and wishful ideation among the critical factors that may determine the retrieval of false memories in confabulating patients (Feinberg, 2001; Gilboa et al., 2006; Johnson et al., 2000; Kopelman, 1999; Metcalf et al., 2007). Acknowledging the role of emotion in confabulation also has pivotal clinical consequences (see Fotopoulou, 2008a for review). It thus seems that at least some authors have recognized that emotion may have a determining role in confabulation and that only its interaction with the neurocognitive factors yields the total psychological picture of the confabulatory-amnesic syndrome.

Thus, far we have emphasized that confabulation may not result from the exaggeration of psychological motivation per se, but rather from an exaggeration of the organically predetermined influence of motivation on memory formation. However, potential individual personality differences should not be excluded from the etiology of confabulation without further study (see Conway and Tacchi, 1996; Fotopoulou et al., 2007a). Some patients may be premorbidly more inclined than others to hold a positive self-regard and distort memories in self-enhancing ways. These individual differences may even be potential candidates for the postmorbid variance in the duration of confabulation; in some patients, confabulation ceases following some days or months, while in others it persists for years (Talland, 1961). In other terms, aside from more universal tendencies, a lesion will influence behavior based also on the kind of person, social environment, and brain that existed prior to the lesion.

Conclusion

Confabulation after ventromedial frontal cortex lesions has been traditionally explained by several cognitive 'deficit' theories, or alternatively by purely psychogenic mechanisms. We have proposed that these theories might best be regarded as complementary rather than competing. The findings from recent experimental studies provide empirical support for the hypothesis that confabulation can in part be 'motivated', or at least show a consistent positive emotional bias. This 'positive' feature of confabulation has not previously received due attention in accounts of the mechanism(s) of confabulation. However, it can readily be considered in parallel with the 'negative' aspects of the cognitive profile, such that a complex combination of damaged (poor retrieval control) and spared (emotionally driven retrieval) procedures apparently interact in generating false memories.

References

Baddeley, A. and Wilson, B. (1986). Amnesia, autobiographical memory and confabulation. In *Autobiographical Memory* (eds. D.C. Rubin). New York, Cambridge University Press. pp. 225–252.

Bartlett, F.C. (1932). *Remembering: A study in Experimental and Social Psychology*. Cambridge, Cambridge University Press.

Bechara, A., Damasio, H., and Damasio, A.R. (2000). Emotion, decision making and the orbitofrontal cortex. *Cerebral Cortex,* **10**, 295–307.

Benson, D.F., Djenderedjian, A., Miller, M.D., Pachana, N.A., Chang, M.D., Itti, L., et al. (1996). Neural basis of confabulation. *Neurology, 46,* 1239–1243.

Bentall, R.B. (2003). The paranoid self. In *The Self in Neuroscience and Psychiatry* (eds. A. Kircher and A. David). Cambridge, Cambridge University Press. pp. 293–318.

Berlin, H.A., Rolls, E.T., and Kischka, U. (2004). Impulsivity, time perception, emotion and reinforcement sensitivity in patients with orbitofrontal cortex lesions. *Brain, 127,* 1108–1126.

Berlyne, N. (1972). Confabulation. *British Journal of Psychiatry, 120,* 31–39.

Berrios, G.E. (1998). Confabulations: A conceptual history. *Journal of the History of the Neurosciences, 7*(3), 225–241.

Betlheim, S., and Hartmann, H. (1924/1951). On parapraxes in the Korsakow psychosis. In *Organisation and Pathology of Thought* (ed. D. Rapaport). New York, Columbia University Press. pp. 289–307.

Burgess, P.W., and McNeil, J.E. (1999). Content-specific confabulation. *Cortex, 35,* 163–182.

Burgess, P.W., and Shallice, T. (1996). Confabulation and the control of recollection. *Memory, 4*(4), 359–411.

Conway, M.A. (1992). A structural model of autobiographical memory. In *Theoretical Perspectives on Autobiographical Memory* (eds. M.A. Conway, D.C. Rubin, H. Spinnier, and W.A. Wagenaar). The Netherlands, Kluwer Academic Publishers. pp. 167–194.

Conway, M.A. (2001). Sensory-perceptual episodic memory and its context: Autobiographical memory. *Philosophical Transactions of The Royal Society of London Series B-Biological Sciences, 356*(1413), 1375–1384.

Conway, M.A. and Fthenaki, A. (2000). Disruption and loss of autobiographical memory. In *Handbook of Neuropsychology: Vol 2* (2nd edition) (eds. F. Boller and J. Grafman). Amsterdam, Elsevier Science. pp. 281–312.

Conway, M.A. and Pleydell-Pearce, C.W. (2000). The construction of autobiographical memories in the self-memory system. *Psychological Review,* **107**(2), 261–288.

Conway, M.A. and Tacchi, P.C. (1996). Motivated confabulation. *Neurocase,* **2**(4), 325–338.

Cunningham, J.M., Pliskin, N.H., Cassissi, J.E., Tsang, B., and Rao, S.M. (1997). Relationship between confabulation and measures of memory and executive function. *Journal of Clinical and Experimental Neuropsychology,* **19**, 867–877.

Dab, S., Claes, T., Morais, J., and Shallice, T. (1999). Confabulation with a selective descriptor process impairment. *Cognitive Neuropsychology,* **16**(3/5), 215–242.

Dalla Barba, G. (1993a). Confabulation: Knowledge and recollective experience. *Cognitive Neuropsychology,* **10**(1), 1–20.

Dalla Barba, G. (1993b). Different patterns of confabulation. *Cortex,* **29**, 567–581.

Dalla Barba, G., Boisse, M.F., Bartolomeo, P., and Bachoud-Levi, A.C. (1997a). Confabulation following rupture of posterior communicative artery. *Cortex,* **33**, 563–570.

Dalla Barba, G., Cappelletti, Y.J., Signorini, M., and Denes, G. (1997b). Confabulation: Remembering 'another' past, planning 'another' future. *Neurocase,* **3**, 425–436.

Dalla Barba, G., Cipolotti, L., and Denes, G. (1990). Autobiographical memory loss and confabulation in Korsakoff's syndrome: A case report. *Cortex,* **26**(4), 525–534.

Damasio, A.R., Graff-Radford, N.R., Eslinger, P.J., Damasio, H., and Kassell, N. (1985). Amnesia following basal forebrain lesions. *Archives of Neurology,* **42**, 263–271.

Davidson, G.M. (1948). Psychosomatic aspects of the Korsakoff. *Psychiatry Quarterly,* **22**, 1–17.

Delbecq-Derouesne, J., Beauvois, M.F., and Shallice, T. (1990). Preserved recall versus impaired recognition: A case study. *Brain,* **113**, 1045–1074.

DeLuca, J. (1993). Predicting neurobehavioral patterns following anterior communicating artery aneurysm. *Cortex,* **29**(4), 639–647.

DeLuca, J. (2000). A cognitive perspective on confabulation. *Neuro-Psychoanalysis,* **2**(2), 119–132.

DeLuca, J. and Cicerone, K.D. (1991). Confabulation following aneurysm of the anterior communicating artery. *Cortex,* **27**, 417–423.

Downes, J.J. and Mayes, A.R. (1995). How bad memories can sometimes lead to fantastic beliefs and strange visions. In *Broken Memories: Case Studies in the Neuropsychology of Memory* (eds. Campbell and M.A. Conway). Oxford, Blackwell. pp. 115–123.

Feinberg, T.E. (2001). *Altered Egos: How the Brain Creates the Self.* New York, Oxford University Press.

Feinberg, T.E. (2004). Commentary on "Pleasantness of False Beliefs" (Turnbull et al.). *Neuro-psychoanalysis,* **6**, 22–25.

Fischer, R.S., Alexander, M.P., D'Esposito, M., and Otto, R. (1995). Neuropsychological and neuroanatomical correlates of confabulation. *Journal of Clinical and Experimental Neuropsychology,* **17**, 20–28.

Fotopoulou, A. (2008). False-selves in neuropsychological rehabilitation: The challenge of confabulation. *Neuropsychological Rehabilitation,* **18**(5-6). pp. 541–565.

Fotopoulou, A. The affective neuropsychology of confabulation and delusion. *Cognitive Neuropsychiatry,* in press.

Fotopoulou, A. and Conway, M.A. (2004). Confabulations pleasant and unpleasant. *Neuropsychoanalysis,* **6**(1), 26–33.

Fotopoulou, A., Solms, M., and Turnbull, O. (2004). Wishful reality distortions in confabulation: A case report. *Neuropsychologia, 42*(6), 727–744.

Fotopoulou, A, Conway, M.A., Griffiths, P., Birchall, D., and Tyrer, S. (2007a). Self-enhancing confabulation: Revising the motivational hypothesis. *Neurocase, 13*, 6–15.

Fotopoulou, A., Conway, M.A., and Solms, M. (2007b). Confabulation: Motivated reality monitoring. *Neuropsychologia, 45*, 2180–2190.

Fotopoulou, A. Conway, M.A., Tyrer, S., Birchall, D., Griffiths, P., and Solms, M. (2008a). Positive emotional biases in confabulation: An experimental study. *Cortex, 44*(7), 764–72.

Fotopoulou, A. Conway, M.A., Solms, M., Tyrer, S., and Kopelman, M. (2008b). Self-serving confabulation in prose recall. *Neuropsychologia, 46*(5), 1429–1441.

Freud, S. (1915). The Unconscious. In *S.E.* Vol. 14, p. 161.

Gainotti, G. (1972). Emotional behaviour and hemispheric side of the lesion. *Cortex, 8*, 41–55.

Gainotti, G. (1975). Confabulation of denial in senile dementia: An experimental study. *Psychiatria Clinica, 8*, 99–108.

Gilboa, A. and Moscovitch, M. (2002). The cognitive neuroscience of confabulation: A review and a model. In *Handbook of Memory Disorders* (2nd edition) (eds. A. Baddeley, M. Kopelman and B. Wilson). Chichester (UK), John Wiley. pp. 315–342.

Gilboa, A., Alain, C., Stuss, D.T., Melo, B., Miller, S., and Moscovitch, M. (2006). Mechanisms of spontaneous confabulations: A strategic retrieval account. *Brain, 129*(6), 1399–1414.

Gudjonsson, G.H. and Sigurdsson, J.F. (1995). The relationship of confabulation to the memory, intelligence, suggestibility and personality of prison inmates. *Nordic Journal of Psychiatry, 49*, 373–378.

Hirstein, W. (2005). *Brain Fiction: Self-Deception and the Riddle of Confabulation.* Cambridge, MA, MIT Press.

Johnson, M.K. (1991). Reality Monitoring: Evidence from confabulation in organic brain disease patients. In *Awareness of Deficit After Brain Injury* (eds. G.P. Prigatano and D.L. Schacter). Oxford, Oxford University Press. pp. 176–197.

Johnson, M.K. (2000). Commentary on ' A Cognitive Perspective of Confabulation'. *Neuro-psychoanalysis, 2*, 150–157.

Johnson, M.K., Hayes, S.M., D'Esposito, M., and Raye, C. (2000). Confabulation. In *Handbook of Neuropsychology: Vol 2: Memory and its Disorders* (2nd edition) (eds. F. Boller and J. Grafman). Amsterdam, Netherlands, Elsevier Science. pp. 383–407.

Johnson, M.K., O'Connor, M., and Cantor, J. (1997). Confabulation, memory deficits, and frontal dysfunction. *Brain and Cognition, 34*(2), 189–206.

Johnson, M.K., and Raye, C.L. (1998). False memories and confabulation. *Trends in Cognitive Sciences, 2*(2), 137–145.

Jorn, M.L. and Rybarczyk, B. (1995). Interpreting the confabulations of geriatric medical inpatients: Two case studies. *Clinical Gerontologist, 16*, 59–62.

Joseph, R. (1999). Frontal lobe psychopathology: Mania, depression, confabulation, catatonia, perseveration, obsessive compulsions, and schizophrenia. *Psychiatry, 62*(2), 138–172.

Kandel, E.R. (1999). Biology and the future of psychoanalysis: A new intellectual framework for psychiatry revisited. *American Journal of Psychiatry, 156*(4), 505–524.

Kaplan-Solms, K. and Solms, M. (2000). *Clinical Studies in Neuro-psychoanalysis: Introduction to a Depth Neuropsychology*. Madison, CT, International Universities Press.

Kapur, N., and Coughlan, A.K. (1980). Confabulation after frontal lobe dysfunction. *Journal of Neurology Neurosurgery, and Psychiatry*, **43**, 461–463.

Kinsbourne, M. (2000). The mechanism of confabulation: A commentary. *Neuro-psychoanalysis*, **2**, 158–162.

Kinsbourne, M. (2004). Commentary on "Pleasantness of False Beliefs" (Turnbull et al.). *Neuro-psychoanalysis*, **6**, 33–36.

Kopelman, M.D. (1987). Two types of confabulation. *Journal of Neurology, Neurosurgery, and Psychiatry*, **50**(11), 1482–1487.

Kopelman, M.D. (1997). Anomalies of autobiographical memory: Retrograde amnesia, confabulation, delusional memory, psychogenic amnesia, and false memories. In *Recollections of Trauma: Scientific Research and Clinical Practice* (eds. J.D. Read and D.S. Lindsay). New York, Plenum Press. pp. 273–303

Kopelman, M.D. (1999). Varieties in false memory. *Cognitive Neuropsychology*, **16**, (3/4/5) 197–214.

Kopelman, M.D. (2002). Disorders of memory. *Brain*, **125**, 2152–2190.

Kopelman, M.D., Ng, N., and Van den Brouke, O. (1997). Confabulation extending across episodic, personal, and general semantic memory. *Cognitive Neuropsychology*, **14**(5), 683–712.

Korsakoff, S.S. (1889/1996). Medico-psychological study of a memory disorder. *Consciousness and Cognition*, **5**, 2–21.

Loftus, E.F. (1993). The reality of repressed memories. *American Psychologist*, **48**, 518–537.

Luria, A.R. (1973). *The Working Brain: An Introduction to Neuropsychology*. Hasrmondsworth, UK, Penguin Books.

Luria, A.R. (1976). *The Neuropsychology of Memory*. New York, Wiley.

Mather, M. and Carstensen, L.L. (2005). Aging and motivated cognition: The positivity effect in attention and memory. *Trends in Cognitive Sciences*, **9**, 10, 496–502.

McAdams, D.P. (2001). The psychology of life stories. *Review of General Psychology*, **5**(2), 100–122.

McKay, R., Langdon, R., and Coltheart, M. (2005). "Sleights of mind": Delusions, defenses and self-deception. *Cognitive Neuropsychiatry*, **10**(4), 305–326.

Mercer, B., Wapner, W., Gardner, H., and Benson, D.F. (1977). A study of confabulation. *Archives of Neurology*, **34**(7), 429–433.

Metcalf, K., Langdon, R., and Coltheart, M. (2007). Models of confabulation: A critical review and a new framework. *Cognitive Neuropsychology*, **24**(1), 23–47.

Moll, J.M. (1915). The "amnestic" or "KorsakoffR1" syndrome, with alcoholic aetiology: An analysis of thirty cases. *Journal of Mental Sciences*, **61**, 424–443.

Moscovitch, M. (1989). Confabulation and the frontal system: Strategic versus associative retrieval in neuropsychological theories of memory. In *Varieties of Memory and Consciousness: Essays in the Honour of Endel Tulving* (eds. H.L. Roediger and C.F.I). Hillsdale, Lawrence Erlbaum Associates. pp. 133–160.

Moscovitch, M. (1995). Confabulation. In *Memory Distortion* (eds. D. Schacter, J.T. Coyle, M.M. Fischbach, Mesulam and L.E. Sullivan) Cambridge, Harvard University Press.

Moscovitch, M., and Melo, B. (1997). Strategic retrieval and the frontal lobes: Evidence from confabulation and amnesia. *Neuropsychologia*, **35**(7), 1017–1034.

Nedjam, Z., Dalla Barba, G., and Pillon, B. (2000). Confabulation in a patient with frontotemporal dementia and a patient with Alzheimer's disease. *Cortex, 36*(4), 561–577.

Papagno, C. and Baddeley, A.D. (1997). Confabulation and dysexecutive patient: Implications for models of retrieval. *Cortex, 33*, 743–752.

Papagno, C. and Muggia, S. (1996). Confabulation: Dissociation between everyday life and neuropsychological performance. *Neurocase, 2*(2), 111–118.

Parkin, A.J. (1984). Amnesic syndrome: A lesion-specific disorder. *Cortex, 20*, 479–503.

Pillemer, D.B. (2001). Momentous events and the life story. *Review of General Psychology, 5*, 123–134.

Ross, M. (1989). Relation of implicit theories to the construction of personal histories. *Psychological Review, 96*, 341–357.

Sabhesan, S., and Natarajan, M. (1988). Fantastic confabulations after head injury. *Indian Journal of Psychological Medicine, 11*, 29–32.

Schacter, D.L., Harbluk, J.L., and McLachlan, D.R. (1984). Retrieval without recollection: An experimental analysis of source amnesia. *Journal of Verbal Learning and Verbal Behaviour, 23*, 593–611.

Schacter, D.L., Norman, K.A., and Koutstaal, W. (1998). The cognitive neuroscience of memory. *Annual Review of Psychology, 49*, 289–318.

Schnider, A. (2003). Spontaneous confabulation and the adaptation of thought to ongoing reality. *Nature Reviews Neuroscience, 4*, 662–671.

Schnider, A. (2004). Commentary on "The Pleasantness of False Beliefs" (Turnbull et al). *Neuro-psychoanalysis, 6*, 37–39.

Schnider, A., Valenza, N., Morand, S., and Michel, C.M. (2002). Early cortical distinction between memories that pertain to ongoing reality and memories that don't. *Cerebral Cortex, 12*(1), 54–61.

Schnider, A., von Däniken, C., and Gutbrod, K. (1996). The mechanisms of spontaneous and provoked confabulations. *Brain; a journal of neurology, 119*(4), 1365–1375.

Shapiro, B.E., Alexander, M.P., Gardner, H., and Mercer, B. (1981). Mechanisms of confabulation. *Neurology, 31*(9), 1070–1076.

Shimamura, A.P., Janowsky, J.S., and Squire, L.R. (1990). Memory for temporal order in patients with frontal lobe lesions and patients with amnesia. *Neuropsychologia, 28*, 803–813.

Singer, J.A., and Salovey, P. (1993). *The Remembered Self: Emotion and Memory in Personality*. New York, Free Press.

Solms, M. (2000). A Psychoanalytic Perspective on Confabulation. *Neuro-psychoanalysis, 2*, 133–143.

Solms, M. and Turnbull, O.H. (2002). *The Brain and the Ineer World*. London, Karnac Books.

Stuss, D.T., Alexander, M.P., Lieberman, A., and Levine, H. (1978). An extraordinary form of confabulation. *Neurology, 28*(11), 1166–1172.

Stuss, D.T. and Benson, D.F. (1986). *The Frontal Lobes*. New York, Raven Press.

Talland, G.A. (1961). Confabulation in the wernicke-korsakoff syndrome. *Journal of Nervous and Mental Disease, 132*(5), 361–381.

Talland, G.A. (1965). *Deranged Memory*. London, Academic Press.

Talland, G.A., Sweet, W.H., and Ballantine, H.T. (1967). Amnestic syndrome with anterior communicating artery aneurysm. *The Journal of Nervous and Mental Disease, 145*, 179–192.

Turnbull, O.H., Berry, H., and Evans, C.E. (2004a). A positive emotional bias in confabulatory false beliefs about place. *Brain and cognition,* **55**(3), 490–494.

Turnbull, O.H., Jenkins, S., and Rowlwy, M.L. (2004b). The Pleasantness of False Beliefs: An Emotion Account of Confabulation. *Neuro-psychoanalysis,* **6**, 5–15.

Van der Horst, L. (1932). Ueber die Psychologie des Korsakowsyndromes. *Psychiatry and Neurology,* **83**, 65–84.

Villiers, C.D., Zent, R., Eastman, R.W., and Swingler, D. (1996). A flight of fantasy: False memories in frontal lobe disease. *Journal of Neurology, Neurosurgery and Psychiatry,* **61**, 652–653.

Walker, W.R., Skowronski, J.J., and Thompson, C.P. (2000). Life is pleasant-and memory helps to keep it that way. *Review of General Psychology,* **7**(2), 203–210.

Weinstein, E.A. (1996). Symbolic aspects of confabulation following brain injury: Influence of premorbid personality. *Bulletin of the Menninger Clinic,* **60**, 331–350.

Weinstein, E.A. and Kahn, R.L. (1955). *Denial of Illness: Symbolic and Physiological Aspects.* Springfield IL, Charles C. Thomas.

Weinstein, E.A., Kahn, R.L., and Malitz, S. (1956). Confabulation as a social-process. *Psychiatry,* **19**(4), 383–396.

Weinstein, E.A. and Lyerly, O.G. (1968). Confabulation following brain injury. Its analogues and sequelae. *Archives of General Psychiatry,* **18**(3), 348–354.

Whitlock, F.A. (1981). Some observations on the meaning of confabulation. *The British Journal of Medical Psychology,* **54**(Pt) 3, 213–218.

Whitty, C.W.M. and Lewin, W. (1957). Vivid day-dreaming: An unusual form of confusion following anterior cingulectomy. *Brain,* **80**, 72–76.

Williams, H.W. and Rupp, C. (1938). Observations on confabulation. *American Journal of Psychiatry,* **95**, 395–405.

Wilson, A.E. and Ross, M. (2003). The identity function of autobiographical memory: Time is on our side. *Memory,* **11**, 137–149.

Woike, B., Gershkovich, I., Piorkowski, R., and Polo, M. (1999). The role of motives in the content and structure of autobiographical memory. *Journal of Personality and Social Psychology,* **76**, 600–612.

Wyke, M. and Warrington, E. (1960). An experimental analysis of confabulation in the case of Korsakoff's syndrome using a tachistoscopic method. *Journal of Neurology, Neurosurgery and Psychiatry,* **17**, 115–123.

Subject Index

Author Index